Essentials
of
Business
Mathematics

Essentials
of
Business
Mathematics

Fourth Edition

W. ALTON PARISH
WILLIAM L. KINDSFATHER

TARRANT COUNTY JUNIOR COLLEGE

Star

PUBLISHING COMPANY
P.O. BOX 68
BELMONT, CALIFORNIA 94002
(415) 591-3505

Printed in the United States of America

ISBN: 0-89863-120-3

Contents

Preface

Essentials of Business Mathematics, Fourth Edition is intended to provide students with practical concepts and skills that will be useful in a business career, in functioning as a consumer, and in other business and related courses.

The employee who is knowledgeable about mathematical procedures is more likely to attain promotions and have a greater degree of personal satisfaction from work than the employee who is not so knowledgeable.

Students who develop an understanding of this book will have a head start in other business courses, especially introduction to business, accounting, marketing, finance, and economics. In other courses, they can devote their study time to attaining an understanding of concepts, without becoming burdened with learning mathematics as the course proceeds. The student should find the chapters "Marketing Applications," "Financial Applications," "Accounting Applications," and "Management Applications" especially useful for accounting and economics courses.

The individual as a consumer in contemporary times needs to be enlightened about methods of calculating interest, methods of calculating markups and markdowns, and the international (metric) system of measurement.

Essentials of Business Mathematics, Fourth Edition has been constructed in such a way that any chapter can be omitted without sacrificing continuity or logical progression. The only chapter that the authors consider an absolute necessity for background is Chapter 4, "Percentages." The first three chapters are entirely for review, and it is expected that some instructors will choose to omit them. The 14-chapter format is intended to fit a typical 16-week semester. (The first week is generally devoted to registration and the last week to final examinations.)

Each chapter of this book begins with a list of objectives the student should meet. If the student accomplishes these objectives, it can be assumed that both the student and the chapter have been successful. Each assignment is preceded by an explanation of the concept, an example of such a problem, and a solution to the problem in the example. At the end of every chapter is a group of mixed-format problems that puts the chapter material to practice in a more realistic context than the usual drill-type problems. Students are also furnished with the answers to all odd-numbered problems.

These features make *Essentials of Business Mathematics, Fourth Edition* an almost self-teaching text and its own best teaching aid.

WAP
WLK

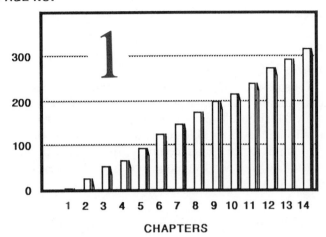

CHAPTERS

Fundamental Arithmetic Operations

Student Objectives

Upon completion of this chapter, the student should be able to

1. **Convert** *a number written out in words to a decimal number.*
2. **Add, subtract, multiply,** *and* **divide** *with decimal numbers.*
3. **Multiply** *or* **divide** *by 10 or multiples of 10.*
4. **Round off** *numbers.*
5. **Define** *or* **illustrate:**

addend	estimating	quotient
sum, or total	factor	dividend
minuend	decimal	remainder
subtrahend	product	rounding off
difference	divisor	

Fundamental Arithmetic Operations

Decimal System

Reading and Writing Whole Numbers

American and world businesses and governments buy and sell billions of dollars worth of goods and services annually. The yearly gross national product in the United States today is approximately $3 trillion. The use of very large numbers has become common, and the ability of individuals to be able to read, write, and understand them has become essential. To simplify such a task, commas are placed at three-digit intervals, called *eras*, starting at the right and moving to the left.* Study Table 1-1 to learn decimal place value names.

Table 1-1 Decimal Place Value Names	Trillions	Billions	Millions	Thousands	Units
	0 0 0,	0 0 0,	0 0 0,	0 0 0,	0 0 0
	Hundred trillions / Ten trillions / Trillions	Hundred billions / Ten billions / Billions	Hundred millions / Ten millions / Millions	Hundred thousands / Ten thousands / Thousands	Hundreds / Tens / Units / Decimal point

Example

Write two million, eight hundred sixty-seven thousand, three hundred ten in decimal form with the commas in the proper positions.

Solution

2,867,310

Assignment 1-1

Write the following numbers in decimal form with the commas in the proper positions:

1. Eight thousand, seven hundred sixty-three

2. Four hundred thirty-five thousand, two hundred six

3. Forty-nine trillion, four hundred twelve million, twenty-seven

4. Five hundred two

5. One million, two hundred fifteen

*The comma is often omitted in four-digit numbers. In this text, we shall omit the comma in four-digit numbers except when they accommpany numbers having five or more digits.

Reading and Writing Decimal Fractions

The decimal numbering system allows the writing of fractions. As in the writing of whole numbers, decimal fractions are positional. Their value depends upon the position they occupy to the right of the decimal point. Table 1-2 illustrates the values of the decimal positions.

Table 9-1

Common Fraction Equivalent

Decimal point	Tenths $\frac{1}{10}$	Hundredths $\frac{1}{100}$	Thousandths $\frac{1}{1000}$	Ten thousandths $\frac{1}{10,000}$	Hundred thousandths $\frac{1}{100,000}$	Millionths $\frac{1}{1,000,000}$	Ten millionths $\frac{1}{10,000,000}$	Hundred millionths $\frac{1}{100,000,000}$	Billionths $\frac{1}{1,000,000,000}$

Example   Write one hundred five ten-thousandths in decimal fraction form.

Solution   .0 1 0 5

    tenths / hundredths / thousandths / ten thousandths

Example   Read .163 and write it properly as it is read.

Solution   The number is read "one hundred sixty-three thousandths."

    .1 6 3

    tenths / hundredths / thousandths

Assignment 1-2

Write the following decimal fractions in proper form:

1. Two tenths

2. Thirty-six hundredths

3. Five ten-thousandths

4. Fifty-four thousand, six hundred five millionths

5. One hundred two thousandths

Read the following decimal fractions and write them as they are read:

6. .014

7. .15

8. .8765

9. .000120

10. .72341

Combination of Whole Numbers and Decimal Fractions

It is often necessary to combine whole numbers and decimal fractions. Table 1-3 illustrates the values of decimal positions.

Table 1-3 Whole Numbers and Decimal Fraction Value Names

Billions	Hundred millions	Ten millions	Millions	Hundred thousands	Ten thousands	Thousands	Hundreds	Tens	Units	. (read "and")	Tenths	Hundredths	Thousandths	Ten thousandths	Hundred thousandths	Millionths	Ten millionths	Hundred millionths	Billionths
0,	0	0	0,	0	0	0,	0	0	0	.	0	0	0	0	0	0	0	0	0

Example Write fifteen thousand five and thirty-eight thousandths in decimal form.

Solution

Ten thousands	Thousands	Hundreds	Tens	Units	(and)	Tenths	Hundredths	Thousandths
1	5,	0	0	5	.	0	3	8

Example Read 398,156.1325 and write it properly as read.

Solution The number is read "three hundred ninety-eight thousand, one hundred fifty-six and one thousand three hundred twenty-five ten-thousandths."

Hundred thousands	Ten thousands	Thousands	Hundreds	Tens	Units	(and)	Tenths	Hundredths	Thousandths	Ten thousandths
3	9	8,	1	5	6	.	1	3	2	5

Assignment 1-3

Write the following numbers in proper decimal form:

1. One and six hundredths

2. Five hundred fifteen and thirty-three hundredths

3. Three million twenty-five and two hundred one ten-thousandths

4. Eight thousand three hundred twenty and four tenths

5. Seventy-nine and one thousand two ten-thousandths

Read the following decimal numbers and write them as they are read.

6. 23.41

7. 1215.003 (or 1,215.003)

8. 78,046.91385

9. 167.9

10. 3,620,005.7382

Rounding
A number is often rounded off because either it is unnecessary to be perfectly accurate or it is not feasible to determine the exact number. The following rules should be followed in rounding off.*

1. If the first digit to the right of the number to be rounded is 5 or larger, the digit to be rounded should be increased by 1 and all digits to the right of it should be replaced by zeros.

2. If the first digit to the right of the digit to be rounded is 4 or smaller, it and all digits to the right of it should be replaced by zeros.

*In this text, unless otherwise stated, all answers will be rounded to the nearest thousandth, except dollar amounts. They will be rounded to the nearest cent (hundredth).

Example   Round off 653,729 to the nearest thousand.

Solution   654,000

Explanation
The number 3 is in the thousand position. The first digit to its right is 7, which is larger than 4. Thus the 3 should be raised to 4, and 7, 2, and 9 replaced by zeros.

Example   Round off 67,843,921 to the nearest hundred thousand.

Solution   67,800,000

Explanation
The number 8 is in the hundred-thousand position. The first digit to its right is 4, which is less than 5. Thus the 4 and all digits to its right are replaced by zeros.

Example   Round off 14.761 to the nearest tenth.

Solution   14.8

Explanation
The number 7 is in the tenth position. The number to its right is 6 (in the hundredth position). Thus the 7 should be raised to 8. The 6 and the 1 are removed. When reading a rounded decimal fraction number, the place value of the last digit will correspond to the desired accuracy; i.e., 14.761 rounded to the nearest tenth is fourteen and eight *tenths*.

Assignment 1-4

Round off the following numbers as indicated:

1. 5412 to the nearest thousand

2. 16,124 to the nearest ten-thousand

3. 576,942,318,731,673 to the nearest trillion

4. 4623 to the nearest hundred

5. 57 to the nearest ten

6. 965 to the nearest hundred

7. 572,135 to the nearest thousand

8. 683,896 to the nearest thousand

9. 1267 to the nearest ten

10. 580 to the nearest hundred

11. .102 to the nearest hundredth

12. .0658 to the nearest thousandth

13. 16.05 to the nearest tenth

14. 2384.87648 to the nearest thousandth

15. 1,410,394.621 to the nearest hundred

16. .014327 to the nearest ten-thousandth

17. $18.087 to the nearest hundredth

18. 12.583 to the nearest unit

19. $38.2832 to the nearest cent

20. 215,024.68 to the nearest hundred

Fundamental Operations Using the Decimal System

Addition

Definition

All numbers to be added are called *addends*. The consequence of addition is called the *sum* or *total*.

```
  52   addend
  29   addend
 +47   addend
 128   sum or total
```

Position of Decimal

As has already been demonstrated, the decimal system is positional. The value of a digit depends on its position as well as on its value. When adding, it is necessary to align the decimal points in the addends. *If no decimal point appears in the addend, it is understood to be at the right end of the addend.* For example, 4 is understood to be 4., even though the decimal point does not appear.

Example   Find the sum of 4.36 + 27 + 72.893 + 632.01 + 102.

Solution
```
  4.36
 27.
 72.893
632.01
102.
838.263  sum
```

Assignment 1-5

Add the following decimal numbers by placing them in columns with the decimal points aligned:

1. .087 + 168.069 + .0023 + .44 + 28.0526 + 4.6028

2. 4.3 + 25.6 + 246.52 + .057 + 21.7003 + 18

3. 7.2168 + 3728.107 + 30.062

4. .7216 + 372.8107 + 3.0062

5. 862.71 + 9.3170 + 86.27 + 96

6. 496.22 + 17.3543 + .27 + 1.3

7. 4.9622 + 173.543 + 27 + 13

8. 4962.2 + 1735.43 + .027 + .013

9. Blackman's Incorporated sells motorcycles. The firm's assets consist of cash in the bank, $22.89; cash on hand, $37.69; receivables, $12,788.43; repair equipment, $47,932.12; merchandise inventory, $52,812.37; supplies, $8,611.34; prepaid insurance, $841. What are the total assets of the firm?

10. J.P. Morgan Incorporated has the following monthly payroll: $2768.13, $5236.07, $3258.33, $6755.26, $8157.61, $9946.15, $1678.42, $7785.23, $5587.20, $746.88, $237.80, $2344.28. Calculate the monthly payroll.

Estimating Addition Problems

When solving business mathematics problems, common sense is often the best tool available. Everyone makes an occasional mistake, such as hitting the wrong key on a calculator. Common sense indicates that all people should develop a way to estimate mathematical solutions to which actual calculations can be compared. Estimations will verify that the calculation is in the ballpark.

Solutions to addition problems can be estimated by a process called *rounding all the way*. Rounding all the way means that there will be only one non-zero digit left. For example, 19,489 would become 20,000, the 2 being the only non-zero digit. By rounding all the way, the estimate may not be very close to exact. If a greater degree of accuracy is necessary, round to a more specific digit. For example, round to the nearest hundred. 19,489 would then be rounded to 19,500.

Example   Add 1416 + 21.89 + 104.2 + 3642.915. Find both the actual and estimated figures by rounding all the way.

Solution

Actual	Estimated
1416.	1000
21.89	20
104.2	100
3642.915	4000
5185.005	5120

Assignment 1-6

Add the following decimal numbers and estimate the solution using rounding all the way.

1. 14 + 98 + 731

2. 125.6 + 179.304 + 1382.997

3. Cecile Brown owns four restaurants. Last week, profits were: $3619.44, $326.50, $4142.96, and $57.31. What were the total actual and estimated profits?

4. Susan had a garage sale. After the first hour, she had sold a painting for $14, a sofa for $75, and a golf cart for $425. Calculate Susan's actual and estimated total sales receipts.

5. Stan and Joan operate S & J Stamp Redemption Center. The previous five customers traded for merchandise costing 8.25 books, 17.5 books, 12 books, 115 books, and 24.5 books. What is the total number of books of stamps that have been redeemed? Give the actual and estimated figures.

Subtraction

Definition

Subtraction involves finding the difference between two numbers. Thus, the result of reducing one number, the "*minuend*," by another number, the "*subtrahend*," is called the "*difference*" or "*remainder*."

      75 minuend
    − 32 subtrahend
      43 difference or remainder

Position of Decimal

Subtraction requires that the decimal points be aligned. The rules apply exactly as with addition. However, when the minuend contains fewer positions to the right of the decimal point than does the subtrahend, zeros are usually added in the minuend. They are placed to the immediate right of the minuend, and as many as necessary are added until the same number of positions are occupied to the right of the decimal point in the minuend and in the subtrahend.

Example   Subtract 41.31242 from 5628.23

Solution   5628.23000
             −   41.31242
               5586.91758

Assignment 1-7

Solve the following subtraction problems (be sure to align the decimal points and add zeros in the minuend when necessary):

1.   3612
    − 315

2.   8721
    − 7635

3.   15.3
    − 3.2

4.   253.5834
    − 1.642513

5.   47.6938
    − 47.6937

6.   38.7453
    − 3.87453

7.   3612.418
   − 3000.418

8.   164.2513
    − 25.35834

9. Speedy's Print Shop has a production capacity of 50,000 units per week. The daily production last week was Monday: 3274; Tuesday, 2492; Wednesday, 3194; Thursday, 6436; Friday, 5432. Determine the difference between actual production and production capacity.

10. The Friendly Bank and Trust had a cash balance of $24,926,375.18 one morning. During the day, the bank received deposits of $2,758,548.36 and paid out $3,944,729.56. What was the closing balance at the end of the day?

Estimating Subtraction Problems
Estimating subtraction problems is often necessary. As in addition, the digit to which rounding is done will be dictated by the need for estimating accuracy. For ballpark figures, however, rounding all the way is recommended.

Example   Subtract: 4893.148 − 151.9. Find both the actual and the estimated figures by rounding all the way.

Solution

Actual	Estimated
4893.148	5000
− 151.9	− 200
4741.248	4800

Assignment 1-8

Subtract the following decimal numbers and estimate the solution using rounding all the way.

1. 14,321.89 − 4896.215

2. 1498 − 346.41

3. 7798.42 − 2344.2856

4. Robin Cole Enterprises tries to keep an inventory of 325 pipes on hand. At the end of business Friday, there were 86 pipes on display and 128 pipes in the storage room. How many pipes would have to be ordered to adjust the inventory to the desired level?

5. O'Casey's Bookstore begins each day with $240 in petty cash. During one busy day, $4943 was added to petty cash and $3348 was taken out. Calculate the amount of cash that would be deposited into the bank to maintain the desired petty cash level for the start of business the next day.

Multiplication

**Table 1-4
Multiplication
Table**

	2	3	4	5	6	7	8	9	12
2	$\times 2$	$\times 2$	$\times 2$	$\times 2$	$\times 2$	$\times 2$	$\times 2$	$\times 2$	$\times 2$
	4	6	8	10	12	14	16	18	24
	2	3	4	5	6	7	8	9	12
3	$\times 3$	$\times 3$	$\times 3$	$\times 3$	$\times 3$	$\times 3$	$\times 3$	$\times 3$	$\times 3$
	6	9	12	15	18	21	24	27	36
	2	3	4	5	6	7	8	9	12
4	$\times 4$	$\times 4$	$\times 4$	$\times 4$	$\times 4$	$\times 4$	$\times 4$	$\times 4$	$\times 4$
	8	12	16	20	24	28	32	36	48
	2	3	4	5	6	7	8	9	12
5	$\times 5$	$\times 5$	$\times 5$	$\times 5$	$\times 5$	$\times 5$	$\times 5$	$\times 5$	$\times 5$
	10	15	20	25	30	35	40	45	60
	2	3	4	5	6	7	8	9	12
6	$\times 6$	$\times 6$	$\times 6$	$\times 6$	$\times 6$	$\times 6$	$\times 6$	$\times 6$	$\times 6$
	12	18	24	30	36	42	48	54	72
	2	3	4	5	6	7	8	9	12
7	$\times 7$	$\times 7$	$\times 7$	$\times 7$	$\times 7$	$\times 7$	$\times 7$	$\times 7$	$\times 7$
	14	21	28	35	42	49	56	63	84
	2	3	4	5	6	7	8	9	12
8	$\times 8$	$\times 8$	$\times 8$	$\times 8$	$\times 8$	$\times 8$	$\times 8$	$\times 8$	$\times 8$
	16	24	32	40	48	56	64	72	96
	2	3	4	5	6	7	8	9	12
9	$\times 9$	$\times 9$	$\times 9$	$\times 9$	$\times 9$	$\times 9$	$\times 9$	$\times 9$	$\times 9$
	18	27	36	45	54	63	72	81	108
	2	3	4	5	6	7	8	9	12
12	$\times 12$	$\times 12$	$\times 12$	$\times 12$	$\times 12$	$\times 12$	$\times 12$	$\times 12$	$\times 12$
	24	36	48	60	72	84	96	108	144

Definition

Multiplication is essentially a short-cut method of addition that is used when a series of addends have the same value. It is imperative that the student have the multiplication table (Table 1-4) memorized.

```
   234   factor
×  24   factor
   936   partial product
   468   partial product
  5616   product
```

In multiplication, the order of the factors can be reversed; for example, 4×5 will result in the same product as 5×4.

Example   Multiply 24 by 4132.

Solution

```
       24                                          4132
    ×4132                                       ×    24
       48     It would be simpler to work as:    16528
       72                                         8264
       24                                        99,168
       96
     99,168
```

Multiplication with Decimal Fractions

The number of decimal places in the product is equal to the sum of the decimal places in the factors.

Example   Multiply 3.251 by 21.36.

Solution

```
      3.251    (3 decimal positions)
    ×21.36   (+ 2 decimal positions)
     19506
      9753
      3251
      6502
    69.44136   (5 decimal positions)
```

Explanation

There are three decimal positions occupied in the first factor and two decimal positions occupied in the second factor. Thus 3 + 2 = 5 decimal positions are occupied in the product.

Assignment 1-9

Find the product in the following multiplication problems (do not round off your answers):

1. 37
    ×326

2. 94
    ×129

3. 7518
    ×9836

4. 2.716
    ×382.9

5. 47.352
    × 63.5

6. 511.23
    × 583.1

7. .6453
    × 2756

8. 1.0076
    × .1012

9. Alan's earnings of $9447.30 are subject to a state income tax of .052. Calculate his state income tax.

10. Argyle socks cost $1.863 per pair to produce and sell for $2.631 per pair. Determine the profit on 163 pairs.

Multiplication by 10 or Powers of 10

In multiplying any multiple of 10, it is only necessary to move the decimal one place *to the right* for every zero in the 10-multiple factor.

Example   Multiply 426 by 1000.

Solution
$$
\begin{array}{r}
426 \\
\times 1000 \\
\hline
000 \\
000 \\
000 \\
426 \\
\hline
426{,}000
\end{array}
$$

The same product could have been found by moving the decimal in the first factor (426) three spaces to the right (remember that 426 and 426.000 are equal):

$$426.000 \times 1000 = 426.000.$$

When either factor ends in one or more zeros, it is not necessary to multiply by zeros. It is simpler to multiply all the other digits together and bring down the total number of zeros of the factors.

Example   Multiply 4200 by 140.

Solution
$$
\begin{array}{r}
4200 \\
\times\ 140 \\
\hline
168 \\
42 \\
\hline
588{,}000
\end{array}
$$

Multiply the following:

1.	295 ×1000	**2.**	462 ×10,000	**3.**	6780 × 427
4.	736,000 × 12,700	**5.**	2903 × 300	**6.**	47,050 × 2,000

7. $$\begin{array}{r} 4,650 \\ \times 10,000 \\ \hline \end{array}$$

8. $$\begin{array}{r} 92,700 \\ \times \quad 100 \\ \hline \end{array}$$

9. $$\begin{array}{r} 600 \\ \times 101 \\ \hline \end{array}$$

10. $$\begin{array}{r} 65,000 \\ \times \ 1,001 \\ \hline \end{array}$$

Estimating Multiplication Problems

Estimating multiplication problems is especially desirable because of the potential for sizable errors. Rounding all the way is recommended.

Example   Multiply 56 × 193 × 32. Find both the actual and estimated figures by rounding all the way.

Solution

Actual

$$\begin{array}{r} 193 \\ \times \ \ 56 \\ \hline 1158 \\ 965 \ \ \\ \hline 10,808 \end{array}$$
$$\begin{array}{r} 10,808 \\ \times \quad 32 \\ \hline 21616 \\ 32424 \ \ \\ \hline 345,856 \end{array}$$

Estimated

$$\begin{array}{r} 200 \\ \times \ \ 60 \\ \hline 12,000 \end{array}$$
$$\begin{array}{r} 12,000 \\ \times \quad 30 \\ \hline 360,000 \end{array}$$

Assignment 1-11

Multiply the following problems and estimate the solutions by rounding all the way.

1. 36 × 72

2. 14.9 × 45.15

3. 12 × 30.5 × 7

4. Tony Pear sold a business for $47 per square foot. The building measured 23,512 square feet. What was the selling price?

5. A girl's softball team went to an out-of-town tournament. The Sleep Tight Motel rented the team 8 rooms at $54 each per night. The girls stayed for 6 nights. What was the total amount of the motel room bill?

Definition

Division is the inverse of multiplication; the finding of a quantity (the quotient), which when multiplied by a given quantity (the divisor) gives another given quantity (the dividend). This will ascertain how many times a number or quantity is contained in another.

Division

$$
\begin{array}{r}
78 \\
6\overline{)469} \\
42 \\
\hline
49 \\
48 \\
\hline
1
\end{array}
$$

divisor 6)469 dividend — quotient 78 — remainder 1

The remainder is commonly expressed as a fraction by placing it over the value of the divisor. The quotient in the above problem would be expressed $78\frac{1}{6}$.

Division by 10 or Powers of 10

When the divisor is 10 or any multiple of 10, division can be accomplished by moving the decimal point *to the left* as many places as there are zeros in the divisor.

Example   Divide 2816 by 10 and 3820 by 1000.

Solution $2816 \div 10 = 281.6$.

$3820 \div 1000 = 3.820$.

Principle

The quotient will be the same if both the divisor and the dividend are divided by the same number. For example,

$$\frac{24}{6} \div \frac{3}{3} = \frac{8}{2} = 4$$

Thus $\frac{24}{6} = 4$ and, after dividing 24 by 3 and 6 by 3, $\frac{8}{2} = 4$.

Because of this principle, when the divisor and the dividend both contain zeros at the end, an equal number of zeros can be removed from the dividend and divisor. This will not change the quotient. The procedure is the same as dividing both the divisor and the dividend by 10, 100, 1000, or any other power of 10.

Example   Divide 643,200 by 2400.

Solution

```
              268
     2400)643200
          4800
          16320
          14400
           19200
           19200
```

This could be simplified to

```
        268
    24)6432
       48
       163
       144
       192
       192
```

by removing two zeros from 2400 and two from 643,200.

Assignment 1-12

Divide the following:

1. 2480 ÷ 10

2. .263 ÷ 100

3. 37.82 ÷ 1000

4. 36,264 ÷ 100

5. 3 ÷ 10,000

6. 94,120 ÷ 3900

7. 140,600 ÷ 3800

8. 907,200 ÷ 2100

9. 531,300 ÷ 2100

10. 117,600 ÷ 120

Division When There is a Decimal Fraction in the Divisor
When the divisor contains a decimal fraction, it must be cleared before performing the calculation. The decimal point in the divisor is moved to the far right end of the divisor, and the decimal point in the dividend is moved to the right the same number of spaces.

Example   291.4544 ÷ 182.159

Solution   3 places 3 places

```
    182.159.)291.454.4


                  1.6
    182159)291454.4
           182159
           109295 4
           109295 4
```

Example   12.3 ÷ 6.15

Solution

$$\begin{array}{r} 2 \\ 6.15.\overline{)12.30.} \end{array}$$

Explanation
When the dividend does not have as many decimal positions occupied as does the divisor, zeros must be added to the dividend until it does.

Assignment 1-13

Divide the following (round to thousandths if necessary):

1. 237 ÷ 2.8

2. 22.5 ÷ 301

3. .736 ÷ 5.36

4. .6530 ÷ .473

5. 475 ÷ .427

6. 8496 ÷ 43.02

7. McDonald Incorporated has a computerized payroll department. The computer has the capacity of processing 168.5 payroll checks per minute. Calculate the computer time necessary to process 26,960 employee checks.

8. The new Burbank school system consumes 22,275 pounds of milk each year. If 1 gallon of milk weighs 8.25 pounds, how many gallons of milk does the school system consume?

Proving Multiplication and Division
Since multiplication is the inverse operation of division, multiplying the quotient by the divisor should render a product that is the dividend. In the same way, multiplication can be proved by dividing the product by one of the factors. The resulting quotient will be the other factor.

Example   Multiply and prove 312 × 38.

Solution

$$\begin{array}{r} 312 \\ \times\ 38 \\ \hline 2496 \\ 936\ \\ \hline 11,856 \end{array}$$

$$\begin{array}{r} 312 \\ 38)\overline{11856} \\ 114\ \ \\ \hline 45\ \\ 38\ \\ \hline 76 \\ 76 \end{array}$$

Example   Divide and prove 962 ÷ 26.

Solution

$$\begin{array}{r}37\\26\overline{)962}\\78\\\hline182\\182\\\hline\end{array}$$

$$\begin{array}{r}37\\\times26\\\hline222\\74\\\hline962\end{array}$$

Estimating Division Problems
Estimating all the way can also provide ballpark figures for division problems.

Example   Divide 428 ÷ 64. Find both the actual and the estimated figures.

Solution

Actual
$$\begin{array}{r}8\\6.6875\\64\overline{)428.0000}\\384\\\hline440\\384\\\hline560\\512\\\hline480\\448\\\hline320\\320\\\hline\end{array}$$

Estimated

$$60\overline{)400}$$

simplify to:

$$6.66\overline{6}\\6\overline{)40.0000}$$

Assignment 1-14

Divide the following problems. Find the actual and estimated solutions and prove the answer. **NOTE:** When estimating, it is not necessary to carry a solution to fractional form.

1. 1845 ÷ 15

2. 1422 ÷ 66

3. 1,062,600 ÷ 1050

4. Todd King bought a lawnmower for $547 plus $65.45 interest. Assuming Todd paid for the mower monthly for one year, how much was each payment?

5. Becky has started a computer service for small businesses. She bills her time at $55 per hour. One client was billed $123.75 in October. How many hours did the client need?

Chapter 1   Self-Testing Exercises

   1. Express the following as numerals with commas inserted:

   a. Sixty-two billion, five hundred-thousand, eight hundred twenty-six

   b. Thirty-seven million, one hundred twenty-three thousand

   c. Eight hundred seventy-one thousand, one hundred

   d. Four hundred million, one thousand, one

   e. Forty-three billion, three hundred-thousand, two hundred fifty-seven and forty-one hundredths

   f. Three hundred sixty-two thousand, three hundred and thirty-three thousandths

   g. Twenty-two million, nine hundred seventy-six thousand and five hundred twenty-seven thousandths

   2. Round off the following to the place indicated:

   a. 36,826 to the nearest thousand

   b. 87,536,598 to the nearest hundred-thousand

   c. 69,431 to the nearest thousand

   d. 8,964,328 to the nearest hundred

   e. 1.1235 to the nearest tenth

f. 6286.4938 to the nearest thousandth

g. 14.9853 to the nearest hundredth

h. 12,976.58 to the nearest unit

3. Add the following decimal numbers. Find the actual and the estimated solutions.

a. 87.3
      4.57
      41.5
      7.71
      9.13
      23.9

b. 428.6
       60.63
       9.207
       495.4
       6.806
       1.003

c. 84,312.6
       41.836
       18,974
       9.101
       12.8
       181.666

d. 101.5
       2728
       31.382
       5.87
       1.899
       987

4. Subtract the following decimal numbers. Find the actual and the estimated solutions.

a.   392.86
       −67.055

b.   5738.6
       −473.24

5. Multiply the following decimal numbers. Find the actual and the estimated solutions.

a.   732.1
       × 6.35

b.   87.612
       × 9.37

c.   725,000
       ×   600

6. Divide the following decimal numbers. Find the actual and the estimated solutions.

   a. $6.5\overline{)69.465}$ b. $.182\overline{)57}$

   c. $6500\overline{)78000}$ d. $2100\overline{)63.000}$

7. Percy had trouble keeping a job and was employed by six different firms last year. His W-2 forms revealed that he had the following earnings: $319.41; $2418.35; $652.28; $129; $1847.28; $11.86. What were his total earnings for the year?

8. Sandra owns an apartment building which she cannot keep leased since she is such a disagreeable landlord. The vacant apartments are of the following sizes: 632 square feet, 1430 square feet, 982 square feet, 896 square feet. How much space is vacant?

9. Honest John's Used Cars paid $1500 for a particular car. It had to be delivered from another state at a cost of $125. Upon receipt of the car, it was discovered that the engine block was cracked. Honest John's had superficial repairs done at a cost of $65. How much gross profit did the company make if the car was sold for $2400?

10. An enterprising student at Atlantic U. tried to earn some money by importing pinatas from Mexico and selling them at a profit during the Thanksgiving holidays. Since pinatas are for Christmas celebrations rather than Thanksgiving, she lost money. She paid $140.60 for 200 pinatas, $16.25 for import duties, and $31.80 for transportation charges. She sold them in town for $182.50, but had to pay a $4.12 delivery charge to one customer. How much did the student lose?

11. The college library had 87,000 volumes at the beginning of the year. In the first quarter, the library purchased 472, during the second quarter 731, during the third quarter 1241, and during the fourth quarter 216. During the year, students and faculty either lost, stole, or destroyed 261 of them. How many volumes did the library contain at the end of the year?

12. A machine produces 124 Frisbees per hour. How many units can it produce in 40 hours?

13. At the pawn shop, a customer gave the clerk a $5 bill to pay for purchases of $.33, $1.29, $.88, and $.45. How much change should the customer receive?

14. Maria received a paycheck for $375, and Harry's check was for $295.60. If Maria worked an average of 40 hours per week for 4 weeks and Harry worked an average of 30 hours per week during the 4-week period, which employee is paid more per hour and by how much? (Round off to the nearest cent.)

15. If 3 cups of molasses are required to make a pecan pie, how many pies can be made with 96 cups of molasses?

16. The total cost for 206.75 pounds of chewing gum was $78.565. What was the cost per pound?

17. A recipe for beer calls for 2.5 cups of sugar and 2 tablespoons of malt, among other ingredients. If this recipe will serve 4, how many cups of sugar and tablespoons of malt would be necessary to serve 8? to serve 16?

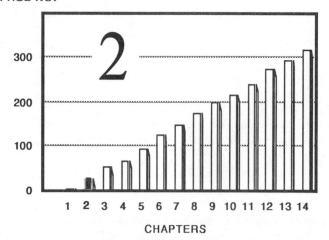

Common and Decimal Fractions

Student Objectives

Upon completion of this chapter, the student should be able to

1. **List** and **illustrate** *the three types of common fractions.*
2. **Convert** *mixed numbers to improper fractions.*
3. **Convert** *improper fractions to mixed numbers.*
4. **Reduce** *fractions, using the trial-and-error method.*
5. **Compute** *the greatest common divisor.*
6. **Reduce** *fractions, using the greatest common divisor.*
7. **Raise** *fractions to equivalent fractions.*
8. **Determine** *the lowest common denominator.*
9. **Distinguish** *between the lowest common denominator and the greatest common divisor.*
10. **Add, subtract, multiply,** and **divide** *common fractions.*
11. **Differentiate** *between reduction of fractions and cancellation of fractions.*
12. **Convert** *a decimal fraction to a common fraction.*
13. **Convert** *a common fraction to a decimal fraction.*
14. **Define** or **illustrate:**

numerator	*conversion*	*prime number*
denominator	*inversion*	*greatest common divisor*
proper fraction	*reducing*	*lowest common denominator*
improper fraction	*lowest terms*	*cancellation*
mixed number		

24

Common Fractions

Common fractions and decimal fractions are used every day by many millions of individuals in thousands of businesses. A glance at any newspaper on any day will illustrate this common usage. For example, "Wool plaid casual jackets—broken sizes. Were $24 and $38. One third off!" "Cash specials, $4 \times 8 \times \frac{3}{8}$-inch particle board, $4 \times 8 \times \frac{5}{8}$-inch exterior plywood." "2.52 acres, high on a hill. Pretty view. 7 miles south of Granbury. Access to Brazos River. $4195, owner financed, $395 down, $49.18 monthly."

These advertisements, and thousands of others like them that appear daily, have one thing in common. They all make reference to numbers that are parts of a whole. In today's society, it is essential to have a clear understanding of fractions to function properly in a business organization or simply in daily living.

Whole numbers are often divided into parts as illustrated above. Fractions indicate that division. The line, or bar, between the top number and the bottom number means "divided by." The top number is the *numerator* and the bottom number is the *denominator*.

$$\begin{aligned} 3 \quad &\text{numerator} \\ - \quad &\text{divided by} \\ 8 \quad &\text{denominator} \end{aligned}$$

The bar, signifying division, is sometimes drawn diagonally, /, but it still means "divided by." Therefore, 3/8 is the same as $\frac{3}{8}$.

Types of Fractions

There are three types of common fractions: proper, improper, and mixed.

Proper Fractions
A *proper fraction* is one in which the numerator, the top number, is smaller than the denominator, the bottom number. Thus $\frac{3}{8}$, $\frac{5}{6}$, $\frac{2}{21}$, $\frac{1}{2}$, and $\frac{61}{123}$ are all examples of proper fractions.

Improper Fractions
Fractions in which the numerator is larger than or equal to the denominator are called *improper fractions*. Examples are $\frac{16}{3}$, $\frac{3}{2}$, $\frac{146}{31}$, $\frac{2}{2}$, $\frac{9}{8}$.

Mixed Numbers
Mixed numbers are combinations of a whole number and a proper fraction, such as $1\frac{3}{5}$, $16\frac{3}{8}$, $126\frac{7}{8}$, $6\frac{5}{16}$, and $3\frac{1}{9}$.

Assignment 2-1

Identify the following fractions as to whether they are proper, improper, or mixed (write P for proper, I for improper, or M for mixed in the space provided):

1. $\frac{6}{5}$ 2. $1\frac{2}{3}$ 3. $\frac{5}{4}$

4. $\frac{2}{31}$ 5. $\frac{21}{16}$ 6. $4\frac{1}{2}$

7. $\frac{19}{19}$ 8. $\frac{263}{142}$ 9. $195\frac{3}{16}$

10. $\frac{6}{7}$

Converting Mixed Numbers to Improper Fractions

A mixed number can be changed into an improper fraction by multiplying the whole number by the denominator of the fraction, adding the numerator to that product, and putting that sum over the fraction denominator.

Example   Convert $3\frac{5}{9}$ to an improper fraction.

Solution $3 \diagdown \frac{5}{9}$ multiply the whole number by the denominator of the fraction

$27 + 5 = 32$ add the numerator of the fraction to the product from the first step

$\frac{32}{9}$ place the resultant sum over the fraction denominator

Assignment 2-2

Convert the following mixed numbers to improper fractions:

1. $2\frac{5}{6}$ 2. $6\frac{11}{12}$ 3. $4\frac{1}{3}$

4. $121\frac{14}{23}$ 5. $85\frac{2}{9}$

Converting Improper Fractions to Mixed Numbers

Improper fractions can be converted to mixed numbers by dividing the numerator by the denominator and placing the remainder over the denominator (the divisor).

Example   Convert $\frac{121}{14}$ to a mixed number.

Solution $14\overline{)121}$ $\overset{8}{}$ divide the numerator by the denominator and place the remainder
             $\underline{112}$ over the divisor
                9

$8\frac{9}{14}$ answer

Assignment 2-3

Convert the following improper fractions to mixed numbers:

1. $\frac{16}{5}$ 2. $\frac{11}{4}$ 3. $\frac{58}{3}$

4. $\frac{256}{27}$ 5. $\frac{1165}{519}$

Reducing Fractions

Fractions should always be reduced to their *lowest terms*. This means that the numerator and denominator of a fraction should be the *smallest numbers possible without changing the original value* of the fraction being reduced. To do this, the numerator and the denominator must be divided by the largest number that will go evenly into both.

Trial-and-Error Method

With many fractions, reduction can be done by inspection because most people have memorized the multiplication table through at least 9 × 9. This process is called *trial and error.*

In this method, an attempt is made to divide both the numerator and the denominator by the same number. If both numerator and denominator cannot be evenly divided by that number, another number is selected and tried. To speed up the process of trial-and-error reduction, there are certain aids to remember (Table 2-1).

Table 2-1
Rules for
Trial-and-
Error
Reduction
Method

1. If the numerator will divide evenly into the denominator, the numerator is the greatest common divisor.
2. If both numerator and denominator end with an even number, both can be divided by 2.
3. If both numerator and denominator end with 0, they can be divided by 10.
4. If both numerator and denominator end with 5 or one ends with 5 and the other ends with 0, they can be divided by 5.
5. If the sums of the digits in both numerator and denominator are multiples of 3 (that is, 6, 9, 12, 15, and so on), they can be divided by 3.

Example   Reduce $\frac{18}{48}$ to lowest terms.

Solution   The numbers 18 and 48 satisfy the requirements of both the second rule and the fifth rule; that is, both end in even numbers and the sums of the digits of both numbers are multiples of 3:

$1 + 8 = 9$ (numerator)
$4 + 8 = 12$ (denominator)

Both 9 and 12 are evenly divisible by 3. Therefore, since $2 \times 3 = 6$, both 18 and 48 are divisible by 6:

$$\frac{18}{6} = 3 \text{ and } \frac{48}{6} = 8 \quad \text{or} \quad \frac{18}{48} = \frac{18 \div 6}{48 \div 6} = \frac{3}{8}$$

NOTE: To reduce a fraction to lowest terms, divide the numerator and denominator of the fraction by the largest common factor.

Assignment 2-4

Using the trial-and-error method, reduce the following fractions to lowest terms:

1. $\frac{16}{32}$ 　　　　　　　　　　　　2. $\frac{82}{100}$

3. $\frac{16}{56}$ 　　　　　　　　　　　　4. $\frac{7}{49}$

5. $\frac{75}{175}$ 　　　　　　　　　　　6. $\frac{21}{222}$

7. $\frac{65}{200}$ 　　　　　　　　　　　8. $\frac{105}{126}$

9. $\frac{80}{90}$ 　　　　　　　　　　　10. $\frac{1200}{4200}$

Prime Numbers

Sometimes it is not easy to determine what numbers can be multiplied together to arrive at a product that is the same as the numerator in the fraction to be reduced. At other times, it becomes quite tedious because there are so many numbers that must be included.

One of the reasons for the difficulty is that there are some *numbers that can be divided evenly only by themselves and by one.* These numbers are called *prime numbers.* Examples of prime numbers are 2, 3, 5, 7, 11, 13, 17, 19, 23, 29, 31, and 37.

If the numerator of a fraction is a prime number, the fraction can be reduced only if the denominator can be divided evenly by the numerator. If the denominator is a prime number, the fraction can be reduced only if the numerator can be divided evenly by the denominator.

The difficulty in reducing fractions by trial and error is created when two fairly large prime numbers are the only two numbers that can be multiplied together to obtain the numerator. For example, the fraction $\frac{1147}{1891}$ can be reduced, but it should be apparent that to discover the proper number to divide evenly into both the numerator and the denominator would be difficult and quite unlikely. Fortunately, an alternative method is available for reducing fractions that does not rely upon trial and error.

Greatest Common Divisor

Since the number being sought is the largest number that will divide evenly into the numerator and denominator, that number is called the *greatest common divisor.* To determine the greatest common divisor, follow these steps.

1. Divide the larger number (usually the denominator) by the smaller number (usually the numerator).
2. If there is a remainder from step 1, divide the remainder into the previous divisor.

3. Continue this process until there is no remainder or until there is a remainder of 1.
4. If there is no remainder, the last divisor is the greatest common divisor.
5. Divide both the numerator and the denominator by the greatest common divisor. The result will be the reduction of the fraction to lowest terms.
6. If there is a remainder of 1, the fraction is already at lowest terms.

Example   Reduce $\frac{1147}{1891}$ to lowest terms.

Solution   *Step 1*   Divide the numerator into the denominator:

$$
\begin{array}{r}
1 \\
1147\overline{)1891} \\
\underline{1147} \\
744
\end{array}
$$

Step 2   Divide the previous divisor by the previous remainder:

$$
\begin{array}{r}
1 \\
744\overline{)1147} \\
\underline{744} \\
403
\end{array}
$$

Step 3   Continue the process begun in step 2:

$$
\begin{array}{r}
1 \\
403\overline{)744} \\
\underline{403} \\
341
\end{array}
$$

$$
\begin{array}{r}
1 \\
341\overline{)403} \\
\underline{341} \\
62
\end{array}
$$

$$
\begin{array}{r}
5 \\
62\overline{)341} \\
\underline{310} \\
31
\end{array}
$$

$$
\begin{array}{r}
2 \\
31\overline{)62} \\
\underline{62} \\
0
\end{array}
$$

The greatest common divisor is 31 since it is the divisor when the remainder is 0.

Step 4   Divide both the numerator and the denominator by the greatest common divisor, 31:

$$\frac{1147}{1891} \div \frac{31}{31} = \frac{37}{61} \quad \text{lowest terms}$$

Assignment 2-5

Using the greatest-common-divisor method, reduce the following fractions to lowest terms:

1. $\dfrac{26}{91}$

2. $\dfrac{57}{76}$

3. $\dfrac{43}{172}$

4. $\dfrac{93}{248}$

5. $\dfrac{235}{517}$

6. $\dfrac{1441}{2992}$

7. $\dfrac{153}{170}$

8. $\dfrac{323}{589}$

9. $\dfrac{161}{253}$

10. $\dfrac{145}{203}$

Raising Fractions

Just as fractions can be reduced by dividing both the numerator and the denominator by the same number, they can also be raised by multiplying both the numerator and the denominator by the same number. This is done to obtain a desired denominator, generally for addition or subtraction of fractions. Often the desired denominator is known, and to determine what number to multiply the numerator by to maintain the original value of the fraction, the desired denominator is divided by the original denominator and the quotient is then multiplied by the numerator. This results in what is known as *equivalent fractions* (a resulting fraction having equal value with the original fraction).

Example   Raise $\frac{7}{8}$ to a fraction with a denominator of 32.

Solution $\frac{7}{8} = \frac{}{32}$

$32 \div 8 = 4$ divide the desired denominator by the original denominator

$\frac{7}{8} \times \frac{4}{4} = \frac{28}{32}$ multiply the numerator by the resultant quotient

Assignment 2-6

Raise the following fractions to fractions with the same value but with the indicated denominator:

1. $\frac{3}{5} = \frac{}{20}$ **2.** $\frac{1}{2} = \frac{}{40}$ **3.** $\frac{13}{22} = \frac{}{66}$

4. $\frac{2}{17} = \frac{}{136}$ **5.** $\frac{35}{61} = \frac{}{1037}$

Lowest Common Denominator

To add or subtract fractions, all of them must have the same denominator. The method for determining the lowest common denominator is as follows:

1. Set up a chart with the denominators of the fractions to be added or subtracted listed across the top.
2. Determine a prime number that will divide evenly into one or more of the denominators, and place it in the column to the left of the chart.
3. Divide the prime number into all the denominators listed across the top of the chart.
4. If the prime number will not divide evenly into a denominator, place the denominator directly below itself and directly across from the prime number in the chart.
5. If the prime number divides evenly into the denominator, place the quotient in the appropriate position in the chart.
6. Continue determining prime numbers that will divide evenly into one or more of the numbers of the preceding row of numbers in the chart until the quotients of all the divisions are 1, that is, until the final row across from the final prime number contains all 1's.
7. Multiply all the prime numbers together.
8. The product is the lowest common denominator.

Example   Find the lowest common denominator for the fractions $\frac{1}{3}, \frac{3}{4}, \frac{5}{6}$.

Solution

denominators

		3	4	6
prime	2	3	2	3
numbers	3	1	2	1
	2	1	1	1

$2 \times 3 \times 2 = \boxed{12}$ lowest common denominator

Assignment 2-7

Find the lowest common denominator for the following sets of fractions:

1. $\frac{1}{5}, \frac{1}{8}, \frac{1}{6}$

2. $\frac{3}{4}, \frac{2}{7}, \frac{1}{8}$

3. $\frac{1}{9}, \frac{2}{15}, \frac{5}{18}$

4. $\frac{4}{5}, \frac{8}{9}, \frac{2}{3}, \frac{8}{21}$

5. $\frac{1}{7}, \frac{1}{28}, \frac{1}{4}, \frac{1}{16}$

6. $\frac{5}{8}, \frac{7}{12}, \frac{47}{60}, \frac{3}{5}$

Addition of Fractions

Addition of fractions is a combination of finding the lowest common denominator and then raising the fractions. Once the lowest common denominator has been found and all fractions have been raised, if necessary, to equivalent fractions, all that remains is to add the numerators together. The sum of the numerators over the lowest common denominator, reduced to its lowest terms, is the answer.

Example   Add $\frac{1}{3} + \frac{6}{7} + \frac{3}{4} + \frac{3}{8}$.

Solution   Find the lowest common denominator:

$$
\begin{array}{r|cccc}
 & 3 & 7 & 4 & 8 \\
\hline
3 & 1 & 7 & 4 & 8 \\
7 & 1 & 1 & 4 & 8 \\
2 & 1 & 1 & 2 & 4 \\
2 & 1 & 1 & 1 & 2 \\
2 & 1 & 1 & 1 & 1 \\
\end{array}
$$

$3 \times 7 \times 2 \times 2 \times 2 = \boxed{168}$ lowest common denominator

Raise all fractions to equivalent fractions with denominators of 168:

$$\frac{1}{3} = \frac{}{168} \quad 168 \div 3 = 56 \quad 56 \times 1 = 56 \quad \frac{56}{168}$$

$$\frac{6}{7} = \frac{}{168} \quad 168 \div 7 = 24 \quad 24 \times 6 = 144 \quad \frac{144}{168}$$

$$\frac{3}{4} = \frac{}{168} \quad 168 \div 4 = 42 \quad 42 \times 3 = 126 \quad \frac{126}{168}$$

$$\frac{3}{8} = \frac{}{168} \quad 168 \div 8 = 21 \quad 21 \times 3 = 63 \quad \frac{63}{168}$$

Put the numerators over 168 and add them together:

$$\frac{56 + 144 + 126 + 63}{168} = \frac{389}{168} = 2\frac{53}{168}$$

Assignment 2-8

Add the following fractions:

1. $\frac{1}{2} + \frac{3}{8}$

2. $\frac{5}{6} + \frac{1}{4} + \frac{2}{3}$

3. $\frac{5}{9} + \frac{14}{15} + \frac{13}{18}$

4. $\frac{2}{5} + \frac{8}{15} + \frac{24}{35}$

5. $\frac{5}{64} + \frac{3}{32} + \frac{7}{16}$

6. $\frac{3}{7} + \frac{3}{28} + \frac{1}{4} + \frac{5}{16}$

7. A carpet that is $\frac{5}{8}$ inch thick is laid on top of a mat that is $\frac{3}{16}$ thick. What is the total thickness of the mat and carpet?

8. Three components used in the manufacture of a stereo set weigh $\frac{7}{8}$ pound, $\frac{2}{3}$ pound, and $\frac{11}{12}$ pound. What is the total component weight?

Addition of Mixed Numbers
To add mixed numbers, follow these steps:

1. Add the fractions together.
2. Add the whole numbers together.
3. Add the sum of the fractional parts of whole numbers and the sum of the whole numbers together.
4. Express in lowest terms.

Example   Add $13\frac{1}{4} + 16\frac{3}{8} + 3\frac{5}{6}$.

Solution   Find the lowest common denominator for the fractions:

$$
\begin{array}{c|ccc}
 & 4 & 8 & 6 \\
\hline
2 & 2 & 4 & 3 \\
2 & 1 & 2 & 3 \\
2 & 1 & 1 & 3 \\
3 & 1 & 1 & 1 \\
\end{array}
$$

$2 \times 2 \times 2 \times 3 = \boxed{24}$ lowest common denominator

Change to equivalent fractions and add the numerators:

$$\frac{1}{4} = \frac{6}{24}$$

$$\frac{3}{8} = \frac{9}{24}$$

$$\frac{5}{6} = \frac{20}{24}$$

$$\frac{6 + 9 + 20}{24} = \frac{35}{24} = 1\frac{11}{24}$$

Add the whole numbers together:

$$
\begin{array}{r}
13 \\
16 \\
\underline{3} \\
32
\end{array}
$$

Add the two sums together:

$$
\begin{array}{r}
32 \\
1\frac{11}{24} \\
\hline
33\frac{11}{24}
\end{array}
$$

Assignment 2-9

Add the following mixed numbers:

1. $1\frac{1}{3} + 2\frac{1}{4} + 6\frac{1}{6}$

2. $14\frac{2}{3} + 1\frac{4}{9}$

3. $3\frac{1}{8} + 5\frac{6}{7} + 9\frac{1}{4}$

4. $16\frac{2}{3} + 7\frac{1}{9}$

5. $37\frac{7}{8} + 8\frac{7}{16} + 17\frac{9}{20}$

6. $23\frac{5}{16} + 42\frac{5}{6} + 51\frac{2}{3}$

7. $79\frac{7}{15} + 38\frac{4}{5} + 383\frac{3}{5} + 68\frac{8}{15}$

8. $25\frac{7}{8} + 14\frac{6}{13} + 121\frac{1}{4} + \frac{7}{24}$

9. $\frac{1}{16} + \frac{5}{8} + 13\frac{2}{9} + \frac{4}{27}$

10. $16\frac{7}{10} + 44\frac{5}{8} + 12\frac{5}{16}$

11. Three bins have capacities of $24\frac{1}{2}$ pounds, $13\frac{1}{8}$ pounds, and $18\frac{3}{4}$ pounds. What is the total capacity of the three bins?

12. The lengths of the walls in an office are $16\frac{7}{16}$ feet, $24\frac{3}{32}$ feet, $18\frac{5}{8}$ feet, and $26\frac{3}{4}$ feet. What is the perimeter of (the distance around) the room?

13. To get from Edenburg to Jonesville, a driver must pass through Central City, Plymouth, Breakitdown, and Symond. From Edenburg to Central City is $22\frac{3}{10}$ miles, from Central City to Plymouth is $8\frac{1}{2}$ miles, from Plymouth to Breakitdown is $28\frac{7}{8}$ miles, from Breakitdown to Symond is $10\frac{7}{15}$ miles, and from Symond to Jonesville is $23\frac{1}{5}$ miles. How far is it from Edenburg to Jonesville?

14. The payroll clerk was to deposit the monthly payroll. She first had to compute the total number of hours worked by the five hourly employees. The total hours for the month per employee were as follows: $152\frac{1}{4}$, $135\frac{3}{8}$, $129\frac{1}{2}$, $185\frac{2}{3}$, and $29\frac{1}{6}$. Determine the total number of hours worked by the five employees.

Subtraction of Fractions

As with the addition of fractions, subtraction of fractions can take place only when they have a common denominator. The procedure for subtracting fractions is as follows:

1. Find the lowest common denominator for the fractions.
2. Change the fractions to equivalent fractions.
3. Subtract the numerators.
4. Write the difference over the common denominator.
5. Reduce to lowest terms.

Example   Subtract $\frac{5}{6} - \frac{3}{32}$

Solution   Find the lowest common denominator:

$$
\begin{array}{r|rr}
 & 32 & 6 \\
3 & 32 & 2 \\
2 & 16 & 1 \\
16 & 1 & 1 \\
\end{array}
$$

NOTE: When all numbers in a row are 1's except one — in this case, the number 16 — there is no reason to continue using prime numbers. The goal is to have 1's all across the last row.

$3 \times 2 \times 16 = \boxed{96}$

Change to equivalent fractions:

$$\frac{3}{32} = \frac{9}{96}$$

$$\frac{5}{6} = \frac{80}{96}$$

Subtract the numerators:

$80 - 9 = 71$

Write the difference over the common denominator:

$$\frac{71}{96}$$

Reduce to lowest terms if necessary:

$\frac{71}{96}$ already in lowest terms

Assignment 2-10

Subtract the following fractions:

1. $\frac{6}{7} - \frac{1}{7}$ 2. $\frac{4}{5} - \frac{1}{3}$

3. $\frac{2}{9} - \frac{2}{21}$ 4. $\frac{7}{6} - \frac{2}{5}$

5. $\frac{3}{4} - \frac{2}{3}$ 6. $\frac{7}{10} - \frac{8}{15}$

7. $\frac{5}{6} - \frac{5}{12}$ 8. $\frac{7}{8} - \frac{3}{32}$

9. Samuel had $\frac{1}{2}$ box of candy. He gave Mary $\frac{1}{3}$ of what had been the original box of candy. What portion of the original box of candy did he have left?

10. A customer of Central City Department Store ordered $\frac{2}{3}$ dozen socks. The store could send only $\frac{1}{6}$ dozen. What part of a dozen was still owed to the customer?

11. A machine shop has to complete a job by tomorrow. When it began work this morning, it had $\frac{3}{4}$ of the job uncompleted. Today it completed $\frac{1}{3}$ of the job. What portion must be completed tomorrow?

Subtraction of Mixed Numbers
To subtract mixed numbers, it is often necessary to convert the whole number 1 into a fraction. Any fraction in which the numerator and denominator are the same number equals 1. For example, $\frac{15}{15} = 1$, $\frac{2}{2} = 1$, $\frac{167}{167} = 1$.

Borrowing
When the value of the fraction in the subtrahend is greater than the value of the fraction in the minuend, it is necessary to borrow from the whole number in the minuend. To do this, use the following steps:

1. Find the lowest common denominator (if necessary) for the fractional parts in the problem.
2. Convert the fractions.
3. If borrowing is necessary, borrow one unit from the whole number in the minuend and convert it to a fraction with the common denominator.
4. Subtract the whole numbers.

5. Subtract the fractions.
6. Reduce to lowest terms.

Example   Subtract $20\frac{1}{4} - 13\frac{5}{8}$.

Solution $20\frac{1}{4} = 20\frac{2}{8}$ convert $\frac{1}{4}$ to $\frac{2}{8}$ since the lowest common denominator is 8

$-13\frac{5}{8} = -13\frac{5}{8}$

Since $\frac{5}{8}$ cannot be subtracted from $\frac{2}{8}$, one unit must be borrowed from the whole number 20:

borrow $\frac{8}{8}$ from $20\frac{2}{8}$ $\overset{19}{20}\frac{2}{8} + \frac{8}{8} = 19\frac{10}{8}$

$-13\frac{5}{8} \quad = -13\frac{5}{8}$ subtract $13\frac{5}{8}$ from $19\frac{10}{8}$

$\underline{\phantom{-13\frac{5}{8}}}$

$6\frac{5}{8}$

Assignment 2-11

Subtract the following mixed numbers (use borrowing only when necessary):

1. $8\frac{3}{5} - 4\frac{1}{5}$ 2. $2\frac{3}{8} - 1\frac{1}{4}$

3. $22\frac{7}{9} - 12\frac{2}{15}$ 4. $16\frac{2}{7} - 13\frac{6}{15}$

5. $3\frac{3}{4} - \frac{4}{5}$ 6. $123\frac{1}{15} - 47\frac{2}{9}$

7. $113\frac{1}{2} - 14\frac{5}{16}$ 8. $1\frac{1}{10} - \frac{1}{2}$

9. $39 - 2\frac{2}{3}$ 10. $27\frac{3}{8} - 7\frac{3}{4}$

11. A metal pipe $16\frac{3}{8}$ inches long was cut into two pieces. One piece was $6\frac{7}{16}$ inches long. What was the length of the second piece?

12. In a class in economics, the students received an average grade of $74\frac{3}{10}$ on one examination. One of the students received a grade of $65\frac{1}{2}$. What was the difference between the average grade and the student's grade?

13. The federal prison nearest Washington, D.C., is 20 miles from that city. John is $3\frac{7}{10}$ miles closer to the city than to the prison. How far is he from Washington, D.C.?

Multiplication of Fractions
There are three steps in multiplying fractions:

1. Multiply the numerators.
2. Multiply the denominators.
3. Reduce to lowest terms.

Cancellation
One of the most commonly made errors in fraction multiplication is converting the fractions to be multiplied into fractions with the lowest common denominator. This need not be done. In fact, *calcellation*, which saves time and work, is actually only *another way of reducing fractions to their lowest terms* before multiplying.

The third step listed above is to reduce the fraction that results from the multiplication of the numerators and the denominators. However, if calcellation is performed prior to the multiplication, the resultant product will be in lowest terms. Canceling is accomplished in almost the same manner as trial-and-error fraction reduction. The difference is that *cancellation involves "reducing" the numerator of one fraction with the denominator of another*. The steps are as follows.

1. Select a number that will divide evenly into both a numerator and a denominator.
2. Divide the numerator and the denominator by that number.
3. Continue canceling numerators and denominators as long as a number can be found that will divide evenly into both.
4. Multiply the numerators.
5. Multiply the denominators.

Example Multiply $\frac{2}{3} \times \frac{3}{4} \times \frac{8}{9}$.

Solution Find a number that will divide evenly into both a numerator and a denominator. The number 3 will divide evenly into the numerator 3 and the denominator 3:

$$\frac{2}{3} \times \frac{\overset{1}{3}}{4} \times \frac{8}{9}$$

The number 4 will divide evenly into the numerator 8 and the denominator 4:

$$\frac{2}{1} \times \frac{1}{4} \times \frac{\overset{2}{8}}{9}$$
$$\underset{1}{}$$

Multiply the numerators together and the denominators together:

$$\frac{2 \times 1 \times 2}{1 \times 1 \times 9} = \frac{4}{9}$$

Assignment 2-12

Multiply the following fractions:

1. $\frac{2}{3} \times \frac{3}{4}$

2. $\frac{1}{12} \times \frac{3}{20}$

3. $\frac{4}{15} \times \frac{7}{10} \times \frac{3}{4}$

4. $\frac{5}{6} \times \frac{5}{16} \times \frac{2}{5}$

5. $\frac{3}{20} \times \frac{5}{36} \times \frac{7}{12} \times \frac{1}{21}$

6. $\frac{3}{5} \times \frac{1}{2} \times \frac{2}{3} \times \frac{5}{21}$

7. $\frac{8}{12} \times \frac{2}{3} \times \frac{4}{16} \times \frac{3}{8}$

8. $\frac{14}{15} \times \frac{19}{21} \times \frac{3}{7} \times \frac{5}{6}$

9. $\frac{5}{100} \times \frac{4}{5} \times \frac{8}{9} \times \frac{15}{16}$

10. $\frac{1}{25} \times \frac{3}{75} \times \frac{100}{101} \times \frac{25}{27}$

11. Sam owns $\frac{1}{3}$ of the XYZ Corporation. If he sells $\frac{1}{4}$ of his interest in the firm to Joe, how much of XYZ will Joe own?

12. An oil tank was $\frac{2}{3}$ full on Wednesday. Of the $\frac{2}{3}$-full tank, $\frac{3}{4}$ was drained that day. What fractional part of the entire tank was drained on Wednesday?

Multiplication of Fractions and Whole Numbers
To multiply a fraction and a whole number follow these steps:

1. Put the whole number over a denominator of 1. For example, the whole number 3 would be written $\frac{3}{1}$.
2. Cancel if possible.
3. Multiply the numerators.
4. Multiply the denominators.
5. Convert if necessary.

Multiplication of Mixed Numbers
To multiply mixed numbers, they must all first be converted into improper fractions. After converting, proceed as with multiplication of fractions.

Example   Multiply $6\frac{2}{5} \times 3\frac{4}{7} \times 2$.

Solution $6\frac{2}{5} \times 3\frac{4}{7} \times 2$

$\frac{32}{\underset{1}{5}} \times \frac{\overset{5}{25}}{7} \times 2$ convert to improper fractions and cancel

$\frac{32}{1} \times \frac{5}{7} \times \frac{2}{1} = \frac{320}{7}$ multiply numerators by numerators and denominators by denominators

$\frac{320}{7} = 45\frac{5}{7}$ convert to a mixed number

Assignment 2-13

Multiply the following mixed numbers, fractions, and whole numbers:

1. $4\frac{4}{9} \times 6\frac{6}{5}$

2. $5\frac{5}{6} \times 3\frac{2}{3}$

3. $1\frac{1}{7} \times 3\frac{1}{2}$

4. $2\frac{1}{4} \times 1\frac{2}{7} \times \frac{4}{27}$

5. $1\frac{7}{8} \times 1\frac{1}{15} \times 1\frac{1}{2} \times 5$

6. $\frac{3}{4} \times 1\frac{1}{4} \times 2\frac{1}{2} \times \frac{16}{25} \times 4$

7. $1\frac{1}{2} \times \frac{3}{4} \times 1\frac{1}{4} \times \frac{4}{9} \times \frac{1}{6} \times 8$

8. Grace invested $1500 last year. Her investment is now worth $\frac{2}{3}$ more than it was then. How much more is the investment worth.

9. A new Ford cost $9000 last year. This year, the same Ford sells for $\frac{1}{10}$ more. How much was the price increase?

10. Three business partners share profits as follows: Robert, $\frac{1}{2}$; John, $\frac{1}{3}$; and Mike $\frac{1}{6}$. If the firm's profits this year were $60,000, how much will each partner receive?

11. A clothing manufacturer bought $3\frac{1}{2}$ bolts of material, each containing $51\frac{2}{3}$ yards. How many yards of material did the firm buy?

12. If a car gets $33\frac{1}{3}$ miles per gallon of gasoline, how far can it travel on $4\frac{4}{5}$ gallons?

13. In a shipment of merchandise, $\frac{1}{5}$ was damaged in transit and had to be sold at $\frac{1}{2}$ its cost. What fraction of the entire cost did the damaged merchandise sell for?

Division of Fractions

To divide fractions, the divisor or divisors must first be inverted. A *divisor* is a number that is divided into another number. To invert a divisor, make the numerator the denominator and make the denominator the numerator. Then proceed as in multiplication.

Example   Divide $\frac{3}{8} \div \frac{3}{4}$

Solution $\frac{3}{8} \div \frac{3}{4}$

$\frac{3}{8} \times \frac{4}{3}$ invert divisor

$\frac{\overset{1}{\cancel{3}}}{\underset{2}{\cancel{8}}} \times \frac{\overset{1}{\cancel{4}}}{\underset{1}{\cancel{3}}} = \frac{1}{2}$ cancel and multiply

When there are more than two fractions in a division problem, all except the first one are divisors and must be inverted.

Example Divide $\frac{3}{8} \div \frac{3}{4} \div \frac{1}{6}$.

Solution $\frac{3}{8} \div \frac{3}{4} \div \frac{1}{6}$

$\frac{3}{8} \times \frac{4}{3} \times \frac{6}{1}$ invert divisors

$\frac{\overset{1}{\cancel{3}}}{\underset{2}{\cancel{8}}} \times \frac{\overset{1}{\cancel{4}}}{\underset{1}{\cancel{3}}} \times \frac{\overset{3}{\cancel{6}}}{1} = \frac{3}{1}$ cancel and multiply

$\frac{3}{1} = 3$

Assignment 2-14

Solve the following division problems:

1. $\frac{3}{5} \div \frac{5}{21}$

2. $\frac{9}{16} \div \frac{3}{4}$

3. $\frac{21}{31} \div \frac{1}{7}$

4. $\frac{2}{5} \div \frac{1}{8} \div \frac{3}{5}$

5. $\frac{4}{7} \div \frac{9}{10} \div \frac{3}{16}$

6. $\frac{3}{10} \div \frac{1}{12} \div \frac{24}{25} \div \frac{5}{49} \div \frac{9}{10}$

7. A recipe calls for $\frac{3}{4}$ cup of sugar. George divided the sugar into portions containing $\frac{1}{4}$ cup each. How many portions are there?

8. A gasoline can contains $\frac{7}{8}$ gallon of gasoline. How many lawnmowers can be filled if each holds $\frac{2}{7}$ gallon? (Round off to the nearest whole number.)

Division of Fractions by Whole Numbers
When dividing a fraction by a whole number, the whole number is the divisor and must be inverted. First, place the whole number over 1, and then invert and multiply.

Example Divide $\frac{3}{25} \div 5$.

Solution $\frac{3}{25} \div 5 = \frac{3}{25} \div \frac{5}{1}$ put the whole number over 1

$\frac{3}{25} \div \frac{5}{1} = \frac{3}{25} \times \frac{1}{5}$ invert divisor

$\frac{3}{25} \times \frac{1}{5} = \frac{3}{125}$ multiply numerators together and denominators together

Division of Mixed Numbers

Division of mixed numbers is accomplished in three steps:

1. Convert all mixed numbers to improper fractions.
2. Invert the divisor.
3. Proceed as in multiplication

Example   Divide $6\frac{3}{8} \div 3\frac{9}{10}$.

Solution $6\frac{3}{8} \div 3\frac{9}{10} = \frac{51}{8} \div \frac{39}{10}$ convert to improper fractions

$\frac{51}{8} \div \frac{39}{10} = \frac{51}{8} \times \frac{10}{39}$ invert divisor

$\overset{17}{\underset{4}{\cancel{51}}} \times \overset{5}{\underset{13}{\cancel{10}}} = \frac{85}{52}$ cancel and multiply

$\frac{85}{52} = 1\frac{33}{52}$ convert to a mixed number

Assignment 2-15

Divide the following fractions, mixed numbers, and whole numbers:

1. $15 \div 3\frac{4}{7}$

2. $4\frac{2}{3} \div 7\frac{3}{5}$

3. $5\frac{4}{7} \div 10\frac{2}{3}$

4. $23\frac{1}{4} \div 13\frac{2}{7}$

5. $\frac{2}{3} \div 76$

6. $\frac{9}{16} \div \frac{1}{14} \div 1\frac{1}{2}$

7. $5\frac{5}{8} \div 5 \div 2\frac{1}{4}$

8. $\frac{3}{16} \div 1\frac{1}{4} \div 5\frac{1}{3} \div \frac{9}{320}$

9. $4\frac{1}{8} \div 1\frac{2}{21} \div 1\frac{4}{12} \div 2\frac{3}{4}$

10. $83\frac{1}{2} \div 12\frac{7}{8} \div 20\frac{7}{8}$

11. An electrical motor manufacturer needs copper wire in lengths of $6\frac{1}{4}$ feet. How many such lengths can be cut from a roll of wire 200 feet long?

12. The average family size in Tulok County is $4\frac{3}{5}$ people. If the total population is 46,000, determine the number of families living there.

13. Compute the average number of copies printed per hour on a printing press that turned out 1000 papers in $2\frac{1}{2}$ hours.

14. If it takes $23\frac{1}{4}$ gallons of water to fill a container, how many of these containers can be filled *to capacity* by 3441 gallons of water?

15. Joan is paid $\frac{5}{6}$ as much as Ann. Joan's salary is \$825 per month. Find Ann's salary.

Decimal Fractions

Fractions are parts of a whole. Common fractions are those written with a numerator divided by a denominator. In many situations, it is preferable to use decimal fractions rather than common fractions.

Converting Decimal Fractions to Common Fractions

When a decimal fraction is read correctly, it is a simple matter to convert it into a common fraction. For example, .35 is properly read "thirty-five hundredths." That indicates $\frac{35}{100}$. A method of converting a decimal fraction into a common fraction is as follows.

1. Count the number of spaces to the right of the decimal point.
2. Place that many zeros in the denominator position for a common fraction.
3. Place a 1 in the position at the left of the zeros.
4. Place the fraction in the numerator position and remove the decimal point.
5. Reduce to lowest terms.

Example   Convert .875 into a common fraction.

Solution
1. Count the number of spaces to the right of the decimal point. This example, .875, contains three such spaces.
2. Place that many zeros in the denominator position for a common fraction: $\overline{000}$.
3. Place a 1 in the position at the left of the zeros: $\overline{1000}$.
4. Place the fraction in the numerator position and remove the decimal point: $\frac{875}{1000}$.
5. Reduce to lowest terms:
$$\frac{875}{1000} = \frac{7}{8}$$

Example   Convert 3.465 to a common fraction.

Solution $3\frac{}{000}$ 3 is a whole number and will remain intact after the conversion

$3\frac{}{1000}$ place a 1 to the left of the zeros

$3\frac{465}{1000}$ place the fraction in the numerator position and remove the decimal point

$3\frac{93}{200}$ reduce to lowest terms

Assignment 2-16

Convert the following decimal fractions to common fractions:

1. .26   **2.** .305

3. .375   **4.** .25

5. .125   **6.** .3357

7. .18725   **8.** .194

9. .4260   **10.** 1.8

Converting Common Fractions to Decimal Fractions
Conversion of common fractions into decimal fractions is accomplished by dividing the numerator by the denominator.

Example   Convert $\frac{6}{7}$ to a decimal. (Round to three places.)

Solution
$$\frac{6}{7} = 7)\overline{6.0000}^{\;.8571} = .857 \text{ answer}$$

$$
\begin{array}{r}
.8571 \\
7)\overline{6.0000} \\
\underline{56} \\
40 \\
\underline{35} \\
50 \\
\underline{49} \\
10 \\
\underline{7}
\end{array}
$$

A whole number and a fraction can be converted in the same manner. Remember that whether it appears or not, there is always a decimal point after the whole number that appears in the unit position.

Example   Convert $6\frac{3}{8}$ to a decimal fraction.

Solution $6\frac{3}{8} = 6.\frac{3}{8}$

$$
\begin{array}{r}
.375 \\
6 \text{ and } 8)\overline{3.000} \\
\underline{24} \\
60 \\
\underline{56} \\
40 \\
\underline{40}
\end{array}
$$

6.375 answer

Assignment 2-17

Convert the following common fractions to decimal fractions (round to three places if necessary):

1. $\frac{2}{5}$ 2. $\frac{5}{9}$

3. $\frac{6}{11}$ 4. $1\frac{21}{31}$

5. $3\frac{8}{9}$ 6. $212\frac{1}{12}$

7. $15\frac{5}{8}$ 8. $2\frac{1}{7}$

9. $388\frac{5}{6}$ 10. $103\frac{2}{9}$

Chapter 2 Self-Testing Exercises

1. Perform the following indicated operations:

a. $115\frac{3}{8} - 109\frac{1}{2}$
b. $4\frac{7}{6} \div \frac{1}{3}$

c. $\frac{1}{2} + \frac{5}{9} + \frac{3}{2} + 4\frac{1}{16}$
d. $\frac{5}{6} + \frac{2}{3}$

e. $4\frac{16}{19} \div 3\frac{3}{13}$
f. $21 - 12\frac{3}{4}$

g. $\frac{1}{3} \times 4\frac{6}{7} \times \frac{9}{4}$
h. $\frac{3}{16} - \frac{1}{8}$

i. $\frac{1}{3} + \frac{2}{5} + \frac{4}{15} - \frac{1}{5}$
j. $\frac{5}{14} \times \frac{3}{5} \times 3\frac{1}{16}$

k. $37\frac{15}{16} - 18\frac{3}{4}$
l. $\frac{1}{4} \div \frac{2}{3}$

m. $\frac{1}{8} \times \frac{6}{7} \times \frac{7}{3} \times 4$
n. $2\frac{1}{3} \div \frac{3}{4}$

o. $1\frac{3}{8} - \frac{5}{12}$
p. $\frac{1}{12} \times \frac{7}{8}$

q. $1\frac{3}{7} \div \frac{4}{5} \div \frac{2}{3} \div \frac{1}{2}$

2. Convert the following fractions to decimal fractions:

a. $\frac{3}{8}$
b. $\frac{2}{3}$

c. $\frac{15}{16}$
d. $\frac{1}{20}$

e. $\frac{2}{7}$
f. $\frac{1}{56}$

g. $\frac{2}{9}$ h. $13\frac{5}{6}$

i. $216\frac{3}{5}$ j. $8\frac{7}{15}$

3. Reduce the following to lowest terms:

a. $\frac{56}{48}$ b. $\frac{48}{72}$

c. $\frac{135}{216}$ d. $\frac{84}{108}$

e. $\frac{45}{54}$ f. $\frac{189}{504}$

g. $\frac{209}{589}$ h. $\frac{40}{56}$

i. $\frac{217}{287}$ j. $\frac{186}{1984}$

4. Convert the following decimal fractions to common fractions and reduce to lowest terms.

a. 0.23   b. 1.4785

c. 1.2   d. 115.115

e. .3165   f. .12

g. .375   h. 2.138

i. .167   j. 58.110

5. A car can be driven for 14 hours on a tank of gas. If it gets $25\frac{9}{10}$ miles per gallon of gas and is driven at an average rate of speed of $55\frac{1}{2}$ miles per hour, determine the gasoline tank capacity.

6. A length of pipe measuring $72\frac{3}{4}$ inches was cut into five pices. Four of the cuts as follows: $5\frac{1}{2}$ inches, $12\frac{3}{32}$ inches, $16\frac{5}{6}$ inches, and $15\frac{7}{8}$ inches. Calculate the length of the remaining piece.

7. The area of a rectangle is found by multiplying the length of two adjacent sides. If a rectangle has sides measuring $12\frac{3}{4}$ inches and $6\frac{2}{3}$ inches, what is the area? (Your answer will be in square inches.)

8. If molding strips necessary for a job are to be $3\frac{1}{2}$ feet long, how many can be cut from a strip 28 feet long?

9. What is the total capacity of a bus if seven people represent $\frac{1}{8}$ capacity?

10. A plot of land has the following dimensions:

    | first side | 24 feet | third side | $18\frac{1}{2}$ feet |
    | second side | $36\frac{2}{3}$ feet | fourth side | $21\frac{1}{6}$ feet |

    What is the perimeter of the land (the distance around)?

11. A machine that a company uses only during peak periods operates, on the average, $\frac{1}{4}$ of the year. Its average output when in operation is 22.5 units per week. How many units will this machine contribute to the company's output in a year?

12. The total cost for painting a warehouse wall 300 feet long and 48 feet high was $224. Compute the cost per square yard.

13. For every yard of material used in an industrial process, $\frac{1}{10}$ is lost to shrinkage and waste. If the total amount of material available for a job is 270 yards, how much usable material is available?

14. A job requires $235\frac{2}{3}$ man-hours of labor. The first day, $\frac{1}{3}$ of the job was completed. The second day, 75.75 man-hours were used. How many man-hours remain to complete the job?

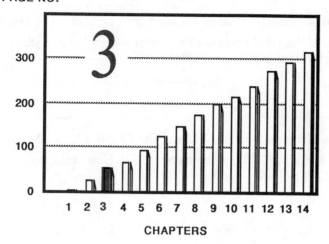

CHAPTERS

Basic Algebra

Student Objectives

Upon completion of this chapter, the student should be able to

1. **Add** *positive and negative numbers.*
2. **Multiply** *positive and negative numbers.*
3. **Divide** *positive and negative numbers.*
4. **Convert** *an equation using addition and subtraction.*
5. **Convert** *an equation using multiplication and division.*
6. **Cross-multiply.**
7. **Define** *or* **illustrate**

   positive   *equation*
   negative   *cross-multiplication*
   unknown

Positive and Negative (Signed) Numbers

Almost daily, we are confronted with both positive and negative numbers. A weather report may give the temperature in one locale as 20° below zero and in another as 40° above zero. This could just as easily be expressed as a negative 20° and a positive 40°. Some businesses make money one month and lose money the next. It is then both convenient and necessary to understand that numbers can be expressed as either negative or positive.

On a straight line, a continuum, both positive and negative numbers can be illustrated as in Figure 3-1.

Figure 3-1
Positive and
Negative
Number
Continuum

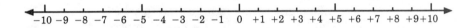

This line is continuous, and both the positive and negative numbers are unending—that is, they are *infinite*.

Addition of Positive and Negative Numbers

When adding numbers with mixed (that is, unlike) signs, determine the difference between the numbers and prefix the difference with the sign of the larger number. If several numbers are to be added, some with positive signs (any unsigned number is assumed to be a positive number) and some with negative signs, it may be necessary to add the numbers of like signs independently and then determine the difference between the two sums, prefixing the difference with the sign of the larger absolute value. (The *absolute value* of a number is the number itself regardless of its sign. The absolute value of both −5 and +5 is 5.)

Example Add −2 +8 −16 −3 +5.

Solution Add numbers with like signs:

$$
\begin{array}{rr}
-\ 2 & +\ 8 \\
-16 & +\ 5 \\
-\ 3 & \overline{+13} \\
\overline{-21} &
\end{array}
$$

Find the difference between the two sums and prefix the difference with the sign of the larger absolute value:

$$
\begin{array}{r}
-21 \\
+13 \\
\hline
-\ 8
\end{array}
$$

Assignment 3-1

Add the following:

1. −4 +6 −8   2. +3 −9 +10

3. −4 −5 −6 +4 −18 +3   **4.** 218 −65 +78 −99

5. 5264 −1994 +6000 −813   **6.** −488 −674 +4615 −123

Multiplication of Signed Numbers
Multiplication of positive and negative numbers is not difficult if the basic rules are remembered:
1. Like signs result in a positive product.
2. Unlike signs result in a negative product.

Example   Multiply +6 by +8. In algebra, this might be written $(+6)(+8)$ or $6 \cdot 8$. This is done because the letter X is often used as a symbol for a numeric value.

Solution $(+6)(+8) = +48$ like signs yield a positive product

---

Example   Multiply $(-6)(+8)$.

Solution $(-6)(+8) = -48$ unlike signs yield a negative product

---

Example   Multiply $(-6)(-8)$.

Solution $(-6)(-8) = +48$ like signs yield a positive product

---

Example   Multiply $(+6)(-8)$.

Solution $(+6)(-8) = -48$ unlike signs yield a negative product

---

Assignment 3-2

Multiply the following (remember that an unsigned number is assumed to be positive):

1. $(6)(7)$ **2.** $(6)(-7)$

3. $(-6)(7)$ **4.** $(-6)(-7)$

5. $(12)(-8)$ **6.** $(-18)(-7)$

7. $(21)(-7)$ **8.** $(-24)(-4)$

9. $(9)(7)$ **10.** $(-14)(10)$

Division of Signed Numbers

Division follows exactly the same rules of signs as multiplication, since it is the opposite process:

1. Like signs result in a positive quotient.
2. Unlike signs result in a negative quotient.

Thus, the following results will occur when dividing signed numbers:

1. Division of a *positive* number by a *positive* number *results in a positive* quotient.
2. Division of a *positive* number by a *negative* number *results in a negative* quotient.
3. Division by a *negative* number by a *positive* number *results in a negative* quotient.
4. Division of a *negative* number by a *negative* number *results in a positive* quotient.

Example   Divide $+6 \div +2$ (which can be written $2\overline{)6}$, $6 \div 2$, or $\frac{6}{2}$).

Solution $\frac{6}{2} = 3$

Example   Divide $-6 \div 2$ ($2\overline{)-6}$, $-6 \div 2$, or $\frac{-6}{2}$).

Solution $\frac{-6}{+2} = -3$

Example   Divide $-6 \div -2$ ($-2\overline{)-6}$, $-6 \div -2$, or $\frac{-6}{-2}$).

Solution $\frac{-6}{-2} = 3$

Assignment 3-3

Divide the following:

1. $\frac{+18}{-3}$ **2.** $\frac{-18}{-3}$ **3.** $\frac{18}{3}$

4. $\frac{-18}{+3}$ **5.** $\frac{804}{-6}$ **6.** $\frac{-62}{-31}$

7. $\dfrac{-75}{15}$ 8. $\dfrac{72}{-8}$ 9. $\dfrac{+72}{+9}$

10. $\dfrac{451}{-7}$

Formula and Equation Conversion

Many business problems are solved with the aid of a formula or equation. Formulas or equations are merely ways of expressing equal relationships that always exist between two or more numbers. They use mathematical symbols or letters instead of words. For example, the formula for computing simple interest is $I = P \times R \times T$. This formula states that the interest (I) can always be determined by multiplying principal (P) by rate (R) and time (T). It is entirely possible, however, that any of the "ingredients" of the formula could be unknown. So long as the other three are known, the unknown can be calculated.

The purpose of this unit is to demonstrate how formulas or equations can be converted so that once the basic formula is known, any unknown value within the formula or equation can be computed. This will be very helpful throughout the remainder of this book and, more important, it will be very valuable in the business world.

Determining the Unknown in Equations

To determine the unknown in any equation, the letter representing that unknown must be left by itself on one side of the equal sign. To isolate the unknown on one side of the equation, one of a series of mathematical operations (addition, subtraction, multiplication, and/or division) may have to be performed. The equality of the equation must be maintained at all times, which means that whatever is done to one side of the equation must also be done to the other side.

Letters are almost always used in equations, but their use should not cause any problems. The letters represent numbers and are handled the same way as numbers.

Equation Conversion Using Addition or Subtraction

If the same number is added to or subtracted from both sides of an equation, the equality is maintained.

Example   Net sales of a business equal its gross sales minus sales returns. What were the gross sales of the Stephen Corporation if net sales were $125,000 and sales returns were $2,500?

Solution   Using N for net sales, G for gross sales, and R for sales returns, the problem states that $N = G - R$.

However, we are looking for gross sales (G). Therefore, we want G by itself on one side of the equation. Since sales returns (R) are subtracted from gross sales (G), we can remove sales returns from the right side of the equation by performing the opposite operation—that is, by adding SR to both sides of the equation. We now have

$$N = G - R$$

$$N + R = G - R + R$$

Performing the indicated operation results in the following:

$$N \; + \; R = G$$

Substituting the numbers into the formula, we have

$$\$125{,}000 + \$2{,}500 = G$$

$$\$127{,}500 = G$$

Example Assets equal liabilities plus capital. Determine the capital if assets are $27,500 and liabilities are $18,750.

Solution A = assets
L = liabilities
C = capital

The basic formula (equation) is

$$A = L + C$$

Isolate C:

$$A - L = L + C - L \quad \text{subtract } L \text{ from both sides}$$
$$A - L = C$$

Substitute numbers into the equation:

$$\$27{,}500 - \$18{,}750 = C$$
$$\$8750 = C$$

Assignment 3-4

Find the unknowns in the following:

1. $A + 12 = 21$ **2.** $X - 5 = 82$

3. $N + 14 = 41$ **4.** $GP + 36 - 10 = 43$

5. $\frac{1}{8} + \frac{1}{10} + L = \frac{3}{5}$

6. What number increased by 60 gives 90?

7. What number decreased by 14 gives 27?

8. Revenues minus expenses equals net income. Determine the revenues if net income is −$25,000 (a loss) and expenses are $316,000.

9. Net invoice equals total cost of merchandise purchased, plus freight charges, less sales returns, less sales allowance. Given the following information, determine the freight charges:
   net invoice $158
   four tables at $50 each
   one table damaged and returned for full credit
   sales allowance $4.50

Equation Conversion Using Multiplication or Division

In the previous section, if the equation showed something added to the unknown we wished to isolate, we had to subtract that value from both sides. If subtraction was indicated, then we added the value to both sides.

Multiplication is the opposite of division. Therefore, if the unknown is multiplied by some value, it can be isolated by dividing both sides of the equation by that value. The reverse is also true. To remove a value which the unknown is divided by in an equation, multiply both sides of the equation by that value.

It can now be stated that *if both sides of an equation are multiplied by or divided by the same number, equality is maintained.*

Example $P = B \times R$. Find R. (**Note:** This could be written as P = BR*)

Solution R is the unknown we want to isolate. Since R is multiplied by B in the original equation, then to remove B from the left side of the equation, divide both sides of the equation by B:

$$P = B \times R$$

$$\frac{P}{B} = \frac{B \times R}{B}$$

Now cancel:

$$\frac{P}{B} = \frac{\overset{1}{B} \times R}{\underset{1}{B}}$$

Rewrite:

$$R = \frac{P}{B}$$

*Unless otherwise defined, letters written together without a mathematical symbol between them will indicate multiplication.

Example $T = \frac{D}{S}$. Find D.

Solution D is the unknown we want to isolate. Since D is divided by S in the original equation, then to remove S from the right side of the equation, multiply both sides of the equation by S:

$$T = \frac{D}{S}$$

$$T \times S = \frac{D}{S} \times S$$

Now cancel:

$$T \times S = \frac{D}{\cancel{S}} \times \frac{\overset{1}{\cancel{S}}}{\underset{1}{1}}$$

Rewrite:

$$D = T \times S$$

Cross Multiplication

Sometimes the unknown to be isolated appears in the denominator of a fraction—that is, it is a divisor. Following the rules given so far, the result would be the *reciprocal* (the inverse—that is, the number turned upside down) of the desired result. For example, given $T = \frac{D}{S}$, find S. To remove D, we must divide both sides of the equation by D. This would result in $\frac{T}{D} = \frac{1}{S}$. Since we want to find S (or $\frac{S}{1}$), *we invert both sides of the equation* since $\frac{1}{S}$ is the reciprocal of what we want. Doing so would provide the corect answer: $\frac{D}{T} = S$.

Finding the reciprocal sometimes can become a complicated procedure, especially if the equation involves several operations. An alternative method to solve for unknowns when they appear as divisors in an equation is *cross multiplication*. Cross multiplication means multiplying the numerator of one side of the equal in an equation by the denominator of the other side. Since the unknown is a denominator, we always multiply it by the numerator on the other side of the equal sign. This operation will not yield the final answer but, if it is done, it is usually easier to see what operations remain to be performed.

Example $T = \frac{D}{S}$. Find S.

Solution S is the unknown and is a divisor (a denominator):

$$T = \frac{D}{S}$$

Rewrite:

$$\frac{T}{1} = \frac{D}{S}$$

Cross-multiply:

$\frac{T}{1} \bowtie \frac{D}{S}$ multiply $T \times S$ and $D \times 1$

$$T \times S = D$$

S is the unknown and must be isolated; therefore divide both sides by T:

$$\frac{T \times S}{T} = \frac{D}{T}$$

$$S = \frac{D}{T}$$

Assignment 3-5

Find the indicated unknowns:

1. $20N = 240$

2. $18 = \frac{270}{X}$

3. $66 = \frac{Y}{66}$

4. $52Z = 416$

5. $NM = G$; find M

6. $\frac{R}{S} = T$; find R

7. $\frac{R}{S} = T$; find S

8. What number multiplied by 8 gives 56?

9. What number divided by 90 gives 40?

10. Interest equals principal times rate times time. Find the principal if interest on a loan is $100, the rate is $\frac{9}{100}$, and the time is 2 years.

11. Tax equals the assessed valuation multiplied by the tax rate. If the tax is $600 and the assessed valuation is $20,000, what is the rate?

Parentheses and Brackets

In some algebra problems, there are problems within the problem. Sometimes these problems are set apart by parentheses ( ) or brackets [ ].

The purpose of the parentheses or brackets is to guide the student toward the order of the solution to the problem. The portion of a problem within the parentheses is solved first, then the portion within the brackets, and finally the portion outside the brackets. In such problems, it is common to omit the use of the sign × for multiplication or to substitute · for ×.

Example Solve for N:
$$N = 3[(4 + 5)(7 + 1)]$$

Solution $N = 3[9 \cdot 8]$
$N = 3 \cdot 72$
$N = 216$

Example Solve for D:

$$D = \frac{2[(5 + 3)(3 \cdot 5)]}{-4[(6 + 2) - (4 + 1)]}$$

Solution $D = \frac{2[8 \cdot 15]}{-4[8 - 5]}$

$D = \frac{2 \cdot 120}{-4 \cdot 3}$

$D = \frac{240}{-12}$

$D = -20$

Assignment 3-6

Find N in the following:

1. $N = (3 \cdot 5) + (4 \cdot 1)$

2. $N = 5 \cdot [(4 + 1) - (7 \cdot 2)]$

3. $N \cdot 6 = 2[(4 \cdot 5) + (4 + 6)]$

4. $6 + 2 = \dfrac{N \cdot 3}{(3 \cdot 7) + (3 + 1)}$

5. $N \cdot B = (L + S) \cdot (C - Z)$

6. $N = \dfrac{(17 \cdot 2) + (17 \cdot 3)}{(11 \cdot 7) - (6 \cdot 12)}$

7. $N = 5[(6 \cdot 2) - (2 \cdot 5)]$

8. $N = [6 + (4 \cdot 2)] + [(7 \cdot 3) - 4]$

9. $\dfrac{N}{B} = (D + S) - (Z \cdot Y)$

10. $N = [(9 \cdot 5) - (2 \cdot 7)] \, [(7 \cdot 11) + (13 \cdot 2)]$

11. $4 \times 7 = \dfrac{14N}{(3 \cdot 6) \, (4 - 1)}$

Solving for Unknowns by Combining Arithmetic Operations

Assignment 3-7 is a combination of different kinds of problems using the information from preceding assignments.

Assignment 3-7

1. Stan Wright and Carla Rong sell real estate. Together, they sold 44 lots. Carla sold three times as many lots as Stan. How many did each sell?

2. Rusty ran twice as many pages of photocopy as Bill. Sorita ran 6 more pages than Bill. The total number of pages of photocopy was 366. Calculate the number each person ran.

3. The cost of electricity is $2\frac{1}{2}$ times the cost of gas. This month's telephone bill is $34 more than the bill for electricity. The total cost of utilities and telephone was $1864. What was the cost of each.

4. One case of disposable syringes costs $100. Disposable needles cost $40 per case. If an order of 24 cases totals $2100, what was the cost for syringes and needles?

5. A soup manufacturer produces 5 times as many cans of soup on shift 1 as on shift 2. Shift 3 produces 47 fewer cans than shift 2. A total of 4153 cans was produced. How many were produced on each shift?

Chapter 3   Self-Testing Exercises

1. Perform the indicated operations:

a. $(-4)(18)$

b. $-30 \div -6$

c. Add $-4 + 8 - 5$

d. $48 \div -6$

e. Add 2 and 4

f. $(-8)(-24)$

g. Add -4 and -16

h. Add $+6 +17 -21 +2 -28$

i. $\frac{-21}{3}(-4)$

j. $\frac{(6)(14)}{(-3)(2)}$

2. Find the value of the unknown:

a. $6 \times N = 18$ **b.** $G + 16 = 27$

c. $A + 3 - 8 = -2$ **d.** $5 \times R = \frac{3}{5}$

e. $N - 3 - 6 = 8$ **f.** $14M = 126$

g. $\frac{F}{5} = 75$ **h.** $\frac{Z}{(4)(8)} = 96$

i. $\frac{15}{N} = 3$ **j.** $4 + P - 16 = 34$

3. Find T in each of the following:

a. $T - Z = P$ **b.** $\frac{T}{H} = Z$

c. $T + R - Q = S$ **d.** $T \cdot U = R \cdot S$

e. $\frac{T \cdot Z}{B} = C$ **f.** $1 + P - Z = T \cdot Y$

g. $M \cdot R = \frac{H}{T}$ **h.** $Y - T - X = D$

i. $H + Z = T - K$ **j.** $A \cdot B = \frac{B}{T}$

k. $4T + 5 = T + 20$ **l.** $-8 + T = 3T + 16$

4. Given $P = B \times R$,

   a. Find B **b.** Find R

5. Given $I = P \cdot R \cdot T$.

   a. Find P **b.** Find Find R

   c. Find T

6. Given $T = V \cdot R$,

   a. Find V **b.** Find R

7. Solve for M:

   a. $M = (5 \cdot 2) + 4$ **b.** $M = 42 - (2 \cdot 6)$

   c. $M = 4(5 + 3)$ **d.** $M = 8(12 - 5)$

   e. $M = (2 \cdot 3) + (5 \cdot 7)$ **f.** $M = (7 \cdot 8) - (4 \cdot 4)$

   g. $M = \dfrac{36 - 6}{12 - 3}$ **h.** $M = \dfrac{11 + 9}{2 \times 5}$

   i. $5 \times 3 = \dfrac{2M}{(2 \cdot 4)(4 + 1)}$ **j.** $\dfrac{M}{S} = (R \cdot P) - (B + T)$

8. During the last quarter of the year, sales declined to \$4,385,000 from \$4,403,500. Calculate the amount of decline.

9. Abe's sales were twice as much as Jill's. Jill sold \$2385 worth of merchandise. What were Abe's sales?

10. What number divided by 5 gives $\frac{5}{43}$?

11. Sally Stewart's batting average went down .120 points after a particularly bad week at the plate. Her new average is .294. What was the batting average at the beginning of last week?

12. Susan is eight years older than Joe. Susan is 18. How old is Joe?

13. During an eight hour shift, Dewitt Manufacturing produced 8,640 units. Determine the average number of units produced per hour.

14. A customer ordered a table and 5 chairs from a retailer. The total selling price was $230. The chairs sold for $90 total. What was the price of the table?

15. Mulhaven is four times as far from Brookhollow as it is from Shady Oaks. If Mulhaven is 80 miles from Shady Oaks, how far is it from Brookhollow?

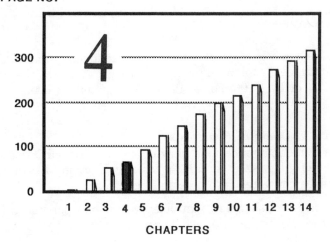

Percentages

Student Objectives

Upon completion of this chapter, the student should be able to

1. **Convert** *percents to decimal fractions.*
2. **Convert** *decimal fractions to percents.*
3. **Convert** *percents to common fractions.*
4. **Convert** *common fractions to percents.*
5. **Calculate** *a percentage when given a base and rate.*
6. **Calculate** *a rate when given a percentage and base.*
7. **Calculate** *a base when given a rate and percentage.*
8. **Calculate** *the amount when given a base and rate.*
9. **Calculate** *the difference when given a base and rate.*
10. **Calculate** *the rate when given a base and amount.*
11. **Calculate** *the rate when given a base and difference.*
12. **Define** *or* **illustrate**

percent	*rate*
percentage	*amount*
base	*difference*

Percentages

The percent sign %, has a mathematical value. It represents one hundredth, .01, or 1/100. Thus, when a number is followed by a percent sign, it means the number is being multiplied by .01 or by 1/100. For example, 25% actually means 25 x .01 or 25 x 1/100.

Converting Percents to Decimal Fractions

To use percents in arithmetic applications, they must be converted into decimal or common fractions. When the percent contains a common fraction, the common fractional part must first be converted into a decimal fraction.

When the decimal point is not shown in a value expressed as a percent, it is always understood to be at the right of the last whole number.

To convert a percent to a decimal fraction, remove the percent sign and move the decimal point two spaces to the left. This is done because the number being converted is actually being multiplied by .01.

Example Convert the following percents to decimal fractions:

a. 4%   b. $73\frac{1}{2}\%$ c. 8%

Solution

a. $4\% = 4 \times .01 = .04$ or $4\% = .04. = .04$

b. $73\frac{1}{2}\% = 73.5 \times .01 = .735$ or $73\frac{1}{2}\% = .73.5 = .735$

c. $.8\% = .8 \times .01 = .008$ or $.8\% = .00.8 = .008$

Assignment 4-1

Convert the following percents to decimal fractions (do not round off your answers):

1. 8%   2. 26%

3. $\frac{1}{2}\%$ 4. 4%

5. $12\frac{1}{4}\%$ 6. 318%

7. $2429\frac{3}{4}\%$ 8. .0007%

Converting Decimal Fractions to Percents

To convert a decimal fraction to a percent, move the decimal point two places to the right and add a percent sign. Any common fractions must be converted to decimal fractions if there are fewer than two spaces to the right of the decimal point in the decimal fraction (for example, $2.5\frac{1}{8} = 2.5125$).

Example   Convert the following decimal fractions to percents:

a. .03   b. .325   c. $.41\frac{2}{3}$ d. $3.6\frac{1}{4}$

Solution   a. $.03 = 3\%$ b. $.325 = 32.5\%$

c. $41\frac{2}{3} = 41\frac{2}{3}\%$ d. $3.6\frac{1}{4} = 3.625 = 362.5\%$

Assignment 4-2

Convert the following decimal fractions to percents:

1. .01

2. .19

3. .002

4. 2.05

5. 42.12

6. .37

7. $.3\frac{2}{5}$

8. $.28\frac{4}{7}$

Converting Percents to Common Fractions

To convert a percent to a common fraction, remove the percent sign and place the resulting number over 100. This is done because the number being converted is actually being multiplied by 1/100. Any common fractions within the percent must first be converted to decimal fractions.

Example   Convert the following percents to common fractions:

a. 75%   b. 6%   c. $5\frac{1}{2}\%$

Solution   a. $75\% = \frac{75}{1} \times \frac{1}{100} = \frac{75}{100} = \frac{3}{4}$ or $75\% = \frac{75}{100} = \frac{3}{4}$

b. $6\% = \frac{6}{1} \times \frac{1}{100} = \frac{6}{100} = \frac{3}{50}$ or $6\% = \frac{6}{100} = \frac{3}{50}$

c. $5\frac{1}{2}\% = \frac{5.5}{1} \times \frac{1}{100} = \frac{5.5}{100} = \frac{5.5}{100.0.} = \frac{11}{200}$ or

$$5\frac{1}{2}\% = \frac{5.5}{100} = \frac{55}{1000} = \frac{11}{200}$$

If a percent is greater than 100%, the conversion will result in a mixed number.

Example   Convert 260% to a common fraction.

Solution $260\% = \frac{260}{100} = 2\frac{60}{100} = 2\frac{3}{5}$

Assignment 4-3

Convert the following percents to common fractions (reduce to lowest terms):

1. 25%

2. 140%

3. 5%

4. .05%

5. .3%

6. $68\frac{3}{4}\%$

7. $2\frac{1}{2}\%$

8. 2600%

Converting Common Fractions to Percents
To convert a common fraction to a percent, first convert the common fraction to a decimal fraction. Then proceed as with converting decimal fractions to percents.

Example   Convert $\frac{4}{5}$ to a percent.

Solution $5)\overline{4.0}^{\,.8} = .80. = 80\%$

Assignment 4-4

Convert the following common fractions to percents:

1. $\frac{2}{5}$

2. $\frac{1}{3}$

3. $\frac{3}{25}$

4. $\frac{5}{8}$ **5.** $1\frac{1}{2}$ **6.** $\frac{1}{16}$

7. $\frac{1}{4}$ **8.** $\frac{1}{2}$

Solving Percentage Problems Using Formulas

There are three components in all percentage problems: base *(B)*, rate *(R)*, and percentage *(P)*.

Definitions
1. *Base*   The starting point representing the whole amount. It is the amount to which comparisons are made and is always that part of a problem representing 100%.
2. *Rate*   The expression of the relationship between the percentage and the base. The rate is expressed as a percent and can always be recognized by the percent sign written beside it.
3. *Percentage*   A part of the base. Although percentage is correctly defined this way, it can be greater than the base if the rate is greater than 100%.

NOTE: In many percentage problems, the term *percent* is used interchangeably with the term *rate*. *Percent* is NOT the same as *percentage*.

The *base* and the *percentage* are always expressed in terms of things or amounts, such as dolls, footballs, questionnaires, dollars, pounds, or miles. The *rate* is always expressed as a percent.

A *base* is considered to be the total number or the number to be compared, and can always be represented by 100%. A *percentage* and a *rate* are both part of a *base*. However, one is expressed in units (the *percentage*), whereas the other is expressed as a percent (the *rate*). If the rate is less than 100%, the percentage will be smaller than the base. If the rate equals 100%, the percentage will equal the base. If the rate is greater than 100%, the percentage will be larger than the base.

Percentage

The basic percentage formula is

percentage = base × rate

Since $P = B \times R$, the three percentage formulas that apply to all percentage problems are

$$P = B \times R$$

$$B = \frac{P}{R}$$

$$R = \frac{P}{B}$$

To succeed in solving percentage problems, these three formulas must be memorized.

Many percentage problems involve finding the percentage when the base and rate are known. This requires using the formula $P = B \times R$.

Example   What is 40% of 380?

Solution

$? = 40\% \times 380$

The base comes after the word *of*. The word *of* indicates that a multiplication is to take place.

$B = 380$

$R = 40\%$

$P = ?$

$P = B \times R$

$P = 380 \times 40\%$

$P = 380 \times .4$

$P = 152$

Example   A capping machine caps 3000 soft drink bottles each hour of operation. It chips the tip of the bottle an average 3% per hour. How many unusable bottles are produced in an average hour?

Solution

$B = 3000$ total number of bottles

$R = 3\%$ percent of unusable bottles

$P = ?$ number (percentage) of unusable bottles

$P = B \times R$

$P = 3000 \times 3\%$

$P = 3000 \times .03$

$P = 90$

Example   Ms. Rodriguez placed $1000 in her savings account 20 years ago. It contains 150% more now than it did 20 years ago. How much more does her banking account contain?

Solution

$B = \$1000$ original savings deposit

$R = 150\%$ percent of increase in savings

$P = ?$ amount (percentage) of increase in savings

$P = B \times R$

$P = \$1000 \times 150\%$

$P = \$1000 \times 1.5$

$P = \$1500$

Assignment 4-5

Solve the following percentage problems:

1.

		Base	Rate	Percentage
	a.	$450	5%	_____
	b.	$569	18%	_____
	c.	$360	7%	_____
	d.	$12,469	.01%	_____
	e.	$6	$3\frac{1}{2}\%$	_____
	f.	$32	125%	_____
	g.	$8500	$5\frac{1}{4}\%$	_____
	h.	$563	47%	_____
	i.	$75	$33\frac{1}{3}\%$	_____
	j.	$13	329%	_____

2. Ralph earned $196.80 for one week. Payroll deductions were 35%. How much was deducted?

3. A dock worker dropped a container of goods valued at $1640. The resulting damage required reducing the price by 32%. How much was the price reduction?

4. A crate of tomatoes weighed 36 pounds. The ones on the bottom were squashed. If the squashed tomatoes were 5% of the total crate weight, how many pounds were squashed?

5. New cars increased in price this year by 12%. A new compact sold for $7800 last year. How much was the price increase?

6. The sales tax rate is $5\frac{1}{2}\%$. Murray buys $120 worth of merchandise. How much is the sales tax?

7. Three percent of the gasoline in Carrie's gas tank evaporated. The tank had contained 10 gallons. How many gallons evaporated?

8. Jason's Printing offered a 2% discount for business cards ordered during December. The average price per 100 cards is $15. How much will the average discount be?

9. Sales for Howard Publications have increased by 225% in the past 10 years. Sales 10 years ago were $180,000. Calculate the amount of increase.

10. An index fell .5% last week. At the beginning of the week, it was 940. How many points did it decline?

11. A diamond bracelet cost a jewelry store owner $1085. He plans to add 100% to the cost when he sells it. Determine the amount to be added.

12. Susan uses her automobile to deliver fresh flowers. She anticipates that the car will lose 20% of its original value every year. If the automobile cost $10,000 new, how much value will it lose each year?

13. Utility rates have increased 380%. Previous average billings during the year for residential customers were $60 per month. What is the amount of increase?

14. Executive Fashions, Inc., has decided to reduce the price of its $400 suits by 25%. Calculate the amount of reduction.

15. Ten percent of all dolls sold by Toys Galore are male dolls. Last month, 80 dolls were sold. How many were male dolls?

Rate

Many percentage problems involve finding the rate when the base and percentage are given. This requires the use of the formula

$$R = \frac{P}{B}$$

Example   26 is what percent of 104?

Solution

$26 = ? \times 104$

$B = 104$

$R = ?$

$P = 26$

$R = \dfrac{P}{B}$

$R = \dfrac{26}{104} = \dfrac{1}{4} = 4\overline{)1.00}^{\,.25}$

$R = .25 = 25\%$

Example   A quarterback completed 24 of 40 pass attempts. What was his completion rate?

Solution

$B = 40$ total pass attempts
$R = ?$ percent of pass completions
$P = 24$ amount (percentage) of pass completions

$R = \dfrac{P}{B}$

$R = \dfrac{24}{40} = \dfrac{3}{5} = 5\overline{)3.00}^{\,.60}$

$R = .60 = 60\%$

Example   Standard Auto Glass has an old machine that can cut 40 sheets of glass every minute. A new machine will cut 64 additional sheets per minute. Determine the rate of increase.

Solution

$B = 40$ original cuts of glass
$R = ?$ percent of additional sheets
$P = 64$ amount (percentage) of additional sheets

$R = \dfrac{P}{B}$

$R = \dfrac{64}{40} = \dfrac{8}{5} = 5\overline{)8.00}^{\,1.60}$

$R = 1.60 = 160\%$

Assignment 4-6

Solve the following rate problems:

1.

	Base	Rate	Percentage
a.	$8	_____	$2
b.	$1247	_____	$2494

c.	$6	_____	$4.80
d.	$2494	_____	$1247
e.	$428	_____	$21.40
f.	$2532	_____	$3798
g.	$3182.50	_____	$25.46
h.	$3798	_____	$2532
i.	$60	_____	$40
j.	$160	_____	$1

2. A large grocery chain bought a truckload of kumquats that weighed 1425 pounds; 114 pounds rotted before they made it to the store shelves. What percent rotted?

3. A Yo-Yo sales representative received a commission of $900 for selling $15,000 worth of Yo-Yos. What was the commission rate?

4. L. D. Skinner Incorporated has the following office expenses each month: rent $480, coffee for employees $360, salaries $120, miscellaneous expenses $240. Calculate the percent of the total budget that each expenditure represents.

5. In a class of 40 students, 32 passed business math. What percent passed?

6. In the 1988 election, 70,000,000 people voted for President of the United States. There were 100,000,000 registered voters. What percent voted?

7. Janice answered 90 questions correctly on a test that contained 120 questions. What percent did she answer correctly?

8. An inspection of the radar equipment in an airline fleet disclosed the fact that 8 of the 40 units were defective. What percent was defective?

9. The cost of a major economics textbook has increased by $14. The original price was $28. Determine the rate of increase.

10. Of 30,000,000 new television sets sold worldwide by U.S. manufacturers last year, 25,500,000 were color sets. Calculate the rate of color set sales.

11. A new company is experiencing tremendous sales increases. As a consequence, employees must be paid overtime. Hourly employees are averaging $5 an hour more. They previously earned $12.50 per hour. What is the rate of increase?

12. Two hundred live oak trees were planted in a special ecology project. Twenty-eight of them died in the first year. What percent died?

13. In a recent survey, a hair products company found that 1 out of 30 women used a hair color product. What percent of the women colored their hair?

14. Union employees voted to strike. Two thousand of the 16,000 employees continued to work. Determine the rate of employees still working.

15. In 1967, bread cost $.22 a loaf. It now costs $.78 a loaf. Figure the rate of increase. (*Hint:* Remember, the rate and the percentage are parts of the same thing. In this problem, they should both represent the *increase* in the cost of bread.)

Base

Some percentage problems involve finding the base when the percentage and rate are known. This requires the use of the formula

$$B = \frac{P}{R}$$

Example   18 is 3% of what number?

Solution

$18 = 3\% \times ?$

$B = ?$

$R = 3\%$

$P = 18$

$B = \frac{P}{R}$

$B = \frac{18}{3\%} = \frac{18}{.03}$

$B = 600$

Example In the doctor's office where she works, Barbara gives shots to the patients needing them. At the end of one day, she had used 12% of the penicillin available. She had used 24 cc. How much penicillin was available at the beginning of the day?

Solution $B = ?$ total units of penicillin available
$R = 12\%$ percent of penicillin used
$P = 24$ cc   amount of penicillin used

$$B = \frac{P}{R}$$

$$B = \frac{24}{12\%} = \frac{24}{.12} = .12\overline{)24.00}. \quad \frac{200}{}$$

$$B = 200 \text{ cc}$$

Example Sales for Youngstown Auto increased 122% this year over last year. Sales were $793,000 this year. Calculate last year's sales.

Solution $B = ?$ last year's sales
$R = 122\%$ percent of increase in sales
$P = \$793,000$ amount of increase in sales

$$B = \frac{P}{R}$$

$$B = \frac{\$793,000}{122\%} = \frac{793,000}{1.22} = 1.22\overline{)793000.00}. \quad \frac{\$650000}{}$$

$$B = \$650,000$$

Assignment 4-7

Solve the following base problems:

1.

Base	Rate	Percentage
a. _____	6%	$25.20
b. _____	50%	$6142
c. _____	2%	$.40
d. _____	150%	$165
e. _____	25%	$6.70
f. _____	60%	$180
g. _____	1.2%	$9.60
h. _____	75%	$2685
i. _____	200%	$6142
j. _____	.01%	$25.63

2. A welder uses welding rods in which 7% of the total weight is brass. The rods used last month contained 42 pounds of brass. How much did the welding rods weigh?

3. An employee is upset because $25.80 was withheld from her check last week. If this was 30% of her total earnings for the week, how much was her gross pay?

4. The price of new foreign cars increased $2\frac{1}{2}\%$ over last year. The increase averaged $242.50 per car. What was the average price of last year's model?

5. Richard paid income tax of $1290 last year. This was 12% of his total income. What was his total income last year?

6. A well-to-do citizen recently bought a used Cadillac. She made a down payment of $984 which was 6% of the full purchase price. How much did the Cadillac cost?

7. The student population of Eastfield College is 52% female. If 13,000 of the students are female, how many students are there in Eastfield College?

8. Four percent of the book value of machinery owned by Acey Deucey Machine Shop will be depreciated this year. The depreciation will be $3200. What is the book value of the machinery?

9. A mutual fund company purchased 3 million shares of Shannon Products, Inc. The purchase gave the mutual fund company 2.5% of the total outstanding stock. How many total shares are outstanding?

10. Three thousand square feet of floor space at Save-More Fashions is devoted to selling and display of merchandise. This is 60% of the total floor space. Calculate the total amount of floor space.

11. A collection agency collected $1500 which was 75% of a delinquent account. What was the total amount owed?

12. Mr. Potter had his home appraised. One realtor quoted a price of $88,000 which was 320% of the original purchase price. Determine the original price.

13. *Universal News* magazine has reached 64% of its annual subscription goal. Thus far, 256,000 copies have been subscribed to. What is *Universal's* subscription goal?

14. Ms. Browning, owner of Rene's Pet Shop, keeps track of parakeet sales by color. She sold 35 green birds last week, which accounted for 70% of all parakeet sales. How many parakeets were sold last week?

15. Smoke and water damage sustained during a fire required sale of merchandise at 55% of its original value. The auction company handling the sale received $33,000 for the merchandise. What was the original value of the merchandise?

Amount

When a base number is increased by a percent of itself, the percentage is added to the base to obtain what is called the *amount*. The formula for amount is

amount = base + percentage

$A = B + P$

Example   This year's sales exceeded last year's by 18%. Last year, $1264 worth of goods was sold. How much was sold this year?

Solution   The percentage must be calculated using the formula $P = B \times R$, then add the percentage to the base $A = B + P$:

$B = \$1264$ last year's sales

$R = 18\%$ percent of increase in sales.

$P = ?$ increase in sales

$A = ?$ (last year's sales) plus (increase in sales)

$P = B \times R$	$A = P + B$
$P = \$1264 \times 18\%$	$A = \$227.52 + \$1264$
$P = \$1264 \times .18$	$A = \$1491.52$
$P = \$227.52$	

An alternative, faster method of solving amount problems is to add 100% to the rate and multiply the resulting sum by the base.

Example   This year's sales exceeded last year's by 18%. Last year, $1264 worth of goods was sold. How much was sold this year?

Solution

18%	$1264
+100%	× 118%
118%	$1491.52

Assignment 4-8

Solve the following amount problems:

1.

	Base	Rate	Amount
a.	$320	5%	_____
b.	$378	$33\frac{1}{3}\%$	_____
c.	$.65	40%	_____
d.	$2.80	16%	_____
e.	$1400	8.125%	_____
f.	$23	47%	_____
g.	$4563.20	$7\frac{1}{2}\%$	_____
h.	$.79	1%	_____
i.	$126	200%	_____
j.	$.02	150%	_____

2.   Jane purchased some stock for $2100. Two years later, the stock had increased in market value by 124%. How much was the stock then worth?

3.   Sam's sales were up 10% this year. Last year, he sold $43,000 worth of goods. How much did he sell this year?

4.   Enrollment at Atlantic State University is 16,450. It is expected that enrollment will increase 42% in 3 years. What will the expected enrollment be at that time?

5.   The price of gasoline went up 220% in 1 year. Donna paid $.39 per gallon before the increase. How much must she pay now? (Do not round your answer.)

6.   Larry was contributing $60 per month to his church. He increased his contribution by 8%. How much does he now contribute monthly?

7. The price of new Fords increased 24% this year. Last year, a new Ford cost $7000. How much does it cost now?

8. A wholesaler adds 60% to the amount he pays manufacturers for cameras. One model cost $140. What was the wholesaler's selling price?

9. Management at Carra's Electronics Corp. has just concluded that its $200,000 inventory should be increased 32% to meet increased sales requirements. Calculate the new inventory value.

10. Because interest rates have risen to such high levels, the UAW union has increased its bond holdings of $85,500,000 by 25%. Determine the new bond holding level.

11. An incentive clause in "Slamming Sammy" Argon's baseball contract calls for an 8.5% salary increase if Sammy hits 40 home runs in a season. Sammy hit number 38 last night. His base contract figure is $650,000. What will Sammy's salary be after he hits his 40th?

12. Renner Department Stores wants to increase catalog sales. Last year, it mailed 34,000 catalogs to residents of Oak Park. This year, 15% more will be mailed. How many catalogs will be mailed this year?

13. Newly developed fabrics have extended the average life of sofa cushions 30%. If the previous expectancy was 90 months, calculate the present life expectancy.

14. Computer home video game sales are booming. Ideal Games, Inc., presently has 28 game discs. This year, 18% more new games will be marketed by Ideal. How many games will Ideal then have available? (Round your answer to the nearest unit.)

15. During the Super Bowl, hotels raised their rates an average of 210%. The normal rate for double-occupancy rooms was $65 at the better hotels. What was the average during the Super Bowl?

Difference
When a base number is decreased by a percent of itself, the percentage is subtracted from the base to obtain what is called the *difference*. The formula for difference is

difference = base − percentage

$$D = B - P$$

Example   Marcia's income is subject to deductions of 20%. Calculate her net pay for a month in which she earned $826.

Solution   The percentage is not given and must be calculated using the formula $P = B \times R$, then the percentage must be subtracted from the base $D = B - P$:

$B = 826 total pay
$R = 20\%$ of deductions
$P = ?$ amount of deductions
$D = ?$ net pay (total pay less deductions)

$P = B \times R$ $D = B - P$

$P = $826 \times 20\%$ $D = $826 - 165.20

$P = $826 \times .2$ $D = 660.80

$P = 165.20

An alternative, faster method of solving difference problems is to subtract the rate from 100% and multiply the resulting difference by the base.

Example   Marcia's income is subject to deductions of 20%. Calculate her net pay for a month in which she earned $826.

Solution

```
    100%       80% = .8        $826
  −  20%                     ×    .8
    80%                       $660.80
```

Assignment 4-9

Solve the following difference problems:

1.

	Base	Rate	Difference
a.	$185	4%	_____
b.	$1286	2%	_____
c.	$.40	60%	_____
d.	$1290	94%	_____
e.	$1905	8%	_____
f.	$125	.05%	_____
g.	$1426.80	12.5%	_____
h.	$24	50%	_____
i.	$6482	75%	_____
j.	$6882	25%	_____

2. A city of 263,500 declined in population by 18%. How large was the city after the decline?

3. Myrtle bought 200 shares of Old Faithful stock for $2000. After four months, the market price of the stock had declined by 14%. What was the stock worth after the decline?

4. It is estimated that 25% of the cloth used in producing men's suits is lost in cutting. If a suit requires 4 yards of fabric before cutting begins, how many yards of cloth do finished suits actually contain?

5. Bob and Helen have decided to have a swimming pool installed in their backyard. The pool will cost $20,000. After making a down payment of 16%, how much will they owe?

6. Kate bought a new sewing machine which Sears had marked down 20%. The original selling price was $160. How much did Kate pay?

7. Pat bought a new pickup truck that gets 10% less gasoline mileage than her old pickup. The old pickup would go 20 miles on a gallon of gasoline. How far will the new one go on a gallon of gasoline?

8. Attendance at Shakespeare in the Park is down 6% from last year's record average of 1200 people per day. What is this year's average daily attendance?

9. Medcare Corporation is considering offering special room rates to persons who opt to have elective surgery on Friday. This is being considered after a record check revealed that hospital utilization on Fridays declined 41% from the normal Monday-through-Thursday average of 4700 persons. Calculate the average Friday hospital utilization.

10. Sales of nonfilter cigarettes have declined 64% since the Surgeon General's report. If total non-filter sales totaled 1,950,000,000 packages annually before the decline, how many packages are now sold each year?

11. Because of poor economic conditions, retail sales this Christmas are expected to be down 11%. Last year's Christmas season resulted in total sales of $850,000 for one chain. Determine this year's expected sales.

12. High interest rates have resulted in a decline in new department store construction. R.C. Dime Stores has had to reduce its planned 175 openings by 12%. How many new stores does Dime now intend to open?

13. Downtime for machine maintenance has been reduced 40% after a newly instituted employee-training program. The average weekly downtime for all machines was 12 hours. What is it after training?

14. Violent crime was reduced 14.6% in one year after an intensive advertising campaign on crime prevention. If 8500 violent crimes were committed in the year before the campaign, what was that number one year later?

15. Henry's Designer Shirts reduced the price of short-sleeved shirts 20%. One style previously sold for $39.95. Calculate the price after the reduction.

Calculating the Rate in Amount and Difference Problems

Often, the rate of increase or the rate of decrease must be calculated when both the base and the amount or difference are known. In either case, the first step in solving for the rate of increase or the rate of decrease is to find the percentage. In amount problems, the percentage is the amount of increase. In difference problems, the percentage is the amount of decrease. The rate can then be calculated:

$$\text{rate of increase or decrease} = \frac{\text{amount of increase or decrease}}{\text{original amount}}$$

$$R = \frac{P}{B}$$

Example   Profits at the Gossage Garage have increased from $24,000 last year to $30,000 this year. Calculate the rate of increase.

Solution $R = \dfrac{A - B}{B}$

$R = \dfrac{\$30,000 - \$24,000}{\$24,000}$ amount of increase
original profit

$R = \dfrac{\$6,000}{\$24,000} = \dfrac{1}{4} = 25\%$ rate of increase

or

$R = \dfrac{P}{B}$

$R = \dfrac{\$6,000}{\$24,000}$ amount of increase
original profit

$R = \dfrac{1}{4} = 25\%$ rate of increase

Example   The manufacturer's suggested retail price for one of the calculators in its line has decreased from $20 to $16 this year. What is the rate of decrease?

Solution $R = \dfrac{B - D}{B}$

$R = \dfrac{\$20 - \$16}{\$20}$ amount of decrease
original price

$R = \dfrac{\$\ 4}{\$20} = \dfrac{1}{5} = 20\%$ rate of decrease

or

$R = \dfrac{P}{B}$

$R = \dfrac{\$\ 4}{\$20}$ amount of decrease
original price

$R = \dfrac{1}{5} = 20\%$ rate of decrease

Assignment 4-10

1. Solve for the rate of increase in the following problems:

	Base	Amount	Rate of Increase
a.	$80	$90	_____
b.	$4000	$9000	_____
c.	$125	$160	_____

d. $40 $50   _____

e. $360 $720   _____

f. $300,000 $900,000   _____

g. $.52 $.65   _____

h. $480 $660   _____

i. $12.50 $18.75   _____

j. $108 $120   _____

2. Solve for the rate of decrease in the following problems:

Base	Difference	Rate of Decrease
a. $108,000	$60,000	_____
b. $180,000	$150,000	_____
c. $30,000	$20,000	_____
d. $200	$140	_____
e. $24	$12	_____
f. $1,000,000	$750,000	_____
g. $280	$201.60	_____
h. $25,500	$17,340	_____
i. $.12	$.03	_____
j. $414	$186.30	_____

3. High photocopying costs forced Stanham's Secretarial Service to use alternate reproduction methods. In the past month, photocopying costs have declined from $2000 to $1500. Calculate the rate of decline.

4. The water level in a lake has declined from 27 feet to 18 feet in the last 6 months. What is the rate of decline?

5. Demand for air conditioners is forecast to increase from 2,400,000 to 3,200,000 units. Determine the rate of increase.

6. A veterinarian is quite concerned because known rabies cases have increased from an average of two each month to nine this month. What is the rate of increase?

7. Advertising expenditures have been increased from $34 million to $51 million by a supermarket chain to change its poor consumer image. Calculate the rate of increase.

8. Jewel Coffee Manufacturers employs a total of 650 persons. Of these, 533 are males. A woman's organization has filed a protest stating that Jewel does not hire a large enough percent of women. What is the percent of women employed?

9. Federal Distributing Corp. leases space in its buildings to specialty sellers such as camera shops, tobacco shops, travel agencies, and optometrists. Federal charges a flat fee plus a percent of sales each month. One camera shop had sales last month of $3500. After deducting the $300 flat fee and the rate charged by Federal, the camera shop realized $3130. What rate was charged by Federal?

10. A major wholesaler has increased its hours of operation from 8 hours a day/5 days per week to 10 hours a day/Monday through Friday and 5 hours on Saturday. Determine the rate of increase in total hours per week.

Chapter 4   Self-Testing Exercises

1. Find the unknowns in the following table:

	Base	Rate	Percentage
a.	235	15%	_____
b.	1000	_____	1650
c.	_____	7%	56
d.	2300	236%	_____
e.	670	_____	120.60
f.	_____	12%	84
g.	536	26%	_____
h.	_____	$3\frac{1}{2}\%$	4.375
i.	112.38	_____	6.7428
j.	14.95	_____	15.6975

2. Schmaltz, Inc., deducts 6% from the gross pay of all employees for the retirement fund. If $720 was withheld one week, what was the gross payroll of Schmaltz, Inc.?

3. Sara has found that if she drives slowly, her Pierce-Arrow gets 15 miles per gallon of gasoline. When she drives faster, the same car gets 10 miles per gallon. What percent of gasoline savings does she realize when she drives slowly?

4. Hicksville Savings and Loan pays a $5\frac{1}{2}$% simple annual rate of interest. If an account earned $550 interest one year, what was the amount of the balance before the interest was earned?

5. Gas Equipment Testing Service offers 2% discount to customers who pay promptly. If all customers pay promptly and the total billings for the month are $58,000, what is the amount customers will pay?

6. Of 1500 marketing questionnaires mailed, 330 were returned. What was the rate of response?

7. Automobile insurance rates have increased $33\frac{1}{3}$% in the past 10 years. If the cost of a policy 10 years ago was $240, what is the cost of the same policy today?

8. An investor in the stock market found that a $2500 investment had declined 15% in value. How much is the investment worth now?

9. Jones and Company reduced its inventory from $45,000 to $41,625. What was the percent of reduction?

10. Enrollment at Mayville Community College was up 22% this year. If last year's enrollment was 1970, what was the enrollment this year?

11. A store marks up merchandise 40% above cost. If the cost for an electric hair-brush is $12.50, what is the markup on the item? What is the selling price?

12. A chemical formula consists of 2 liters of sulfuric acid for every 24 liters of the compound. What percent of the compound is sulfuric acid?

13. Convert the following problems as indicated:

    a. 35% to a decimal fraction   **k.** 150% to a common fraction

    b. .025 to a percent   **l.** $5\frac{1}{2}$% to a decimal fraction

    c. $3\frac{1}{4}$ to a percent   **m.** 2150% to a decimal fraction

    d. 22% to a common fraction   **n.** .215 to a percent

    e. $5\frac{2}{5}$% to a common fraction   **o.** 85% to a common fraction

    f. $.2\frac{1}{4}$ to a percent   **p.** $1.6\frac{4}{5}$% to a decimal fraction

    g. $\frac{3}{50}$ to a percent   **q.** 12% to a common fraction

    h. $1\frac{1}{8}$ to a percent   **r.** .013% to a decimal fraction

    i. $\frac{15}{150}$ to a percent   **s.** $.1\frac{24}{25}$% to a decimal fraction

    j. .65% to a decimal fraction   **t.** $62\frac{3}{4}$% to a common fraction

14. Find the unknowns in the following problems:

	Base	Rate	Percentage	Difference
a.	_____	_____	$24	$6
b.	_____	12%	$84	_____
c.	$3000	3%	_____	_____
d.	$16	_____	_____	$2
e.	$900	_____	$300	_____
f.	_____	_____	$2850	$1425
g.	_____	55%	$330	_____
h.	_____	_____	$171	$621
i.	$360	22%	_____	_____
j.	$44	_____	_____	$13.20
k.	$1350	_____	$1053	_____

15. A dance studio's management is planning an advertising campaign to attract men to take lessons. Only 18% of the 200 students presently enrolled are men. How many are men? How many are women?

16. Twenty-five of every 40 people entering Johnson's Curio Shop to browse purchase something. What percent make purchases?

17. Find the unknowns in the following problems:

	Base	Rate	Percentage	Amount
a.	_____	_____	$504	$1304
b.	_____	5.5%	$82.50	_____
c.	$990	_____	$148.50	_____
d.	$325	60%	_____	_____
e.	$625	_____	_____	$875
f.	_____	_____	$1.47	$22.47
g.	_____	45%	$9	_____
h.	$270	_____	$14.58	_____
i.	$40,500	143%	_____	_____
j.	$41.80	_____	_____	$85.69

18. Country Girl Cosmetics sold $82,000 worth of nail polish. Total company sales were $656,000. What percent of total sales was nail polish?

19. Leslie Steel earned $3705 one year cutting lawns. This accounted for 28.5% of her total lawn care income. Calculate Leslie's gross income.

20. Sales Boosters, Inc., earned net income of $43,000 last year. This year's net income is $61,060. Determine the rate of increase.

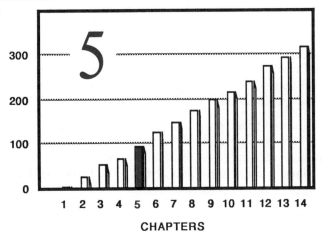

CHAPTERS

Marketing Applications

Student Objectives

Upon completion of this chapter, the student should be able to

1. **Calculate** *markup.*
2. **Calculate** *markup percent based on cost.*
3. **Calculate** *markup percent based on retail.*
4. **Figure** *the cost when the markup percent, the retail price, and the base are known.*
5. **Determine** *the retail price when the markup percent, the cost, and the base are known.*
6. **Calculate** *average markup rates.*
7. **Calculate** *markdown rates.*
8. **Calculate** *cash discounts from date of invoice, from EOM, or from ROG.*
9. **Use, define** *or* **illustrate**

markup	*markdown*	*ROG*
markup percent	*cash discount*	*trade discount*
average markup	*EOM*	

Markups and Markup Percents

Success or failure in business will ultimately depend on how successfully a firm markets its products. Prices must be set high enough to assure enough return to cover expenses plus a reasonable profit. On the other hand, they must be set low enough to guarantee adequate buyer appeal.

Markups must be calculated based on the best knowledge available about the value of the merchandise in the market and the needs of the firm to cover its expenses. Markdown (sales) must be calculated on the basis of how important it is to a retailer to sell merchandise that did not sell at the original retail price, and how great a loss the firm can withstand.

A number of procedures are used in making price calculations in retailing, but certainly markup percents are among the most important.

Individual Markup

Note: The terms *retail price* and *selling price* are used interchangeably.

Markup problems are applied uses of the percentage problems covered in Chapter 4. The term *markup* refers to the amount a seller charges for a good in excess of the amount the seller paid for the good. Hence:

$$\begin{array}{ll} \text{selling price} & \text{often referred to as } \textit{retail price} \\ \underline{-\text{cost}} & \text{amount seller paid} \\ =\text{markup} & \end{array}$$

It follows logically from the above equation that

$$\begin{array}{ccc} \text{cost} & & \text{selling price} \\ \underline{+\text{markup}} & \text{and} & \underline{-\text{markup}} \\ =\text{selling price} & & =\text{cost} \end{array}$$

Although the student should be able to instantly recognize all the preceding equations, it is more useful if the equation is always written

$$\begin{array}{l} SP \\ \underline{-C} \\ =M \end{array}$$

as will be evident later when markup percent is discussed.

Example   A retail store buys clocks for $8 each and sells them for $12 each. How much is the markup on each clock?

Solution
$$\begin{array}{lll} SP & = & \$12 \\ \underline{-C} & = & \underline{-\ 8} \\ =M & & \$\ 4 \end{array}$$

Assignment 5-1

1. A clothing store buys men's suits for $76 and sells them for $110. How much is the markup on each suit?

2. A furniture store sells chairs for $89 each. The markup on each chair is $31. How much does each chair cost the store?

3. A retailer pays $128 for refrigerators and marks them up $56. What is the retail price?

4. Fill in the blanks in the following retail, cost, and markup problems:

	Retail	−	*Cost*	=	*Markup*
a.	$647		$463		_____
b.	$59		_____		$28
c.	_____		$1284		$948
d.	$48		$32		_____
e.	_____		$3.18		$5.28
f.	$175		_____		$75
g.	$1475.45		$1000		_____
h.	$1856.45		_____		$1027.35
i.	_____		$2489		$1833
j.	$6.07		$2.18		_____

Markup Percent

Although it is necessary to know the dollar amount of markup, people involved in marketing are more concerned with the markup percent. It might be wise to review the percentage formulas:

$$\text{percentage} = \text{base} \times \text{rate} \quad P = B \times R$$

$$\text{base} = \frac{\text{percentage}}{\text{rate}} \quad\quad B = \frac{P}{R}$$

$$\text{rate} = \frac{\text{percentage}}{\text{base}} \quad\quad R = \frac{P}{B}$$

In problems dealing with retail, cost, and markup, either cost or retail will always be given as base. By definition, in percentage problems *base is always 100%*. The *markup percent* equals the *markup divided by* the *selling price (retail)* or the *cost*, whichever is given as base in the problem.

Example   A department store buys records for $4 and resells them for $6.

1. What is the percent of markup based on *retail?*

2. What is the percent of markup based on *cost?*

Note: The key words here are *on retail* and *on cost.* Later, the word *based* will be eliminated.

Solution   1. Since markup is based on retail, retail is base and 100%. The markup is determined by subtracting the cost, $4, from the selling price, $6. $6 − $4 = $2.

	Amount	Percent	Part represented
SP	$6	100%	base
−C	$4		percentage
=M	$2		percentage

NOTE: Percentages are parts of the base. Thus, there can be more than one percentage.

To find the percent of markup, use the formula for finding a percent:

B = retail or selling price
R = markup percent based on selling price
P = amount of markup

$$R = \frac{P}{B}$$

(markup %) $R = \frac{\$2 \ (\text{markup})}{\$6 \ (\text{selling price})}$

$$R = 33\frac{1}{3}\%$$

After finding the percent of base that the markup represents, the *cost percent* can be determined by subtracting the percent of markup from the base:

	Amount	Percent	Part represented
SP	$6	100%	base
−C	$4		percentage
=M	$2	$33\frac{1}{3}\%$	percentage

$$\begin{array}{rl} 100\% & \text{retail percent (base)} \\ -33\frac{1}{3}\% & \text{markup percent} \\ \hline = 66\frac{2}{3}\% & \text{cost percent} \end{array}$$

	Amount	Percent
SP	$6	100%
−C	$4	$66\frac{2}{3}\%$
=M	$2	$33\frac{1}{3}\%$

← This was not required as part of the answer, but it will become important later.

Solution 2. Since markup is based on cost, cost is base and 100%. The markup is still $2: $6 − $4 = $2.

	Amount	Percent	Part represented
SP	$6		percentage
−C	$4	100%	base
=M	$2		percentage

To find the percent of markup, use the formula for finding a percent:

B = cost

R = markup percent based on cost

P = amount of markup

$R = \dfrac{P}{B}$

(markup %) $R = \dfrac{\$2}{\$4}$ (amount of markup) (cost)

$R = 50\%$

After finding the percent of base that the markup represents, the *retail percent* can be calculated by adding the percent of markup to the base:

	Amount	Percent	Part represented
SP	$6		percentage
−C	$4	100%	base
=M	$2	50%	percentage

50% + 100% = 150% retail percent

	Amount	Percent
SP	$6	150%
−C	$4	100%
=M	$2	50%

← This was not required as part of the answer, but again, it will become important later.

Assignment 5-2

1. An electric toothbrush retails for $15. It costs the retailer $10. What is the percent of markup based on

    a. retail _____   **b.** cost _____

2. A coffeepot costs a retailer $12. She marks it up $4. What is the percent of markup based on

    a. retail _____   **b.** cost _____

3. Shirts sell for $10 each at Garfinkel's Department Store. The store buys the shirts in cartons containing a dozen each and pays $72 for a carton. What is the percent of markup on each shirt based on

    a. retail _____   **b.** cost _____

4. A radio costs $8.50 and retails for $13.50. What is the percent of markup based on

    a. retail _____   **b.** cost _____

5. A color television set retails for $680. It is marked up $120. What is the percent of markup based on

    a. retail _____   **b.** cost _____

6. Fill in the blanks:

	Retail	−	*Cost*	=	*Markup*	*Markup % based on* retail	cost
a.	$100		$80		_____	_____	_____
b.	$43		_____		$14.50	_____	_____
c.	_____		$12.50		$3.50	_____	_____
d.	$300		$150		_____	_____	_____
e.	$.75		_____		$.25	_____	_____
f.	$15		_____		$10	_____	_____
g.	_____		$1.33		$2	_____	_____
h.	$10		$7.50		_____	_____	_____

Finding the Unknowns in Retailing

There may be instances in which the amount of only one of the three (retail, cost, or markup) is known, yet a firm needs further information. When two of the six parts of markup problems are given and the base for markup is known, the other parts can be derived by subtracting, adding, and using percentage formulas. This is illustrated in the following examples.

Finding the Unknowns When the Cost and Markup Percent on Retail are Given

Example   Find all the unknowns if a suitcase cost the seller $21 and is marked up 30% on retail.

Note: The following solution will show a very careful step-by-step process. The marketing formula used to find the selling price when the markup percent is *based on retail* is

$$SP = \frac{C}{100\% - M\%} \quad (M\% = \text{markup } \%)$$

Solution   Using the information given, the following parts of the problem are known before any calculations are made (remember that retail = 100% because markup is based on *retail*):

	Amount	Percent	Part represented
SP		100%	base
−C	$21		percentage
=M		30%	percentage

The percent of cost can be found by subtracting the percent of markup from the percent of base (percent of base is always 100%):

$$100\% - 30\% = 70\%$$

	Amount	Percent
SP		100%
−C	$21 ÷	70%
=M		30%

When the known *amount* (in this case, the $21) is *not* the base, it is *divided* by its *percent* to find the base.

The amount of retail can be determined by using the formula for finding the base (in this problem, *retail* was given as base):

$$B = \frac{P}{R}$$

$$B = \frac{\$21}{70\%} \quad \frac{\text{amount of cost}}{\text{percent of cost}}$$

$$B = \$30 \quad \text{amount of retail}$$

OR

$$SP = \frac{C}{100\% - M\%}$$

$$SP = \frac{\$21}{100\% - 30\%}$$

$$SP = \frac{\$21}{70\%}$$

$$SP = \$30$$

The amount of cost can be subtracted from the amount of retail to find the amount of markup—that is, $30 − $21 = $9. Upon entering $9 for the amount of markup, the problem is complete.

	Amount	Percent
SP	$30	100%
−C	$21	70%
=M	$ 9	30%

Assignment 5-3

1.   Find the unknowns in the following table:

	Retail −	Cost =	Markup	Markup %	Cost %	Base
a.	_____	$45	_____	25%	_____	retail
b.	_____	$60	_____	40%	_____	retail
c.	_____	$280	_____	30%	_____	retail
d.	_____	$12	_____	$33\frac{1}{3}\%$	_____	retail
e.	_____	$30	_____	50%	_____	retail
f.	_____	$4960	_____	20%	_____	retail
g.	_____	$325	_____	35%	_____	retail
h.	_____	$56.40	_____	40%	_____	retail
i.	_____	$26.25	_____	25%	_____	retail
j.	_____	$49.60	_____	38%	_____	retail

2.   Find the retail price of a model car that costs the dealer $6 and will carry a markup of 40% on retail.

3.   Jonesborough's Furniture pays $35 for a coffee table. Its markup on furniture is 30% on retail. What is the retail price to Jonesborough's customers?

4.   Washington Whitley's Telaco Station carries automobile accessories. One style of slip-on seat covers costs Mr. Whitley $16. He has decided to mark them up 20% on retail to attract new customers. What will be his retail price?

5.   Determine the retail price of a record that costs $3.20 and is marked up 60% on retail.

Finding the Unknowns When the Retail Price and Markup Percent on Retail Are Given

Example   Find the unknowns if a typewriter that retails for $140 is marked up 40% on retail.

NOTE: A very careful step-by-step solution is presented below. The following formula is used to find the cost when the markup percent is *based on retail:*

$$SP = \frac{C}{100\% - M\%}$$

$$\frac{SP}{1} \bowtie \frac{C}{(100\% - M\%)} \quad \text{(cross multiply)}$$

$$SP \times (100\% - M\%) = C$$

or

$$C = SP \times (100\% - M\%)$$

Solution   Using the information given, the following parts of the problem are known before any calculations are made:

	Amount	Percent	Part represented
SP	$140	100%	base
−C			percentage
=M		40%	percentage

The percent of cost can be found by subtracting the percent of markup from the percent of retail:

$$100\% - 40\% = 60\%$$

	Amount	Percent
SP	$140	100%
−C		60%
=M		40%

When the known *amount* is the base, it is *multiplied* by the *percent* of the *unknown amount* to find the percentage.

The amount of cost can be determined by applying the percentage formula for finding a percentage (*retail* has been given as base):

$$P = B \times R$$

$$P = \begin{array}{l} \$140 \quad \text{amount of retail} \\ \underline{\times\, 60\%} \quad \text{percent of cost} \end{array}$$

$$P = \$140 \times .6$$

$$P = \$84 \quad \text{amount of cost}$$

OR

$$C = SP \times (100\% - M\%)$$

$$C = \$140 \times (100\% - 40\%)$$

$$C = \$140 \times 60\%$$

$$C = \$84$$

	Amount	Percent
SP	$140	100%
− C	$ 84	60%
= M		40%

The problem can be completed by subtracting the amount of cost from the amount of retail to find the amount of markup:

$140 − $84 = $56

	Amount	Percent
SP	$140	100%
− C	$ 84	60%
= M	$ 56	40%

Assignment 5-4

1. Find the unknowns in the following table:

Retail	− Cost =	Markup	Markup %	Cost %	Base
a. $25	____	____	40%	____	retail
b. $300	____	____	25%	____	retail
c. $70	____	____	50%	____	retail
d. $2	____	____	60%	____	retail
e. $16	____	____	35%	____	retail
f. $2000	____	____	45%	____	retail
g. $55	____	____	30%	____	retail
h. $.80	____	____	40%	____	retail
i. $7	____	____	38%	____	retail
j. $21	____	____	26%	____	retail

2. Suzanne's Typing Service has found that it must charge customers $7 per hour for typing business letters to achieve the desired 50% markup on retail. What is Suzanne's hourly cost?

3. Calculate the cost for a typewriter that retails for $320 and is marked up 40% on retail.

4. Golf clubs retail for $170. The Par Golf Shop marks clubs up 38% on retail. How much do the clubs cost?

5. Merchandise sells for $2300 and has a markup of 25% on retail. How much did the retailer pay for it?

Finding the Unknowns When the Retail Price and Markup Percent on Cost Are Given

Example Find the unknowns when a radio that sells for $96 is marked up 20%, based on cost.

Note: A step-by-step solution is presented below. The marketing formula for calculating the cost when the markup percent is *based on cost* is:

$$C = \frac{SP}{100\% + M\%}$$

Solution Using the information given, the following parts of the problem are known before any calculations are made:

	Amount	Percent	Part represented
SP	$96		percentage
−C		100%	base
=M		20%	percentage

The percent of retail can be found by adding the percent of markup to the percent of cost:

20% + 100% = 120%

	Amount	Percent
SP	$96	120%
−C		100%
=M		20%

When the known *amount* is the *not* the base, it is *divided* by *its percent* to find the base.

104   *Marketing Applications*

The amount of cost can be found by applying the percentage formula for finding the base (*cost* has been given as base):

$$B = \frac{P}{R}$$

$$B = \frac{\$96}{120\%} \quad \frac{\text{amount of retail}}{\text{percent of retail}}$$

$$B = \frac{\$96}{1.2}$$

$$B = \$80 \text{ amount of cost}$$

OR

$$C = \frac{SP}{100\% + M\%}$$

$$C = \frac{\$96}{100\% + 20\%}$$

$$C = \frac{\$96}{120\%}$$

$$C = \$80$$

	Amount	Percent
SP	$96 —÷→	120%
−C	$80	100%
=M		20%

The amount of markup can be found either by subtracting, $96 − 80 = $16, or by using the percentage formula:

$$P = B \times R$$

$$P = \$80 \times 20\%$$

$$P = \$80 \times .2$$

$$P = \$16$$

	Amount	Percent
SP	$96 —÷→	120%
−C	$80	100%
=M	$16	20%

Assignment 5-5

1. Find the unknowns in the following table:

	Retail −	Cost =	Markup	Markup %	Retail %	Base
a.	$60	___	___	50%	___	cost
b.	$20	___	___	60%	___	cost
c.	$12.50	___	___	25%	___	cost
d.	$200	___	___	$66\frac{2}{3}\%$	___	cost
e.	$3	___	___	50%	___	cost
f.	$63	___	___	40%	___	cost
g.	$28	___	___	$33\frac{1}{3}\%$	___	cost
h.	$2000	___	___	60%	___	cost
i.	$.50	___	___	25%	___	cost
j.	$15	___	___	65%	___	cost

2.   Dominici's Hardware marks hand tools up 70% on cost. A power drill retails for $34. How much is Dominici's cost?

3.   Find the cost for a toy that retails for $18 when it has been marked up 60% on cost.

4.   Karl's Home Cookin' charges $2.30 for chicken-fried steak. The manager attempts to maintain a markup percent of 100% on cost. Calculate the cost.

5.   Determine the cost on a product carrying a 75% markup-on-cost which sells for $175.

Finding the Unknowns When the Cost and Markup Percent on Cost Are Given

Example   Find the unknowns for a CB radio that costs a retailer $120 and is marked up 60% on cost.

Note: A careful step-by-step solution is presented below. The formula used to calculate the selling price when the markup percent is *based on cost* is

$$C = \frac{SP}{100\% + M\%}$$

$$\frac{C}{1} \diagdown \frac{SP}{(100\% + M\%)} \quad \text{(cross multiply)}$$

$$C \times (100\% + M\%) = SP$$

or

$$SP = C \times (100\% + M\%)$$

Solution   Using the information given, the following parts of the problem are known before any calculations are made:

	Amount	Percent	Part represented
SP			percentage
− C	$120	100%	base
= M		60%	percentage

The percent of retail can be found by adding the percent of markup to the percent of cost:

60% + 100% = 160%

	Amount	Percent
SP	← = − 160%	
− C	$120	100%
= M		60%

When the known *amount* is the base, it is *multiplied* by the *percent* of the *unknown amount* to find the percentage.

The amount of retail can be found by using the percentage formula for finding a percentage (*cost* has been given as base):

$P =$ B amount of cost

     $\times R$ percent of retail

$P = \$120 \times 160\%$ **OR**

$P = \$120 \times 1.6$

$P = \$192$ amount of retail

$SP = C \times (100\% + M\%)$

$SP = \$120 \times (100\% + 60\%)$

$SP = \$120 \times 160\%$

$SP = \$192$

	Amount	Percent
SP	$192 ← = − 160%	
− C	$120	100%
= M		60%

The amount of markup can be found by subtracting the amount of cost from the amount of retail:

$192 − $120 = $72

	Amount	Percent
SP	$192 ← = − 160%	
− C	$120	100%
= M	$ 72	60%

Assignment 5-6

1. Find the unknowns in the following table:

	Retail −	Cost =	Markup	Markup %	Retail %	Base
a. _____	$5	_____	100%	_____	cost
b. _____	$25	_____	70%	_____	cost
c. _____	$15	_____	60%	_____	cost
d. _____	$30	_____	55%	_____	cost
e. _____	$7	_____	40%	_____	cost
f. _____	$850	_____	65%	_____	cost
g. _____	$350	_____	45%	_____	cost
h. _____	$55	_____	30%	_____	cost
i. _____	$175	_____	90%	_____	cost
j. _____	$180	_____	85%	_____	cost

2. The Days Inn estimates its costs at $10 per room. The markup desired by management is 80% on cost. What do guests at the inn pay?

3. Calculate the retail price for a suit costing the retail clothing stores $80, if the markup percent is 70% on cost.

4. Determine the retail price for a dozen eggs costing grocery stores $.65, if the markup percent is 30% on cost.

5. Ye Olde Pub marks liquor up 110% on cost. A bottle of aged Scotch costs the pub $9.50. For how much will the bottle sell?

Review
The following problems are designed to test your comprehension of the preceding assignments.

Assignment 5-7

1. Kelly's Gun Shop sells a rifle for $126. If the markup based on cost is 40%, what is the cost?

2. What is the amount of the markup on a sofa that sells for $298 if the markup percent is 42% of retail?

3. What is the selling price of a used television set that cost $75 and is marked up 45% on cost?

4. Joe Garcia's Restaurant charges $4.50 for an enchilada dinner. The cost of preparing the dinner is $3. What percent markup is there on the selling price?

5. A carpet sells for $200 and is marked up 50% on cost. What is the cost?

6. A haberdasher sells a shirt for $13.50. If the markup percent on retail is 42%, what is the cost of the shirt?

7. A football costs $25 and sells for $45. What is the markup percent on retail?

8. A ten-speed bicycle retails for $160. The markup percent is 30% on retail. What is the cost to the retailer?

9. Honest Joe, who sells used cars, sold an old Dodge for $600. The car had been marked up $33\frac{1}{3}$% on retail. What was the cost?

10. A hardware dealer pays 1.9¢ each for screws and sells them for 3.5¢ each. What is the markup percent based on cost?

11. A buyer for a supermarket chain marks up produce 84% on cost. If she pays $287 for a purchase of potatoes, for how much will she sell them?

12. Fill in the following blanks:

	Base	Retail	Cost	Markup	Retail %	Cost %	Markup %
a. retail	$17	_____	$10		_____	_____	_____
b. cost	_____	$65	_____	130%	_____	_____	
c. retail	_____	_____	$146	_____	60%	_____	
d. cost	$49	_____	_____	_____	_____	15%	
e. retail	_____	$1235	_____	_____	42%	_____	
f. cost	_____	_____	$927	150%	_____	_____	
g. retail	$35,600	_____	_____	_____	80%	_____	
h. cost	_____	$1.25	_____	_____	_____	35%	
i. retail	_____	_____	$.15	_____	70%	_____	
j. cost	$35	_____	_____	_____	_____	110%	

Average Markup

The markup problems up to this point have all been markups on single items. Retailers do not ordinarily buy one item at a time. Some items by their nature require higher markups than others. Expensive luxury goods do not have a large market and are likely to have higher markups than staple necessity goods which do have a large market.

A retailer attempts to maintain an *average* markup for a department or for a whole store. The percent of markup necessary to cover operating expenses and guarantee a reasonable profit is determined, and the prices for merchandise are adjusted to return the needed markup percent.

A company's buyers work from a budget. They have a specific dollar amount to spend, and they must keep accurate records of their expenditures. In addition, when a buyer purchases merchandise, care must be taken to ensure that the desired average markup is attained. Merchandise is typically bought in different amounts, at various costs, and at different times. The following procedure is used.

1. The total budget is determined and recorded as *total planned purchases*. The total budget is recorded at both cost and retail.
2. When purchases are made, they are subtracted from the total planned purchases, at both cost and retail. The difference between *total planned purchases* and *purchases to date* gives the *balance remaining to buy* at cost and at retail.
3. The *markup percent* on the *balance remaining to buy* at cost and at retail is calculated. This markup percent will be required on the remaining purchases if the retailer is to achieve the desired average markup on the total planned purchases.

Example A buyer plans to buy $2000 worth of clothes at retail for the women's department in a department store. The merchandise is to have an average markup of 60% on retail. The first purchases made will have a low markup to attract customers to the department. The first purchases will retail at $400 and have a markup of 30% on retail. What percent must the balance of the total purchase be marked up in order to attain the desired average markup?

Solution The parts of the problem should be organized as follows:

	Retail	−	Cost	=	Markup	Markup %
total planned purchases	$2000					60%
−purchases to date	400		___		___	30%
=balance to buy						

Note: Markup percent on total planned purchases minus markup percent on purchases to date does *not* equal markup percent on balance to buy.

The part of the problem that needs to be solved is *markup percent of balance to buy*. To find this, the retail value of balance to buy and the markup of balance to buy must be determined and compared. (Note that the markup percent is based *on retail*.)

The retail balance to buy can be determined by subtracting retail value of purchases to date from retail value of total planned purchases:

$2000 retail value of total planned purchases
−   400 retail value of purchases to date
=$1600 retail value of balance to buy

	Retail	−	Cost	=	Markup	Markup %
total planned purchases	$2000					60%
−purchases to date	400		___		___	30%
=balance to buy	$1600					

The cost percent of the total planned purchases is determined by subtracting the markup percent from the retail percent:

100% retail percent
− 60% markup percent
= 40% cost percent

	Amount	Percent
SP	$2000	100%
−C		40%
=M		60%

The cost of the total planned purchases is determined by using the percentage formula:

$P = B \times R$

$P =$ $2000 amount of retail
$\times$ 40% percent of cost

$P = \$2000 \times .4$

$P = \$800$ amount of cost

OR

$C = SP(100\% - m\%)$

$C = \$2000(100\% - 60\%)$

$C = \$2000 \times 40\%$

$C = \$800$

	Retail	–	Cost	=	Markup	Markup %
total planned purchases	$2000		$800			60%
−purchases to date	400					30%
=balance to buy	$1600					

The cost percent of purchases to date is determined by subtracting the markup percent from the retail percent:

      100% retail percent
   − 30% markup percent
   = 70% cost percent

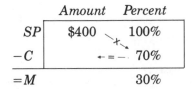

The cost of purchases to date is determined by using the percentage formula:

$P = B \times R$

$P = 400 amount of retail

   $\times$ 70%   cost percent

$P = $400 \times .7$

$P = 280 amount of cost

OR

$C = SP \times (100\% - M\%)$

$C = $400 \times (100\% - 30\%)$

$C = $400 \times 70\%$

$C = 280

	Retail	–	Cost	=	Markup	Markup %
total planned purchases	$2000		$800			60%
−purchases to date	400		280			30%
=balance to buy	$1600					

The cost value of the balance to buy is found by subtracting the cost value of purchases to date from the cost value of total planned purchases:

      $800
   − 280
   =$520

	Retail	–	Cost	=	Markup	Markup %
total planned purchases	$2000		$800			60%
−purchases to date	400		280			30%
=balance to buy	$1600		$520			

Balance-to-buy markup is determined by subtracting cost value of balance to buy from retail value of balance to buy:

      $1600
   − 520
   =$1080

	Retail	–	Cost	=	Markup	Markup %
total planned purchases	$2000		$800			60%
−purchases to date	400		280			30%
=balance to buy	$1600		$520		$1080	

The markup percent of the balance to buy can now be determined by using the percentage formula for finding rates:

$$R = \frac{P}{B}$$

markup % $R = \dfrac{\$1080}{\$1600}$ markup value of balance to buy / retail value of balance to buy

$R = .675$

$R = 67.5\%$ markup percent of balance to buy

	Retail	–	Cost	=	Markup	Markup %
total planned purchases	$2000		$800			60%
−purchases to date	400		280			30%
=balance to buy	$1600		$520		$1080	67.5%

Assignment 5-8

1. A buyer plans to buy merchandise costing $50,000 for a department store, to be marked up 50% on retail. He has already bought merchandise costing $40,000 that will retail for $70,000. What must be the percent of markup on retail for the remaining purchases in order to achieve the desired average markup percent?

2. A buyer for a hardware store needs to buy goods costing $36,000 to sell for $60,000. She went to the Dallas market and started buying. At the end of the first day, she had made purchases costing $16,000, which will be marked up 20% on retail. What percent will she need to mark up the remaining purchases to attain the desired average markup?

3. Garfinkel's Department Store attempts to maintain a 40% average markup on retail on all merchandise. A buyer for the store has already spent $60,000 for merchandise that will retail for $98,000. The buyer intends to spend $90,000 *more*. What will be the percent of markup on retail for the remaining purchases?

4. A retailer plans to make purchases costing $80,000. She has determined that a 70% markup on cost is necessary to cover operating expenses and earn an adequate profit. The head buyer is visiting the trade show in New York. To date, he has purchased merchandise costing $30,000. It will be sold for $48,000. What will the markup percent on cost have to be for the remaining purchases in order to achieve the desired average markup?

5. Barney's Shoes maintains an average markup percent of 60% on cost. Barney Oldfoot plans to have merchandise retailing for $20,000 on hand at the beginning of spring. To date, he has made purchases costing $4000, which he will retail for $6400. Calculate the markup percent on cost required for the remaining purchases in order to achieve the 60% average markup.

6. A dress buyer has a budget of $300,000 cost to be sold for $495,000. She has purchased merchandise costing $75,000 as of today. That merchandise has been marked up 50% on cost. Determine the markup percent required on the remaining purchases to be made in order to attain the desired average markup percent.

7. Find the percent of markup-on-retail of the balance to buy, using the following information. (*Note:* It is not necessary to fill in the information in every block, only the last column on the right of the *balance to buy*.) All problems are based on retail.

	Total purchases in $				Purchases to date in $				Balance to buy in $			
	Retail	*Cost*	*Markup*	%	*Retail*	*Cost*	*Markup*	%	*Retail*	*Cost*	*Markup*	%
a.		1,800	1,200			900			1,000			
b.		12,500		50	17,500	10,000						
c.			20,000	60	10,000					9,000		
d.	18,000		10,000			6,000		25				
e.			300	25			150	30				
f.	500					100		35		200		
g.	100,000			90		5,000		80				

Discounts

Business people must make several decisions on the discounts that they will offer or take. Discounts are offered as part of the pricing "package." Managers charged with the responsibility of pricing products must include their company's discount policy when setting price levels.

Each type of discount has a specific purpose. The purpose for, and effects of, offering discounts must be understood if realistic pricing policies are to be followed. In most industries, a traditional discount policy exists and usually must be followed if a firm expects to be competitive. Three types of discounts will be discussed in this section: markdown, cash discounts, and trade discounts.

Markdown

Although a retailer would always rather obtain the full price for everything, quite often some items must be marked down. Markdown may be the result of a retailer's having stock which, for a number of reasons, will not sell, or it may be the result of an effort to lure bargain hunters into the store.

The difference between the *original price* and the *actual selling price* is the *markdown*. Generally, however, retailers state the markdown on merchandise as a percent, such as 25% off. Consumers naturally assume that the markdown percent is based on the original retail price. Thus, if an article had sold for $100 and was marked down 25%, the assumption would be that the sales price would be $75 ($100 × 25% = $25; $100 − $25 = $75). Most retailers do base their markdowns on the original retail price, and the calculation is a simple difference problem (as discussed in Chapter 4). However, many retailers base markdown percents on the actual selling price of merchandise. The result of that practice is a larger markdown percent. For example, using our previous numbers, the actual selling price after the merchandise was marked down would be $75. The markdown percent based on the selling price would be

$$\frac{\$25}{\$75} \quad \frac{\text{markdown}}{\text{actual selling price}} = 33\tfrac{1}{3}\% \quad \begin{array}{l}\text{instead of 25\% when based on}\\\text{original selling price}\end{array}$$

Example   A store owner decides to reduce the selling price of her inventory 20% of original retail. The inventory is worth $6000 at retail. What is the markdown percent based on actual sales if she sells out the entire inventory?

Solution

1. Calculate the amount of markdown:

original retail × markdown percent
$6000 × 20% = $6000 × .2 = $1200

2. Calculate the actual sale price:

original retail − amount of markdown = actual sale price
$6000 − $1200 = $4800

3. Calculate the markdown percent on actual sale price:

$$\text{markdown \%} = \frac{\text{amount of markdown}}{\text{actual sale price}}$$

$$\text{markdown \%} = \frac{\$1200}{\$4800} = .25$$

markdown % = 25%

Alternate
Solution

While the solution given above is the proper way to calculate the markdown percent, a very simple short-cut method is possible. It consists of the following steps:

1. Subtract the markdown percent based on the original sales price from 100%.
2. Divide the markdown percent based on the original retail price by the result obtained in Step 1.

Step 1	Step 2

Step 1

$$100\%$$
$$-\ \ 20\%$$
$$\overline{\ \ \ 80\%}$$

Step 2

$$\frac{20\%}{80\%} = \frac{1}{4} = 25\%$$

Assignment 5-9

1. A dealer reduces the price of the merchandise in his store by 25% of retail. The original value at retail was $120,000. What is the markdown percent on actual sales, assuming all merchandise is sold?

2. With cold weather approaching, Bimble's Department Store attempts to get rid of the swimsuits in stock. The original retail value of the stock is $6000. The price is reduced by 40% of original retail. What is the markdown percent on actual sales, assuming the swimsuits are sold out?

3. A pet shop owner wants to get rid of the guppies in stock. There are now 325 guppies in the guppy tank, and they are priced at $.49 each. If the pet shop owner reduces the price by 30% of original retail and sells them all, what will be the markdown percent on actual sales?

4. Chuck Kent, the owner of a men's clothing store, heard from a reliable source that coats with large lapels would be out of style this fall. Chuck lowered the price of his inventory of men's coats by 15%. The original selling price was $12,643.18. If Chuck was able to sell off the unwanted stock, what was the markdown percent on actual sales?

5. The high-fashion section of a department store near the U.C. campus in Berkeley, California, was going broke because of a lack of customers. The manager lowered the $13,500 price of his inventory by $33\frac{1}{3}\%$ and somehow sold it all. What was the markdown percent on actual sales?

6.   Find the markdown percent on actual sales for the following:

Original retail price	Markdown percent of original retail	Markdown percent on actual sales
a. $242	40%	_____
b. $1816.25	12%	_____
c. $180,000	35%	_____
d. $.29	20%	_____
e. $27,432	10%	_____

Cash Discounts

Most manufacturers and wholesalers provide their customers with a *discount for prompt payment*. A discount of this type is a *cash discount*. An explanation and an example for each of the three most frequently used types of cash discounts are given below.

2/10, n/30   A 2% discount is allowed if the invoice is paid within 10 days of the invoice date (represented by the 2/10). The net amount of the invoice is due within 30 days (n/30).

Example   How much would have to be paid on an invoice of $500 with terms of 3/10, n/45 if paid within the discount period?

Solution   base = amount of credit to be received

rate = 100% minus discount rate (rate to be paid)

percentage = amount to be paid

$P = B \times R$

$P = \$500 \times (100\% - 3\%) = \$500 \times 97\%$

$P = \$500 \times 97\% = \$485$

2/10, n/30 EOM   A 2% discount is allowed if the invoice is paid by the tenth of the month following the month in which the invoice was received. The initials EOM stand for "end of month." Thus, the discount payment period does not begin until the end of the month in which the invoice is dated. The net amount of the invoice is due 30 days later.

Example   How much would have to be paid on an invoice of $2000 dated September 6 and paid on October 8, if terms are 3/10, n/30 EOM?

Solution $P = B \times R$

$P = \$2000 \times (100\% - 3\%) = \$2000 \times 97\%$

$P = \$1940$

2/10, n/30 ROG   The letters ROG mean "receipt of goods." The discount period begins when the merchandise is received by the buyer instead of on the date of the invoice.

Example   An invoice of $700 dated September 6 was received in the mail on September 8. Merchandise shipped by rail on September 6 arrived on September 23. If terms were 3/10, n/30 ROG, on what date would the discount period expire? What would be the last date for paying the net amount of the invoice? What amount would have to be paid if the invoice was paid within the discount period?

Solution   1. Merchandise received on September 23 would have to be paid for by October 3 (10 days after receipt) to take advantage of the discount.
2. The net amount of the invoice would be due on October 23 (30 days after September 23).
3. $P = B \times R$

$P = \$700 \times (100\% - 3\%) = \$700 \times 97\%$

$P = \$679$

The cash discount is applied *only on the merchandise that is retained* by the buyer. If part of the merchandise is returned because it was damaged in shipment or was not the merchandise ordered, or if freight charges are included in the invoice, then these must be subtracted from the net invoice before the discount is calculated. Freight charges, in total, must be added back to determine the amount of payment.

Assignment 5-10

1. A $350 invoice with terms 3/10, n/30 was dated January 4. If the debt was paid on January 11, how much was the payment?

2. An invoice with terms 2/10, 1/30, n/60 was dated March 3. The net invoice is $680. How much is owed if the invoice is paid on March 6? How much if paid on April 1? How much if paid on April 4?

   Note: The seller is offering two discount periods and terms. The discount is 2% if paid within 10 days, 1% if paid between the 11th day and the 30th day.

3. An invoice with terms 2/10, n/30 was dated October 14. The invoice listed merchandise of $540 and $5 shipping costs. There was $25 worth of damage, and the damaged merchandise had to be returned. How much is due if the debt is paid on October 18?

4. An invoice with terms 3/10, 2/30, n/60 dated February 23 contained the following items:

    20 beer steins @ $7 each
    10 dozen wine glasses @ $36 per dozen
    10 brandy snifters @ $4.50 each

    In the shipment, two brandy snifters and four beer steins were broken and had to be returned to the sender. Freight charges totaled $18. How much is owed if the bill is paid on:
    a. March 30 _____   b. March 18 _____   c. March 1 _____

5. Merchandise valued at $1000 was received by Ned Banks Industries on September 15. What would be the date by which a discount must be taken if terms were 2/10, n/30 EOM? If terms were 2/10, n/30 ROG? If payment was made within the discount period using either cash discount policy, what would be the required payment?
    EOM _____   ROG _____   payment _____

6. A manufacturer gave terms of 8/10 EOM. An invoice of $4500 dated December 28 was paid on January 9. What amount should have been paid? When was the net bill due under these terms?

Trade Discounts

Trade discounts are offered to different classes of customers at different rates. A manufacturer has to sell to wholesalers at a lower rate than to retailers. The manufacturer might also sell to an export agent. The discount to the agent would be greater than the discount to wholesalers.

Production costs for catalogs describing the manufacturer's product offerings are expensive. Rather than print three separate catalogs identical except for the prices, the manufacturer can print one catalog. The prices in the catalog are *list prices*, the suggested retail prices to be charged to final customers. A discount sheet can then be inserted into the catalog so that all classes of customers will be able to calculate their costs when buying from the manufacturer.

For example, the manufacturer might sell to retailers at 40% off list:

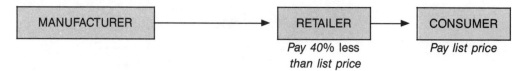

MANUFACTURER → RETAILER → CONSUMER

Pay 40% less than list price   Pay list price

Discounts are often offered in series. For example, the manufacturer might sell to wholesalers for 40, 15 [effectively, (100% − 40%) × (100% − 15%), or 60% × 85%, or *51% of list price*, which is a *discount of 49%*]:

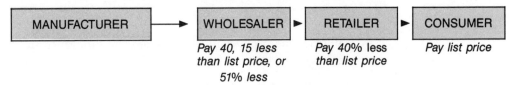

When selling to an agent, the discount might be 40, 15, 10 [effectively, (100% − 40%) × (100% − 15%) × (100% − 10%), or 60% × 85% × 90%, or *45.9% of list price*, which is a *discount of 54.1%*]:

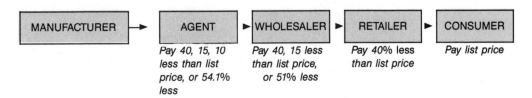

When a single discount is given, such as 40%, the calculation for finding the discount is a simple percentage problem. For finding the cost to the middleman (agent, wholesaler, or retailer), the calculation is a difference problem.

The best way to find the middleman's cost when the list price and a series of trade discounts are given is as follows:

1. Subtract each each discount in the series from 100%.
2. Multiply the results of the subtractions in Step 1 together.
3. Multiply the product found in Step 2 by the list price.

Example Find the cost to an agent for an item that lists for $2000. Agent discounts are 30,20,10.

Solution

$$\begin{array}{ccc} 100\% & 100\% & 100\% \\ -\ 30\% & -\ 20\% & -10\% \\ \hline 70\% \times & 80\% \times & 90\% \end{array} = .7 \times .8 \times .9 = .504$$

.504 × $2000 = $1008 = cost to agent

Alternate Solution

For some people, the method of solving trade discount problems presented below is preferable.

1. Multiply the list price by the first discount:

$2000
×30%
$ 600

2. Subtract the result in Step 1 from the list price:

$2000
− 600
$1400

3. Multiply the difference obtained in Step 2 by the second discount:

$1400
× 20%
$ 280

4. Subtract the product in Step 3 from the difference in Step 2:

$1400
−   280
$1120

5. Multiply the difference obtained in Step 4 by the third discount:

$1120
× 10%
$ 112

6. Subtract the product in Step 5 from the difference in Step 4 to obtain the final answer:

$1120
−   112
$1008   cost to agent

Assignment 5-11

1. Nicholas Toy Company allows trade discounts of 30, 20, 4 to wholesalers. How much will a wholesaler pay for an order that lists for $8000?

2. Alonzo's Winery allows trade discounts of 40, 10, 5 to wholesalers. How much does a wholesaler owe on an order with a list price of $1200?

3. Merlin's Magic Tricks allows trade discounts of 30%, 20%, 10% to wholesalers and discounts of 25%, 15%, 5% to retailers. On an order with a list price of $25,000, how much would a wholesaler pay? How much would a retailer pay?

4. An agent purchased merchandise listing for $100,000 to export to the European market. Trade discounts offered by the manufacturer were 40, 10, 10. The merchandise was received by the agent on August 14. The invoice listed terms of 6/10 EOM. The full invoice amount, less applicable discounts, was paid on September 6. How much did the agent have to pay?

5. Merchandise listing for $800 was purchased with trade discounts of 20, 10, 5. The merchandise arrived on July 28. An attached invoice was dated July 18 and was paid on August 1. What amount was paid if cash terms were:

    a. 3/10 EOM   b. 3/10, n/30, ROG   c. 3/10, n/30

Chapter 5 Self-Testing Exercises

1. A knife costs $1.50 and retails for $2. What is the markup percent on retail?

2. Merchandise damaged in shipment is marked down 50%. If the original retail value was to have been $7000 and the merchandise was completely sold out after offered for sale, what is the markdown percent on actual sales?

3. A buyer plans to purchase merchandise costing a total of $50,000 for the upcoming season, to carry an average markup of 42% on retail. To date, he has purchased merchandise costing $10,000 to be used as a come-on to the store's customers. It has been marked up 35% on retail. What must the remaining purchases be marked up, and what is the markup percent required to achieve the desired average markup?

4. A shirt costs $15 and retails for $22. What is the markup percent on cost?

5. A dress retails for $55 and carries a 30% markup on retail. What is the cost?

6. Stockings are purchased at $90 for 12 dozen. They are marked up 65% on cost. What is the retail price per pair?

7. Merchandise of $25,000 has been purchased to retail at $40,000. Remaining purchases to be made are $50,000 at cost. The desired average markup is 60% on cost. What must the markup percent on cost be for the remaining purchases?

8. A chair costs $56 and retails for $75.60. What is the markup percent on cost?

9. Candy retails for $5 per box and is marked up 50% on cost. What is the cost?

10. Lipstick costs $.78 per tube. It is marked up 75% on retail. What is the retail price?

11. Suits are marked down 15% from the normal retail price of $130. What will be the markdown percent based on each sale?

12. Ties sell for $7.50 each and cost $72 per dozen. What is the markup percent on retail?

13. The Irving Company of The Bronx, New York, ordered merchandise listing for $420. Trade discounts for the order are 20%, 10%, 5%. How much will the Irving Company be required to pay?

14. Swanson Department Store purchased furniture listing for $75,000. Trade discounts were 20%, 15%, 10%. Terms of payment were 3/10, n/45. If the invoice was dated 3/18 and was paid on 3/23, what amount should be paid?

15. An invoice dated March 6 with terms 4/10 EOM is for $400. On April 10, the debt was paid. What was the amount of payment?

16. International Distribution, Inc., ordered merchandise listing for $50,000 on May 3. Trade discounts were 40%, 20%. On May 8, an invoice arrived bearing cash terms of 2/10, n/30 ROG. The carload of goods arrived at International's off-loading dock on June 8. What is the last date International can pay for the merchandise and still take advantage of the cash discount? Assuming the debt is paid within this discount period, what amount must be remitted?

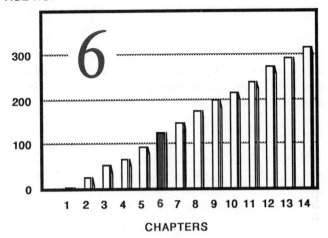

CHAPTERS

Banking Applications

Student Objectives

Upon completion of this chapter, the student should be able to

1. **Calculate** simple interest.
2. **Calculate** the principal.
3. **Calculate** the rate.
4. **Calculate** the time.
5. **Calculate** the interest, net proceeds, and true rate of interest on a discounted note.
6. **Calculate** the effective rate of interest on a personal loan.
7. **Calculate** the effective rate of interest on installment purchases.
8. **Calculate** the APR.
9. **Define, illustrate,** or **use**

simple interest	ordinary time
principal	exact interest
exact time	true rate of interest

Simple Interest

Simple Interest Formula

Interest is the charge made for using a certain amount of money (called the *principal*) for a definite period of time on the basis of a percent (called the *rate of interest*). The formula for calculating interest is

$$I = P \times R \times T$$

where

I = interest, the amount charged for the use of money

P = principal, the amount loaned or borrowed

R = rate of interest, the percent charged for the use of money on an annual basis

T = time, the time allowed or taken to pay back the principal and interest, stated in years, months, or days

Stated in Years

Since the rate of interest is always expressed on an annual basis, the actual time for which the money is being used is important. If the time is expressed in years, interest calculation is as shown in the following example.

Example   Calculate the interest on a loan of $500 at 12% for 1 year and for $\frac{1}{2}$ year.

Solution   For 1 year:

$$I = P \times R \times T$$

$$I = \$500 \times 12\% \times 1$$

$$I = \$500 \times .12 \times 1$$

$$I = \$500 \times \frac{12}{100} \times 1$$

$$I = \$5 \times 12 \times 1$$

$$I = \$60$$

For $\frac{1}{2}$ year:

$$I = P \times R \times T$$

$$I = \$500 \times 12\% \times \frac{1}{2} \quad \text{or} \quad I = \$500 \times .12 \times \frac{1}{2}$$

$$I = \$500 \times \frac{12}{100} \times \frac{1}{2} \qquad\qquad I = \$60 \times \frac{1}{2}$$

$$I = \$5 \times 12 \times \frac{1}{2} \qquad\qquad I = \$30$$

$$I = \$60 \times \frac{1}{2}$$

$$I = \$30$$

Assignment 6-1

1. Solve for interest in the following problems:

	Principal	Rate	Time	Interest
a.	$ 500	18%	1 year	_____
b.	240	9%	$\frac{1}{6}$ year	_____
c.	1500	10%	$\frac{1}{3}$ year	_____
d.	50	16%	$\frac{1}{2}$ year	_____
e.	175	12%	$\frac{2}{3}$ year	_____

2. Determine the interest on a loan of $2000 at 8% for 2 years.

3. Burns, Inc., charges 12% on payments for merchandise one fourth of a year after the bill is due. How much interest does a borrower owe on a bill for $200 at the end of 3 months?

Stated in Months If time is stated in monthly terms, then it is written as a fraction with the number of months in the interest period as the numerator and 12, the number of months in a year, as the denominator.

Example Calculate the amount of interest on a loan of $300 at 12% for 4 months.

Solution

$$I = P \times R \times T$$

$I = \$300 \times 12\% \times 4 \text{ months}$ or $I = \$300 \times .12 \times \frac{4}{12}$

$I = \$300 \times .12 \times \frac{1}{3}$

$I = \$300 \times \frac{12}{100} \times \frac{4}{12}$ $I = \$36 \times \frac{1}{3}$

$I = \$3 \times 1 \times 4$ $I = \$12$

$I = \$12$

Assignment 6-2

1. Solve for interest in the following problems:

	Principal	Rate	Time	Interest
a.	$ 250	12%	8 months	_____
b.	600	14%	6 months	_____

c.	$1300	6%	2 months	_____
d.	975	24%	18 months	_____
e.	550	18%	15 months	_____

2. On a loan of $1500 at 12% for 7 months, calculate the interest.

3. The Sharp Savings and Loan Association pays $5\frac{3}{4}$% on savings accounts. If Alan Sneed left $1000 in savings for 9 months, how much interest did his money earn?

Stated in Days   When time is stated in days, there are two methods commonly used to calculate the time:

1. *Exact time, ordinary interest.* Exact number of calendar days—360 days in a year
2. *Exact time, exact interest.* Exact number of calendar days—365 days in a year.

Exact time, ordinary interest* is sometimes referred to as *banker's interest*. The time fraction using this method has the exact number of days in the payment period as the numerator and a denominator of 360 days. (February is always assumed to contain 28 days.) This is the most commonly used method for calculating simple interest.

In determining the rediscount rate, the federal government and the federal reserve banks make interest computations on an exact time, exact interest basis. This method is usually referred to as *exact interest*. In this method, the exact number of days in each month in the interest period is counted and becomes the numerator of the time fraction, with a denominator of 365 days.

Example   What is the banker's interest on a note that has a face value of $500 at 9% per annum for 60 days?

Solution

$$I = P \times R \times T$$

$$I = \$500 \times 9\% \times 60 \text{ days}$$

$$I = \$500 \times \frac{\overset{3}{\cancel{9}}}{100} \times \frac{\overset{1}{\cancel{60}}}{\underset{\underset{2}{\cancel{6}}}{360}} \quad \text{or} \quad I = \$500 \times .09 \times \frac{60}{360}$$

$$I = \$500 \times .09 \times \frac{1}{6}$$

---

*This method of calculation will be used when the exact number of days or dates is given in a problem, unless otherwise stated.

$$I = \frac{\$5 \times 3 \times 1}{2} \qquad\qquad I = \$45 \times \frac{1}{6}$$

$$I = \frac{\$15}{2} \qquad\qquad\qquad I = \$7.50$$

$$I = \$7.50$$

Example   A loan of $1000 at 12% was made on April 16; it was due on August 16. Determine the amount of interest using (1) exact time, ordinary interest and (2) exact time, exact interest.

Solution   1. *Exact time, ordinary interest.* The exact number of days in each month must be calculated and then added together. There are 30 days in April, but the note was not taken out until April 16. Therefore,

April 16 to April 30

$= 30 - 16 =$ 14 days in April
31 days in May
30 days in June
31 days in July
16 days in August

total   122 days

Ordinary interest assumes 360 days in a year:

$$I = P \times R \times T$$

$$I = \$1000 \times 12\% \times \frac{122}{360} \quad \text{or} \quad I = \$1000 \times .12 \times \frac{122}{360}$$

$$I = \$1000 \times \frac{12}{100} \times \frac{122}{\underset{30}{360}} \qquad I = \$1000 \times .12 \times \frac{61}{180}$$

$$\qquad\qquad\qquad\qquad\qquad I = \$120 \times \frac{61}{180}$$

$$I = \frac{\$122}{3} \qquad\qquad\qquad\qquad I = \$40.67$$

$$I = \$40.67$$

2. *Exact time, exact interest.* In the previous solution, the exact time between April 16 and August 16 was determined to be 122 days. Since exact interest is calculated at 365 days in a year, the time fraction will now be $\frac{122}{365}$.

$$I = P \times R \times T$$

$$I = \$1000 \times 12\% \times \frac{122}{365} \quad \text{or} \quad I = \$1000 \times .12 \times \frac{122}{365}$$

$$\qquad\qquad\qquad\qquad\qquad I = \$120 \times \frac{122}{365}$$

$$I = \$1000 \times \frac{12}{100} \times \frac{122}{\underset{73}{365}} \qquad I = \frac{\$14,640}{365}$$

$$I = \$2 \times 12 \times \frac{122}{73} \qquad\qquad I = \$40.11$$

$$I = \frac{\$2928}{73}$$

$$I = \$40.11$$

Finding the Time

To find the number of days in the interest period, the following steps should be followed:

1. Find the day of the month on which the interest period begins in the leftmost column of Table 6-1.
2. Go across the row of the day found in Step 1 to the column headed by the month in which the interest period begins and record that number.
3. Find the day of the month on which the interest period ends in the leftmost column.
4. Go across the row of the day found in Step 3 to the column headed by the month in which the interest period ends and record that number.
5. Subtract the number of days found in Step 2 from the number of days found in Step 4.

Example   Find the number of days between March 3 and May 6.

Solution

1. The day of the beginning month is 3; therefore, find 3 in the leftmost column of Table 6-1.
2. The month is March; go across row 3 until you come to the column headed March.
3. Record that number, 62.
4. The day of the ending month is 6; find 6 in the left column.
5. The month is May; go across row 6 until you come to the column headed May.
6. Record that number, 126.
7. Subtract 62 from 126.

$$\begin{array}{r} 126 \\ -\ 62 \\ \hline = 64 \ \text{days} \end{array}$$

Assignment 6-3

1. Find the interest in the following using the exact time, ordinary interest method:

	Principal	Rate	Time	Interest
a.	$1000	18%	May 10-July 9	_____
b.	390	24%	September 5-December 14	_____
c.	200	12%	March 21-September 17	_____
d.	880	12.5%	July 4-August 3	_____
e.	3200	7%	October 16-December 15	_____

2. Find the interest in the following using the exact time, exact interest method:

	Principal	Rate	Time	Interest
a.	$ 185	8%	January 2-March 16	_____
b.	1825	11.5%	June 12-September 20	_____
c.	390	10%	February 16-March 28	_____
d.	730	13%	October 4-December 18	_____
e.	1095	12%	March 12-September 28	_____

3. Minnie's Plumbing Company borrowed $750 on July 26, to be paid back on October 26 with interest calculated at 16%. Determine the amount of interest using exact time, ordinary interest and exact time, exact interest.

Table 6-1 *Exact Number of Days from Beginning of Year to Any Date*

Day of Month	Jan.	Feb.	Mar.	April	May	June	July	Aug.	Sept.	Oct.	Nov.	Dec.	Day of Month
1	1	32	60	91	121	152	182	213	244	274	305	335	1
2	2	33	61	92	122	153	183	214	245	275	306	336	2
3	3	34	62	93	123	154	184	215	246	276	307	337	3
4	4	35	63	94	124	155	185	216	247	277	308	338	4
5	5	36	64	95	125	156	186	217	248	278	309	339	5
6	6	37	65	96	126	157	187	218	249	279	310	340	6
7	7	38	66	97	127	158	188	219	250	280	311	341	7
8	8	39	67	98	128	159	189	220	251	281	312	342	8
9	9	40	68	99	129	160	190	221	252	282	313	343	9
10	10	41	69	100	130	161	191	222	253	283	314	344	10
11	11	42	70	101	131	162	192	223	254	284	315	345	11
12	12	43	71	102	132	163	193	224	255	285	316	346	12
13	13	44	72	103	133	164	194	225	256	286	317	347	13
14	14	45	73	104	134	165	195	226	257	287	318	348	14
15	15	46	74	105	135	166	196	227	258	288	319	349	15
16	16	47	75	106	136	167	197	228	259	289	320	350	16
17	17	48	76	107	137	168	198	229	260	290	321	351	17
18	18	49	77	108	138	169	199	230	261	291	322	352	18
19	19	50	78	109	139	170	200	231	262	292	323	353	19
20	20	51	79	110	140	171	201	232	263	293	324	354	20
21	21	52	80	111	141	172	202	233	264	294	325	355	21
22	22	53	81	112	142	173	203	234	265	295	326	356	22
23	23	54	82	113	143	174	204	235	266	296	327	357	23
24	24	55	83	114	144	175	205	236	267	297	328	358	24
25	25	56	84	115	145	176	206	237	268	298	329	359	25
26	26	57	85	116	146	177	207	238	269	299	330	360	26
27	27	58	86	117	147	178	208	239	270	300	331	361	27
28	28	59	87	118	148	179	209	240	271	301	332	362	28
29	29	—	88	119	149	180	210	241	272	302	333	363	29
30	30	—	89	120	150	181	211	242	273	303	334	364	30
31	31	—	90	—	151	—	212	243	—	304	—	365	31

Other Uses of the Simple Interest Formula

Calculating the Principal
If the interest, the rate, and the time are known, the principal can be found by dividing the interest by the product of the rate and the time.

The original interest formula, $I = P \times R \times T$, can be converted to an equation in which the principal P is the unknown:

$$I = P \times R \times T$$

$$\frac{I}{R \times T} = \frac{P \times R \times T}{R \times T} \quad \text{divide both sides of the equation by } R \times T$$

$$\frac{I}{R \times T} = \frac{P \times R \times T}{R \times T} \quad \text{cancel}$$

$$\frac{I}{R \times T} = P \quad \text{rewrite}$$

Example Find the principal of a loan that earned $57 at a rate of 12% for 90 days.

Solution $P = \dfrac{I}{R \times T}$

$$P = \frac{\$57}{12\% \times 90 \text{ days}} \quad \text{or} \quad P = \frac{\$57}{.12 \times \dfrac{90}{360}}$$

$$P = \frac{\$57}{\dfrac{12}{100} \times \dfrac{90}{360}} \qquad P = \frac{\$57}{.12 \times \dfrac{1}{4}}$$

$$P = \frac{\$57}{\dfrac{12}{100} \times \dfrac{1}{4}} \qquad P = \frac{\$57}{.03}$$

$$P = \frac{\$57}{\dfrac{3}{100}} \qquad\qquad P = \$1900$$

$$P = \$57 \times \frac{100}{3}$$

$$P = \$19 \times 100$$

$$P = \$1900$$

Assignment 6-4

1. Find the principal in the following:

	Principal	Rate	Time	Interest
a.	_____	10%	90 days	$ 16
b.	_____	14%	45 days	14
c.	_____	24%	240 days	300
d.	_____	6%	270 days	45
e.	_____	8%	60 days	4
f.	_____	12%	30 days	20

g. _____	18%	180 days	369
h. _____	15%	January 6-October 13	49
i. _____	17%	March 14-June 12	102
j. _____	$12\frac{1}{2}$%	April 26-August 4	380

2. A. R. Jones put money in his bank savings account for his vacation in July. If he earned $66 interest in 180 days and the bank pays $5\frac{1}{2}$% on passbook savings accounts, how much money did Mr. Jones place in savings?

3. Mortgage Guarantee Corporation charges 3% on payments that arrive late each month. In June, the firm collected $587 in late-payment fees. Calculate the total amount of late payments for the month of June.

4. Lois Lane used her credit card for purchases. She was billed for her purchases, plus 30 days' interest of $15. The store from which the purchases were made charges 18%. What was the original charge, before interest?

5. Clark Kent earned $341 interest on bonds of the *Daily Planet*. He bought the bonds on January 19, and the interest was paid on April 19. The bonds earn interest at the rate of 16%. What was the value of the bonds Clark bought?

Calculating the Rate

Many times, the amount of the principal, the interest, and the time period are known, but a determination of the rate of interest is desired. In order to calculate the rate of interest, the simple interest formula, $I = P \times R \times T$, can be manipulated to isolate the rate R:

$$I = P \times R \times T$$

$$\frac{I}{P \times T} = \frac{P \times R \times T}{P \times T} \quad \text{divide both sides of the equation by } P \times T$$

$$\frac{I}{P \times T} = \frac{P \times R \times T}{P \times T} \quad \text{cancel}$$

$$\frac{I}{P \times T} = R \quad \text{rewrite}$$

Example   Calculate the rate of interest on a loan of $2500 for 90 days if the interest earned was $62.50.

Solution

$$R = \frac{I}{P \times T}$$

$$R = \frac{\$62.50}{\$2500 \times \frac{90}{360}}$$

$$R = \frac{\$62.50}{\overset{\$625}{\cancel{\$2500}} \times \frac{\overset{1}{\cancel{90}}}{\underset{\underset{1}{4}}{\cancel{360}}}}$$

$$R = \frac{\$62.50}{\$625 \times \frac{1}{1}}$$

$$R = \frac{\$62.50}{\$625}$$

$$R = \frac{1}{10}$$

$$R = 10\%$$

Assignment 6-5

1.   Find the rate in each of the following:

	Principal	Rate	Time	Interest
a.	$ 2,460	_____	60 days	$ 41.00
b.	150	_____	72 days	2.00
c.	3,264	_____	45 days	32.64
d.	292	_____	90 days	8.04
e.	150	_____	180 days	9.00
f.	14,292	_____	240 days	1,524.48
g.	1,596	_____	30 days	23.94
h.	360	_____	August 4-November 20	10.80
i.	2,000	_____	July 15-December 12	50.00
j.	1,500	_____	February 6-June 18	47.76

2.   Determine the rate of interest on a note of $2500 that returns $25 in 30 days.

3.   Thrift, Inc., offers credit terms for all purchases. In September, Tom Stayhorn was charged $5 interest for purchases of $325 on his monthly installment. What is the interest rate?

4. Book Binders Corporation pays its bills quarterly. For the previous 90-day period, the firm owed $31,360. Interest was $1254.40. What was the rate of interest?

Calculating the Time

Time can be calculated by a variation of the simple interest formula:

$$I = P \times R \times T$$

$$\frac{I}{P \times R} = \frac{P \times R \times T}{P \times R} \quad \text{divide both sides of the equation by } P \times R$$

$$\frac{I}{P \times R} = \frac{P \times R \times T}{P \times R} \quad \text{cancel}$$

$$\frac{I}{P \times R} = T \quad \text{rewrite}$$

This relationship, $T = \dfrac{I}{P \times R}$, will result in a fraction. The fraction represents a portion of a year. Therefore, if time is desired in days, the resulting fraction must be multiplied by 360 if ordinary interest is being used, or by 365 if exact interest is being used.

Example   Find the time in days on a note of $3500 that earned $35 interest at 12%.

Solution

$$T = \frac{I}{P \times R}$$

$$T = \frac{\$35}{\$3500 \times \frac{12}{100}} \times 360 \qquad or \qquad T = \frac{\$35}{\$3500 \times .12} \times 360$$

$$T = \frac{\overset{1}{\cancel{\$35}}}{\underset{1}{\cancel{\$3500}} \times \frac{12}{100}} \times 360 \qquad\qquad T = \frac{35}{420} \times 360$$

$$T = \frac{1}{1 \times \frac{12}{1}} \times 360 \qquad\qquad\qquad T = \frac{1}{12} \times 360$$

$$T = \frac{1}{12} \times 360 \qquad\qquad\qquad\qquad T = 30 \text{ days}$$

$$T = 30 \text{ days}$$

Assignment 6-6

1. Find the time in days, using ordinary interest in each of the following:

	Principal	Rate	Time	Interest
a.	$ 3,000	12%	_____	$ 20.00
b.	2,000	14%	_____	35.00
c.	6,500	9%	_____	71.50
d.	1,750	6%	_____	3.50
e.	2,140	12%	_____	32.10
f.	9,165	$17\frac{1}{2}$%	_____	400.97
g.	426	20%	_____	14.20
h.	800	8%	_____	3.20
i.	750	8%	_____	5.00
j.	14,500	18%	_____	261.00

2.   Determine the time on a note for $720 that earned $7.68 at 16%.

3.   Janson's Jewelry received a check for $613.20 in full payment of a loan for $600 at 12%. How long was the loan period?

4.   Calculate the number of days for which $425 was loaned if the rate was 12% and the interest paid was $5.10.

5.   A bank pays 12% on savings. If C. Geronimo's account contained $2800 before interest was added and $2828 after the addition of interest, how many days were in the interest period?

Discounting Notes

Business people sometimes find it necessary to obtain cash for a short time. There are several ways in which this needed cash can be obtained. One method is to borrow funds from a commercial bank. The bank either will lend the funds on a short-term basis for a simple interest charge or will discount a note.

A discounted note is much like a loan charging simple interest. The difference is that *discounting a note* means that interest is collected in advance rather than simple interest being paid at maturity. The note being discounted may be non-interest-bearing or interest-bearing.

Simple Interest and Discounts

The formula for calculating the amount of the discount is the same as that for calculating simple interest if the note is non-interest-bearing. In that case, the maturity value of the note will be the same as the principal. In this section, we will always assume that the note being discounted is non-interest-bearing.

$I = P \times R \times T$ interest formula
$D = MV \times R \times T$ discount formula

However, since discounts are taken in advance, the proceeds (the amount received by the borrower) are less, which makes the true rate of interest slightly higher for discounted notes than for notes bearing simple interest.

Example   Determine the true rate of interest that would be charged on a bank discount for a $1000 loan at 12% for 60 days.

Solution

$D = MV \times R \times T$

$D = \$1000 \times 12\% \times 60 \text{ days}$ or $D = \$1000 \times .12 \times \frac{60}{360}$

$D = \$1000 \times \frac{12}{100} \times \frac{60}{360}$ $D = \$1000 \times .12 \times \frac{1}{6}$

$D = \$1000 \times \frac{\overset{2}{\cancel{12}}}{100} \times \frac{\overset{1}{\cancel{60}}}{\underset{\underset{1}{6}}{\cancel{360}}}$ $D = \$120 \times \frac{1}{6}$

$D = \$20$ $D = \$20$

Since the discount is $20 and is taken in advance, the net proceeds would be $980:

net proceeds = maturity value − discount

$NP = \$1000 - \$20$

$NP = \$980$

Since the maker of the note, the borrower, has use of only $980 for the 60 days, not $1000, the true rate of interest can be determined as follows:

$$R = \frac{D}{NP \times T}$$

$$R = \frac{\$20}{\$980 \times \frac{60}{360}}$$

$$R = \frac{\overset{1}{\cancel{\$20}}}{\underset{\underset{6}{}}{\cancel{\$980}} \times \frac{\overset{1}{\cancel{60}}}{\cancel{360}}}$$

$$R = \frac{1}{\frac{49}{6}}$$

$$R = 1 \times \frac{6}{49}$$

$$R = \frac{6}{49}$$

$$R = .1224$$

$$R = 12.2\%$$

Assignment 6-7

1. Calculate the amount of the discount and the net proceeds for the following non-interest-bearing notes:

	Maturity Value	Rate	Time	Discount	Net Proceeds
a.	$ 1,000	12%	120 days	_____	_____
b.	500	9%	60 days	_____	_____
c.	20,000	16%	45 days	_____	_____
d.	5,000	14%	72 days	_____	_____
e.	1,500	24%	30 days	_____	_____

2. Determine the true rate of interest on a note for $1800 discounted at 10% for 90 days.

3. Hams For Sale, Limited, discounted a $3000 note at Ben E. Edward Financial for 45 days at a rate of 14%. Find the amount of discount, the net proceeds, and the true interest rate.

Effective Interest and APR

Since the end of World War II, borrowing from financial institutions and buying of goods on credit from retail outlets have increased tremendously. Americans today borrow from commercial banks, loan companies, credit unions, and pawnbrokers. Similarly, people are buying goods in retail establishments—ranging from large department stores to small specialized outlets—at an ever-increasing rate with the use of credit cards and other credit arrangements.

With the increase in the assortment of extenders of credit, abuses became common. Thus in 1969, Congress passed legislation to standardize the calculation of interest. This standardization enabled consumers to make comparisons of interest rates among lenders, thus making the industry more competitive.

The standardization of interest calculation is of such monumental importance to individuals as consumers that to neglect its mastery is to do oneself a disservice.

It is not too outlandish today to state that simple interest formulas have become outdated for consumers. Since 1969, all extenders of credit must reveal to the borrower what the effective interest rate (interest on the unpaid balance) is. It is referred to as the APR (Annual Percentage Rate).

Effective-Interest Formula

A formula can be constructed for calculating effective interest (interest on the unpaid balance). The formula is used to *estimate* the APR. It is as follows:

$$\text{effective interest rate} = \frac{2 \times \text{number of pay periods in 1 year} \times \text{total interest}}{\text{principal} \times (\text{number of payments} + 1)}$$

Definitions:
1. *Number of pay periods in 1 year* does not refer to the length of the loan. It refers to the frequency of pay periods. For example, the number of pay periods for a loan that is to be paid back in five monthly installments is 12, since the payments are monthly and there are 12 months in a year.
2. *Total interest* refers to all charges in excess of the principal. Regardless of the title given to such charges by retailers (service charges, etc.), for calculative purposes, it is interest. To find the amount of interest, it is necessary to find the total amount to be paid and subtract the amount of the principal:
   a. amount to be paid = number of payments × amount per payment
   b. principal = amount borrowed
   c. total interest = amount to be paid − principal

Personal Loans

Using the above formulas and information, effective interest can be calculated for personal loans as follows:

Example   Find the rate of interest on a loan of $375 to be repaid in ten equal monthly installments of $43 each.

Solution   a.   amount to be paid = number of payments × amount per payment

amount to be paid = 10 × $43 = $430

b.   principal = $375

c.   total interest = amount to be paid − principal

$$I = \$430 - \$375 = \$55$$

$$\text{effective interest rate} = \frac{2 \times \text{number of pay periods in 1 year} \times \text{total interest}}{\text{principal} \times (\text{number of payments} + 1)}$$

$$R = \frac{2 \times 12 \times \$55}{\$375 \times (10 + 1)}$$

$$R = \frac{2 \times 12 \times \overset{1}{\underset{1}{\cancel{55}}}}{\underset{75}{\cancel{375}} \times 11} \quad \text{or} \quad R = \frac{24 \times 55}{375 \times 11}$$

$$R = \frac{24}{75} \qquad\qquad R = \frac{1320}{4125}$$

$$R = .32 \qquad\qquad R = .32$$

$$R = 32\% \qquad\qquad R = 32\%$$

Note: Interest rates, when calculated on an effective-rate basis, are often very high. So long as you are applying the formula correctly, do not be concerned when rates seem unreasonably high. They often are.

Assignment 6-8

1. Calculate the effective interest rates on the following loans (round off to the nearest percent):

	Amount of loan	Amount of each payment	Number of payments	Frequency of payments	Total amount to be paid	Total interest	Effective interest rate
a.	$ 375	$ 52.00	8	monthly	_____	_____	_____
b.	400	32.08	15	monthly	_____	_____	_____
c.	750	50.00	16	weekly	_____	_____	_____
d.	460	60.00	9	quarterly	_____	_____	_____
e.	1,500	50.00	36	monthly	_____	_____	_____
f.	895	26.00	36	weekly	_____	_____	_____
g.	9,200	3,000.00	4	semi-annually	_____	_____	_____
h.	12,000	280.00	48	monthly	_____	_____	_____
i.	698	60.00	12	quarterly	_____	_____	_____
j.	45	8.00	6	monthly	_____	_____	_____

2. What is the effective interest rate on a $250 loan to be paid in ten equal monthly installments of $27.50? (Round off to the nearest percent.)

3.   John pays his life insurance premiums quarterly. If the total cost of the insurance is $300 per year and he makes payments of $78, what is the effective rate of interest for the privilege of paying quarterly?

4.   Al Gentry borrowed $200 from the Three-Ball Pawnshop, to be repaid with 14 weekly payments of $14.50 and one payment of $14.75. What is the effective rate of interest that Al must pay?

5.   Paul MacDougal borrowed $300 from the Sharkstown Bank. He agreed to pay five equal monthly installments of $52 each and one of $51.62. What is the effective rate of interest?

6.   Elnora bought a dishwasher for $500. Sears financed it for 24 months at $25 per payment. What is the effective rate of interest? (Round off to the nearest percent.)

Annual Percentage Rate (APR)

Remember, the effective interest rate formula is used to estimate the APR. It can be used when you do not have access to APR tables. Table 6-2, the annual percentage rate table, is more accurate. The Truth in Lending Act requires that the APR, when stated, must be accurate to the nearest $\frac{1}{4}$ of 1%.

Example   Find the rate of interest on a loan of $380 to be repaid in ten equal monthly installments of $41.20 each.

Solution   Table 6-2 is used by following the procedure below:

1. Amount to be paid = number of payments × amount per payment
   Amount to be paid = 10 × $41.20 = $412

2. Total interest = amount to be paid − principal
   Total interest = $412 − $380 = $32

3. $\frac{\text{Total interest}}{\text{Principal}} \times 100$ (Table 6-2 is based on $100 of financing.)

4. In Table 6-2, go down the left column to the number of payments, 10. Go across to 8.42. You will not find exactly 8.42 when reading across the table. It is between 17.75% and 18.00%, but is closest to 18.00%, so use 18%.

Assignment 6-9

Use Table 6-2 to find the APR in the following problems.

1. Alice Jones purchased a new color TV. The selling price of the TV was $500. Alice will pay $45 per month for one year. Calculate the APR.

2. Alan Brown bought a new van to use in his business. The cash price for the van is $14,500. Alan is trading in a car as a down payment. The dealer is allowing a trade-in value of $2500. Alan's payments will be $320 per month for 48 months. What is the APR?

3. Red Johnson bought a $500 stereo. He paid $50 down and financed the remainder for 10 equal monthly payments of $49 each. Determine the APR.

4. Ralph Lawer charged an $850 watch. He agreed to make 6 equal monthly payments of $150 each. What APR will Ralph pay?

5. A new sofa retailed for $1255. Becky Glass paid $275 down and will pay $95 per month for one year. Calculate the APR.

Interpolation
A process called interpolation (finding immediate terms in a series of terms) can be used to obtain more accurate APR figures.

Example Find the APR, using interpolation if necessary, for a loan of $5000 which will be paid off in 3 years. Monthly payments will be $180 each.

Solution
1. $36 \times \$180 = \$6480$ total installment cost
2. $\$6480 - \$5000 = \$1480$ interest
3. $\frac{\$1480}{\$5000} \times 100 = 29.6$ (number to be found in APR Table)
4. APR is between 17.5% and 17.75%.

Table 6-2 Annual Percentage Rate Table (Monthly Payments)

Number Of Payments	Annual Percentage Rate (Fiance Charge per $100 of Amount Financed)															
	10.00%	10.25%	10.50%	10.75%	11.00%	11.25%	11.50%	11.75%	12.00%	12.25%	12.50%	12.75%	13.00%	13.25%	13.50%	13.75%
1	0.83	0.85	0.87	0.90	0.92	0.94	0.96	0.98	1.00	1.02	1.04	1.06	1.08	1.10	1.12	1.15
2	1.25	1.28	1.31	1.35	1.38	1.41	1.44	1.47	1.50	1.53	1.57	1.60	1.63	1.66	1.69	1.72
3	1.67	1.71	1.76	1.80	1.84	1.88	1.92	1.96	2.01	2.05	2.09	2.13	2.17	2.22	2.26	2.30
4	2.09	2.14	2.20	2.25	2.30	2.35	2.41	2.46	2.51	2.57	2.62	2.67	2.72	2.78	2.83	2.88
5	2.51	2.58	2.64	2.70	2.77	2.83	2.89	2.96	3.02	3.08	3.15	3.21	3.27	3.34	3.40	3.46
6	2.94	3.01	3.08	3.16	3.23	3.31	3.38	3.45	3.53	3.60	3.68	3.75	3.83	3.90	3.97	4.05
7	3.36	3.45	3.53	3.62	3.70	3.78	3.87	3.95	4.04	4.12	4.21	4.29	4.38	4.47	4.55	4.64
8	3.79	3.88	3.98	4.07	4.17	4.26	4.36	4.46	4.55	4.65	4.74	4.84	4.94	5.03	5.13	5.22
9	4.21	4.32	4.43	4.53	4.64	4.75	4.85	4.96	5.07	5.17	5.28	5.39	5.49	5.60	5.71	5.82
10	4.64	4.76	4.88	4.99	5.11	5.23	5.35	5.46	5.58	5.70	5.82	5.94	6.05	6.17	6.29	6.41
11	5.07	5.20	5.33	5.45	5.58	5.71	5.84	5.97	6.10	6.23	6.36	6.49	6.62	6.75	6.88	7.01
12	5.50	5.64	5.78	5.92	6.06	6.20	6.34	6.48	6.62	6.76	6.90	7.04	7.18	7.32	7.46	7.60
13	5.93	6.08	6.23	6.38	6.53	6.68	6.84	6.99	7.14	7.29	7.44	7.59	7.75	7.90	8.05	8.20
14	6.36	6.52	6.69	6.85	7.01	7.17	7.34	7.50	7.66	7.82	7.99	8.15	8.31	8.48	8.64	8.81
15	6.80	6.97	7.14	7.32	7.49	7.66	7.84	8.01	8.19	8.36	8.53	8.71	8.88	9.06	9.23	9.41
16	7.23	7.41	7.60	7.78	7.97	8.15	8.34	8.53	8.71	8.90	9.08	9.27	9.46	9.64	9.83	10.02
17	7.67	7.86	8.06	8.25	8.45	8.65	8.84	9.04	9.24	9.44	9.63	9.83	10.03	10.23	10.43	10.63
18	8.10	8.31	8.52	8.73	8.93	9.14	9.35	9.56	9.77	9.98	10.19	10.40	10.61	10.82	11.03	11.24
19	8.54	8.76	8.98	9.20	9.42	9.64	9.86	10.08	10.30	10.52	10.74	10.96	11.18	11.41	11.63	11.85
20	8.98	9.21	9.44	9.67	9.90	10.13	10.37	10.60	10.83	11.06	11.30	11.53	11.76	12.00	12.23	12.46
21	9.42	9.66	9.90	10.15	10.39	10.63	10.88	11.12	11.36	11.61	11.85	12.10	12.34	12.59	12.84	13.08
22	9.86	10.12	10.37	10.62	10.88	11.13	11.39	11.64	11.90	12.16	12.41	12.67	12.93	13.19	13.44	13.70
23	10.30	10.57	10.84	11.10	11.37	11.63	11.90	12.17	12.44	12.71	12.97	13.24	13.51	13.78	14.05	14.32
24	10.75	11.02	11.30	11.58	11.86	12.14	12.42	12.70	12.98	13.26	13.54	13.82	14.10	14.38	14.66	14.95
25	11.19	11.48	11.77	12.06	12.35	12.64	12.93	13.22	13.52	13.81	14.10	14.40	14.69	14.98	15.28	15.57
26	11.64	11.94	12.24	12.54	12.85	13.15	13.45	13.75	14.06	14.36	14.67	14.97	15.28	15.59	15.89	16.20
27	12.09	12.40	12.71	13.03	13.34	13.66	13.97	14.29	14.60	14.92	15.24	15.56	15.87	16.19	16.51	16.83
28	12.53	12.86	13.18	13.51	13.84	14.16	14.49	14.82	15.15	15.48	15.81	16.14	16.47	16.80	17.13	17.46
29	12.98	13.32	13.66	14.00	14.33	14.67	15.01	15.35	15.70	16.04	16.38	16.72	17.07	17.41	17.75	18.10
30	13.43	13.78	14.13	14.48	14.83	15.19	15.54	15.89	16.24	16.60	16.95	17.31	17.66	18.02	18.38	18.74
31	13.89	14.25	14.61	14.97	15.33	15.70	16.06	16.43	16.79	17.16	17.53	17.90	18.27	18.63	19.00	19.38
32	14.34	14.71	15.09	15.46	15.84	16.21	16.59	16.97	17.35	17.73	18.11	18.49	18.87	19.25	19.63	20.02
33	14.79	15.18	15.57	15.95	16.34	16.73	17.12	17.51	17.90	18.29	18.69	19.08	19.47	19.87	20.26	20.66
34	15.25	15.65	16.04	16.44	16.85	17.25	17.65	18.05	18.46	18.86	19.27	19.67	20.08	20.49	20.90	21.31
35	15.70	16.11	16.53	16.94	17.35	17.77	18.18	18.60	19.01	19.43	19.85	20.27	20.69	21.11	21.53	21.95
36	16.16	16.58	17.01	17.43	17.86	18.29	18.71	19.14	19.57	20.00	20.43	20.87	21.30	21.73	22.17	22.60
37	16.62	17.06	17.49	17.93	18.37	18.81	19.25	19.69	20.13	20.58	21.02	21.46	21.91	22.36	22.81	23.25
38	17.08	17.53	17.98	18.43	18.88	19.33	19.78	20.24	20.69	21.15	21.61	22.07	22.52	22.99	23.45	23.91
39	17.54	18.00	18.46	18.93	19.39	19.86	20.32	20.79	21.26	21.73	22.20	22.67	23.14	23.61	24.09	24.56
40	18.00	18.48	18.95	19.43	19.90	20.38	20.86	21.34	21.82	22.30	22.79	23.27	23.76	24.25	24.73	25.22
41	18.47	18.95	19.44	19.93	20.42	20.91	21.40	21.89	22.39	22.88	23.38	23.88	24.38	24.88	25.38	25.88
42	18.93	19.43	19.93	20.43	20.93	21.44	21.94	22.45	22.96	23.47	23.98	24.49	25.00	25.51	26.03	26.55
43	19.40	19.91	20.42	20.94	21.45	21.97	22.49	23.01	23.53	24.05	24.57	25.10	25.62	26.15	26.68	27.21
44	19.86	20.39	20.91	21.44	21.97	22.50	23.03	23.57	24.10	24.64	25.17	25.71	26.25	26.79	27.33	27.88
45	20.33	20.87	21.41	21.95	22.49	23.03	23.58	24.12	24.67	25.22	25.77	26.32	26.88	27.43	27.99	28.55
46	20.80	21.35	21.90	22.46	23.01	23.57	24.13	24.69	25.25	25.81	26.37	26.95	27.51	28.08	28.65	29.22
47	21.27	21.83	22.40	22.97	23.53	24.10	24.68	25.25	25.82	26.40	26.98	27.56	28.14	28.72	29.31	29.89
48	21.74	22.32	22.90	23.48	24.06	24.64	25.23	25.81	26.40	26.99	27.58	28.18	28.77	29.37	29.97	30.57
49	22.21	22.80	23.39	23.99	24.58	25.18	25.78	26.38	26.98	27.59	28.19	28.80	29.41	30.02	30.63	31.24
50	22.69	23.29	23.89	24.50	25.11	25.72	26.33	26.94	27.56	28.18	28.80	29.42	30.04	30.67	31.29	31.92
51	23.16	23.78	24.40	25.02	25.64	26.26	26.89	27.52	28.15	28.78	29.41	30.05	30.68	31.32	31.96	32.60
52	23.64	24.27	24.90	25.53	26.17	26.81	27.45	28.09	28.73	29.38	30.02	30.67	31.32	31.98	32.63	33.29
53	24.11	24.76	25.40	26.05	26.70	27.35	28.00	28.66	29.32	29.98	30.64	31.30	31.97	32.63	33.30	33.97
54	24.59	25.25	25.91	26.57	27.23	27.90	28.56	29.23	29.91	30.58	31.25	31.93	32.61	33.29	33.98	34.66
55	25.07	25.74	26.41	27.09	27.77	28.44	29.13	29.81	30.50	31.18	31.87	32.56	33.26	33.95	34.65	35.35
56	25.55	26.23	26.92	27.61	28.30	28.99	29.69	30.39	31.09	31.79	32.49	33.20	33.91	34.62	35.33	36.04
57	26.03	26.73	27.43	28.13	28.84	29.54	30.25	30.97	31.68	32.39	33.11	33.83	34.56	35.28	36.01	36.74
58	26.51	27.23	27.94	28.66	29.37	30.10	30.82	31.55	32.27	33.00	33.74	34.47	35.21	35.95	36.69	37.43
59	27.00	27.72	28.45	29.18	29.91	30.65	31.39	32.13	32.87	33.61	34.36	35.11	35.86	36.62	37.37	38.13
60	27.48	28.22	28.96	29.71	30.45	31.20	31.96	32.71	33.47	34.23	34.99	35.75	36.52	37.29	38.06	38.83

Table 6-2 Annual Percentage Rate Table (Monthly Payments)

Number Of Payments	Annual Percentage Rate (Fiance Charge per $100 of Amount Financed)															
	14.00%	14.25%	14.50%	14.75%	15.00%	15.25%	15.50%	15.75%	16.00%	16.25%	16.50%	16.75%	17.00%	17.25%	17.50%	17.75%
1	1.17	1.19	1.21	1.23	1.25	1.27	1.29	1.31	1.33	1.35	1.37	1.40	1.42	1.44	1.46	1.48
2	1.75	1.78	1.82	1.85	1.88	1.91	1.94	1.97	2.00	2.04	2.07	2.10	2.13	2.16	2.19	2.22
3	2.34	2.38	2.43	2.47	2.51	2.55	2.59	2.64	2.68	2.72	2.76	2.80	2.85	2.89	2.93	2.97
4	2.93	2.99	3.04	3.09	3.14	3.20	3.25	3.30	3.36	3.41	3.46	3.51	3.57	3.62	3.67	3.73
5	3.53	3.59	3.65	3.72	3.78	3.84	3.91	3.97	4.04	4.10	4.16	4.23	4.29	4.35	4.42	4.48
6	4.12	4.20	4.27	4.35	4.42	4.49	4.57	4.64	4.72	4.79	4.87	4.94	5.02	5.09	5.17	5.24
7	4.72	4.81	4.89	4.98	5.06	5.15	5.23	5.32	5.40	5.49	5.58	5.66	5.75	5.83	5.92	6.00
8	5.32	5.42	5.51	5.61	5.71	5.80	5.90	6.00	6.09	6.19	6.29	6.38	6.48	6.58	6.67	6.77
9	5.92	6.03	6.14	6.25	6.35	6.46	6.57	6.68	6.78	6.89	7.00	7.11	7.22	7.32	7.43	7.54
10	6.53	6.65	6.77	6.88	7.00	7.12	7.24	7.36	7.48	7.60	7.72	7.84	7.96	8.08	8.19	8.31
11	7.14	7.27	7.40	7.53	7.66	7.79	7.92	8.05	8.18	8.31	8.44	8.57	8.70	8.83	8.96	9.09
12	7.74	7.89	8.03	8.17	8.31	8.45	8.59	8.74	8.88	9.02	9.16	9.30	9.45	9.59	9.73	9.87
13	8.36	8.51	8.66	8.81	8.97	9.12	9.27	9.43	9.58	9.73	9.89	10.04	10.20	10.35	10.50	10.66
14	8.97	9.13	9.30	9.46	9.63	9.79	9.96	10.12	10.29	10.45	10.62	10.78	10.95	11.11	11.28	11.45
15	9.59	9.76	9.94	10.11	10.29	10.47	10.64	10.82	11.00	11.17	11.35	11.53	11.71	11.88	12.06	12.24
16	10.20	10.39	10.58	10.77	10.95	11.14	11.33	11.52	11.71	11.90	12.09	12.28	12.46	12.65	12.84	13.03
17	10.82	11.02	11.22	11.42	11.62	11.82	12.02	12.22	12.42	12.62	12.83	13.03	13.23	13.43	13.63	13.83
18	11.45	11.66	11.87	12.08	12.29	12.50	12.72	12.93	13.14	13.35	13.57	13.78	13.99	14.21	14.42	14.64
19	12.07	12.30	12.52	12.74	12.97	13.19	13.41	13.64	13.86	14.09	14.31	14.54	14.76	14.99	15.22	15.44
20	12.70	12.93	13.17	13.41	13.64	13.88	14.11	14.35	14.59	14.82	15.06	15.30	15.54	15.77	16.01	16.25
21	13.33	13.58	13.82	14.07	14.32	14.57	14.82	15.06	15.31	15.56	15.81	16.06	16.31	16.56	16.81	17.07
22	13.96	14.22	14.48	14.74	15.00	15.26	15.52	15.78	16.04	16.30	16.57	16.83	17.09	17.36	17.62	17.88
23	14.59	14.87	15.14	15.41	15.68	15.96	16.23	16.50	16.78	17.05	17.32	17.60	17.88	18.15	18.43	18.70
24	15.23	15.51	15.80	16.08	16.37	16.65	16.94	17.22	17.51	17.80	18.09	18.37	18.66	18.95	19.24	19.53
25	15.87	16.17	16.46	16.76	17.06	17.35	17.65	17.95	18.25	18.55	18.85	19.15	19.45	19.75	20.05	20.36
26	16.51	16.82	17.13	17.44	17.75	18.06	18.37	18.68	18.99	19.30	19.62	19.93	20.24	20.56	20.87	21.19
27	17.15	17.47	17.80	18.12	18.44	18.76	19.09	19.41	19.74	20.06	20.39	20.71	21.04	21.37	21.69	22.02
28	17.80	18.13	18.47	18.80	19.14	19.47	19.81	20.15	20.48	20.82	21.16	21.50	21.84	22.18	22.52	22.86
29	18.45	18.79	19.14	19.49	19.83	20.18	20.53	20.88	21.23	21.58	21.94	22.29	22.64	22.99	23.35	23.70
30	19.10	19.45	19.81	20.17	20.54	20.90	21.26	21.62	21.99	22.35	22.72	23.08	23.45	23.81	24.18	24.55
31	19.75	20.12	20.49	20.87	21.24	21.61	21.99	22.37	22.74	23.12	23.50	23.88	24.26	24.64	25.02	25.40
32	20.40	20.79	21.17	21.56	21.95	22.33	22.72	23.11	23.50	23.89	24.28	24.68	25.07	25.46	25.86	26.25
33	21.06	21.46	21.85	22.25	22.65	23.06	23.46	23.86	24.26	24.67	25.07	25.48	25.88	26.29	26.70	27.11
34	21.72	22.13	22.54	22.95	23.37	23.78	24.19	24.61	25.03	25.44	25.86	26.28	26.70	27.12	27.54	27.97
35	22.38	22.80	23.23	23.65	24.08	24.51	24.94	25.36	25.79	26.23	26.66	27.09	27.52	27.96	28.39	28.83
36	23.04	23.48	23.92	24.35	24.80	25.24	25.68	26.12	26.57	27.01	27.46	27.90	28.35	28.80	29.25	29.70
37	23.70	24.16	24.61	25.06	25.51	25.97	26.42	26.88	27.34	27.80	28.26	28.72	29.18	29.64	30.10	30.57
38	24.37	24.84	25.30	25.77	26.24	26.70	27.17	27.64	28.11	28.59	29.06	29.53	30.01	30.49	30.96	31.44
39	25.04	25.52	26.00	26.48	26.96	27.44	27.92	28.41	28.89	29.38	29.87	30.36	30.85	31.34	31.83	32.32
40	25.71	26.20	26.70	27.19	27.69	28.18	28.68	29.18	29.68	30.18	30.68	31.18	31.68	32.19	32.69	33.20
41	26.39	26.89	27.40	27.91	28.41	28.92	29.44	29.95	30.46	30.97	31.49	32.01	32.52	33.04	33.56	34.08
42	27.06	27.58	28.10	28.62	29.15	29.67	30.19	30.72	31.25	31.78	32.31	32.84	33.37	33.90	34.44	34.97
43	27.74	28.27	28.81	29.34	29.88	30.42	30.96	31.50	32.04	32.58	33.13	33.67	34.22	34.76	35.31	35.86
44	28.42	28.97	29.52	30.07	30.62	31.17	31.72	32.28	32.83	33.39	33.95	34.51	35.07	35.63	36.19	36.76
45	29.11	29.67	30.23	30.79	31.36	31.92	32.49	33.06	33.63	34.20	34.77	35.35	35.92	36.50	37.08	37.66
46	29.79	30.36	30.94	31.52	32.10	32.68	33.26	33.84	34.43	35.01	35.60	36.19	36.78	37.37	37.96	38.56
47	30.48	31.07	31.66	32.25	32.84	33.44	34.03	34.63	35.23	35.83	36.43	37.04	37.64	38.25	38.86	39.46
48	31.17	31.77	32.37	32.98	33.59	34.20	34.81	35.42	36.03	36.65	37.27	37.88	38.50	39.13	39.75	40.37
49	31.86	32.48	33.09	33.71	34.34	34.96	35.59	36.21	36.84	37.47	38.10	38.74	39.37	40.01	40.65	41.29
50	32.55	33.18	33.82	34.45	35.09	35.73	36.37	37.01	37.65	38.30	38.94	39.59	40.24	40.89	41.55	42.20
51	33.25	33.89	34.54	35.19	35.84	36.49	37.15	37.81	38.46	39.12	39.79	40.45	41.11	41.78	42.45	43.12
52	33.95	34.61	35.27	35.93	36.60	37.27	37.94	38.61	39.28	39.96	40.63	41.31	41.99	42.67	43.36	44.04
53	34.65	35.32	36.00	36.68	37.36	38.04	38.72	39.41	40.10	40.79	41.48	42.17	42.87	43.57	44.27	44.97
54	35.35	36.04	36.73	37.42	38.12	38.82	39.52	40.22	40.92	41.63	42.33	43.04	43.75	44.47	45.18	45.90
55	36.05	36.76	37.46	38.17	38.88	39.60	40.31	41.03	41.74	42.47	43.19	43.91	44.64	45.37	46.10	46.83
56	36.76	37.48	38.20	38.92	39.65	40.38	41.11	41.84	42.57	43.31	44.05	44.79	45.53	46.27	47.02	47.77
57	37.47	38.20	38.94	39.68	40.42	41.16	41.91	42.65	43.40	44.15	44.91	45.66	46.42	47.18	47.94	48.71
58	38.18	38.93	39.68	40.43	41.19	41.95	42.71	43.47	44.23	45.00	45.77	46.54	47.32	48.09	48.87	49.65
59	38.89	39.66	40.42	41.19	41.96	42.74	43.51	44.29	45.07	45.85	46.64	47.42	48.21	49.01	49.80	50.60
60	39.61	40.39	41.17	41.95	42.74	43.53	44.32	45.11	45.91	46.71	47.51	48.31	49.12	49.92	50.73	51.55

Table 6-2 Annual Percentage Rate Table (Monthly Payments)

Number Of Payments	18.00%	18.25%	18.50%	18.75%	19.00%	19.25%	19.50%	19.75%	20.00%	20.25%	20.50%	20.75%	21.00%	21.25%	21.50%	21.75%
	Annual Percentage Rate (Fiance Charge per $100 of Amount Financed)															
1	1.50	1.52	1.54	1.56	1.58	1.60	1.62	1.65	1.67	1.69	1.71	1.73	1.75	1.77	1.79	1.81
2	2.26	2.39	2.32	2.35	2.38	2.41	2.44	2.48	2.51	2.54	2.57	2.60	2.63	2.66	2.70	2.73
3	3.01	3.06	3.10	3.14	3.18	3.23	3.27	3.31	3.35	3.39	3.44	3.48	3.52	3.56	3.60	3.65
4	3.78	3.83	3.88	3.94	3.99	4.04	4.10	4.15	4.20	4.25	4.31	4.36	4.41	4.47	4.52	4.57
5	4.54	4.61	4.67	4.74	4.80	4.86	4.93	4.99	5.06	5.12	5.18	5.25	5.31	5.37	5.44	5.50
6	5.32	5.39	5.46	5.54	5.61	5.69	5.76	5.84	5.91	5.99	6.06	6.14	6.21	6.29	6.36	6.44
7	6.09	6.18	6.26	6.35	6.43	6.52	6.60	6.69	6.78	6.86	6.95	7.04	7.12	7.21	7.29	7.38
8	6.87	6.96	7.06	7.16	7.26	7.35	7.45	7.55	7.64	7.74	7.84	7.94	8.03	8.13	8.23	8.33
9	7.65	7.76	7.87	7.97	8.08	8.19	8.30	8.41	8.52	8.63	8.73	8.84	8.95	9.06	9.17	9.28
10	8.43	8.55	8.67	8.79	8.91	9.03	9.15	9.27	9.39	9.51	9.63	9.75	9.88	10.00	10.12	10.24
11	9.22	9.35	9.49	9.62	9.75	9.88	10.01	10.14	10.28	10.41	10.54	10.67	10.80	10.94	11.07	11.20
12	10.02	10.16	10.30	10.44	10.59	10.73	10.87	11.02	11.16	11.31	11.45	11.59	11.74	11.88	12.02	12.17
13	10.81	10.97	11.12	11.28	11.43	11.59	11.74	11.90	12.05	12.21	12.36	12.52	12.67	12.83	12.99	13.14
14	11.61	11.78	11.95	12.11	12.28	12.45	12.61	12.78	12.95	13.11	13.28	13.45	13.62	13.79	13.95	14.12
15	12.42	12.59	12.77	12.95	13.13	13.31	13.49	13.67	13.85	14.03	14.21	14.39	14.57	14.75	14.93	15.11
16	13.22	13.41	13.60	13.80	13.99	14.18	14.37	14.56	14.75	14.94	15.13	15.33	15.52	15.71	15.90	16.10
17	14.04	14.24	14.44	14.64	14.85	15.05	15.25	15.46	15.66	15.86	16.07	16.27	16.48	16.68	16.89	17.09
18	14.85	15.07	15.28	15.49	15.71	15.93	16.14	16.36	16.57	16.79	17.01	17.22	17.44	17.66	17.88	18.09
19	15.67	15.90	16.12	16.35	16.58	16.81	17.03	17.26	17.49	17.72	17.95	18.18	18.41	18.64	18.87	19.10
20	16.49	16.73	16.97	17.21	17.45	17.69	17.93	18.17	18.41	18.66	18.90	19.14	19.38	19.63	19.87	20.11
21	17.32	17.57	17.82	18.07	18.33	18.58	18.83	19.09	19.34	19.60	19.85	20.11	20.36	20.62	20.87	21.13
22	18.15	18.41	18.68	18.94	19.21	19.47	19.74	20.01	20.27	20.54	20.81	21.08	21.34	21.61	21.88	22.15
23	18.98	19.26	19.54	19.81	20.09	20.37	20.65	20.93	21.21	21.49	21.77	22.05	22.33	22.61	22.90	23.18
24	19.82	20.11	20.40	20.69	20.98	21.27	21.56	21.86	22.15	22.44	22.74	23.03	23.33	23.62	23.92	24.21
25	20.66	20.96	21.27	21.57	21.87	22.18	22.48	22.79	23.10	23.40	23.71	24.02	24.32	24.63	24.94	25.25
26	21.50	21.82	22.14	22.45	22.77	23.09	23.41	23.73	24.04	24.36	24.68	25.01	25.33	25.65	25.97	26.29
27	22.35	22.68	23.01	23.34	23.67	24.00	24.33	24.67	25.00	25.33	25.67	26.00	26.34	26.67	27.01	27.34
28	23.20	23.55	23.89	24.23	24.58	24.92	25.27	25.61	25.96	26.30	26.65	27.00	27.35	27.70	28.05	28.40
29	24.06	24.41	24.77	25.13	25.49	25.84	26.20	26.56	26.92	27.28	27.64	28.00	28.37	28.73	29.09	29.46
30	24.92	25.29	25.66	26.03	26.40	26.77	27.14	27.52	27.89	28.26	28.64	29.01	29.39	29.77	30.14	30.52
31	25.78	26.16	26.55	26.93	27.32	27.70	28.09	28.47	28.86	29.25	29.64	30.03	30.42	30.81	31.20	31.59
32	26.65	27.04	27.44	27.84	28.24	28.64	29.04	29.44	29.84	30.24	30.64	31.05	31.45	31.85	32.26	32.67
33	27.52	27.93	28.34	28.75	29.16	29.57	29.99	30.40	30.82	31.23	31.65	32.07	32.49	32.91	33.33	33.75
34	28.39	28.81	29.24	29.66	30.09	30.52	30.95	31.37	31.80	32.23	32.67	33.10	33.53	33.96	34.40	34.83
35	29.27	29.71	30.14	30.58	31.02	31.47	31.91	32.35	32.79	33.24	33.68	34.13	34.58	35.03	35.47	35.92
36	30.15	30.60	31.05	31.51	31.96	32.42	32.87	33.33	33.79	34.25	34.71	35.17	35.63	36.09	36.56	37.02
37	31.03	31.50	31.97	32.43	32.90	33.37	33.84	34.32	34.79	35.26	35.74	36.21	36.69	37.16	37.64	38.12
38	31.92	32.40	32.88	33.37	33.85	34.33	34.82	35.30	35.79	36.28	36.77	37.26	37.75	38.24	38.73	39.23
39	32.81	33.31	33.80	34.30	34.80	35.30	35.80	36.30	36.80	37.30	37.81	38.31	38.82	39.32	39.83	40.34
40	33.71	34.22	34.73	35.24	35.75	36.26	36.78	37.29	37.81	38.33	38.85	39.37	39.89	40.41	40.93	41.46
41	34.61	35.13	35.66	36.18	36.71	37.24	37.77	38.30	38.83	39.36	39.89	40.43	40.96	41.50	42.04	42.58
42	35.51	36.05	36.59	37.13	37.67	38.21	38.76	39.30	39.85	40.40	40.95	41.50	42.05	42.60	43.15	43.71
43	36.42	36.97	37.52	38.08	38.63	39.19	39.75	40.31	40.87	41.44	42.00	42.57	43.13	43.70	44.27	44.84
44	37.33	37.89	38.46	39.03	39.60	40.18	40.75	41.33	41.90	42.48	43.06	43.64	44.22	44.81	45.39	45.98
45	38.24	38.82	39.41	39.99	40.58	41.17	41.75	42.35	42.94	43.53	44.13	44.72	45.32	45.92	46.52	47.12
46	39.16	39.75	40.35	40.95	41.55	42.16	42.76	43.37	43.98	44.58	45.20	45.81	46.42	47.03	47.65	48.27
47	40.08	40.69	41.30	41.92	42.54	43.15	43.77	44.40	45.02	45.64	46.27	46.90	47.53	48.16	48.79	49.42
48	41.00	41.63	42.26	42.89	43.52	44.15	44.79	45.43	46.07	46.71	47.35	47.99	48.64	49.28	49.93	50.58
49	41.93	42.57	43.22	43.86	44.51	45.16	45.81	46.46	47.12	47.77	48.43	49.09	49.75	50.41	51.08	51.74
50	42.86	43.52	44.18	44.84	45.50	46.17	46.83	47.50	48.17	48.84	49.52	50.19	50.87	51.55	52.23	52.91
51	43.79	44.47	45.14	45.82	46.50	47.18	47.86	48.55	49.23	49.92	50.61	51.30	51.99	52.69	53.38	54.08
52	44.73	45.42	46.11	46.80	47.50	48.20	48.89	49.59	50.30	51.00	51.71	52.41	53.12	53.83	54.55	55.26
53	45.67	46.38	47.08	47.79	48.50	49.22	49.93	50.65	51.37	52.09	52.81	53.53	54.26	54.98	55.71	56.44
54	46.62	47.34	48.06	48.79	49.51	50.24	50.97	51.70	52.44	53.17	53.91	54.65	55.39	56.14	56.88	57.63
55	47.57	48.30	49.04	49.78	50.52	51.27	52.02	52.76	53.52	54.27	55.02	55.78	56.54	57.30	58.06	58.82
56	48.52	49.27	50.03	50.78	51.54	52.30	53.06	53.83	54.60	55.37	56.14	56.91	57.68	58.46	59.24	60.02
57	49.47	50.24	51.01	51.79	52.56	53.34	54.12	54.90	55.68	56.47	57.25	58.04	58.84	59.63	60.43	61.22
58	50.43	51.22	52.00	52.79	53.58	54.38	55.17	55.97	56.77	57.57	58.38	59.18	59.99	60.80	61.62	62.43
59	51.39	52.20	53.00	53.80	54.61	55.42	56.23	57.05	57.87	58.68	59.51	60.33	61.15	61.98	62.81	63.64
60	52.36	53.18	54.00	54.82	55.64	56.47	57.30	58.13	58.96	59.80	60.64	61.48	62.32	63.17	64.01	64.86

Table 6-2 Annual Percentage Rate Table (Monthly Payments)

Number Of Payments	Annual Percentage Rate (Finance Charge per $100 of Amount Financed)															
	22.00%	22.25%	22.50%	22.75%	23.00%	23.25%	23.50%	23.75%	24.00%	24.25%	24.50%	24.75%	25.00%	25.25%	25.50%	25.75%
1	1.83	1.85	1.87	1.90	1.92	1.94	1.96	1.98	2.00	2.02	2.04	2.06	2.08	2.10	2.12	2.15
2	2.76	2.79	2.82	2.85	2.88	2.92	2.95	2.98	3.01	3.04	3.07	3.10	3.14	3.17	3.20	3.23
3	3.69	3.73	3.77	3.82	3.86	3.90	3.94	3.98	4.03	4.07	4.11	4.15	4.20	4.24	4.28	4.32
4	4.62	4.68	4.73	4.78	4.84	4.89	4.94	5.00	5.05	5.10	5.16	5.21	5.26	5.32	5.37	5.42
5	5.57	5.63	5.69	5.76	5.82	5.89	5.95	6.02	6.08	6.14	6.21	6.17	6.34	6.40	6.46	6.53
6	6.51	6.59	6.66	6.74	6.81	6.89	6.96	7.04	7.12	7.19	7.27	7.34	7.42	7.49	7.57	7.64
7	7.47	7.55	7.64	7.73	7.81	7.90	7.99	8.07	8.16	8.24	8.33	8.42	8.51	8.59	8.68	8.77
8	8.42	8.52	8.62	8.72	8.82	8.91	9.01	9.11	9.21	9.31	9.40	9.50	9.60	9.70	9.80	9.90
9	9.39	9.50	9.61	9.72	9.83	9.94	10.04	10.15	10.26	10.37	10.48	10.59	10.70	10.81	10.92	11.03
10	10.36	10.48	10.60	10.72	10.84	10.96	11.08	11.21	11.33	11.45	11.57	11.69	11.81	11.93	12.06	12.18
11	11.33	11.47	11.60	11.73	11.86	12.00	12.13	12.26	12.40	12.53	12.66	12.80	12.93	13.06	13.20	13.33
12	12.31	12.46	12.60	12.75	12.89	13.04	13.18	13.33	13.47	13.62	13.76	13.91	14.05	14.20	14.34	14.49
13	13.30	13.46	13.61	13.77	13.93	14.08	14.24	14.40	14.55	14.71	14.87	15.03	15.18	15.34	15.50	15.66
14	14.29	14.46	14.63	14.80	14.97	15.13	15.30	15.47	15.64	15.81	15.98	16.15	16.32	16.49	16.66	16.83
15	15.29	15.47	15.65	15.83	16.01	16.19	16.37	16.56	16.74	16.92	17.10	17.28	17.47	17.65	17.83	18.02
16	16.29	16.48	16.68	16.87	17.06	17.26	17.45	17.65	17.84	18.03	18.23	18.42	18.62	18.81	19.01	19.21
17	17.30	17.50	17.71	17.92	18.12	18.33	18.53	18.74	18.95	19.16	19.36	19.57	19.78	19.99	20.20	20.40
18	18.31	18.53	18.75	18.97	19.19	19.41	19.62	19.84	20.06	20.28	20.50	20.72	20.95	21.17	21.39	21.61
19	19.33	19.56	19.79	20.02	20.26	20.49	20.72	20.95	21.19	21.42	21.65	21.89	22.12	22.35	22.59	22.82
20	20.35	20.60	20.84	21.09	21.33	21.58	21.82	22.07	22.31	22.56	22.81	23.05	23.30	23.55	23.79	24.04
21	21.38	21.64	21.90	22.16	22.41	22.67	22.93	23.19	23.45	23.71	23.97	24.23	24.49	24.75	25.01	25.27
22	22.42	22.69	22.96	23.23	23.50	23.77	24.04	24.32	24.59	24.86	25.13	25.41	25.68	25.96	26.23	26.50
23	23.46	23.74	24.03	24.31	24.60	24.88	25.17	25.45	25.74	26.02	26.31	26.60	26.88	27.17	27.46	27.75
24	24.51	24.80	25.10	25.40	25.70	25.99	26.29	26.59	26.89	27.19	27.49	27.79	28.09	28.39	28.69	29.00
25	25.56	25.87	26.18	26.49	26.80	27.11	27.43	27.74	28.05	28.36	26.68	28.99	29.31	29.62	29.94	30.25
26	26.62	26.94	27.26	27.59	27.91	28.24	28.56	28.89	29.22	29.55	29.87	30.20	30.53	30.86	31.19	31.52
27	27.68	28.02	28.35	28.69	29.03	29.37	29.71	30.05	30.39	30.73	31.07	31.42	31.76	32.10	32.45	32.79
28	28.75	29.10	29.45	29.80	30.15	30.51	30.86	31.22	31.57	31.93	32.28	32.64	33.00	33.35	33.71	34.07
29	29.82	30.19	30.55	30.92	31.28	31.65	32.02	32.39	32.76	33.13	33.50	33.87	34.24	34.61	34.98	35.36
30	30.90	31.28	31.66	32.04	32.42	32.80	33.18	33.57	33.95	34.33	34.72	35.10	35.49	35.88	36.26	36.65
31	31.98	32.38	32.77	33.17	33.56	33.96	34.35	34.75	35.15	35.55	35.95	36.35	36.75	37.15	37.55	37.95
32	33.07	33.48	33.89	34.30	34.71	35.12	35.53	35.94	36.35	36.77	37.18	37.60	38.01	38.43	38.84	39.26
33	34.17	34.59	35.01	35.44	35.86	36.29	36.71	37.14	37.57	37.99	38.42	38.85	39.28	39.71	40.14	40.58
34	35.27	35.71	36.14	36.58	37.02	37.46	37.90	38.34	38.78	39.23	39.67	40.11	40.56	41.01	41.45	41.90
35	36.37	36.83	37.28	37.73	38.18	38.64	39.09	39.55	40.01	40.47	40.92	41.38	41.84	42.31	42.77	43.23
36	37.49	37.95	38.42	38.89	39.35	39.82	40.29	40.77	41.24	41.71	42.19	42.66	43.14	43.61	44.09	44.57
37	38.60	39.08	39.56	40.05	40.53	41.02	41.50	41.99	42.48	42.96	43.45	43.94	44.43	44.93	45.42	45.91
38	39.72	40.22	40.72	41.21	41.71	42.21	42.71	43.22	43.72	44.22	44.73	45.23	45.74	46.25	46.75	47.26
39	40.85	41.36	41.87	42.39	42.90	43.42	43.93	44.45	44.97	45.49	46.01	46.53	47.05	47.57	48.10	48.62
40	41.98	42.51	43.04	43.56	44.09	44.62	45.16	45.69	46.22	46.76	47.29	47.83	48.37	48.91	49.45	49.99
41	43.12	43.66	44.20	44.75	45.29	45.84	46.39	46.94	47.48	48.04	48.59	49.14	49.69	50.25	50.80	51.36
42	44.26	44.82	45.38	45.94	46.50	47.06	47.62	48.19	48.75	49.32	49.89	50.46	51.03	51.60	52.17	52.74
43	45.41	45.98	46.56	47.13	47.71	48.29	48.87	49.45	50.03	50.61	51.19	51.78	52.36	52.95	53.54	54.13
44	46.56	47.15	47.74	48.33	48.93	49.52	50.11	50.71	51.31	51.91	52.51	53.11	53.71	54.31	54.92	55.52
45	47.72	48.33	48.93	49.54	50.15	50.76	51.37	51.98	52.59	53.21	53.82	54.44	55.06	55.68	56.30	56.92
46	48.89	49.51	50.13	50.75	51.37	52.00	52.63	52.26	53.89	54.52	55.15	55.78	56.42	57.05	57.69	58.33
47	50.06	50.69	51.33	51.97	52.61	53.25	53.89	54.54	55.18	55.83	56.48	57.13	57.78	58.44	59.09	59.75
48	51.23	51.88	52.54	53.19	53.85	54.51	55.16	55.83	56.49	57.15	57.82	58.49	59.15	59.82	60.50	61.17
49	52.41	53.08	53.75	54.42	55.09	55.77	56.44	57.12	57.80	58.48	59.16	59.85	60.53	61.22	61.91	62.60
50	53.59	54.28	54.96	55.65	56.34	57.03	57.73	58.42	59.12	59.81	60.51	61.21	61.92	62.62	63.33	64.03
51	54.78	55.48	56.19	56.89	57.60	58.30	59.01	59.73	60.44	61.15	61.87	62.59	63.31	64.03	64.75	65.47
52	55.98	56.69	57.41	58.13	58.86	59.58	60.31	61.04	61.77	62.50	63.23	63.97	64.70	65.44	66.18	66.92
53	57.18	57.91	58.65	59.38	60.12	60.87	61.61	62.35	63.10	63.85	64.60	65.35	66.11	66.86	67.62	68.38
54	58.38	59.13	59.88	60.64	61.40	62.16	62.92	63.68	64.44	65.21	65.98	66.75	67.52	68.29	69.07	69.84
55	59.59	60.36	61.13	61.90	62.67	63.45	64.23	65.01	65.79	66.57	67.36	68.14	68.93	69.72	70.52	71.31
56	60.80	61.59	62.38	63.17	63.96	64.75	65.54	66.34	67.14	67.94	68.74	69.55	70.36	71.16	71.97	72.79
57	62.02	62.83	63.63	64.44	65.25	66.06	66.87	67.68	68.50	69.32	70.14	70.96	71.78	72.61	73.44	74.27
58	63.25	64.07	64.89	65.71	66.54	67.37	68.20	69.03	69.86	70.70	71.54	72.38	73.22	74.06	74.91	75.76
59	64.48	65.32	66.15	67.00	67.84	68.68	69.53	70.38	71.23	72.09	72.94	73.80	74.66	75.52	76.39	77.25
60	65.71	66.57	67.42	68.28	69.14	70.01	70.87	71.74	72.61	73.48	74.35	75.23	76.11	76.99	77.87	78.76

Table 6-2 Annual Percentage Rate Table (Monthly Payments)

Number Of Payments	Annual Percentage Rate (Finance Charge per $100 of Amount Financed)															
	26.00%	26.25%	26.50%	26.75%	27.00%	27.25%	27.50%	27.75%	28.00%	28.25%	28.50%	28.75%	29.00%	29.25%	29.50%	29.75%
1	2.17	2.19	2.21	2.23	2.25	2.27	2.29	2.31	2.33	2.35	2.37	2.40	2.42	2.44	2.46	2.48
2	3.26	3.29	3.32	3.36	3.39	3.42	3.45	3.48	3.51	3.54	3.58	3.61	3.64	3.67	3.70	3.73
3	4.36	4.41	4.45	4.49	4.53	4.58	4.62	4.66	4.70	4.74	4.79	4.83	4.87	4.91	4.96	5.00
4	5.47	5.53	5.58	5.63	5.69	5.74	5.79	5.85	5.90	5.95	6.01	6.06	6.11	6.17	6.22	6.27
5	6.59	6.66	6.72	6.79	6.85	6.91	6.98	7.04	7.11	7.17	7.24	7.30	7.37	7.43	7.49	7.56
6	7.72	7.79	7.87	7.95	8.02	8.10	8.17	8.25	8.32	8.40	8.48	8.55	8.63	8.70	8.78	8.85
7	8.85	8.94	9.03	9.11	9.20	9.29	9.37	9.46	9.55	9.64	9.72	9.81	9.90	9.98	10.07	10.16
8	9.99	10.09	10.19	10.29	10.39	10.49	10.58	10.68	10.78	10.88	10.98	11.08	11.18	11.28	11.38	11.47
9	11.14	11.25	11.36	11.47	11.58	11.69	11.80	11.91	12.03	12.14	12.25	12.36	12.47	12.58	12.69	12.80
10	12.30	12.42	12.54	12.67	12.79	12.91	13.03	13.15	13.28	13.40	13.52	13.64	13.77	13.89	14.01	14.14
11	13.46	13.60	13.73	13.87	14.00	14.13	14.27	14.40	14.54	14.67	14.81	14.94	15.08	15.21	15.35	15.48
12	14.64	14.78	14.93	15.07	15.22	15.37	15.51	15.66	15.81	15.95	16.10	16.25	16.40	16.54	16.69	16.84
13	15.82	15.97	16.13	16.29	16.45	16.61	16.77	16.93	17.09	17.24	17.40	17.56	17.72	17.88	18.04	18.20
14	17.00	17.17	17.35	17.52	17.69	17.86	18.03	18.20	18.37	18.54	18.72	18.89	19.06	19.23	19.41	19.58
15	18.20	18.38	18.57	18.75	18.93	19.12	19.30	19.48	19.67	19.85	20.04	20.22	20.41	20.59	20.78	20.96
16	19.40	19.60	19.79	19.99	20.19	20.38	20.58	20.78	20.97	21.17	21.37	21.57	21.76	21.96	22.16	22.36
17	20.61	20.82	21.03	21.24	21.45	21.66	21.87	22.08	22.29	22.50	22.71	22.92	23.13	23.34	23.55	23.77
18	21.83	22.05	22.27	22.50	22.72	22.94	23.16	23.39	23.61	23.83	24.06	24.28	24.51	24.73	24.96	25.18
19	23.06	23.29	23.53	23.76	24.00	24.23	24.47	24.71	24.94	25.18	25.42	25.65	25.89	26.13	26.37	26.61
20	24.29	24.54	24.79	25.04	25.28	25.53	25.78	26.03	26.28	26.53	26.78	27.04	27.29	27.54	27.79	28.04
21	25.53	25.79	26.05	26.32	26.58	26.84	27.11	27.37	27.63	27.90	28.16	28.43	28.69	28.96	29.22	29.49
22	26.78	27.05	27.33	27.61	27.88	28.16	28.44	28.71	28.99	29.27	29.55	29.82	30.10	30.38	30.66	30.94
23	28.04	28.32	28.61	28.90	29.19	29.48	29.77	30.07	30.36	30.65	30.94	31.23	31.53	31.82	32.11	32.41
24	29.30	29.60	29.90	30.21	30.51	30.82	31.12	31.43	31.73	32.04	32.34	32.65	32.96	33.27	33.57	33.88
25	30.57	30.89	31.20	31.52	31.84	32.16	32.48	32.80	33.12	33.44	33.76	34.08	34.40	34.72	35.04	35.37
26	31.85	32.18	32.51	32.84	33.18	33.51	33.84	34.18	34.51	34.84	35.18	35.51	35.85	36.19	36.52	36.86
27	33.14	33.48	33.83	34.17	34.52	34.87	35.21	35.56	35.91	36.26	36.61	36.96	37.31	37.66	38.01	38.36
28	34.43	34.79	35.15	35.51	35.87	36.23	36.59	36.96	37.32	37.68	38.05	38.41	38.78	39.15	39.51	39.88
29	35.73	36.10	36.48	36.85	37.23	37.61	37.98	38.36	38.74	39.12	39.50	39.88	40.26	40.64	41.02	41.40
30	37.04	37.43	37.82	38.21	38.60	38.99	39.38	39.77	40.17	40.56	40.95	41.35	41.75	42.14	42.54	42.94
31	38.35	38.76	39.16	39.57	39.97	40.38	40.79	41.19	41.60	42.01	42.42	42.83	43.24	43.65	44.06	44.48
32	39.68	40.10	40.52	40.94	41.36	41.78	42.20	42.62	43.05	43.47	43.90	44.32	44.75	45.17	45.60	46.03
33	41.01	41.44	41.88	42.31	42.75	43.19	43.62	44.06	44.50	44.94	45.38	45.82	46.26	46.70	47.15	47.59
34	42.35	42.80	43.25	43.70	44.15	44.60	45.05	45.51	45.96	46.42	46.87	47.33	47.79	48.24	48.70	49.16
35	43.69	44.16	44.62	45.09	45.56	46.02	46.49	46.96	47.43	47.90	48.37	48.85	49.32	49.79	50.27	50.74
36	45.05	45.53	46.01	46.49	46.97	47.45	47.94	48.42	48.91	49.40	49.88	50.37	50.86	51.35	51.84	52.33
37	46.41	46.90	47.40	47.90	48.39	48.89	49.39	49.89	50.40	50.90	51.40	51.91	52.41	52.92	53.42	53.93
38	47.77	48.29	48.80	49.31	49.82	50.34	50.86	51.37	51.89	52.41	52.93	53.45	53.97	54.49	55.02	55.54
39	49.15	49.68	50.20	50.73	51.26	51.79	52.33	52.86	53.39	53.93	54.46	55.00	55.54	56.08	56.62	57.16
40	50.53	51.07	51.62	52.16	52.71	53.26	53.81	54.35	54.90	55.46	56.01	56.56	57.12	57.67	58.23	58.79
41	51.92	52.48	53.04	53.60	54.16	54.73	55.29	55.86	56.42	56.99	57.56	58.13	58.70	59.28	59.85	60.42
42	53.32	53.89	54.47	55.05	55.63	56.21	56.79	57.37	57.95	58.54	59.12	59.71	60.30	60.89	61.48	62.07
43	54.72	55.31	55.90	56.50	57.09	57.69	58.29	58.89	59.49	60.09	60.69	61.30	61.90	62.51	63.11	63.72
44	56.13	56.74	57.35	57.96	58.57	59.19	59.80	60.42	61.03	61.65	62.27	62.89	63.51	64.14	64.76	65.39
45	57.55	58.17	58.80	59.43	60.06	60.69	61.32	61.95	62.59	63.22	63.86	64.50	65.13	65.77	66.42	67.06
46	58.97	59.61	60.26	60.90	61.55	62.20	62.84	63.49	64.15	64.80	65.45	66.11	66.76	67.42	68.08	68.74
47	60.40	61.06	61.72	62.38	63.05	63.71	64.38	65.05	65.71	66.38	67.06	67.73	68.40	69.08	69.75	70.43
48	61.84	62.52	63.20	63.87	64.56	65.24	65.92	66.60	67.29	67.98	68.67	69.36	70.05	70.74	71.44	72.13
49	63.29	63.98	64.68	65.37	66.07	66.77	67.47	68.17	68.87	69.58	70.29	70.99	71.70	72.41	73.13	73.84
50	64.74	65.45	66.16	66.88	67.59	68.31	69.03	69.75	70.47	71.19	71.91	72.64	73.37	74.10	74.83	75.56
51	66.20	66.93	67.66	68.39	69.12	69.86	70.59	71.33	72.07	72.81	73.55	74.29	75.04	75.78	76.53	77.28
52	67.67	68.41	69.16	69.91	70.66	71.41	72.16	72.92	73.67	74.43	75.19	75.95	76.72	77.48	78.25	79.02
53	69.14	69.90	70.67	71.43	72.20	72.97	73.74	74.52	75.29	76.07	76.85	77.62	78.41	79.19	79.97	80.76
54	70.62	71.40	72.18	72.97	73.75	74.54	75.33	76.12	76.91	77.71	78.50	79.30	80.10	80.90	81.71	82.51
55	72.11	72.91	73.71	74.51	75.31	76.12	76.92	77.73	78.55	79.36	80.17	80.99	81.81	82.63	83.45	84.27
56	73.60	74.42	75.24	76.06	76.88	77.70	78.53	79.35	80.18	81.02	81.85	82.68	83.52	83.46	85.20	86.04
57	75.10	75.94	76.77	77.61	78.45	79.29	80.14	80.98	81.83	82.68	83.53	84.39	85.24	86.10	86.96	87.82
58	76.61	77.46	78.32	79.17	80.03	80.89	81.75	82.62	83.48	84.35	85.22	86.10	86.97	87.85	88.72	89.60
59	78.12	78.99	79.87	80.74	81.62	82.50	83.38	84.26	85.15	86.03	86.92	87.81	88.71	89.60	90.50	91.40
60	79.64	80.53	81.42	82.32	83.21	84.11	85.01	85.91	86.81	87.72	88.63	89.54	90.45	91.37	92.28	93.20

5. Since the number 29.6 does not appear in Table 6-2, an accurate APR must be interpolated.

6. Find the difference between the two numbers the 29.6 falls between:

> 17.75% is above   29.70
> 17.5% is above $-$29.25
> Difference   .45

7. Find the difference between the desired number, 29.6, and the lower number found in the table, 29.25.

> 29.60
> $-$29.25
> .35

8. 29.6 is $\frac{.35}{.45}$ of the difference between 17.5% and 17.75%.

> 17.75%
> $-$17.50% $\frac{.35}{.45} \times .25\% = .194\%$
> .25%

9. Add 17.5% and .194% to obtain a more accurate APR.

> 17.5% + .194% = 17.694% or 17.7%

Assignment 6-10

1. Use Table 6-2 to find the APR in the following problems. Use interpolation, if necessary, and round to the nearest thousandth.

	Amount of loan	Amount of each payment	Number of payments	Frequency of payments	Total amount to be paid	Total interest	APR
a.	$ 500	$ 53	10	monthly	_____	_____	_____
b.	4600	185	30	monthly	_____	_____	_____
c.	350	23	18	monthly	_____	_____	_____
d.	12,400	265	60	monthly	_____	_____	_____
e.	85,000	2500	48	monthly	_____	_____	_____

Chapter 6 Self-Testing Exercises

1. What is the simple rate of interest for a payment totaling $450 in 6 months for a note of $420?

2. Determine the exact number of days between July 7 and October 20.

3. Ceiling Street, Inc., purchased $25,000 worth of 3-month, $5\frac{1}{2}\%$ government securities. How much interest will the company earn?

4. Calculate the interest rate on a loan of $7230, drawing interest of $72.30 for 4 months.

5. Determine the principal of a loan that earns $12 in 30 days at 16%.

6. Determine the net proceeds and the amount of discount on a $1500 note discounted at 18% for 60 days.

7. Determine the true rate of interest on a $900 note discounted at 12% for 90 days.

8. Using exact time, ordinary interest, determine the amount of principal if 6.6% bonds yield $33 in interest between January 1 and March 2.

9. An investment of $6750 in 12% corporate bonds produced interest of $101.25. For how long were the bonds held?

10. What rate of interest is required to yield $700 if the principal is $16,000 and the time is 72 days?

11. The Trusty Bank of Cicero made a loan of $2950 at 16% on June 21. Using exact time, exact interest, find the interest if the loan was to be repaid on September 1.

12. Jose bought a motorcycle for $750. He borrowed the money from the Friendly Loan Co., and the loan is to be paid in 22 monthly installments of $53 each. Determine the effective rate of interest Jose will pay.

13. Suzie borrowed $750 from Dave's Pawnshop. She agreed to pay $50 per week for 16 weeks to repay the loan. What is the effective rate of interest Suzie will pay?

14. Ms. Carson wants to buy some property for $16,200. Her monthly payments will be $480 for 5 years. Calculate the APR and interpolate, if necessary, for an exact answer.

15. Determine the amount of time it will take $1500 to earn $45 at a 9% interest rate.

16. Determine the principal on a note that earns $50 in 4 months at 12%.

17. Sam Lattimer made a deposit in the Bank of Alaska on April 11. Sam had earned $44 interest when he withdrew his savings on June 23 to prospect for gas and oil. What was the amount deposited if the bank calculates interest on an exact time, exact interest basis at a rate of 10%.

18. Jim is considering the purchase of a pickup truck for his ranch. If the truck costs $10,800, Jim makes a $3000 down payment, and finance terms are for $200 per month for 48 months, then how much is the APR? (Interpolate, if necessary.)

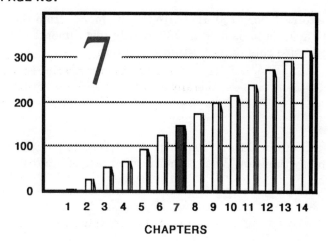

Financial Applications

Student Objectives

Upon completion of this chapter, the student should be able to

1. **Calculate** *the maturity value and total compounded interest arithmetically.*
2. **Calculate** *the maturity value and total compounded interest using a compound interest table.*
3. **Calculate** *the present value of money.*
4. **Determine** *the future value of an ordinary annuity.*
5. **Determine** *the value of an annuity due.*
6. **Determine** *the present value of an annuity.*
7. **Find** *the value of a sinking fund.*
8. **Define, illustrate,** *or* **use**

   present value   *maturity value*
   annuity   *compound interest*
   sinking fund   *future value*

Compound Interest

With simple interest, the payment or charge of interest is made on a short-term basis. Many times, however, interest payments are not made in every period in which they are earned. If interest is not paid, it is generally added to the original principal. Then the next period's interest is calculated on the new principal, that is, the original principal plus the interest earned in the prior period.

Many business calculations are based upon the principle of compound interest. Among these calculations are—to name just a few—present value, life insurance, annuities, discounts, stock investments, and capital equipment investment decisions. Most of these decision-making calculations are covered later in this book. Obviously, since so many financial decisions are based on calculations that are dependent upon the compounding principal, a clear understanding of the concepts involved is essential.

Definitions
1. *Maturity value* is the amount obtained when the total interest earned is added to the original principal $(P + I)$.
2. *Compound interest* is interest earned on the principal and on previously earned interest $(MV - P)$.

To solve compound interest problems, the interest is calculated for each compound period and then added to the principal to find the principal for the next compound period. Hence, it should be recognized that compound interest problems are a series of *amount* problems (see Chapter 4). To solve compound interest problems as amount problems, the rate per compound period and the number of compound periods in the interest period must be determined.

Determining the Rate per Compound Period
The interest rate stated in compound interest problems is nearly always stated in yearly terms. If the interest period for compounding purposes is less than 1 year, such as semiannually or quarterly, the stated interest rate must be divided by the number of interest periods during the year before calculations proceed.

Example What is the interest rate per period if interest is compounded quarterly at 16%?

Solution $\frac{16\%}{4}$ yearly interest / number of compound periods in each year

=4% per period

Assignment 7-1

1. Calculate the interest rate per compound period in the following:

	Rate	Time of loan	Compounded	Period interest rate
a.	16%	1 year	semiannually	_____
b.	12%	1 year	quarterly	_____
c.	20%	1 year	semiannually	_____
d.	18%	1 year	every 4 months	_____
e.	12%	1 year	monthly	_____
f.	8%	1 year	quarterly	_____

Determining the Number of Compound Periods

To determine the number of compound periods in the interest period, multiply the number of years in the interest period by the number of compound periods per year.

Example   Calculate the number of periods in the interest period if the interest is compounded quarterly for 10 years.

Solution

    10 years in interest period
   × 4 number of times interest is compounded per year
  =40 total number of compound periods in interest period

Assignment 7-2

1.   Determine the number of periods in the interest period in the following:

	Time of loan	Compounded	Number of periods
a.	5 years	monthly	_____
b.	15 years	quarterly	_____
c.	3 years	quarterly	_____
d.	20 years	semiannually	_____
e.	12 years	annually	_____
f.	6 years	monthly	_____

Assignment 7-3

1.   Complete the following:

	Rate	Time of loan	Compounded	Number of periods	Period interest rate
a.	6%	8 years	semiannually	_____	_____
b.	8%	4 years	quarterly	_____	_____
c.	4%	2 years	monthly	_____	_____
d.	12%	12 years	semiannually	_____	_____
e.	9%	20 years	every 4 months	_____	_____
f.	10%	15 years	annually	_____	_____
g.	4%	10 years	quarterly	_____	_____
h.	3%	30 years	semiannually	_____	_____
i.	6%	9 years	quarterly	_____	_____
j.	10%	5 years	semiannually	_____	_____

Solving Compound Interest Problems

Example A deposit of $1000 is made in a bank that compounds interest quarterly at 8%. Calculate the maturity value and the interest earned in $1\frac{1}{2}$ years.

Solution 1. Determine the interest rate per compound period:

$\dfrac{8\%}{4}$ yearly interest rate
number of compound periods in 1 year

$=2\%$ interest rate per compound period

2. Add 100% to the interest rate per compound period since this is an *amount* problem:

$\begin{array}{r} 2\% \\ +100\% \\ \hline =102\% \end{array}$

3. Determine the number of compound periods in the interest period:

$1\frac{1}{2}$ years in interest period

$\begin{array}{r} \times 4 \\ \hline =6 \end{array}$ number of times interest is compounded per year
total number of compound periods in interest period

4. Calculate the maturity value and the compound interest:

$\begin{array}{r} \$1000 \\ \times \ 1.02 \\ \hline \end{array}$

$=\$1020$ maturity value at end of first compound period
$\times \ 1.02$

$=\$1040.40$ maturity value at end of second compound period
$\times \quad 1.02$

$=\$1061.21$ maturity value at end of third compound period
$\times \quad 1.02$

$=\$1082.43$ maturity value at end of fourth compound period
$\times \quad 1.02$

$=\$1104.08$ maturity value at end of fifth compound period
$\times \quad 1.02$

$=1126.16$ maturity value at end of sixth compound period

$\begin{array}{r} \$1126.16 \\ -\$1000.00 \\ \hline =\$\ 126.16 \end{array}$ maturity value at end of $1\frac{1}{2}$ years
original principal
interest earned in $1\frac{1}{2}$ years

Assignment 7-4

1. Calculate the maturity value and the compound interest in the following:

	Principal	Rate	Time of loan	Compounded	Maturity value	Compound interest
a.	$ 800	10%	1 year	quarterly	_____	_____
b.	600	6%	1 year	semiannually	_____	_____
c.	3,000	5%	$1\frac{1}{2}$ years	semiannually	_____	_____

d.	500	3%	1 year	quarterly	_____	_____
e.	1,200	10%	2 years	semiannually	_____	_____
f.	200	8%	$\frac{1}{2}$ year	quarterly	_____	_____
g.	300	5%	2 years	annually	_____	_____
h.	10,000	8%	3 years	annually	_____	_____
i.	400	4%	2 years	semiannually	_____	_____
j.	700	6%	1 year	monthly	_____	_____

Compound Interest Tables

Finding the Compound Interest

Computing compound interest manually requires a great deal of drudgery. Fortunately, there are tables for compound interest calculation which are easy to use. Table 7-1, on pages 166 to 175, a compound interest table, is used as follows:

1. Calculate the number of compound periods in the interest period.
2. Determine the interest rate per period.
3. In the tables find the interest rate computed in Step 2.
4. Find the number of periods computed in Step 1 under the column headed *n*.
5. Go across the row found in Step 4 to Table 7-1 (Compound Interest of $1).
6. Multiply the amount found in Table 7-1 by the principal.
7. The answer determined in Step 6 will be the maturity value ($P + I$). Therefore, if interest is desired, subtract the principal from the value obtained in Step 6.

Example Find the maturity value and the amount of compound interest on a loan of $15,000 at 8%, compounded quarterly for 10 years.

Solution

1. Find the number of periods:

   10 years
   × 4 periods per year
   = 40 periods

2. Determine the interest rate per period:

   8% yearly rate
   4 number of periods per year
   = 2% interest rate per period

3. Find the 2% tables on page 167.

4. Find 40 periods in the leftmost column.

5. Go across row 40 to the column headed by Table 7-1. Record that number: 2.20803966.

6. Multiply 2.20803966 by the principal:

   2.20803966
   × $15000
   1104019830000
   220803966
   33120.59490000   =$33,120.59 maturity value

7. Subtract $15,000, the principal, from $33,120.59, the maturity value, to determine the amount of compound interest:

   $33,120.59 MV
   − 15,000.00 P
   =$18,120.59 compound interest

Assignment 7-5

1. Solve the following:

	Principal	Rate	Time of Loan	Compounded	Maturity Value	Compound Interest
a.	$1500	8%	2 years	quarterly	_____	_____
b.	2800	10%	8 years	semiannually	_____	_____
c.	5600	6%	10 years	quarterly	_____	_____
d.	640	12%	4 years	monthly	_____	_____
e.	7100	4%	5 years	quarterly	_____	_____
f.	5500	8%	15 years	semiannually	_____	_____
g.	2500	14%	22 years	semiannually	_____	_____
h.	4800	8%	12 years	quarterly	_____	_____
i.	1200	16%	18 years	semiannually	_____	_____
j.	9620	12%	3 years	monthly	_____	_____

2. Henry Zap put $10,000 into a pension fund for his retirement at age 55. Henry is now 35 years old. The fund guarantees a return of 6%, compounded semi-annually. What is the maturity value of the fund?

3. The Dusky Dealing Corporation negotiated a $100,000 long-term loan with First International State Bank. Interest was to be compounded monthly for 4 years at a rate of 12%. Calculate the maturity value and the compound interest of the loan.

Present Value

Money that is to be received at some future date is not worth as much as it would be if it were received today. Money received today can be 'put to work' earning interest. This is the opposite of paying compound interest. The amount that a future payment of money is worth today is called its *present value*. The present value is less than the future value.

Some of the uses for calculating present value are to determine how much must be put aside now to, for example: (1) start a business in the future, (2) put a child through college, (3) purchase a new machine or other piece of capital equipment, (4) save for a future vacation, or (5) determine the regular or periodic savings necessary to provide a definite retirement income.

Calculation of Present Value
To determine the present value of money, a present-value table is used (Table 7-2). The table gives the present value of $1 at compound interest for various periods at compound interest rates of .5% to 20%. To use the table, follow these steps:

1. Calculate the number of compound periods in the interest period.
2. Determine the interest rate per period.

3. In the tables find the interest rate computed in Step 2.
4. Find the number of periods computed in Step 1 under the leftmost column.
5. Go across the row found in Step 4 to Table 7-2 (Present Value of $1 at Compound Interest).
6. Multiply the amount found in Table 7-2 by the principal, or the amount of money for which the present value is being calculated. The product of the multiplication will be the present value of the money.

Example   Find the amount that must be saved now to provide the estimated $40,000 required to send a child through college in 10 years, if the interest rate is 5% compounded annually.

Solution   1. Find the 5% table on page 170.
2. Since the time period is 10 years, find the number 10 under the leftmost column.
3. Go across row 10 to the column headed Table 7-2. The number that corresponds to ten periods at 5% is .61391325.
4. Multiply the .61391325 found in Step 2 by the amount required in 10 years, $40,0000:

$$\begin{array}{r} .61391325 \quad \text{present value of \$1, ten years hence} \\ \times \quad \$40,000 \quad\quad\quad\quad\quad\quad\quad\quad\quad\quad \\ \hline =\$24,556.53 \quad \text{present value of \$40,000, ten years hence} \end{array}$$

Therefore, $24,556.53 must be placed in an account that will draw 5% interest, compounded annually.

Example   Using the preceding example, calculate the amount that must be saved if the interest is compounded semiannually.

Solution   1. The time period, 10 years, compounded semiannually will contain 20 interest payment periods:

$$\begin{array}{r} 10 \quad \text{years} \\ \times \ 2 \quad \text{interest payments per year (semiannual payments)} \\ \hline =20 \quad \text{interest payments in 10 years} \end{array}$$

2. The annual interest rate is 5%; therefore, the semiannual interest rate is 2.5%.

$\dfrac{5\%}{2}$ annual interest rate
   number of interest payments per year

$=2.5\%$ semiannual interest rate

3. Find the 2.5% table on page 168.
4. Find 20 under the leftmost column.
5. Go across row 20 until you come to the column headed Table 7-2. Record that number: .61027094.
6. Multiply 6.1027094 by $40,000, the amount required in 10 years:

$$\begin{array}{r} .61027094 \quad \text{present value of \$1, ten years hence} \\ \times \quad \$40,000 \quad\quad\quad\quad\quad\quad\quad\quad\quad\quad \\ \hline =\$24,410.8376 \quad \text{present value of \$40,000, ten years hence} \end{array}$$

Therefore, $24,410.84 must be placed in an account paying 5% interest, compounded semiannually.

Assignment 7-6

1. Calculate the present value of the following:

	Amount required	Years	Rate of interest	Compounded	Investment required
a.	$1000	4	5%	annually	$_____
b.	750	2	6%	semiannually	_____
c.	3500	5	8%	quarterly	_____
d.	2000	3	6%	monthly	_____
e.	1250	10	4%	quarterly	_____
f.	800	4	7%	annually	_____
g.	1200	5	$5\frac{1}{2}$%	annually	_____
h.	2500	8	3%	semiannually	_____
i.	600	6	5%	semiannually	_____
j.	1500	12	10%	quarterly	_____

2. If Archie Bunker wants to accumulate $2500 at an interest rate of 4% compounded quarterly to pay his back taxes at the end of 5 years, how much must he invest?

3. An ambitious intern wants to have $44,000 in 4 years to open his doctor's office when he graduates from medical school. Determine how much he will have to invest now at 5% compounded annually.

4. Sally Corbin wants to invest enough money in a mutual fund—promising to pay 6% compounded quarterly—to open a library in 6 years. If she feels that it will require $16,500 to start her library, how much must Sally invest?

5. Susan Lightfoot, a dance instructor, wants to buy her own studio. She needs $2500 to start her business. Interest rates are 6% compounded quarterly. To open in 5½ years, how much will she need to invest now?

Annuities

An annuity is a series of payments, of equal amounts, made or received at regular, stated intervals. Therefore, a home mortgage is an annuity, as regular payments are made for a fixed period of time. This type of annuity is called an *annuity certain* since the payments are for a fixed amount of time.

A retirement annuity from a pension fund pays regular, equal amounts on specified dates during the life of the pension recipient. This type of annuity is called a *contingent annuity* since payments are contingent upon certain conditions—namely, in this case, the life-span of the pension recipient.

Many other examples of annuities could be given. Among these are installment payments, insurance payments, and the regular saving of money for some future obligation (in business—usually called *sinking funds*).

Future Value of Ordinary Annuities

When payments are made regularly at the end of each period, the annuity is called an *ordinary annuity*. It is possible to calculate the value of an ordinary annuity manually or with compound interest tables. However, there are ordinary annuity tables available and these are almost always used for this purpose. Such a table, presented as Table 7-3, is used as follows:

1. Calculate the number of compound periods in the interest period.
2. Determine the interest rate per period.
3. In the tables, find the interest rate computed in Step 2.
4. Find the number of periods computed in Step 1 under the leftmost column.
5. Go across the row found in Step 4 to Table 7-3 (Amount of Ordinary Annuity).
6. Multiply the number found in Step 5 by the amount of the periodic investment. The resulting product will be the total amount of the annuity.

Example   Vito Ganinni invested $500 in an ordinary annual annuity for 5 years at 5%. Find the amount of this annuity.

Solution
1. Find the 5% tables on page 170.
2. Find the number 5, for 5 years, in the leftmost column.
3. Go across row 5 to the column headed Table 7-3.
4. Multiply the number that corresponds to row 5, Table 7-3, 5.52563125, by $500:

5.52563125	amount of annuity for $1
× $500	amount invested
$2762.82	amount of annuity

Example   Jane McDowell was a member of an investment club. She made semiannual investments of $100 for 4 years in an ordinary annuity at 8%. Find the amount.

Solution
1. Multiply the number of years by 2:
   4 years × 2 payments per year = 8 payments
2. Divide the interest rate by 2:
   8% annual interest rate ÷ 2 interest periods = 4% interest per period
3. Find the 4% tables on page 169.
4. Find 8 periods in the leftmost column.
5. Go across row 8 to the column headed Table 7-3. Record that value: 9.21422626.
6. Multiply 9.21422626 by the amount of the periodic investment:

9.21422626	amount of annuity for $1
× $100	amount of periodic investment
$921.42	amount of annuity

Assignment 7-7

1. Calculate the value of the annuity in the following ordinary annuity problems:

	Annuity payment	Payments made	Number of years	Interest rate	Value of annuity
a.	$1000	annually	15	6%	$_____
b.	500	semiannually	6	8%	_____
c.	630	annually	4	5%	_____
d.	750	annually	10	4%	_____
e.	2500	quarterly	5	16%	_____
f.	600	semiannually	3	6%	_____
g.	100	quarterly	2	12%	_____
h.	8000	semiannually	8	8%	_____
i.	150	annually	12	3%	_____
j.	950	quarterly	4	12%	_____

2. Sylvia Mendoza invested $500 semiannually for 4 years at 5% compounded semiannually. Compute the worth of her investment.

3. Sara Teasdale bought a diamond ring. Her installment contract called for quarterly payments of $100 for $1\frac{1}{2}$ years at an annual effective interest of 18%. How much did she have invested in the ring at the end of the $1\frac{1}{2}$ years?

4. George Scott wanted to save $400 per year for 10 years at 6% compounded annually to put his daughter through college. How much did George plan on having for his daughter's education?

Annuities Due

An annuity due is a disbursement transaction wherein the series of payments are made at the *beginning* of the period. The obvious difference between the annuity due and the ordinary annuity is that, for the same number of periods, the annuity due will earn interest for one period more than will the ordinary annuity. In other words, the first principal payment into an ordinary annuity does not earn interest in the first period. All principal payments earn interest with the annuity due. The difference is illustrated in Table 7-6.

Table 7-6

Comparison Between Ordinary Annuity and Annuity Due for $1 at 6% Compound Interest for Five Periods

Period	Annuity Investment Ordinary	Annuity Investment Due	Interest Earned During Period Ordinary	Interest Earned During Period Due	Total of Principal and Interest at End of the Period Ordinary	Total of Principal and Interest at End of the Period Due
1	$1	$1	$0	$.06	$1.00	$1.06
2	1	1	.06	.1836	2.06	2.1836
3	1	1	.1836	.3746	3.1836	3.3746
4	1	1	.3746	.6371	4.3746	4.6371
5	1	1	.6371	.9753	5.6371	5.9753

The amount of an annuity due can be calculated from an ordinary annuity table, as follows:

1. Calculate the number of compound periods in the interest period.
2. Determine the interest rate per period.
3. In the tables find the interest rate computed in Step 2.
4. Find the number of periods computed in Step 1 under the leftmost column.
5. Go across the row found in Step 4 to Table 7-3 (Amount of Ordinary Annuity). Record the whole number part. Move to the next higher period. Record the fractional portion next to the whole number previously recorded.
6. Multiply the value found in Step 5 by the amount of the periodic investment. The resulting product will be the total amount of the annuity.

Example   Peter Donovan invested $750 at the beginning of each year for 5 years. What was the value of his investment at the end of the fifth year if his investment earned 5% compounded annually?

Solution
1. Find the 5% tables on page 170.
2. Find 5 periods in the leftmost column.
3. Go across row 5 to the column headed Table 7-3. Record the whole number (5). Move to row 6 in the leftmost column. Go across to Table 7-3. Record the fractional portion (.80191281) next to the whole number (5) previously recorded (5.80191281).
4. Multiply 5.80191281 by the amount of the annual investment, $750:

$$
\begin{array}{ll}
5.801911281 & \text{annuity for \$1} \\
\times \qquad \$750 & \text{amount invested} \\
\hline
\$ \quad 4351.43 & \text{annuity for \$750 invested at 5\%}
\end{array}
$$

Therefore, an investment of $750 made in an annuity due (at the beginning of each period) for 5 years will be worth $4351.43 at maturity.

Assignment 7-8

1. Calculate the amount of an annuity due in each of the following:

	Annuity payment	Payments made	Number of years	Interest rate	Value of annuity
a.	$1000	annually	15	6%	_____
b.	500	semiannually	6	4%	_____
c.	630	annually	4	5%	_____
d.	750	annually	10	2%	_____
e.	2500	quarterly	5	16%	_____
f.	600	semiannually	3	6%	_____
g.	100	quarterly	2	8%	_____
h.	8000	semiannually	8	8%	_____
i.	150	annually	12	3%	_____
j.	950	quarterly	4	12%	_____

2. Find the difference between an ordinary annuity and an annuity due if the investment is $600 annually at 5% for 5 years.

3. An investment of $100 at the beginning of each quarter at 8% compounded quarterly for 3 years will result in an annuity due of how much?

Present Value of an Annuity

The value of future receipts in terms of today's worth is known as the *present value of an annuity*. That is, the present value of an annuity is the total amount that must be deposited or invested now to provide for the withdrawal of a series of periodic equal payments.

To use a present value of annuity table (Table 7-4), follow the same procedures as for a future value of annuity table:

1. Calculate the number of compound periods in the interest period.
2. Determine the interest rate per period.
3. In the tables find the interest rate computed in Step 2.
4. Find the number of periods computed in Step 1 under the leftmost column.
5. Go across the row found in Step 4 to Table 7-4 (Present Value of Annuity).
6. Multiply the value found in Step 5 by the amount of periodic payments.

Example   I. M. Rich decided to set up a trust fund for his daughter so that she will be able to withdraw $5000 each December for the next 4 years. If the fund will earn 8% compounded annually, find the amount Mr. Rich needs to deposit today.

Solution
1. Find the 8% tables on page 172.
2. Find the number 4 in the leftmost column.
3. Go across row 4 to the column headed Table 7-4. Record that value: 3.31212684.
4. Multiply 3.31212684 by the amount of the annual withdrawal, $5000:

    3.31212684   present value of annuity of $1
    × $5000   amount of withdrawal
    $ 16,560.64   present value of annuity

Mr. Rich needs to deposit $16,560.64 in the trust for his daughter.

Example   Mr. Jones wishes to invest in a bond having a face value of $10,000. The bond agreement calls for 5% interest to be paid annually for the next 5 years. Because the current market rate for similar bonds is 8%, Mr. Jones is not willing to pay the full face amount. Determine how much he should be willing to pay for the bond.

Solution   The solution to this problem involves two operations. The face value of the bond will be repaid in 5 years, so this is a present value problem. The interest payments represent a present value of an annuity problem since Mr. Jones will be receiving $500 (interest = $10,000 × 5%) each year for 5 years. To solve this problem, each operation must be done and then the answers combined.

1. Find the 8% tables on page 172.
2. Find 5, for 5 years, in the leftmost column.
3. Go across row 5 to the column headed Table 7-2. Record that number: .68058320.
4. Multiply .68058320 by the face value of the bond, $10,000:

> .68058320 present value of $1
> × $10,000 face value of bond
> $6805.83 present value of face value of bond

5. In the 8% tables, find 5, for 5 years, in the leftmost column.
6. Go across row 5 to the column headed Table 7-4. Record that number: 3.99271004.
7. Multiply 3.99271004 by the amount of interest payments, $500:

> 3.99271004 present value of annuity of $1
> × $500 annual interest payments
> $ 1996.36 present value of interest payments

8. Add the present value of the face value of the bond to the present value of the interest payments:

> $6805.83 present value of face value of bond
> 1996.36 present value of interest payments
> $8802.19 current market price of bond

Assignment 7-9

1. Calculate the present value of an annuity in the following:

	Periodic withdrawal	Withdrawals made	Number of years	Interest rate	Present value of annuity
a.	$1000	semiannually	16	10%	$_____
b.	500	semiannually	7	16%	_____
c.	2500	annually	26	5%	_____
d.	750	quarterly	5	12%	_____
e.	125	semiannually	5	12%	_____

2. Ace Manufacturers wants to invest in a new process that is expected to reduce net expenses by $10,000 each year for the next 7 years. Money is currently earning 14% compounded semiannually. Find the most Ace should be willing to pay for this process.

3. Find the current value of an installment contract that calls for eight equal annual payments of $2575 if the current interest rate is 6% compounded annually.

4. Lucky Smith was a grand-prize winner in a sweepstakes and was offered a choice between the following prizes:

    $10,000 at the end of each year for 20 years
    $75,000 immediately

   If money is currently earning 12% compounded quarterly, which prize is worth more to Lucky in terms of today's money?

5. Susan wishes to purchase a bond with a face value of $1000. The bond is paying 6% annually for the next 20 years. The current market rate for similar bonds is 8%. Susan won't pay the full face value. How much should she be willing to pay?

Sinking Fund

A person or a company that has a fixed obligation in which an exact sum of money must be raised by a specified time may want to save a certain amount each year rather than try to raise the entire amount at its maturity date. This can be done by setting aside certain amounts of money periodically to accumulate at interest. The resulting money accumulation is called a *sinking fund*. To determine how much must be set aside each period in order to accumulate the desired amount by the date the obligation is due, follow these steps:

1. Calculate the number of compound periods in the interest period.
2. Determine the interest rate per period.
3. In the tables find the interest rate computed in Step 2.
4. Find the number of periods computed in Step 1 under the leftmost column.
5. Go across the row found in Step 4 to Table 7-6 (Sinking Fund).
6. Multiply the value found in Step 5 by the amount of money to be raised. The resulting product will be the funds which must be set aside each period in order to accumulate the desired amount.

Example   A company sold bonds having a face value of $100,000 due in 10 years. The company's management decided to set aside a sinking fund at the end of each year until the vace value of the bonds had to be paid. If management believes it can invest the funds at 6% compounded annually, how much must it set aside each year?

Solution
1. Find the 6% tables on page 171.
2. Find the number 10, for 10 years, under the leftmost column.
3. Go across row 10 to the column headed by Table 7-5. Record that number: .07586796.
4. Multiply .07586796 by the amount to be accumulated, $100,000:

$$\begin{array}{r} .07586796 \\ \times \quad \$100,000 \\ \hline \$7586.80 \end{array} \quad \text{amount to be set aside each year}$$

Therefore, the company will have to set aside $7586.80 at the end of each year for 10 years in order to have $100,000 available to pay the bondholders the face value of the bonds at maturity.

Assignment 7-10

1. Find the amount required for the sinking fund in each of the following:

	Maturity value	Payments made	Number of years	Interest rate	Periodic amount to sinking fund
a.	$ 10,000	annually	5	4%	$_____
b.	50,000	annually	10	5%	_____
c.	100,000	semiannually	10	6%	_____
d.	200,000	annually	15	3%	_____
e.	60,000	semiannually	8	8%	_____
f.	30,000	semiannually	5	4%	_____
g.	80,000	annually	12	6%	_____
h.	75,000	semiannually	7	6%	_____
i.	40,000	annually	9	5%	_____
j.	15,000	quarterly	3	8%	_____

2. The Shamrock Inn wanted to build a new motel in 5 years at an estimated cost of $1,500,000. Management set up a sinking fund to save the amount needed. It estimated that it would receive 6% interest, and it planned to make semi-annual payments into the fund. How much must each payment be?

3. A manufacturer just purchased a machine that has an expected life of 12 years. The company has a policy of setting up a sinking fund to replace machinery at the end of its expected life. The machine cost $58,000 and is expected to have a scrap value at the end of 12 years of $8000. Calculate the annual amount that should go into the sinking fund to replace the machine if prices are expected to remain constant and the company can invest its money at 6% compounded annually.

Chapter 7   Self-Testing Exercises

1. What is the present value of an investment that will return $20,000 in 5 years if the investor can earn 5% compounded annually?

2. Find the value of an investment of $250 made at the beginning of each year for 15 years at 4% interest compounded annually.

3. Laughlin, Inc., issued bonds for $50,000 to be repaid in 7 years. How much must be invested at the end of each year at 5% to pay off the bonds at maturity?

4. Calculate the interest on a 5% note compounded semiannually for 2 years on a principal of $500.

5. Calculate the amount of compound interest on a note of $1000 at 12% compounded quarterly for 2 years.

6. How much will John have if he invests $50 at the end of each year for 30 years in an annuity carrying a $3\frac{1}{2}$% annual compound interest?

7. How much must Jones and Bros., Inc., deposit every 6 months at 8% compounded semiannually to have $20,000 available 6 years from now?

8. Kelly's Bar pays Nowlin Realty $6720 per year rent. After 5 years of payments, what would be the total value of this money to Nowlin Realty if it invested at 6% compounded yearly?

9. Henry has $50 withheld from his salary each month and invested at 12% compounded quarterly. How large will his investment be 2 years from now?

10. Jan plans to invest an annual $500 royalty payment from her book at 5% compounded annually. What is today's value of 16 years worth of such payments?

11. Bob's Equipment Service Co. places $1200 in a savings account every 3 months. The bank pays 16% interest compounded quarterly. How much will be in Bob's account at the end of 7 years?

12. Jackson, Inc., wants to invest in a new machine that will reduce the company's expenses by $5000 annually for the next 4 years. Money is currently earning 14% compounded annually. Find the most Jackson, Inc., should be willing to pay for the machine.

13. Find the current selling price of a $100,000, 7% compounded annually, 10-year bond if similar bonds are presently selling at 8%.

Financial Applications
RATE 1.0%

PERIODS	7-1 COMPOUND INTEREST	7-2 PRESENT VALUE	7-3 AMOUNT OF ORDINARY ANNUITY	7-4 PRESENT VALUE OF ANNUITY	7-5 SINKING FUND
1	1.01000000	0.99009901	1.00000000	0.99009901	1.00000000
2	1.02010000	0.98029605	2.01000000	1.97039506	0.49751244
3	1.03030100	0.97059015	3.03010000	2.94098521	0.33002211
4	1.04060401	0.96098034	4.06040100	3.90196555	0.24628109
5	1.05101005	0.95146569	5.10100501	4.85343124	0.19603980
6	1.06152015	0.94204524	6.15201506	5.79547647	0.16254837
7	1.07213535	0.93271805	7.21353521	6.72819453	0.13862828
8	1.08285671	0.92348322	8.28567056	7.65167775	0.12069029
9	1.09368527	0.91433982	9.36852727	8.56601758	0.10674036
10	1.10462213	0.90528695	10.46221254	9.47130453	0.09558208
11	1.11566835	0.89632372	11.56683467	10.36762825	0.08645408
12	1.12682503	0.88744923	12.68250301	11.25507747	0.07884879
13	1.13809328	0.87866260	13.80932804	12.13374007	0.07241482
14	1.14947421	0.86996297	14.94742132	13.00370304	0.06690117
15	1.16096465	0.86134947	16.09689554	13.86505252	0.06212378
16	1.17257864	0.85282126	17.25786449	14.71787378	0.05794460
17	1.18430443	0.84437749	18.43044313	15.56225127	0.05425806
18	1.19614748	0.83601131	19.61474757	16.39826858	0.05098205
19	1.20810895	0.82773992	20.81089504	17.22600850	0.04805175
20	1.22019004	0.81954447	22.01900399	18.04555297	0.04541531
21	1.23239194	0.81143017	23.23919403	18.85698313	0.04303075
22	1.24471586	0.80339621	24.47158598	19.66037934	0.04086372
23	1.25716302	0.79544179	25.71630183	20.45582113	0.03888584
24	1.26973465	0.78756613	26.97346485	21.24338726	0.03707347
25	1.28243200	0.77976844	28.24319950	22.02315570	0.03540675
26	1.29525631	0.77204796	29.52563150	22.79520366	0.03386888
27	1.30820888	0.76440392	30.82088781	23.55960759	0.03244553
28	1.32129097	0.75683557	32.12909669	24.31644316	0.03112444
29	1.33450388	0.74934215	33.45038766	25.06578530	0.02989502
30	1.34784892	0.74192292	34.78489153	25.80770822	0.02874811
31	1.36132740	0.73457715	36.13274045	26.54228537	0.02767573
32	1.37494068	0.72730411	37.49406785	27.26958947	0.02667089
33	1.38869009	0.72010307	38.86900853	27.98969255	0.02572744
34	1.40257699	0.71297334	40.25769862	28.70266589	0.02483997
35	1.41660276	0.70591420	41.66027560	29.40858009	0.02400368
36	1.43076878	0.69892495	43.07683836	30.10750504	0.02321431
37	1.44507724	0.69200490	44.50764714	30.79950994	0.02246805
38	1.45952724	0.68515337	45.95272361	31.48466330	0.02176150
39	1.47412251	0.67836967	47.41225085	32.16303298	0.02109160
40	1.48886373	0.67165314	48.88637336	32.83468611	0.02045560
41	1.50375237	0.66500311	50.37523709	33.49968922	0.01985102
42	1.51878989	0.65841892	51.87898946	34.15810814	0.01927563
43	1.53397779	0.65189992	53.39777936	34.81000806	0.01872737
44	1.54931757	0.64544546	54.93175715	35.45545352	0.01820441
45	1.56481075	0.63905492	56.48107472	36.09450844	0.01770505
46	1.58045885	0.63272764	58.04588547	36.72723608	0.01722775
47	1.59626344	0.62646301	59.62634432	37.35369909	0.01677111
48	1.61222608	0.62026041	61.22260777	37.97399949	0.01633384
49	1.62834834	0.61411921	62.83483385	38.58807871	0.01591474
50	1.64463182	0.60803882	64.46318218	39.19611753	0.01551273
60	1.81669670	0.55044962	81.66966986	44.95503841	0.01224445
80	2.21671522	0.45111794	121.67152172	54.88820611	0.00821885
100	2.70481383	0.36971121	170.48138294	63.02887877	0.00586574
120	3.30038689	0.30299478	230.03868946	69.70052203	0.00434709
240	10.89255365	0.09180584	989.25536539	90.81941635	0.00101086
360	35.94964133	0.02781669	3494.96413277	97.21833108	0.00028613

RATE 0.5%

PERIODS	7-1 COMPOUND INTEREST	7-2 PRESENT VALUE	7-3 AMOUNT OF ORDINARY ANNUITY	7-4 PRESENT VALUE OF ANNUITY	7-5 SINKING FUND
1	1.00500000	0.99502488	1.00000000	0.99502488	1.00000000
2	1.01002500	0.99007450	2.00500000	1.98509938	0.49875312
3	1.01507513	0.98514876	3.01502500	2.97024814	0.33167221
4	1.02015050	0.98024752	4.03010013	3.95049566	0.24813279
5	1.02525125	0.97537067	5.05025063	4.92586633	0.19800997
6	1.03037751	0.97051808	6.07550188	5.89638441	0.16459546
7	1.03552940	0.96568963	7.10587939	6.86207404	0.14072854
8	1.04070704	0.96088520	8.14140879	7.82295924	0.12282886
9	1.04591058	0.95610468	9.18211583	8.77906392	0.10890736
10	1.05114013	0.95134794	10.22802641	9.73041186	0.09777057
11	1.05639583	0.94661487	11.27916654	10.67702673	0.08865903
12	1.06167781	0.94190534	12.33556237	11.61893207	0.08106643
13	1.06698620	0.93721924	13.39724018	12.55615131	0.07464224
14	1.07232113	0.93255646	14.46422639	13.48870777	0.06913609
15	1.07768274	0.92791688	15.53654752	14.41662465	0.06436436
16	1.08307115	0.92330037	16.61423026	15.33992502	0.06018937
17	1.08848651	0.91870684	17.69730141	16.25863186	0.05650579
18	1.09392894	0.91413616	18.78578791	17.17276802	0.05323173
19	1.09939858	0.90958822	19.87971685	18.08235624	0.05030253
20	1.10489558	0.90506290	20.97911544	18.98741915	0.04766645
21	1.11042006	0.90056010	22.08401101	19.88797925	0.04528163
22	1.11597216	0.89607971	23.19443107	20.78405896	0.04311380
23	1.12155202	0.89162160	24.31040322	21.67568055	0.04113465
24	1.12715978	0.88718567	25.43195524	22.56286622	0.03932061
25	1.13279558	0.88277181	26.55911502	23.44563803	0.03765186
26	1.13845955	0.87837991	27.69191059	24.32401794	0.03611163
27	1.14415185	0.87400986	28.83037015	25.19803779	0.03468565
28	1.14987261	0.86966155	29.97452200	26.06768936	0.03336167
29	1.15562197	0.86533488	31.12439461	26.93302423	0.03212914
30	1.16140008	0.86102973	32.28001658	27.79405397	0.03097892
31	1.16720708	0.85674600	33.44141666	28.65079997	0.02990304
32	1.17304312	0.85248358	34.60862375	29.50328355	0.02889453
33	1.17890833	0.84824237	35.78166686	30.35152592	0.02794727
34	1.18480288	0.84402226	36.96057520	31.19554818	0.02705586
35	1.19072689	0.83982314	38.14537807	32.03537132	0.02621550
36	1.19668052	0.83564492	39.33610496	32.87101624	0.02542194
37	1.20266393	0.83148748	40.53278549	33.70250372	0.02467139
38	1.20867725	0.82735073	41.73544942	34.52985445	0.02396045
39	1.21472063	0.82323455	42.94412666	35.35308900	0.02328607
40	1.22079424	0.81913886	44.15884730	36.17222786	0.02264552
41	1.22689821	0.81506354	45.37964153	36.98729141	0.02203631
42	1.23303270	0.81100850	46.60653974	37.79829991	0.02145622
43	1.23919786	0.80697363	47.83957244	38.60527354	0.02090320
44	1.24539385	0.80295884	49.07877030	39.40823238	0.02037541
45	1.25162082	0.79896402	50.32416415	40.20719640	0.01987117
46	1.25787892	0.79498907	51.57578497	41.00218547	0.01938894
47	1.26416832	0.79103390	52.83366390	41.79321937	0.01892733
48	1.27048916	0.78709841	54.09783222	42.58031778	0.01848503
49	1.27684161	0.78318250	55.36832138	43.36350028	0.01806087
50	1.28322581	0.77928607	56.64516299	44.14278635	0.01765376
60	1.34885015	0.74137220	69.77003051	51.72556075	0.01433280
80	1.49033357	0.67098847	98.06771357	65.80230538	0.01019704
100	1.64666849	0.60728678	129.33369842	78.54264477	0.00773194
120	1.81939673	0.54963273	163.87934681	90.07345333	0.00610205
240	3.31020448	0.30209614	462.04089516	139.58071439	0.00216431
360	6.02257521	0.16604193	1004.51504245	166.79161439	0.00099551
166

RATE 2.0%

PERIODS	7-1 COMPOUND INTEREST	7-2 PRESENT VALUE	7-3 AMOUNT OF ORDINARY ANNUITY	7-4 PRESENT VALUE OF ANNUITY	7-5 SINKING FUND
1	1.02000000	0.98039216	1.00000000	0.98039216	1.00000000
2	1.04040000	0.96116878	2.02000000	1.94156094	0.49504950
3	1.06120800	0.94232233	3.06040000	2.88388327	0.32675467
4	1.08243216	0.92384543	4.12160800	3.80772870	0.24262375
5	1.10408080	0.90573081	5.20404016	4.71345951	0.19215839
6	1.12616242	0.88797138	6.30812096	5.60143089	0.15852581
7	1.14868567	0.87056018	7.43428338	6.47199107	0.13451196
8	1.17165938	0.85349037	8.58296905	7.32548144	0.11650980
9	1.19509257	0.83675527	9.75462843	8.16223671	0.10251544
10	1.21899442	0.82034830	10.94972100	8.98258501	0.09132653
11	1.24337431	0.80426304	12.16871542	9.78684805	0.08217794
12	1.26824179	0.78849318	13.41208973	10.57534122	0.07455960
13	1.29360663	0.77303253	14.68033152	11.34837375	0.06811835
14	1.31947876	0.75787502	15.97393815	12.10624877	0.06260197
15	1.34586834	0.74301473	17.29341692	12.84926350	0.05782547
16	1.37278571	0.72844581	18.63928525	13.57770931	0.05365013
17	1.40024142	0.71416256	20.01207096	14.29187188	0.04996984
18	1.42824625	0.70015937	21.41231238	14.99203125	0.04670210
19	1.45681117	0.68643076	22.84055863	15.67846201	0.04378177
20	1.48594740	0.67297133	24.29736980	16.35143334	0.04115672
21	1.51566634	0.65977582	25.78331719	17.01120916	0.03878477
22	1.54597967	0.64683904	27.29898354	17.65804820	0.03663140
23	1.57689926	0.63415592	28.84496321	18.29220412	0.03466810
24	1.60843725	0.62172149	30.42186247	18.91392560	0.03287110
25	1.64060599	0.60953087	32.03029972	19.52345647	0.03122044
26	1.67341811	0.59757928	33.67090572	20.12103576	0.02969923
27	1.70688648	0.58586204	35.34432383	20.70689780	0.02828309
28	1.74102421	0.57437455	37.05121031	21.28127236	0.02698967
29	1.77584469	0.56311231	38.79223451	21.84438466	0.02577836
30	1.81136158	0.55207089	40.56807921	22.39645555	0.02464992
31	1.84758882	0.54124597	42.37944079	22.93770152	0.02359635
32	1.88454059	0.53063330	44.22702961	23.46833482	0.02261061
33	1.92223140	0.52022873	46.11157020	23.98856355	0.02168653
34	1.96067603	0.51002817	48.03380160	24.49859172	0.02081867
35	1.99988955	0.50002761	49.99447763	24.99861933	0.02000221
36	2.03988734	0.49022315	51.99436719	25.48884248	0.01923285
37	2.08068509	0.48061093	54.03425453	25.96945341	0.01850678
38	2.12229879	0.47118719	56.11493962	26.44064060	0.01782057
39	2.16474477	0.46194822	58.23723841	26.90258883	0.01717114
40	2.20803966	0.45289042	60.40198318	27.35547924	0.01655575
41	2.25220046	0.44401021	62.61002284	27.79948945	0.01597188
42	2.29724447	0.43530413	64.86222330	28.23479358	0.01541729
43	2.34318936	0.42676875	67.15946777	28.66156233	0.01488993
44	2.39005314	0.41840074	69.50265712	29.07996307	0.01438794
45	2.43785421	0.41019680	71.89271027	29.49015987	0.01390962
46	2.48661129	0.40215373	74.33056447	29.89231360	0.01345342
47	2.53570739	0.39426836	76.81717576	30.28658196	0.01301792
48	2.58870039	0.38653761	79.35351927	30.67311957	0.01260184
49	2.63881179	0.37895844	81.94058966	31.05207801	0.01220396
50	2.69158803	0.37152788	84.57940145	31.42360589	0.01182321
60	3.28103079	0.30478227	114.05153942	34.76088668	0.00876797
80	4.87543916	0.20510973	193.77195780	39.74451359	0.00516071
100	7.24464612	0.13803297	312.23230591	43.09835164	0.00320274
120	10.76516303	0.09289223	488.25815171	45.35538655	0.00204810
240	115.88873515	0.00862897	5744.43675765	49.56855168	0.00017408
360	1247.56112775	0.00080156	62328.05638744	49.95992180	0.00001604

RATE 1.5%

PERIODS	7-1 COMPOUND INTEREST	7-2 PRESENT VALUE	7-3 AMOUNT OF ORDINARY ANNUITY	7-4 PRESENT VALUE OF ANNUITY	7-5 SINKING FUND
1	1.01500000	0.98522167	1.00000000	0.98522167	1.00000000
2	1.03022500	0.97066175	2.01500000	1.95588342	0.49627792
3	1.04567837	0.95631699	3.04522500	2.91220042	0.32838296
4	1.06136355	0.94218423	4.09090338	3.85438485	0.24444479
5	1.07728400	0.92826033	5.15226693	4.78264497	0.19408932
6	1.09344326	0.91454219	6.22955093	5.69718717	0.16052521
7	1.10984491	0.90102679	7.32299419	6.59821396	0.13655616
8	1.12649259	0.88771112	8.43283911	7.48592508	0.11858402
9	1.14338998	0.87459224	9.55933169	8.36051732	0.10460982
10	1.16054083	0.86166723	10.70272167	9.22218455	0.09343418
11	1.17794894	0.84893323	11.86326249	10.07111779	0.08429384
12	1.19561817	0.83638742	13.04121143	10.90750521	0.07667999
13	1.21355244	0.82402702	14.23682960	11.73153222	0.07024036
14	1.23175573	0.81184928	15.45038205	12.54338150	0.06472332
15	1.25023207	0.79985150	16.68213778	13.34323301	0.05994436
16	1.26898555	0.78803104	17.93236984	14.13126405	0.05576508
17	1.28802033	0.77638526	19.20135539	14.90764931	0.05207966
18	1.30734064	0.76491159	20.48937572	15.67256089	0.04880578
19	1.32695075	0.75360747	21.79671636	16.42616837	0.04587847
20	1.34685501	0.74247042	23.12366710	17.16863879	0.04324574
21	1.36705783	0.73149795	24.47052211	17.90013673	0.04086550
22	1.38756370	0.72068763	25.83757994	18.62082437	0.03870332
23	1.40837715	0.71003708	27.22514364	19.33086145	0.03673075
24	1.42950281	0.69954392	28.63352080	20.03040537	0.03492410
25	1.45094535	0.68920583	30.06302361	20.71961120	0.03326345
26	1.47270953	0.67902052	31.51396896	21.39863172	0.03173196
27	1.49480018	0.66898574	32.98667850	22.06761746	0.03031527
28	1.51722218	0.65909925	34.48147867	22.72671671	0.02900108
29	1.53998051	0.64935887	35.99870085	23.37607558	0.02777878
30	1.56308022	0.63976243	37.53868137	24.01583801	0.02663919
31	1.58652642	0.63030781	39.10176159	24.64614582	0.02557430
32	1.61032432	0.62099292	40.68828801	25.26713874	0.02457710
33	1.63447918	0.61181568	42.29861233	25.87895442	0.02364144
34	1.65899637	0.60277407	43.93309152	26.48172849	0.02276189
35	1.68388132	0.59386608	45.59208789	27.07559458	0.02193383
36	1.70913954	0.58508974	47.27596921	27.66068431	0.02115240
37	1.73477663	0.57644309	48.98510874	28.23712740	0.02041437
38	1.76079828	0.56792423	50.71988538	28.80501163	0.01971613
39	1.78721025	0.55953126	52.48068366	29.36458288	0.01905463
40	1.81401841	0.55126232	54.26789391	29.91584520	0.01842710
41	1.84122888	0.54311559	56.08191232	30.45896079	0.01783106
42	1.86884712	0.53508925	57.92314100	30.99405004	0.01726426
43	1.89687983	0.52718153	59.79198812	31.52123157	0.01672465
44	1.92533302	0.51939067	61.68886794	32.04062223	0.01621038
45	1.95421301	0.51171494	63.61420096	32.55233718	0.01571976
46	1.98352621	0.50415265	65.56841398	33.05648983	0.01525125
47	2.01327910	0.49670212	67.55194018	33.55319195	0.01480342
48	2.04347826	0.48936170	69.56521929	34.04255365	0.01437500
49	2.07413046	0.48212975	71.60869758	34.52468339	0.01398478
50	2.10524242	0.47500468	73.68282804	34.99968807	0.01357168
60	2.44321978	0.40929597	96.21465171	39.38026888	0.01039343
80	3.29066279	0.30389015	152.71085247	46.40732349	0.00654832
100	4.43204565	0.22562944	228.80304330	51.62470367	0.00437057
120	5.96932287	0.16752319	331.28819149	55.49845411	0.00301852
240	35.63281555	0.02806402	2308.85437027	64.79573209	0.00043312
360	212.70378089	0.00470137	14113.58539279	66.35324174	0.00007085

RATE 3.0%

PERIODS	7-1 COMPOUND INTEREST	7-2 PRESENT VALUE	7-3 AMOUNT OF ORDINARY ANNUITY	7-4 PRESENT VALUE OF ANNUITY	7-5 SINKING FUND
1	1.0300000	0.97087379	1.0000000	0.97087379	1.0000000
2	1.0609000	0.94259591	2.0300000	1.91346970	0.49261084
3	1.09272700	0.91514166	3.0909000	2.82861135	0.32353036
4	1.12550881	0.88848705	4.18362700	3.71709840	0.23902705
5	1.15927407	0.86260878	5.30913581	4.57970719	0.18835457
6	1.19405230	0.83748426	6.46840988	5.41719144	0.15459750
7	1.22987387	0.81309151	7.66246218	6.23028296	0.13050635
8	1.26677008	0.78940923	8.89233605	7.01969219	0.11245639
9	1.30477318	0.76641673	10.15910613	7.78610892	0.09843386
10	1.34391638	0.74409391	11.46387931	8.53020284	0.08723051
11	1.38423387	0.72242128	12.80779569	9.25262411	0.07807745
12	1.42576089	0.70137988	14.19202956	9.95400399	0.07046209
13	1.46853371	0.68095134	15.61779045	10.63495533	0.06402954
14	1.51258972	0.66111781	17.08632416	11.29607314	0.05852634
15	1.55796742	0.64186195	18.59891389	11.93793509	0.05376658
16	1.60470644	0.62316694	20.15688130	12.56110203	0.04961085
17	1.65284763	0.60501645	21.76158774	13.16611847	0.04595253
18	1.70243306	0.58739461	23.41443537	13.75351308	0.04270870
19	1.75350605	0.57028603	25.11686844	14.32379911	0.03981388
20	1.80611123	0.55367575	26.87037449	14.87747486	0.03721571
21	1.86029457	0.53754928	28.67648572	15.41502414	0.03487178
22	1.91610341	0.52189250	30.53678030	15.93691664	0.03274739
23	1.97358651	0.50669175	32.45288370	16.44360839	0.03081390
24	2.03279411	0.49193374	34.42647022	16.93554212	0.02904742
25	2.09377793	0.47760557	36.45926432	17.41314769	0.02742787
26	2.15659127	0.46369473	38.55304225	17.87684242	0.02593829
27	2.22128901	0.45018906	40.70963352	18.32703147	0.02456421
28	2.28792768	0.43707675	42.93092252	18.76410823	0.02329323
29	2.35656551	0.42434636	45.21885020	19.18845459	0.02211467
30	2.42726247	0.41198676	47.57541571	19.60044135	0.02101926
31	2.50008035	0.39982715	50.00267818	20.00042849	0.01999893
32	2.57508276	0.38833703	52.50275852	20.38876553	0.01904662
33	2.65233524	0.37702625	55.07784128	20.76579178	0.01815612
34	2.73190530	0.36604490	57.73017652	21.13183668	0.01732196
35	2.81386245	0.35538340	60.46208181	21.48722007	0.01653929
36	2.89827833	0.34503243	63.27594427	21.83225250	0.01580379
37	2.98522668	0.33498294	66.17422259	22.16723544	0.01511162
38	3.07478348	0.32522615	69.15944927	22.49246159	0.01445934
39	3.16702698	0.31575355	72.23423275	22.80821513	0.01384385
40	3.26203779	0.30655684	75.40125973	23.11477197	0.01326238
41	3.35989893	0.29762800	78.66329753	23.41239997	0.01271241
42	3.46069569	0.28895922	82.02319645	23.70135920	0.01219687
43	3.56451677	0.28054294	85.48389234	23.98190213	0.01169811
44	3.67145227	0.27237178	89.04840911	24.25427392	0.01122985
45	3.78159584	0.26444862	92.71986139	24.51871254	0.01078518
46	3.89504372	0.25673653	96.50145723	24.77544907	0.01036254
47	4.01189503	0.24925876	100.39650095	25.02470783	0.00996051
48	4.13225188	0.24199880	104.40839598	25.26670664	0.00957777
49	4.25621944	0.23495029	108.54064785	25.50165693	0.00921314
50	4.38390602	0.22810708	112.79686729	25.72976401	0.00886549
60	5.89166310	0.16973309	163.05343680	27.67556367	0.00613296
80	10.64089056	0.09397710	321.36301855	30.20076345	0.00311175
100	19.21863198	0.05203284	607.28773270	31.59890534	0.00164667
120	34.71098714	0.02880932	1123.69957119	32.37302261	0.00088992
240	1204.85262793	0.00082998	40128.42093093	33.30566743	0.00002492

RATE 2.5%

PERIODS	7-1 COMPOUND INTEREST	7-2 PRESENT VALUE	7-3 AMOUNT OF ORDINARY ANNUITY	7-4 PRESENT VALUE OF ANNUITY	7-5 SINKING FUND
1	1.0250000	0.97560976	1.0000000	0.97560976	1.0000000
2	1.05062500	0.95181440	2.02500000	1.92742415	0.49382716
3	1.07689062	0.92855941	3.07562500	2.85602356	0.32513717
4	1.10381289	0.90595064	4.15251563	3.76197421	0.24081788
5	1.13140821	0.88385429	5.25632852	4.64582850	0.19024686
6	1.15969342	0.86229687	6.38773673	5.50812536	0.15654997
7	1.18868575	0.84126524	7.54743015	6.34939060	0.13248543
8	1.21840290	0.82074657	8.73611590	7.17013717	0.11446735
9	1.24886297	0.80072836	9.95451880	7.97086553	0.10045689
10	1.28008454	0.78119840	11.20338177	8.75206393	0.08925876
11	1.31208666	0.76214478	12.48346631	9.51420871	0.08010596
12	1.34488882	0.74355589	13.79555297	10.25776460	0.07248713
13	1.37851104	0.72542038	15.14044179	10.98318497	0.06604827
14	1.41297382	0.70772720	16.51895284	11.69091217	0.06063652
15	1.44829817	0.69046556	17.93192666	12.38137773	0.05576646
16	1.48450562	0.67362493	19.38022483	13.05500266	0.05159899
17	1.52161826	0.65719506	20.86473045	13.71219772	0.04792777
18	1.55965872	0.64116591	22.38634871	14.35336363	0.04467008
19	1.59865019	0.62552772	23.94600743	14.97889134	0.04176062
20	1.63861644	0.61027094	25.54465761	15.58916229	0.03914713
21	1.67958185	0.59538629	27.18327405	16.18454857	0.03678733
22	1.72157140	0.58086467	28.86285590	16.76541324	0.03464461
23	1.76461068	0.56669724	30.58442730	17.33211048	0.03269638
24	1.80872595	0.55287535	32.34903798	17.88498583	0.03091282
25	1.85394410	0.53939059	34.15776393	18.42437642	0.02927592
26	1.90029270	0.52623472	36.01170803	18.95061114	0.02776875
27	1.94780002	0.51339973	37.91200073	19.46401087	0.02637687
28	1.99649502	0.50087778	39.85980075	19.96488866	0.02508793
29	2.04640739	0.48866125	41.85629577	20.45354991	0.02389127
30	2.09756758	0.47674269	43.90270316	20.93029259	0.02277764
31	2.15000677	0.46511481	46.00027074	21.39540741	0.02173900
32	2.20375694	0.45377055	48.15027751	21.84917796	0.02076831
33	2.25885086	0.44270298	50.35403445	22.29188094	0.01985938
34	2.31532213	0.43190534	52.61288531	22.72378628	0.01900675
35	2.37320519	0.42137107	54.92820744	23.14515734	0.01820558
36	2.43253532	0.41109372	57.30141263	23.55625107	0.01745158
37	2.49334870	0.40106705	59.73394794	23.95731812	0.01674090
38	2.55568242	0.39128492	62.22729664	24.34860304	0.01607012
39	2.61957448	0.38174139	64.78297906	24.73034443	0.01543615
40	2.68506384	0.37243062	67.40255354	25.10277505	0.01483623
41	2.75219043	0.36334695	70.08761737	25.46612200	0.01426786
42	2.82099569	0.35448483	72.83980781	25.82060683	0.01372876
43	2.89152008	0.34583886	75.66080300	26.16644569	0.01321688
44	2.96380808	0.33740376	78.55232308	26.50384945	0.01273037
45	3.03790328	0.32917440	81.51613116	26.83302386	0.01226751
46	3.11385086	0.32114576	84.55403443	27.15416962	0.01182673
47	3.19169713	0.31331294	87.66788530	27.46748255	0.01140669
48	3.27148956	0.30567116	90.85958243	27.77315371	0.01100599
49	3.35327680	0.29821576	94.13107199	28.07136947	0.01062348
50	3.43710872	0.29094221	97.48434879	28.36231168	0.01025806
60	4.39978975	0.22728359	135.99158995	30.90865649	0.00735340
80	7.20956782	0.13870457	248.38271265	34.45181722	0.00402605
100	11.81371635	0.08464707	432.54865494	36.61410526	0.00231188
120	19.35814983	0.05165783	734.32599335	37.93368683	0.00136179
240	374.73796499	0.00266853	14949.51859948	39.89325875	0.00006689

RATE 4.0 %

PERIODS	7-1 COMPOUND INTEREST	7-2 PRESENT VALUE	7-3 AMOUNT OF ORDINARY ANNUITY	7-4 PRESENT VALUE OF ANNUITY	7-5 SINKING FUND
1	1.0400000	0.96153846	1.0000000	0.96153846	1.0000000
2	1.0816000	0.92455621	2.0400000	1.88609467	0.49019608
3	1.12486400	0.88899636	3.1216000	2.77509103	0.32034854
4	1.16985856	0.85480419	4.24646400	3.62989522	0.23549005
5	1.21665290	0.82192711	5.41632256	4.45182233	0.18462711
6	1.26531902	0.79031453	6.63297546	5.24213686	0.15076190
7	1.31593178	0.75991781	7.89829448	6.00205467	0.12660961
8	1.36856905	0.73069021	9.21422626	6.73274487	0.10852783
9	1.42331181	0.70258674	10.58279531	7.43533161	0.09449299
10	1.48024428	0.67556417	12.00610712	8.11089578	0.08329094
11	1.53945406	0.64958093	13.48635141	8.76047671	0.07414904
12	1.60103222	0.62459705	15.02580546	9.38507376	0.06655217
13	1.66507351	0.60057409	16.62683768	9.98564785	0.06014373
14	1.73167645	0.57747508	18.29191119	10.56312293	0.05466897
15	1.80094351	0.55526450	20.02358764	11.11838743	0.04994110
16	1.87298125	0.53390818	21.82453114	11.65229561	0.04582000
17	1.94790050	0.51337325	23.69751239	12.16566885	0.04219852
18	2.02581652	0.49362812	25.64541288	12.65929697	0.03899333
19	2.10684918	0.47464242	27.67122940	13.13393940	0.03613862
20	2.19112314	0.45638695	29.77807858	13.59032634	0.03358175
21	2.27876807	0.43883360	31.96920172	14.02915995	0.03128011
22	2.36976879	0.42195305	34.24796979	14.45111533	0.02919881
23	2.46471559	0.40572633	36.61788858	14.85684167	0.02730906
24	2.56330416	0.39012147	39.08260412	15.24696314	0.02558683
25	2.66583633	0.37511680	41.64590829	15.62207994	0.02401196
26	2.77246978	0.36068923	44.31174462	15.98276918	0.02256738
27	2.88336858	0.34681657	47.08421440	16.32958575	0.02123854
28	2.99870332	0.33347747	49.96758298	16.66306322	0.02001298
29	3.11865145	0.32065141	52.96628630	16.98371463	0.01887993
30	3.24339751	0.30831867	56.08493775	17.29203330	0.01783010
31	3.37313341	0.29646026	59.32833526	17.58849356	0.01685535
32	3.50805875	0.28505794	62.70146867	17.87355150	0.01594859
33	3.64838170	0.27409417	66.20952742	18.14764567	0.01510357
34	3.79431634	0.26355209	69.85790851	18.41119976	0.01431477
35	3.94608899	0.25341547	73.65222486	18.66461323	0.01357732
36	4.10393255	0.24366872	77.59831385	18.90828195	0.01288688
37	4.26808986	0.23429685	81.70224640	19.14257880	0.01223957
38	4.43881345	0.22528543	85.97033626	19.36786423	0.01163192
39	4.61636599	0.21662061	90.40914971	19.58448484	0.01106083
40	4.80102063	0.20828904	95.02551570	19.79277388	0.01052349
41	4.99306145	0.20027793	99.82653633	19.99305181	0.01001738
42	5.19278391	0.19257493	104.81959778	20.18562674	0.00954020
43	5.40049527	0.18516820	110.01238169	20.37079494	0.00908989
44	5.61651508	0.17804635	115.41287696	20.54884129	0.00866454
45	5.84117568	0.17119841	121.02939204	20.72003970	0.00826246
46	6.07482271	0.16461386	126.87056772	20.88465356	0.00788205
47	6.31781562	0.15828256	132.94539043	21.04293612	0.00752189
48	6.57052824	0.15219476	139.26320604	21.19513088	0.00718065
49	6.83334937	0.14634112	145.83373429	21.34147200	0.00685712
50	7.10668335	0.14071262	152.66708366	21.48218462	0.00655020
60	10.51962741	0.09506040	237.99068520	22.62348997	0.00420185
80	23.04979907	0.04338433	551.24497675	23.91539185	0.00181408
100	50.50494818	0.01980004	1237.62370461	24.50499900	0.00080800
120	110.66256080	0.00903648	2741.56402011	24.77408400	0.00036476
240	12246.2023638	0.00008166	306130.059093	24.99795855	0.00000327

RATE 3.5 %

PERIODS	7-1 COMPOUND INTEREST	7-2 PRESENT VALUE	7-3 AMOUNT OF ORDINARY ANNUITY	7-4 PRESENT VALUE OF ANNUITY	7-5 SINKING FUND
1	1.0350000	0.96618357	1.0000000	0.96618357	1.0000000
2	1.07122500	0.93351070	2.03500000	1.89969428	0.49140049
3	1.10871788	0.90194271	3.10622500	2.80163698	0.32193418
4	1.14752300	0.87144223	4.21494287	3.67307921	0.23725114
5	1.18768631	0.84197317	5.36246588	4.51505238	0.18648137
6	1.22925533	0.81350064	6.55015218	5.32855302	0.15266821
7	1.27227926	0.78599096	7.77940751	6.11454398	0.12854449
8	1.31680904	0.75941156	9.05168677	6.87395554	0.11047665
9	1.36289735	0.73373097	10.36849581	7.60768651	0.09644601
10	1.41059876	0.70891881	11.73139316	8.31660532	0.08524137
11	1.45996972	0.68494571	13.14199192	9.00155104	0.07609197
12	1.51106866	0.66178330	14.60196164	9.66333433	0.06848395
13	1.56395606	0.63940415	16.11303030	10.30273849	0.06206157
14	1.61869452	0.61778179	17.67698636	10.92052028	0.05657073
15	1.67534883	0.59689062	19.29568088	11.51741090	0.05182507
16	1.73398604	0.57670591	20.97102971	12.09411681	0.04768483
17	1.79467555	0.55720378	22.70501575	12.65132059	0.04404313
18	1.85748920	0.53836114	24.49969130	13.18968173	0.04081684
19	1.92250132	0.52015569	26.35718050	13.70983742	0.03794033
20	1.98978886	0.50256588	28.27968181	14.21240330	0.03536108
21	2.05943147	0.48557090	30.26947068	14.69797420	0.03303659
22	2.13151158	0.46915063	32.32890215	15.16712484	0.03093207
23	2.20611448	0.45328563	34.46041373	15.62041047	0.02901880
24	2.28332849	0.43795713	36.66652821	16.05836760	0.02727283
25	2.36324498	0.42314699	38.94985669	16.48151459	0.02567404
26	2.44595856	0.40883767	41.31310168	16.89035226	0.02420540
27	2.53156771	0.39501224	43.75906024	17.28536451	0.02285241
28	2.62017196	0.38165434	46.29062734	17.66701885	0.02160265
29	2.71187798	0.36874815	48.91079930	18.03576700	0.02044538
30	2.80679370	0.35627841	51.62267728	18.39204541	0.01937133
31	2.90503148	0.34423035	54.42947098	18.73627576	0.01837240
32	3.00670759	0.33258971	57.33450247	19.06886547	0.01744150
33	3.11194235	0.32134271	60.34121005	19.39200818	0.01657242
34	3.22086033	0.31047605	63.45315240	19.70068423	0.01575966
35	3.33359045	0.29997686	66.67401274	20.00066110	0.01499835
36	3.45026611	0.28983272	70.00760318	20.29049381	0.01428416
37	3.57102543	0.28003161	73.45786930	20.57052542	0.01361325
38	3.69601132	0.27056194	77.02889472	20.84108736	0.01298214
39	3.82537171	0.26141250	80.72490604	21.10249987	0.01238775
40	3.95925972	0.25257247	84.55027775	21.35507234	0.01182728
41	4.09783381	0.24403137	88.50953747	21.59910371	0.01129822
42	4.24125799	0.23577910	92.60737128	21.83488281	0.01079828
43	4.38970202	0.22780590	96.84862928	22.06268870	0.01032539
44	4.54334160	0.22010231	101.23833130	22.28279102	0.00987768
45	4.70235855	0.21265924	105.78167290	22.49545026	0.00945343
46	4.86694110	0.20546787	110.48403145	22.70091813	0.00905018
47	5.03728404	0.19851968	115.35097255	22.89943787	0.00866919
48	5.21358898	0.19180645	120.38825659	23.09124425	0.00830646
49	5.39606459	0.18532024	125.60184557	23.27656450	0.00796167
50	5.58492686	0.17905337	130.99791016	23.45561787	0.00763371
60	7.87809090	0.12693431	196.51688288	24.94473412	0.00508862
80	15.67573754	0.06379285	419.30678685	26.74877567	0.00238489
100	31.19140798	0.03206011	862.61165666	27.65542540	0.00115927
120	62.06431624	0.01611232	1744.69474973	28.11107663	0.00057317
240	3851.9793504	0.00025961	110027.981440	28.56401123	0.00000909

RATE 5.0%

7-5 SINKING FUND	7-4 PRESENT VALUE OF ANNUITY	7-3 AMOUNT OF ORDINARY ANNUITY	7-2 PRESENT VALUE	7-1 COMPOUND INTEREST	PERIODS
1.00000000	0.95238095	1.00000000	0.95238095	1.05000000	1
0.48780488	1.85941043	2.05000000	0.90702948	1.10250000	2
0.31720856	2.72324803	3.15250000	0.86383760	1.15762500	3
0.23201183	3.54595050	4.31012500	0.82270247	1.21550625	4
0.18097480	4.32947667	5.52563125	0.78352617	1.27628156	5
0.14701747	5.07569207	6.80191281	0.74621540	1.34009564	6
0.12281982	5.78637340	8.14200845	0.71068133	1.40710042	7
0.10472181	6.46321276	9.54910888	0.67683936	1.47745544	8
0.09069008	7.10782168	11.02656432	0.64460892	1.55132822	9
0.07950457	7.72173493	12.57789254	0.61391325	1.62889463	10
0.07038889	8.30641422	14.20678716	0.58467929	1.71033936	11
0.06282541	8.86325164	15.91712652	0.55683742	1.79585633	12
0.05645577	9.39357299	17.71298285	0.53032135	1.88564914	13
0.05102397	9.89864094	19.59863199	0.50506795	1.97993160	14
0.04634229	10.37965804	21.57856359	0.48101710	2.07892818	15
0.04226991	10.83776956	23.65749177	0.45811152	2.18287459	16
0.03869914	11.27406625	25.84036636	0.43629669	2.29201832	17
0.03554622	11.68958690	28.13238467	0.41552065	2.40661923	18
0.03274501	12.08532086	30.53900391	0.39573396	2.52695020	19
0.03024259	12.46221034	33.06595410	0.37688948	2.65329771	20
0.02799611	12.82115271	35.71925181	0.35894236	2.78596259	21
0.02597051	13.16300258	38.50521440	0.34184987	2.92526072	22
0.02413682	13.48857388	41.43047512	0.32557131	3.07152376	23
0.02247090	13.79864179	44.50199887	0.31006791	3.22509994	24
0.02095246	14.09394457	47.72709882	0.29530277	3.38635494	25
0.01956432	14.37518530	51.11345376	0.28124073	3.55567269	26
0.01829186	14.64303362	54.66912645	0.26784832	3.73345632	27
0.01712253	14.89812726	58.40258277	0.25509364	3.92012914	28
0.01604551	15.14107358	62.32271191	0.24294632	4.11613560	29
0.01505144	15.37245103	66.43884750	0.23137745	4.32194238	30
0.01413212	15.59281050	70.76078988	0.22035947	4.53803949	31
0.01328042	15.80267667	75.29882937	0.20986617	4.76494147	32
0.01249004	16.00254921	80.06377084	0.19987254	5.00318854	33
0.01175545	16.19290401	85.06695938	0.19035480	5.25334797	34
0.01107171	16.37419429	90.32030735	0.18129029	5.51601537	35
0.01043446	16.54685171	95.83632272	0.17265741	5.79181614	36
0.00983979	16.71128734	101.62813886	0.16443563	6.08140694	37
0.00928423	16.86789271	107.70954580	0.15660536	6.38547729	38
0.00876462	17.01704067	114.09502309	0.14914797	6.70475115	39
0.00827816	17.15908635	120.79977424	0.14204568	7.03998871	40
0.00782229	17.29436796	127.83976295	0.13528160	7.39198815	41
0.00739471	17.42320758	135.23175110	0.12883962	7.76158756	42
0.00699333	17.54591198	142.99333866	0.12270440	8.14966693	43
0.00661625	17.66277331	151.14300559	0.11686133	8.55715028	44
0.00626173	17.77406982	159.70015587	0.11129651	8.98500779	45
0.00592820	17.88006650	168.51816366	0.10599668	9.43425818	46
0.00561421	17.98101571	178.11942185	0.10094921	9.90597109	47
0.00531843	18.07715782	188.02539294	0.09614211	10.40126965	48
0.00503965	18.16872173	198.42666259	0.09156391	10.92133313	49
0.00477674	18.25592546	209.34799572	0.08720373	11.46739979	50
0.00282818	18.92928953	353.58371788	0.05353552	18.67918589	60
0.00102962	19.59646048	971.22882134	0.02017698	49.56144107	80
0.00038314	19.84791020	2610.02515693	0.00760125	131.50125785	100
0.00014371	19.94267895	6958.23971334	0.00286605	348.91198567	120
0.00000041	19.99983571	2434771.47490	0.00000821	121739.573742	240

RATE 4.5%

7-5 SINKING FUND	7-4 PRESENT VALUE OF ANNUITY	7-3 AMOUNT OF ORDINARY ANNUITY	7-2 PRESENT VALUE	7-1 COMPOUND INTEREST	PERIODS
1.00000000	0.95693780	1.00000000	0.95693780	1.04500000	1
0.48899756	1.87266775	2.04500000	0.91572995	1.09202500	2
0.31877336	2.74896435	3.13702500	0.87629660	1.14116612	3
0.23374365	3.58752570	4.27819112	0.83856134	1.19251860	4
0.18279164	4.38997674	5.47070973	0.80245105	1.24618194	5
0.14887839	5.15787248	6.71689166	0.76789574	1.30226012	6
0.12470147	5.89270094	8.01915179	0.73483846	1.36086183	7
0.10660965	6.59588607	9.38001362	0.70318513	1.42210061	8
0.09257447	7.26879050	10.80211423	0.67290443	1.48609514	9
0.08137882	7.91271818	12.28820837	0.64392768	1.55296942	10
0.07224818	8.52891692	13.84117879	0.61619874	1.62285305	11
0.06466619	9.11858078	15.46403184	0.58966386	1.69588143	12
0.05827535	9.68285242	17.15991327	0.56427164	1.77219610	13
0.05287032	10.22282528	18.93210937	0.53997286	1.85194492	14
0.04811381	10.73954573	20.78405429	0.51672044	1.93528244	15
0.04401537	11.23401505	22.71933673	0.49446932	2.02237015	16
0.04041758	11.70719143	24.74170689	0.47317639	2.11337681	17
0.03723690	12.15999180	26.85508370	0.45280037	2.20847877	18
0.03440734	12.59329359	29.06356246	0.43330179	2.30786031	19
0.03187614	13.00793645	31.37142277	0.41464286	2.41171402	20
0.02960057	13.40472388	33.78313680	0.39678743	2.52024116	21
0.02754565	13.78442476	36.30337795	0.37970089	2.63365201	22
0.02568249	14.14777489	38.93702996	0.36335013	2.75216635	23
0.02398703	14.49547837	41.68919631	0.34770347	2.87601383	24
0.02243903	14.82820896	44.56521015	0.33273060	3.00543446	25
0.02102140	15.14661145	47.57064460	0.31840248	3.14067901	26
0.01971946	15.45130282	50.71132361	0.30469137	3.28280959	27
0.01852081	15.74287351	53.99333317	0.29157069	3.42969999	28
0.01741461	16.02188853	57.42303316	0.27901502	3.58403649	29
0.01639154	16.28888854	61.00706966	0.26700002	3.74531813	30
0.01544345	16.54439095	64.75238779	0.25550241	3.91385745	31
0.01456320	16.78889086	68.66624524	0.24449991	4.08998104	32
0.01374453	17.02286207	72.75622628	0.23397121	4.27403018	33
0.01298191	17.24675796	77.03025646	0.22389589	4.46636154	34
0.01227045	17.46101240	81.49661800	0.21425444	4.66734781	35
0.01160578	17.66604058	86.16396581	0.20502817	4.87737846	36
0.01098402	17.86223979	91.04134427	0.19619921	5.09686049	37
0.01040169	18.04999023	96.13820476	0.18775044	5.32621921	38
0.00985567	18.22965572	101.46442398	0.17966549	5.56589908	39
0.00934315	18.40158442	107.03032306	0.17192870	5.81636454	40
0.00886158	18.56610949	112.84668760	0.16452507	6.07810094	41
0.00840868	18.72354975	118.92478854	0.15744026	6.35161548	42
0.00798235	18.87421029	125.27640402	0.15066054	6.63743818	43
0.00758071	19.01838305	131.91384220	0.14417276	6.93612290	44
0.00720202	19.15634742	138.84996510	0.13796437	7.24824843	45
0.00684471	19.28837074	146.09821353	0.13202332	7.57441961	46
0.00650734	19.41470884	153.67263314	0.12633810	7.91526849	47
0.00618858	19.53660654	161.58750163	0.12089771	8.27145557	48
0.00588722	19.65129813	169.85935720	0.11569158	8.64367107	49
0.00560215	19.76200778	178.50302828	0.11070965	9.03263627	50
0.00345426	20.63802204	289.49795398	0.07128901	14.02740793	60
0.00137069	21.56534493	729.55769854	0.02955948	33.83009643	80
0.00055839	21.94985274	1790.85595627	0.01225663	81.58851803	100
0.00022986	22.10928616	4350.40384897	0.00508212	196.76817320	120
0.00000116	22.22164827	860371.4219077	0.00002583	38717.713986	240

RATE 7.0%

PERIODS	7-1 COMPOUND INTEREST	7-2 PRESENT VALUE	7-3 AMOUNT OF ORDINARY ANNUITY	7-4 PRESENT VALUE OF ANNUITY	7-5 SINKING FUND
1	1.07000000	0.93457944	1.00000000	0.93457944	1.00000000
2	1.14490000	0.87343873	2.07000000	1.80801817	0.48309179
3	1.22504300	0.81629788	3.21490000	2.62431604	0.31105167
4	1.31079601	0.76289521	4.43994300	3.38721126	0.22522812
5	1.40255173	0.71298618	5.75073901	4.10019744	0.17389069
6	1.50073035	0.66634222	7.15329074	4.76653966	0.13979580
7	1.60578148	0.62274974	8.65402109	5.38928940	0.11555322
8	1.71818618	0.58200910	10.25980257	5.97129851	0.09746776
9	1.83845921	0.54393374	11.97798875	6.51523225	0.08348647
10	1.96715136	0.50834929	13.81644796	7.02358154	0.07237750
11	2.10485195	0.47509280	15.78359932	7.49867434	0.06335690
12	2.25219159	0.44401196	17.88845127	7.94268430	0.05590109
13	2.40984500	0.41496445	20.14064286	8.35765074	0.04965085
14	2.57853415	0.38781724	22.55048786	8.74546799	0.04434494
15	2.75903154	0.36244602	25.12902201	9.10791401	0.03979482
16	2.95216375	0.33873460	27.88805355	9.44664860	0.03585765
17	3.15881521	0.31657439	30.84021730	9.76322299	0.03242519
18	3.37993228	0.29586392	33.99903251	10.05908691	0.02941260
19	3.61652754	0.27650833	37.37896479	10.33559524	0.02675301
20	3.86968446	0.25841900	40.99549232	10.59401425	0.02439293
21	4.14056237	0.24151309	44.86517678	10.83552733	0.02228900
22	4.43040174	0.22671317	49.00573916	11.06124050	0.02040577
23	4.74052695	0.21094688	53.43614090	11.27218738	0.01871393
24	5.07236695	0.19714662	58.17667076	11.46933400	0.01718902
25	5.42743264	0.18424918	63.24903772	11.65358318	0.01581052
26	5.80735292	0.17219549	68.67647036	11.82577867	0.01456103
27	6.21386763	0.16093037	74.48382328	11.98670904	0.01342573
28	6.64883836	0.15040221	80.69769091	12.13711125	0.01239193
29	7.11425705	0.14056282	87.34652927	12.27767407	0.01144865
30	7.61225504	0.13136712	94.46078632	12.40904118	0.01058640
31	8.14511290	0.12277301	102.07304137	12.53181419	0.00979691
32	8.71527080	0.11474113	110.21815426	12.64655532	0.00907292
33	9.32533975	0.10723470	118.93342506	12.75379002	0.00840807
34	9.97811354	0.10021934	128.25876481	12.85400936	0.00779674
35	10.67658148	0.09366294	138.23687835	12.94767230	0.00723396
36	11.42394219	0.08753546	148.91345984	13.03520776	0.00671531
37	12.22361814	0.08180884	160.33740202	13.11701660	0.00623685
38	13.07927141	0.07645686	172.56102017	13.19347345	0.00579505
39	13.99482041	0.07145501	185.64029158	13.26492846	0.00538676
40	14.97445784	0.06678038	199.63511199	13.33170884	0.00500914
41	16.02266989	0.06241157	214.60956983	13.39412041	0.00465962
42	17.14425678	0.05832857	230.63223972	13.45244898	0.00433591
43	18.34435475	0.05451268	247.77645125	13.50696167	0.00403590
44	19.62845959	0.05094643	266.12085125	13.55790810	0.00375769
45	21.00245176	0.04761349	285.74931084	13.60552159	0.00349957
46	22.47262338	0.04449859	306.75176260	13.65002018	0.00325996
47	24.04570702	0.04158747	329.22438598	13.69180764	0.00303744
48	25.72890651	0.03886679	353.27008300	13.73047443	0.00283070
49	27.52992997	0.03632410	378.99899951	13.76679853	0.00263853
50	29.45702506	0.03394776	406.52892947	13.80074629	0.00245985
60	57.94642683	0.01725732	813.52038335	14.03918115	0.00122923
80	224.23438758	0.00445962	3189.06267969	14.22200544	0.00031357
100	867.71632557	0.00115245	12381.66179381	14.26925071	0.00008076
120	3357.78838289	0.00029782	47954.11975557	14.28145978	0.00002085

RATE 6.0%

PERIODS	7-1 COMPOUND INTEREST	7-2 PRESENT VALUE	7-3 AMOUNT OF ORDINARY ANNUITY	7-4 PRESENT VALUE OF ANNUITY	7-5 SINKING FUND
1	1.06000000	0.94339623	1.00000000	0.94339623	1.00000000
2	1.12360000	0.88999644	2.06000000	1.83339267	0.48543689
3	1.19101600	0.83961928	3.18360000	2.67301195	0.31410981
4	1.26247696	0.79209366	4.37461600	3.46510561	0.22859149
5	1.33822558	0.74725817	5.63709296	4.21236379	0.17739640
6	1.41851911	0.70496054	6.97531854	4.91732433	0.14336263
7	1.50363026	0.66505711	8.39383766	5.58238144	0.11913502
8	1.59384807	0.62741237	9.89746791	6.20979381	0.10103594
9	1.68947896	0.59189846	11.49131598	6.80169227	0.08702224
10	1.79084770	0.55838478	13.18079494	7.36008705	0.07586796
11	1.89829856	0.52678753	14.97164264	7.88687458	0.06679294
12	2.01219647	0.49696936	16.86994120	8.38384394	0.05927703
13	2.13292826	0.46883902	18.88213767	8.85268296	0.05296011
14	2.26090396	0.44230096	21.01506593	9.29498393	0.04758491
15	2.39655819	0.41726506	23.27596988	9.71224899	0.04296276
16	2.54035168	0.39364628	25.67252808	10.10589527	0.03895214
17	2.69277279	0.37136442	28.21287976	10.47725969	0.03544480
18	2.85433915	0.35034379	30.90565255	10.82760348	0.03235654
19	3.02559950	0.33051301	33.75999170	11.15811649	0.02962086
20	3.20713547	0.31180473	36.78559120	11.46992122	0.02718456
21	3.39956360	0.29415540	39.99272668	11.76407662	0.02500455
22	3.60353742	0.27750510	43.39229028	12.04158172	0.02304557
23	3.81974966	0.26179726	46.99582770	12.30337898	0.02127848
24	4.04893464	0.24697855	50.81557735	12.55035753	0.01967900
25	4.29187072	0.23299863	54.86451200	12.78335616	0.01822672
26	4.54938296	0.21981003	59.15638272	13.00316619	0.01690435
27	4.82334594	0.20736795	63.70576568	13.21053414	0.01569717
28	5.11168670	0.19563014	68.52811162	13.40616428	0.01459255
29	5.41838790	0.18455674	73.63979832	13.59072102	0.01357961
30	5.74349117	0.17411013	79.05818622	13.76483115	0.01264891
31	6.08810064	0.16425484	84.80167739	13.92908599	0.01179222
32	6.45338668	0.15495740	90.88977803	14.08404339	0.01100234
33	6.84058988	0.14618622	97.34316471	14.23022961	0.01027293
34	7.25102528	0.13791153	104.18375460	14.36814114	0.00959843
35	7.68608679	0.13010522	111.43477987	14.49824636	0.00897386
36	8.14725200	0.12274077	119.12086666	14.62098713	0.00839483
37	8.63608712	0.11579318	127.26811866	14.73678031	0.00785743
38	9.15425235	0.10923885	135.90420578	14.84601916	0.00735812
39	9.70350749	0.10305552	145.05845813	14.94907468	0.00689377
40	10.28571794	0.09722219	154.76196562	15.04629687	0.00646154
41	10.90286101	0.09171905	165.04768356	15.13801592	0.00605886
42	11.55703267	0.08652740	175.95054457	15.22454332	0.00568342
43	12.25045463	0.08162942	187.50757724	15.30617294	0.00533312
44	12.98548191	0.07700908	199.75803188	15.38318202	0.00500606
45	13.76461083	0.07265007	212.74351379	15.45583209	0.00470050
46	14.59048748	0.06853781	226.50812462	15.52436990	0.00441485
47	15.46591673	0.06465831	241.09861210	15.58902821	0.00414768
48	16.39387173	0.06099840	256.56452882	15.65002661	0.00389765
49	17.37750403	0.05754566	272.95840055	15.70757227	0.00366356
50	18.42015427	0.05428836	290.33590458	15.76186064	0.00344429
60	32.98769085	0.03031434	533.12818089	16.16142771	0.00187572
80	105.79599348	0.00945215	1746.59989137	16.50913077	0.00057254
100	339.30208351	0.00294723	5638.36805857	16.61754623	0.00017736
120	1088.18774784	0.00091896	18119.79579725	16.65135068	0.00005519

RATE 9.0%

PERIODS	7-1 COMPOUND INTEREST	7-2 PRESENT VALUE	7-3 AMOUNT OF ORDINARY ANNUITY	7-4 PRESENT VALUE OF ANNUITY	7-5 SINKING FUND
1	1.0900000	0.91743119	1.0000000	0.91743119	1.0000000
2	1.18810000	0.84167999	2.0900000	1.75911119	0.47846890
3	1.29502900	0.77218348	3.2781000	2.53129467	0.30505476
4	1.41158161	0.70842521	4.5731290	3.23971988	0.21866866
5	1.53862395	0.64993139	5.98471061	3.88965126	0.16709246
6	1.67710011	0.59626733	7.52333456	4.48591859	0.13291978
7	1.82803912	0.54703424	9.20043468	5.03290284	0.10869052
8	1.99256264	0.50186628	11.02847380	5.53481911	0.09067438
9	2.17189328	0.46042778	13.02103644	5.99524689	0.07679880
10	2.36736367	0.42241081	15.1929972	6.41765770	0.06582009
11	2.58042641	0.38753285	17.56029339	6.80519055	0.05694666
12	2.81266478	0.35553473	20.14071980	7.16072528	0.04965066
13	3.06580461	0.32617865	22.95338458	7.48690392	0.04356656
14	3.34172703	0.29924647	26.01918919	7.78615039	0.03843317
15	3.64248246	0.27453804	29.36091622	8.06068843	0.03405888
16	3.97030588	0.25186976	33.00339668	8.31255819	0.03029991
17	4.32763341	0.23107318	36.97370456	8.54363137	0.02704625
18	4.71712042	0.21199374	41.30133797	8.75562511	0.02421229
19	5.14166125	0.19448967	46.01845839	8.95011478	0.02173041
20	5.60441077	0.17843089	51.16011964	9.12854567	0.01954648
21	6.10880774	0.16369806	56.76453041	9.29224373	0.01761663
22	6.65860043	0.15018171	62.87333815	9.44242544	0.01590499
23	7.25787447	0.13778139	69.53193858	9.58020683	0.01438188
24	7.91108317	0.12640494	76.78981305	9.70661177	0.01302256
25	8.62308066	0.11596784	84.70089623	9.82257960	0.01180625
26	9.39915792	0.10639251	93.32397689	9.92897211	0.01071536
27	10.24508213	0.09760781	102.72313481	10.02657992	0.00973491
28	11.16713952	0.08954845	112.96821694	10.11612837	0.00885205
29	12.17218208	0.08215454	124.13535646	10.19828291	0.00805572
30	13.26767847	0.07537114	136.30753855	10.27365404	0.00733635
31	14.46176953	0.06914783	149.57521702	10.34280187	0.00668560
32	15.76332879	0.06343838	164.03698655	10.40624025	0.00609619
33	17.18202838	0.05820035	179.80031534	10.46444060	0.00556173
34	18.72841093	0.05339481	196.98234372	10.51783541	0.00507660
35	20.41396792	0.04898607	215.71075465	10.56682148	0.00463584
36	22.25122503	0.04494135	236.12472257	10.61176282	0.00423505
37	24.25383528	0.04123059	258.37594760	10.65299342	0.00387033
38	26.43668046	0.03782623	282.62978288	10.69081965	0.00353820
39	28.81598170	0.03470296	309.06646334	10.72552281	0.00323555
40	31.40942005	0.03183758	337.88244504	10.75736020	0.00295961
41	34.23626786	0.02920879	369.29186510	10.78656899	0.00270789
42	37.31753197	0.02679706	403.52813296	10.81336604	0.00247814
43	40.67610984	0.02458446	440.84566492	10.83795050	0.00226837
44	44.33695973	0.02255455	481.52177477	10.86050504	0.00207675
45	48.32728610	0.02069224	525.86873450	10.88119729	0.00190165
46	52.67674185	0.01898371	574.18602060	10.90018100	0.00174160
47	57.41764862	0.01741625	626.86276245	10.91759725	0.00159525
48	62.58523700	0.01597821	684.28041107	10.93357546	0.00146139
49	68.21790833	0.01465891	746.86564807	10.94823436	0.00133893
50	74.35752008	0.01344854	815.08355640	10.96168290	0.00122687
60	176.03129196	0.00568081	1944.79213289	11.04799102	0.00051419
80	986.55166813	0.00101363	10950.5740900	11.09984854	0.00009132
100	5529.04079183	0.00018086	61422.6754630	11.10910152	0.00001628
120	30987.0157492	0.00003227	344289.0638799	11.11075254	0.00000290

RATE 8.0%

PERIODS	7-1 COMPOUND INTEREST	7-2 PRESENT VALUE	7-3 AMOUNT OF ORDINARY ANNUITY	7-4 PRESENT VALUE OF ANNUITY	7-5 SINKING FUND
1	1.08000000	0.92592593	1.0000000	0.92592593	1.0000000
2	1.16640000	0.85733882	2.0800000	1.78326475	0.48076923
3	1.25971200	0.79383224	3.2464000	2.57709699	0.30803351
4	1.36048896	0.73502985	4.5061120	3.31212684	0.22192080
5	1.46932808	0.68058320	5.86660096	3.99271004	0.17045645
6	1.58687432	0.63016963	7.33592904	4.62287966	0.13631539
7	1.71382427	0.58349040	8.92280336	5.20637006	0.11207240
8	1.85093021	0.54026888	10.63662763	5.74663894	0.09401476
9	1.99900463	0.50024897	12.48755784	6.24688791	0.08007971
10	2.15892500	0.46319349	14.48655247	6.71008140	0.06902949
11	2.33163900	0.42888286	16.64548746	7.13896426	0.06007634
12	2.51817012	0.39711376	18.97712646	7.53807802	0.05269502
13	2.71962373	0.36769792	21.49529658	7.90377594	0.04652181
14	2.93719362	0.34046104	24.21492030	8.24423698	0.04129685
15	3.17216911	0.31524170	27.15211393	8.55947869	0.03682954
16	3.42594264	0.29189047	30.32428304	8.85136916	0.03297687
17	3.70001805	0.27026895	33.75022569	9.12163811	0.02962943
18	3.99601950	0.25024903	37.45024374	9.37188714	0.02670210
19	4.31570106	0.23171206	41.44626324	9.60359920	0.02412763
20	4.66095714	0.21454821	45.76196430	9.81814741	0.02185221
21	5.03383372	0.19865575	50.42292144	10.01680316	0.01983225
22	5.43654041	0.18394051	55.45675516	10.20074366	0.01803207
23	5.87146365	0.17031528	60.89329557	10.37105895	0.01642217
24	6.34118074	0.15769934	66.76475922	10.52875828	0.01497796
25	6.84847520	0.14601790	73.10593995	10.67477619	0.01367878
26	7.39635241	0.13520176	79.95441515	10.80997795	0.01250713
27	7.98806147	0.12518682	87.35076836	10.93516477	0.01144810
28	8.62710639	0.11591372	95.33882983	11.05107849	0.01048891
29	9.31727490	0.10732752	103.96593622	11.15840601	0.00961854
30	10.06265689	0.09937733	113.28321111	11.25778334	0.00882743
31	10.86766944	0.09201605	123.34586800	11.34979939	0.00810728
32	11.73708300	0.08520005	134.21353744	11.43499944	0.00745081
33	12.67604964	0.07888893	145.95062044	11.51388837	0.00685163
34	13.69013361	0.07304531	158.62667007	11.58693367	0.00630411
35	14.78534429	0.06763454	172.31680368	11.65456822	0.00580326
36	15.96817184	0.06262458	187.10214797	11.71719279	0.00534467
37	17.24562558	0.05798572	203.07031981	11.77517851	0.00492440
38	18.62527563	0.05369048	220.31594540	11.82886899	0.00453894
39	20.11529768	0.04971341	238.94122103	11.87858240	0.00418518
40	21.72452150	0.04603093	259.05651871	11.92461333	0.00386016
41	23.46248322	0.04262123	280.78104021	11.96723457	0.00356149
42	25.33948187	0.03946411	304.24352342	12.00669867	0.00328684
43	27.36664042	0.03654084	329.58300530	12.04323951	0.00303414
44	29.55597166	0.03383411	356.94964572	12.07707362	0.00280152
45	31.92044939	0.03132788	386.50561738	12.10840150	0.00258728
46	34.47408534	0.02900730	418.42606677	12.13740880	0.00239991
47	37.23201217	0.02685861	452.90015211	12.16426741	0.00220799
48	40.21057314	0.02486908	490.13216428	12.18913649	0.00204027
49	43.42741899	0.02302693	530.34273742	12.21216341	0.00188557
50	46.90161251	0.02132123	573.77015642	12.23348464	0.00174286
60	101.25706367	0.00987585	1253.21329584	12.37655782	0.00079795
80	471.95483426	0.00211885	5886.93542831	12.47351441	0.00016987
100	2199.76125634	0.00045459	27484.5157042	12.49431757	0.00003638
120	10252.9929425	0.00009753	128149.9117813	12.49878084	0.00000780

RATE 12%

PERIODS	7-1 COMPOUND INTEREST	7-2 PRESENT VALUE	7-3 AMOUNT OF ORDINARY ANNUITY	7-4 PRESENT VALUE OF ANNUITY	7-5 SINKING FUND
1	1.12000000	0.89285714	1.00000000	0.89285714	1.00000000
2	1.25440000	0.79719388	2.12000000	1.69005102	0.47169811
3	1.40492800	0.71178025	3.37440000	2.40183127	0.29634898
4	1.57351936	0.63551808	4.77932800	3.03734935	0.20923444
5	1.76234168	0.56742686	6.35284736	3.60477620	0.15740973
6	1.97382269	0.50663112	8.11518904	4.11140732	0.12322572
7	2.21068141	0.45234922	10.08901173	4.56375654	0.09911774
8	2.47596318	0.40388323	12.29969314	4.96763977	0.08130284
9	2.77307876	0.36061002	14.77565631	5.32824979	0.06767889
10	3.10584821	0.32197324	17.54873507	5.65022303	0.05698416
11	3.47854999	0.28747610	20.65458328	5.93769913	0.04841540
12	3.89597599	0.25667509	24.13313327	6.19437423	0.04143681
13	4.36349311	0.22917419	28.02910926	6.42354842	0.03567720
14	4.87511229	0.20461981	32.39260238	6.62816823	0.03087125
15	5.47356576	0.18269626	37.27971466	6.81086449	0.02682424
16	6.13039365	0.16312166	42.75328042	6.97398615	0.02339002
17	6.86604089	0.14564434	48.88367407	7.11963049	0.02045673
18	7.68996589	0.13003959	55.74971496	7.24967008	0.01793731
19	8.61276169	0.11610678	63.43968075	7.36577686	0.01576300
20	9.64629309	0.10366677	72.05244244	7.46944362	0.01387878
21	10.80384826	0.09255961	81.69873554	7.56200324	0.01224009
22	12.10031006	0.08264251	92.50258380	7.64464575	0.01081051
23	13.55234726	0.07378796	104.60289386	7.71843370	0.00955996
24	15.17862893	0.06588210	118.15524112	7.78431581	0.00846344
25	17.00006441	0.05882331	133.33387006	7.84313911	0.00749997
26	19.04007214	0.05252081	150.33393446	7.89565992	0.00665186
27	21.32488079	0.04689358	169.37400660	7.94255350	0.00590409
28	23.88386649	0.04186927	190.69888739	7.98442277	0.00524387
29	26.74993047	0.03738327	214.58275388	8.02180604	0.00466021
30	29.95992212	0.03337792	241.33268434	8.05518397	0.00414366
31	33.55511278	0.02980172	271.29260646	8.08498569	0.00368606
32	37.58172631	0.02660868	304.84771924	8.11159436	0.00328033
33	42.09155347	0.02375775	342.42944555	8.13535211	0.00292031
34	47.14251748	0.02121227	384.52097901	8.15656438	0.00260064
35	52.79961958	0.01893953	431.66349649	8.17550391	0.00231662
36	59.13557393	0.01691029	484.46311607	8.19241421	0.00206414
37	66.23184280	0.01509848	543.59869000	8.20751269	0.00183959
38	74.17966394	0.01348078	609.83053280	8.22099347	0.00163980
39	83.08122361	0.01203641	684.01019674	8.23302988	0.00146197
40	93.05097044	0.01074680	767.09142034	8.24377668	0.00130363
41	104.21708689	0.00959536	860.14239079	8.25337204	0.00116260
42	116.72313732	0.00856728	964.35947768	8.26193932	0.00103696
43	130.72991380	0.00764936	1081.08261500	8.26958868	0.00092500
44	146.41750346	0.00682978	1211.81252880	8.27641846	0.00082521
45	163.98760387	0.00609802	1358.23003226	8.28251648	0.00073625
46	183.66611634	0.00544466	1522.21763613	8.28796115	0.00065694
47	205.70605030	0.00486131	1705.58375247	8.29282245	0.00058621
48	230.39077633	0.00434045	1911.58980276	8.29716290	0.00052312
49	258.03766949	0.00387540	2141.98057909	8.30103831	0.00046686
50	289.00218983	0.00346018	2400.01824858	8.30449849	0.00041666
60	897.59693349	0.00111409	7471.64111243	8.32404929	0.00013384
80	8658.4830008	0.00011549	72145.69250066	8.33237089	0.00001386

RATE 10%

PERIODS	7-1 COMPOUND INTEREST	7-2 PRESENT VALUE	7-3 AMOUNT OF ORDINARY ANNUITY	7-4 PRESENT VALUE OF ANNUITY	7-5 SINKING FUND
1	1.10000000	0.90909091	1.00000000	0.90909091	1.00000000
2	1.21000000	0.82644628	2.10000000	1.73553719	0.47619048
3	1.33100000	0.75131480	3.31000000	2.48685199	0.30211480
4	1.46410000	0.68301346	4.64100000	3.16986545	0.21547080
5	1.61051000	0.62092132	6.10510000	3.79078677	0.16379748
6	1.77156100	0.56447393	7.71561000	4.35526070	0.12960738
7	1.94871710	0.51315812	9.48717100	4.86841882	0.10540550
8	2.14358881	0.46650738	11.43588810	5.33492620	0.08744402
9	2.35794769	0.42409762	13.57947691	5.75902382	0.07364066
10	2.59374246	0.38554329	15.93742460	6.14456711	0.06274539
11	2.85311671	0.35049390	18.53116706	6.49506101	0.05396314
12	3.13842838	0.31863082	21.38428377	6.81369182	0.04676332
13	3.45227121	0.28966438	24.52271214	7.10335620	0.04077852
14	3.79749834	0.26333125	27.97498336	7.36668746	0.03574622
15	4.17724817	0.23939205	31.77248169	7.60607951	0.03147378
16	4.59497299	0.21762914	35.94972986	7.82370864	0.02781662
17	5.05447028	0.19784467	40.54470285	8.02155331	0.02466413
18	5.55991731	0.17985879	45.59917313	8.20141210	0.02193022
19	6.11590904	0.16350799	51.15909204	8.36492009	0.01954687
20	6.72749995	0.14864363	57.27499949	8.51356372	0.01745962
21	7.40024994	0.13513057	64.00249944	8.64869429	0.01562439
22	8.14027494	0.12284597	71.40274939	8.77154026	0.01400506
23	8.95430243	0.11167816	79.54302433	8.88321842	0.01257181
24	9.84973268	0.10152560	88.49732676	8.98474402	0.01129978
25	10.83470594	0.09229600	98.34705943	9.07704002	0.01016807
26	11.91817654	0.08390545	109.18176538	9.16094547	0.00915904
27	13.10999419	0.07627768	121.09994191	9.23722316	0.00825764
28	14.42099361	0.06934335	134.20993611	9.30656651	0.00745101
29	15.86309297	0.06303941	148.63092972	9.36960591	0.00672807
30	17.44940227	0.05730855	164.49402269	9.42691447	0.00607925
31	19.19434250	0.05209868	181.94342496	9.47901315	0.00549621
32	21.11377675	0.04736244	201.13776745	9.52637555	0.00497172
33	23.22515442	0.04305676	222.25154420	9.56943236	0.00449941
34	25.54766986	0.03914251	245.47669862	9.60857487	0.00407371
35	28.10243685	0.03558410	271.02436848	9.64415897	0.00368971
36	30.91268053	0.03234918	299.12680533	9.67650816	0.00334306
37	34.00394859	0.02940835	330.03948586	9.70591651	0.00302994
38	37.40434344	0.02673486	364.04343445	9.73265137	0.00274692
39	41.14477779	0.02430442	401.44777789	9.75695579	0.00249098
40	45.25925557	0.02209493	442.59255568	9.77905072	0.00225941
41	49.78518112	0.02008630	487.85181125	9.79913702	0.00204980
42	54.76369923	0.01826027	537.63699237	9.81739729	0.00185999
43	60.24006916	0.01660025	592.40069161	9.83399753	0.00168805
44	66.26407608	0.01509113	652.64076077	9.84908867	0.00153224
45	72.89048369	0.01371921	718.90483685	9.86280788	0.00139100
46	80.17953205	0.01247201	791.79532054	9.87527989	0.00126295
47	88.19748526	0.01133819	871.97485259	9.88661808	0.00114682
48	97.01723378	0.01030745	960.17233785	9.89692553	0.00104148
49	106.71895716	0.00937041	1057.18957163	9.90629594	0.00094590
50	117.39085288	0.00851855	1163.90852880	9.91481449	0.00085917
60	304.48163954	0.00328427	3034.81639541	9.96715730	0.00032951
80	2048.40021459	0.00048813	20474.00214585	9.99511814	0.00004884
100	13780.6123398	0.00007257	137796.1233982	9.99927434	0.00000726
120	92709.0688178	0.00001079	927080.6881783	9.99989214	0.00000108

RATE 16.%

PERIODS	7-1 COMPOUND INTEREST	7-2 PRESENT VALUE	7-3 AMOUNT OF ORDINARY ANNUITY	7-4 PRESENT VALUE OF ANNUITY	7-5 SINKING FUND
1	1.1600000	0.86206897	1.0000000	0.86206897	1.00000000
2	1.34560000	0.74316290	2.16000000	1.60523187	0.46296266
3	1.56089600	0.64065767	3.5056000	2.24588954	0.28525787
4	1.81063936	0.55229110	5.06649600	2.79818064	0.19737507
5	2.10034166	0.47611302	6.87713536	3.27429365	0.14540938
6	2.43639632	0.41044225	8.97747702	3.68473591	0.11138987
7	2.82621973	0.35382953	11.41387334	4.03856544	0.08761268
8	3.27841489	0.30502546	14.24009307	4.34369090	0.07022426
9	3.80296127	0.26295298	17.51850797	4.60654388	0.05708249
10	4.41143508	0.22668360	21.32146924	4.83322748	0.04690108
11	5.11726469	0.19541690	25.73290432	5.02864438	0.03886075
12	5.93602704	0.16846284	30.85016901	5.19710722	0.03241473
13	6.88579137	0.14522659	36.78619605	5.34233381	0.02718411
14	7.98751799	0.12515534	43.67198742	5.46752915	0.02289797
15	9.26552087	0.10792701	51.65950541	5.57545616	0.01935752
16	10.74800420	0.09304053	60.92502627	5.66849669	0.01641362
17	12.46768488	0.08020735	71.67303048	5.74870404	0.01395225
18	14.46251446	0.06914427	84.14071536	5.81784831	0.01188485
19	16.77651677	0.05960713	98.60322981	5.87745544	0.01014166
20	19.46075945	0.05138546	115.37974658	5.92884090	0.00866703
21	22.57448097	0.04429781	134.84050604	5.97313871	0.00741617
22	26.18639792	0.03818776	157.41498700	6.01132647	0.00635264
23	30.37622159	0.03292049	183.60188492	6.04424696	0.00544658
24	35.23641704	0.02837973	213.97760651	6.07262669	0.00467339
25	40.87424277	0.02446528	249.21402355	6.09709197	0.00401262
26	47.41412277	0.02109076	290.08826732	6.11818273	0.00344723
27	55.00038241	0.01818169	337.50239009	6.13636443	0.00296294
28	63.80044360	0.01567387	392.50277250	6.15203830	0.00254775
29	74.00851458	0.01351196	456.30321610	6.16655026	0.00219153
30	85.84987691	0.01164824	530.31173068	6.17719850	0.00188568
31	99.58585721	0.01004159	616.16160759	6.18724008	0.00162295
32	115.51959437	0.00865654	715.74746480	6.19589662	0.00138914
33	134.00272947	0.00746253	831.26705917	6.20335916	0.00120298
34	155.44316618	0.00643322	965.26978864	6.20979238	0.00103598
35	180.31407277	0.00554588	1120.71295482	6.21533824	0.00089229
36	209.16432441	0.00478093	1301.02702759	6.22011919	0.00076862
37	242.63061632	0.00412149	1510.19135201	6.22424068	0.00066217
38	281.45151493	0.00355301	1752.82196833	6.22779369	0.00057051
39	326.48375193	0.00306294	2034.27348326	6.23085663	0.00049158
40	378.72115849	0.00264047	2360.75724058	6.23349709	0.00042859
41	439.31664385	0.00227626	2739.47839907	6.23577336	0.00036503
42	509.60719087	0.00196230	3178.79494293	6.23773565	0.00031458
43	591.14434141	0.00169163	3688.40213380	6.23942729	0.00027112
44	685.72743603	0.00145831	4279.54647520	6.24088558	0.00023367
45	795.44382580	0.00125716	4965.27391123	6.24214275	0.00020140
46	922.71483793	0.00108378	5760.71773703	6.24322651	0.00017359
47	1070.34921199	0.00093427	6683.43257496	6.24416078	0.00014962
48	1241.60508591	0.00080541	7753.78178695	6.24496619	0.00012897
49	1440.26189966	0.00069432	8995.38687286	6.24566051	0.00011117
50	1670.70380360	0.00059855	10435.64877252	6.24625906	0.00009583
60	7370.20136525	0.00013568	46057.50853281	6.24915199	0.00002171

RATE 14.%

PERIODS	7-1 COMPOUND INTEREST	7-2 PRESENT VALUE	7-3 AMOUNT OF ORDINARY ANNUITY	7-4 PRESENT VALUE OF ANNUITY	7-5 SINKING FUND
1	1.1400000	0.87719298	1.0000000	0.87719298	1.00000000
2	1.2996000	0.76946753	2.1400000	1.64666051	0.46728972
3	1.48154400	0.67497152	3.4396000	2.32163203	0.29073148
4	1.68896016	0.59208028	4.92114400	2.91371230	0.20320478
5	1.92541458	0.51936866	6.61010416	3.43308097	0.15128355
6	2.19497262	0.45558655	8.53551874	3.88866752	0.11715750
7	2.50226879	0.39963732	10.73049137	4.28830484	0.09319238
8	2.85258642	0.35055905	13.23276016	4.63886389	0.07557002
9	3.25194852	0.30750794	16.08534658	4.94637184	0.06216638
10	3.70722131	0.26974381	19.33729510	5.21611565	0.05171354
11	4.22823230	0.23661738	23.04451641	5.45273302	0.04339427
12	4.81790482	0.20755910	27.27074871	5.66029213	0.03666933
13	5.49241149	0.18206939	32.08865353	5.84236151	0.03116388
14	6.26134910	0.15970999	37.58106503	6.00207150	0.02660914
15	7.13793798	0.14009964	43.84241413	6.14216799	0.02288096
16	8.13724930	0.12289165	50.98035211	6.26505964	0.01961540
17	9.27646420	0.10779969	59.11760141	6.37285933	0.01691544
18	10.57516918	0.09456151	68.39406560	6.46742046	0.01462115
19	12.05569287	0.08294836	78.96923479	6.55036883	0.01266316
20	13.74348987	0.07276172	91.02492766	6.62313055	0.01098600
21	15.66757845	0.06382607	104.76841753	6.68695662	0.00954486
22	17.86103944	0.05598778	120.43599598	6.74294441	0.00830317
23	20.36158496	0.04911209	138.29703542	6.79205650	0.00723081
24	23.21220685	0.04308078	158.65862003	6.83513728	0.00630284
25	26.46191581	0.03779016	181.87082723	6.87292744	0.00549841
26	30.16658403	0.03314926	208.33274304	6.90607670	0.00480001
27	34.38990579	0.02907830	238.49932707	6.93515500	0.00419288
28	39.20449260	0.02550728	272.88923268	6.96066228	0.00366449
29	44.69312158	0.02237481	312.09372546	6.98303709	0.00320417
30	50.95015858	0.01962702	356.78684702	7.00266411	0.00280279
31	58.08318078	0.01721669	407.73700561	7.01988080	0.00245256
32	66.21482609	0.01510236	465.82018639	7.03498316	0.00214675
33	75.48490175	0.01324768	532.03501249	7.04823084	0.00187958
34	86.05278799	0.01162077	607.51991423	7.05985161	0.00164604
35	98.10017831	0.01019366	693.57270223	7.07004528	0.00144181
36	111.83420328	0.00894181	791.67288054	7.07898708	0.00126315
37	127.49099173	0.00784369	903.50708382	7.08683078	0.00110680
38	145.34973058	0.00688043	1030.99807555	7.09371121	0.00096993
39	165.68729286	0.00603547	1176.33780613	7.09974667	0.00085010
40	188.88351386	0.00529427	1342.02509898	7.10504094	0.00074514
41	215.32720580	0.00464410	1530.90861284	7.10968504	0.00065321
42	245.47301461	0.00407377	1746.23581864	7.11375880	0.00057266
43	279.83923665	0.00357348	1991.70883325	7.11733228	0.00050208
44	319.01672979	0.00313463	2271.54806990	7.12046692	0.00044023
45	363.67907196	0.00274968	2590.56479969	7.12321659	0.00038602
46	414.59414203	0.00241200	2954.24387165	7.12562659	0.00033850
47	472.63732191	0.00211579	3368.83801368	7.12774438	0.00029684
48	538.80654698	0.00185595	3841.47533559	7.12960033	0.00026032
49	614.23946656	0.00162803	4380.28182058	7.13122836	0.00022830
50	700.23298846	0.00142810	4994.52134614	7.13265646	0.00020022
60	2595.91865966	0.00038572	18535.13328332	7.14010557	0.00005395

RATE 20.%

PERIODS	7-1 COMPOUND INTEREST	7-2 PRESENT VALUE	7-3 AMOUNT OF ORDINARY ANNUITY	7-4 PRESENT VALUE OF ANNUITY	7-5 SINKING FUND
1	1.20000000	0.83333333	1.00000000	0.83333333	1.00000000
2	1.44000000	0.69444444	2.20000000	1.52777778	0.45454545
3	1.72800000	0.57870370	3.64000000	2.10648148	0.27472527
4	2.07360000	0.48225309	5.36800000	2.58873457	0.18628912
5	2.48832000	0.40187757	7.44160000	2.99061214	0.13437970
6	2.98598400	0.33489798	9.92992000	3.32551012	0.10070575
7	3.58318080	0.27908165	12.91590400	3.60459176	0.07742393
8	4.29981696	0.23256804	16.49908480	3.83715980	0.06060942
9	5.15978035	0.19380670	20.79890176	4.03096650	0.04807946
10	6.19173642	0.16150558	25.95868211	4.19247209	0.03852276
11	7.43008371	0.13458799	32.15041853	4.32706007	0.03110379
12	8.91610045	0.11215665	39.58050224	4.43921673	0.02526496
13	10.69932054	0.09346388	48.49660269	4.53268061	0.02062000
14	12.83918465	0.07788657	59.19592323	4.61056717	0.01689306
15	15.40702157	0.06490547	72.03510787	4.67547264	0.01388212
16	18.48842589	0.05408789	87.44212945	4.72956054	0.01143614
17	22.18611107	0.04507324	105.93055534	4.77463378	0.00944015
18	26.62333328	0.03756104	128.11666640	4.81219482	0.00780539
19	31.94799994	0.03130086	154.73999969	4.84349568	0.00646245
20	38.33759992	0.02608405	186.68799962	4.86957973	0.00535653
21	46.00511991	0.02173671	225.02559955	4.89131644	0.00444394
22	55.20614389	0.01811393	271.03071946	4.90943037	0.00368962
23	66.24737267	0.01509494	326.23686335	4.92452531	0.00306526
24	79.49684720	0.01257912	392.48423602	4.93710442	0.00254787
25	95.39621664	0.01048260	471.98108322	4.94758702	0.00211873
26	114.47545997	0.00873550	567.37729986	4.95632252	0.00176250
27	137.37055197	0.00727958	681.85275984	4.96360210	0.00146659
28	164.84466236	0.00606632	819.22331180	4.96966841	0.00122067
29	197.81359483	0.00505526	984.06797417	4.97472368	0.00101619
30	237.37631380	0.00421272	1181.88156900	4.97893640	0.00084611
31	284.85157656	0.00351060	1419.25788280	4.98244700	0.00070459
32	341.82189187	0.00292550	1704.10945936	4.98537250	0.00058682
33	410.18627025	0.00243792	2045.93135123	4.98781042	0.00048877
34	492.22352430	0.00203160	2456.11762148	4.98984201	0.00040715
35	590.66822915	0.00169300	2948.34114577	4.99153501	0.00033917
36	708.80187499	0.00141083	3539.00937493	4.99294584	0.00028256
37	850.56224998	0.00117569	4247.81124991	4.99412154	0.00023542
38	1020.67469998	0.00097974	5098.37349989	4.99510128	0.00019614
39	1224.80963997	0.00081645	6119.04819987	4.99591773	0.00016342
40	1469.77156797	0.00068038	7343.85783985	4.99659811	0.00013617
41	1763.72588156	0.00056698	8813.62940781	4.99716509	0.00011346
42	2116.47105788	0.00047248	10577.35528938	4.99763758	0.00009454
43	2539.76526945	0.00039374	12693.82634725	4.99803131	0.00007878
44	3047.71832334	0.00032811	15233.59161670	4.99835943	0.00006564
45	3657.26198801	0.00027343	18281.30994004	4.99863286	0.00005470
46	4388.71438561	0.00022786	21938.57192805	4.99886071	0.00004558
47	5266.45726273	0.00018988	26327.28631366	4.99905060	0.00003798
48	6319.74871528	0.00015823	31593.74357640	4.99920883	0.00003165
49	7583.69845834	0.00013186	37913.49229168	4.99934069	0.00002638
50	9100.43815000	0.00010988	45497.19075001	4.99945058	0.00002188
60	56347.5143517	0.00001775	281732.5717658	4.99991126	0.00000355

RATE 18.%

PERIODS	7-1 COMPOUND INTEREST	7-2 PRESENT VALUE	7-3 AMOUNT OF ORDINARY ANNUITY	7-4 PRESENT VALUE OF ANNUITY	7-5 SINKING FUND
1	1.18000000	0.84745763	1.00000000	0.84745763	1.00000000
2	1.39240000	0.71818443	2.18000000	1.56564206	0.45871560
3	1.64303200	0.60863087	3.57240000	2.17427293	0.27992386
4	1.93877776	0.51578888	5.21543200	2.69006180	0.19173867
5	2.28775776	0.43710922	7.15420976	3.12717102	0.13977784
6	2.69955415	0.37043154	9.44196752	3.49760256	0.10591013
7	3.18547390	0.31392503	12.14152167	3.81152759	0.08236200
8	3.75885920	0.26603816	15.32699557	4.07756576	0.06524436
9	4.43545386	0.22545607	19.08585477	4.30302183	0.05239482
10	5.23383555	0.19106447	23.52130863	4.49406629	0.04251464
11	6.17592595	0.16191904	28.75514419	4.65600533	0.03477639
12	7.28759263	0.13721953	34.93107014	4.79322486	0.02862781
13	8.59935930	0.11628773	42.21866276	4.90951259	0.02368621
14	10.14724397	0.09854893	50.81802206	5.00806152	0.01967806
15	11.97374789	0.08351604	60.96526603	5.09157756	0.01640278
16	14.12902251	0.07077630	72.93901392	5.16235386	0.01371008
17	16.67224656	0.05997992	87.06803642	5.22233378	0.01148527
18	19.67325094	0.05083044	103.74028298	5.27316422	0.00963946
19	23.21443611	0.04307664	123.41353392	5.31624087	0.00810284
20	27.39303460	0.03650563	146.62797002	5.35274650	0.00681998
21	32.32378083	0.03093698	174.02100463	5.38368347	0.00574643
22	38.14206138	0.02621778	206.34478546	5.40990125	0.00484626
23	45.00763243	0.02221845	244.48684684	5.43211970	0.00409020
24	53.10900627	0.01882905	289.49447928	5.45094890	0.00345430
25	62.66862740	0.01595695	342.60348554	5.46690585	0.00291883
26	73.94898033	0.01352284	405.27211294	5.48042868	0.00246748
27	87.25979679	0.01146003	479.22109327	5.49188872	0.00208672
28	102.96656021	0.00971189	566.48089006	5.50160061	0.00176528
29	121.50054105	0.00823042	669.44745027	5.50983102	0.00149377
30	143.37063844	0.00697493	790.94799132	5.51680595	0.00126431
31	169.17735336	0.00591096	934.31862976	5.52271691	0.00107030
32	199.62927696	0.00500929	1103.49598312	5.52772619	0.00090621
33	235.56254681	0.00424516	1303.12526008	5.53197135	0.00076739
34	277.96380524	0.00359759	1538.68780689	5.53556894	0.00064990
35	327.99729018	0.00304881	1816.65161213	5.53861775	0.00055046
36	387.03680242	0.00258373	2144.64890232	5.54120148	0.00046628
37	456.70342685	0.00218960	2531.68570473	5.54339108	0.00039499
38	538.91004369	0.00185560	2988.38913158	5.54524668	0.00033463
39	635.91385155	0.00157254	3527.29917527	5.54681922	0.00028350
40	750.37834483	0.00133266	4163.21302682	5.54815188	0.00024020
41	885.44644690	0.00112937	4913.59137165	5.54928126	0.00020352
42	1044.82680734	0.00095710	5799.03781854	5.55023835	0.00017244
43	1232.89563246	0.00081110	6843.86462588	5.55104945	0.00014612
44	1454.81684654	0.00068737	8076.76025854	5.55173682	0.00012381
45	1716.68387891	0.00058252	9531.57710507	5.55231934	0.00010491
46	2025.68697712	0.00049366	11248.26098399	5.55281300	0.00008890
47	2390.31063300	0.00041836	13273.94796110	5.55323136	0.00007534
48	2820.56654694	0.00035454	15664.25859410	5.55358580	0.00006384
49	3328.26852539	0.00030046	18484.82514104	5.55388635	0.00005410
50	3927.35685996	0.00025462	21813.09366643	5.55414098	0.00004584
60	20555.1399661	0.00004865	114189.6664783	5.55528528	0.00000876

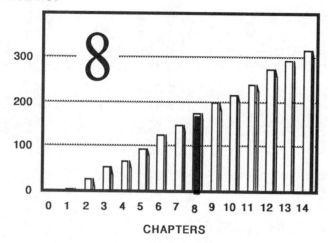

CHAPTERS

Real Estate and Insurance Applications

Student Objectives

Upon completion of this chapter, the student should be able to

*1. **Find** the size of a mortgage payment from a mortgage table.*
*2. **Prepare** a loan repayment schedule for a mortgage.*
*3. **Calculate** life insurance premiums.*
*4. **Calculate** the cash surrender value of life insurance policies.*
*5. **Calculate** fire insurance premiums.*
*6. **Calculate** the refund of premiums when fire insurance policies are canceled.*
*7. **Calculate** the payment for loss under a co-insurance clause.*
*8. **Define, illustrate,** or **use***

    assessment rate   *straight life insurance*
    assessed value   *limited-payment life insurance*
    market value   *co-insurance*
    endowment life insurance

Home Mortgages

In contemporary America, most houses are sold through an arrangement in which there is a down payment and a long-term loan (a mortgage) for the balance. Mortgages are usually paid in monthly installments, each of which includes interest on the unpaid balance and a payment on the principal.

Rarely does anyone attempt to compute the payment on a mortgage. The amount of the payment is instead found in a loan amortization schedule which is a table of monthly payments at various rates of interest, numbers of years, and amounts of loans. An excerpt from a loan amortization schedule is given in Table 8-1.

Assignment 8-1

1. Two builders offer similar new homes for $90,000 each, financed over 30 years. The Edwards Company can acquire 9% financing. The Grunt Company's houses finance at 10%. How much more per month would it cost to buy the Grunt house than the Edwards' house and how much more would it cost in total?

2. Jack and Jill Hill are in the market for a new home. The house on Waits St. costs $65,000 and can be financed at 9% for 30 years. The one on Everest Ave. costs $75,000 and will finance at 8% for 20 years. How much is the difference in the monthly payments and how much difference in the total costs of the houses?

3. Six years ago, Mr. Chan bought a house for $55,000 at 14% financed over 25 years. Interest rates have declined to 11% since then. How much difference would there be in the monthly payments and the total amount to be paid if he bought the same house today?

4. Robbie bought a home with a mortgage of $80,000 for 30 years at 10%. She could have financed it for 25 years but wanted a lower payment. How much lower is the payment and how much more will she pay in finance costs for the additional five years of credit?

5. Steve has been trying to sell his house for three years. The price is $90,000. In that time, interest rates have declined from 12% to 9%. How much difference would that make in a monthly payment and in the total amount a buyer would pay over the life of a 30-year mortgage?

Loan Repayment Schedules (Amortization Schedule)

Loan repayment schedules are available ordinarily from the company that holds the mortgage. The schedule shows the amount of each payment which is applied to the principal and the amount applied to interest. Also, the loan repayment schedule shows the principal balance following each payment.

A loan repayment schedule is constructed after the amount of the monthly payment is determined from an amortization schedule. The formulas used to construct a loan repayment schedule are

1. Interest portion equals balance of loan (P) times interest rate (R) times time (T):
$I = P \times R \times \frac{1}{12}$ (T is always $\frac{1}{12}$).
2. Principal portion is monthly payment minus interest portion.
3. Balance of principal is previous principal balance minus principal portion.

Example

Prepare a loan repayment schedule for the first three payments on a loan of $60,000 at 12% for 30 years.

Solution

Determine the size of the monthly payment from the 12% mortgage table. The payment is $617.17

first payment
interest portion = $60,000 \times .12 \times \frac{1}{12}$ = $600
principal portion = $617.17 − $600 = $17.17
balance of principal = $60,000 − $17.17 = $59,982.83
second payment
interest portion = $59,982.83 \times .12 \times \frac{1}{12}$ = $599.83
principal portion = $617.17 − $599.83 = $17.34
balance of principal = $59,982.83 − $17.34 = $59,965.49
third payment
interest portion = $59,965.49 \times .12 \times \frac{1}{12}$ = $599.65
principal portion = $617.17 − $599.65 = $17.52
balance of principal = $59,965.49 − $17.52 = $59,947.97

Payment number	Size of payment	Interest portion	Principal portion	Balance of principal
1	$617.17	$600.00	$17.17	$59,982.83
2	617.17	599.83	17.34	59,965.49
3	617.17	599.65	17.52	59,947.97

Assignment 8-2

1. Prepare a loan repayment schedule for the first three payments on a loan of $80,000 at 10% for 30 years.

2. Prepare a loan repayment schedule for the first three payments on a loan of $90,000 at 8% for 25 years.

8% MONTHLY PAYMENT
necessary to amortize a loan

Term Amt.	10 Years	12 Years	15 Years	20 Years	25 Years	29 Years	30 Years
25	.31	.28	.24	.21	.20	.19	.19
50	.61	.55	.48	.42	.39	.37	.37
75	.91	.82	.72	.63	.58	.56	.56
100	1.22	1.09	.96	.84	.78	.74	.74
200	2.43	2.17	1.92	1.68	1.55	1.48	1.47
300	3.64	3.25	2.87	2.51	2.32	2.22	2.21
400	4.86	4.33	3.83	3.35	3.09	2.96	2.94
500	6.07	5.42	4.78	4.19	3.86	3.70	3.67
600	7.28	6.50	5.74	5.02	4.64	4.44	4.41
700	8.50	7.58	6.69	5.86	5.41	5.18	5.14
800	9.71	8.66	7.65	6.70	6.18	5.92	5.88
900	10.92	9.75	8.61	7.53	6.95	6.66	6.61
1000	12.14	10.83	9.56	8.37	7.72	7.40	7.34
2000	24.27	21.65	19.12	16.73	15.44	14.80	14.68
3000	36.40	32.48	28.67	25.10	23.16	22.20	22.02
4000	48.54	43.30	38.23	33.46	30.88	29.60	29.36
5000	60.67	54.13	47.79	41.83	38.60	37.00	36.69
6000	72.80	64.95	57.34	50.19	46.31	44.40	44.03
7000	84.93	75.78	66.90	58.56	54.03	51.80	51.37
8000	97.07	86.60	76.46	66.92	61.75	59.20	58.71
9000	109.20	97.43	86.01	75.28	69.47	66.60	66.04
10000	121.33	108.25	95.57	83.65	77.19	74.00	73.38
11000	133.47	119.07	105.13	92.01	84.90	81.40	80.72
12000	145.60	129.90	114.68	100.38	92.62	88.80	88.06
13000	157.73	140.72	124.24	108.74	100.34	96.20	95.39
14000	169.86	151.55	133.80	117.11	108.06	103.60	102.73
15000	182.00	162.37	143.35	125.47	115.78	111.00	110.07
16000	194.13	173.20	152.91	133.84	123.50	118.40	117.41
17000	206.26	184.02	162.47	142.20	131.21	125.80	124.74
18000	218.39	194.85	172.02	150.56	138.93	133.20	132.08
19000	230.53	205.67	181.58	158.93	146.65	140.59	139.42
20000	242.66	216.50	191.14	167.29	154.37	147.99	146.76
21000	254.79	227.32	200.69	175.66	162.09	155.39	154.10
22000	266.93	238.14	210.25	184.02	169.80	162.79	161.43
23000	279.06	248.97	219.80	192.39	177.52	170.19	168.77
24000	291.19	259.79	229.36	200.75	185.24	177.59	176.11
25000	303.32	270.62	238.92	209.12	192.96	184.99	183.45
26000	315.46	281.44	248.47	217.48	200.68	192.39	190.78
27000	327.59	292.27	258.03	225.84	208.40	199.79	198.12
28000	339.72	303.09	267.59	234.21	216.11	207.19	205.46
29000	351.86	313.92	277.14	242.57	223.83	214.59	212.80
30000	363.99	324.74	286.70	250.94	231.55	221.99	220.13
31000	376.12	335.57	296.26	259.30	239.27	229.39	227.47
32000	388.25	346.39	305.81	267.67	246.99	236.79	234.81
33000	400.39	357.21	315.37	276.03	254.70	244.19	242.15
34000	412.52	368.04	324.93	284.39	262.42	251.49	249.48
35000	424.65	378.86	334.48	292.76	270.14	258.89	256.82
40000	485.32	432.99	382.27	334.58	308.73	295.98	293.51
45000	545.98	487.11	430.05	376.40	347.32	332.98	330.20
50000	606.64	541.23	477.83	418.23	385.91	369.98	366.89
55000	667.31	595.35	525.61	460.05	424.50	406.98	403.58
60000	727.97	649.48	573.40	501.87	463.09	443.97	440.26
65000	788.63	703.60	621.18	543.69	501.69	480.97	476.95
70000	849.30	757.72	668.96	585.51	540.28	517.97	513.64
75000	909.96	811.84	716.74	627.34	578.87	554.96	550.33
80000	970.63	865.97	764.53	669.16	617.46	591.96	587.02
85000	1031.29	920.09	812.31	710.98	656.05	628.96	623.70
90000	1091.95	974.21	860.09	752.80	694.64	665.96	660.39
95000	1152.62	1028.33	907.87	794.62	733.23	702.95	697.08
100000	1213.28	1082.46	955.66	836.45	771.82	739.95	733.77

9% MONTHLY PAYMENT
necessary to amortize a loan

Term Amt.	10 Years	12 Years	15 Years	20 Years	25 Years	29 Years	30 Years
25	.32	.29	.26	.23	.21	.21	.21
50	.64	.57	.51	.45	.42	.41	.41
75	.96	.86	.77	.68	.63	.61	.61
100	1.27	1.14	1.02	.90	.84	.82	.81
200	2.54	2.28	2.03	1.80	1.68	1.63	1.61
300	3.81	3.42	3.05	2.70	2.52	2.44	2.42
400	5.07	4.56	4.06	3.60	3.36	3.25	3.22
500	6.34	5.70	5.08	4.50	4.20	4.06	4.03
600	7.61	6.83	6.09	5.40	5.04	4.87	4.83
700	8.87	7.97	7.11	6.30	5.88	5.68	5.64
800	10.14	9.11	8.12	7.20	6.72	6.49	6.44
900	11.41	10.25	9.13	8.10	7.56	7.30	7.25
1000	12.67	11.39	10.15	9.00	8.40	8.11	8.05
2000	25.34	22.77	20.29	18.00	16.79	16.21	16.10
3000	38.01	34.15	30.43	27.00	25.18	24.31	24.14
4000	50.68	45.53	40.58	35.99	33.57	32.41	32.19
5000	63.34	56.91	50.72	44.99	41.96	40.51	40.24
6000	76.01	68.29	60.86	53.99	50.36	48.61	48.28
7000	88.68	79.67	71.00	62.99	58.75	56.72	56.33
8000	101.35	91.05	81.15	71.98	67.14	64.82	64.37
9000	114.01	102.43	91.29	80.98	75.53	72.92	72.42
10000	126.68	113.81	101.43	89.98	83.92	81.02	80.47
11000	139.35	125.19	111.57	98.97	92.32	89.12	88.51
12000	152.02	136.57	121.72	107.97	100.71	97.22	96.56
13000	164.68	147.95	131.86	116.97	109.10	105.33	104.61
14000	177.35	159.33	142.00	125.97	117.49	113.43	112.65
15000	190.02	170.71	152.14	134.96	125.88	121.53	120.70
16000	202.69	182.09	162.29	143.96	134.28	129.63	128.74
17000	215.35	193.47	172.43	152.96	142.67	137.73	136.79
18000	228.02	204.85	182.57	161.96	151.06	145.83	144.84
19000	240.69	216.23	192.72	170.95	159.45	153.93	152.88
20000	253.36	227.61	202.86	179.95	167.84	162.04	160.93
21000	266.02	238.99	213.00	188.95	176.24	170.14	168.98
22000	278.69	250.37	223.14	197.94	184.63	178.24	177.02
23000	291.36	261.75	233.29	206.94	193.02	186.34	185.07
24000	304.03	273.13	243.43	215.94	201.41	194.44	193.11
25000	316.69	284.51	253.57	224.94	209.80	202.54	201.16
26000	329.36	295.89	263.71	233.93	218.20	210.65	209.21
27000	342.03	307.27	273.86	242.93	226.59	218.75	217.25
28000	354.70	318.65	284.00	251.93	234.98	226.85	225.30
29000	367.36	330.03	294.14	260.93	243.37	234.95	233.35
30000	380.03	341.41	304.28	269.92	251.76	243.05	241.39
31000	392.70	352.79	314.43	278.92	260.16	251.15	249.44
32000	405.37	364.17	324.57	287.92	268.55	259.26	257.48
33000	418.04	375.56	334.71	296.91	276.94	267.36	265.53
34000	430.70	386.94	344.86	305.91	285.33	275.46	273.58
35000	443.37	398.32	355.00	314.91	293.72	283.56	281.62
40000	506.71	455.22	405.71	359.90	335.68	324.07	321.85
45000	570.05	512.12	456.42	404.88	377.64	364.58	362.09
50000	633.38	569.02	507.14	449.87	419.60	405.08	402.32
55000	696.72	625.92	557.85	494.85	461.56	445.59	442.55
60000	760.06	682.82	608.56	539.84	503.52	486.10	482.78
65000	823.40	739.72	659.28	584.83	545.48	526.61	523.01
70000	886.74	796.63	709.99	629.81	587.44	567.12	563.24
75000	950.07	853.53	760.70	674.80	629.40	607.62	603.47
80000	1013.41	910.43	811.42	719.79	671.36	648.13	643.70
85000	1076.75	967.33	862.13	764.77	713.32	688.64	683.93
90000	1140.09	1024.23	912.84	809.76	755.28	729.15	724.17
95000	1203.42	1081.13	963.56	854.74	797.24	769.65	764.40
100000	1266.76	1138.04	1014.27	899.73	839.20	810.16	804.63

10% MONTHLY PAYMENT
necessary to amortize a loan

Term Amt.	10 Years	12 Years	15 Years	20 Years	25 Years	29 Years	30 Years
25	.34	.30	.27	.25	.23	.23	.22
50	.67	.60	.54	.49	.46	.45	.44
75	1.00	.90	.81	.73	.69	.67	.66
100	1.33	1.20	1.08	.97	.91	.89	.88
200	2.65	2.40	2.15	1.94	1.82	1.77	1.76
300	3.97	3.59	3.23	2.90	2.73	2.65	2.64
400	5.29	4.79	4.30	3.87	3.64	3.53	3.52
500	6.61	5.98	5.38	4.83	4.55	4.42	4.39
600	7.93	7.18	6.45	5.80	5.46	5.30	5.27
700	9.26	8.37	7.53	6.76	6.37	6.18	6.15
800	10.58	9.57	8.60	7.73	7.27	7.06	7.03
900	11.90	10.76	9.68	8.69	8.18	7.95	7.90
1000	13.22	11.96	10.75	9.66	9.09	8.83	8.78
2000	26.44	23.91	21.50	19.31	18.18	17.65	17.56
3000	39.65	35.86	32.24	28.96	27.27	26.48	26.33
4000	52.87	47.81	42.99	38.61	36.35	35.30	35.11
5000	66.08	59.76	53.74	48.26	45.44	44.13	43.88
6000	79.30	71.71	64.48	57.91	54.53	52.95	52.66
7000	92.51	83.66	75.23	67.56	63.61	61.78	61.44
8000	105.73	95.61	85.97	77.21	72.70	70.60	70.21
9000	118.94	107.56	96.72	86.86	81.79	79.43	78.99
10000	132.16	119.51	107.47	96.51	90.88	88.25	87.76
11000	145.37	131.46	118.21	106.16	99.96	97.08	96.54
12000	158.59	143.41	128.96	115.81	109.05	105.90	105.31
13000	171.80	155.37	139.70	125.46	118.14	114.73	114.09
14000	185.02	167.32	150.45	135.11	127.22	123.55	122.87
15000	198.23	179.27	161.20	144.76	136.31	132.38	131.64
16000	211.45	191.22	171.94	154.41	145.40	141.20	140.42
17000	224.66	203.17	182.69	164.06	154.48	150.03	149.19
18000	237.88	215.12	193.43	173.71	163.57	158.85	157.97
19000	251.09	227.07	204.18	183.36	172.66	167.68	166.74
20000	264.31	239.02	214.93	193.01	181.75	176.50	175.52
21000	277.52	250.97	225.67	202.66	190.83	185.33	184.30
22000	290.74	262.92	236.42	212.31	199.92	194.15	193.07
23000	303.95	274.87	247.16	221.96	209.01	202.97	201.85
24000	317.17	286.82	257.91	231.61	218.09	211.80	210.62
25000	330.38	298.77	268.66	241.26	227.18	220.62	219.40
26000	343.60	310.73	279.40	250.91	236.27	229.45	228.17
27000	356.81	322.68	290.15	260.56	245.35	238.27	236.95
28000	370.03	334.63	300.89	270.21	254.44	247.10	245.73
29000	383.24	346.58	311.64	279.86	263.53	255.92	254.50
30000	396.46	358.53	322.39	289.51	272.62	264.75	263.28
31000	409.67	370.48	333.13	299.16	281.70	273.57	272.05
32000	422.89	382.43	343.88	308.81	290.79	282.40	280.83
33000	436.10	394.38	354.62	318.46	299.88	291.22	289.60
34000	449.32	406.33	365.37	328.11	308.96	300.05	298.38
35000	462.53	418.28	376.12	337.76	318.05	308.87	307.16
40000	528.61	478.04	429.85	386.01	363.49	353.00	351.03
45000	594.68	537.79	483.58	434.26	408.92	397.12	394.91
50000	660.76	597.54	537.31	482.52	454.36	441.24	438.78
55000	726.83	657.30	591.04	530.77	499.79	485.37	482.67
60000	792.91	717.05	644.77	579.02	545.23	529.49	526.55
65000	858.98	776.81	698.50	627.27	590.66	573.62	570.43
70000	925.06	836.56	752.23	675.52	636.10	617.74	614.31
75000	991.14	896.31	805.96	723.77	681.53	661.86	658.18
80000	1057.21	956.07	859.69	772.02	726.97	705.99	702.06
85000	1123.29	1015.82	913.42	820.27	772.40	750.11	745.94
90000	1189.36	1075.58	967.15	868.52	817.84	794.23	789.82
95000	1255.44	1135.33	1020.88	916.78	863.27	838.26	833.70
100000	1321.51	1195.08	1074.61	965.03	908.71	882.48	877.58

11% MONTHLY PAYMENT
necessary to amortize a loan

Term Amt.	10 Years	12 Years	15 Years	20 Years	25 Years	29 Years	30 Years
25	.35	.32	.29	.26	.25	.24	.24
50	.69	.63	.57	.52	.50	.48	.48
75	1.04	.95	.86	.78	.74	.72	.72
100	1.38	1.26	1.14	1.04	.99	.96	.96
200	2.76	2.51	2.28	2.07	1.97	1.92	1.91
300	4.14	3.77	3.41	3.10	2.95	2.87	2.86
400	5.52	5.02	4.55	4.13	3.93	3.83	3.81
500	6.89	6.27	5.69	5.17	4.91	4.79	4.77
600	8.27	7.53	6.82	6.20	5.89	5.74	5.72
700	9.65	8.78	7.96	7.23	6.87	6.70	6.67
800	11.03	10.03	9.10	8.26	7.85	7.66	7.62
900	12.40	11.29	10.23	9.29	8.83	8.61	8.58
1000	13.78	12.54	11.37	10.33	9.81	9.57	9.53
2000	27.56	25.08	22.74	20.65	19.61	19.14	19.05
3000	41.33	37.61	34.10	30.97	29.41	28.70	28.57
4000	55.11	50.15	45.47	41.29	39.21	38.27	38.10
5000	68.88	62.68	56.83	51.61	49.01	47.84	47.62
6000	82.66	75.22	68.20	61.94	58.81	57.40	57.14
7000	96.43	87.75	79.57	72.26	68.61	66.97	66.67
8000	110.21	100.29	90.93	82.56	78.41	76.54	76.19
9000	123.98	112.82	102.30	92.90	88.22	86.10	85.71
10000	137.76	125.36	113.66	103.22	98.02	95.67	95.24
11000	151.53	137.90	125.03	113.55	107.82	105.23	104.76
12000	165.31	150.43	136.40	123.87	117.62	114.80	114.28
13000	179.08	162.97	147.76	134.19	127.42	124.37	123.81
14000	192.86	175.50	159.13	144.51	137.22	133.93	133.33
15000	206.63	188.04	170.49	154.83	147.02	143.50	142.85
16000	220.41	200.57	181.86	165.16	156.82	153.07	152.38
17000	234.18	213.11	193.23	175.48	166.62	162.63	161.90
18000	247.96	225.64	204.59	185.80	176.43	172.20	171.42
19000	261.73	238.18	215.96	196.12	186.23	181.76	180.95
20000	275.51	250.72	227.32	206.44	196.03	191.33	190.47
21000	289.28	263.25	238.69	216.76	205.83	200.90	199.99
22000	303.06	275.79	250.06	227.09	215.63	210.46	209.52
23000	316.83	288.32	261.42	237.41	225.43	220.03	219.04
24000	330.61	300.86	272.79	247.73	235.23	229.60	228.56
25000	344.38	313.39	284.15	258.05	245.03	239.16	238.09
26000	358.16	325.93	295.52	267.38	254.83	248.73	247.61
27000	371.93	338.46	306.89	278.70	264.64	258.29	257.13
28000	385.71	351.00	318.25	289.02	274.44	267.86	266.66
29000	399.48	363.53	329.62	299.34	284.24	277.43	276.18
30000	413.26	376.07	340.98	309.66	294.04	286.99	285.70
31000	427.03	388.61	352.35	319.98	303.84	296.56	295.23
32000	440.81	401.14	363.72	330.31	313.64	306.13	304.75
33000	454.58	413.68	375.08	340.63	323.44	315.69	314.27
34000	468.36	426.21	386.45	350.95	333.24	325.26	323.79
35000	482.13	438.75	397.81	361.27	343.04	334.83	333.32
40000	551.01	501.43	454.64	412.88	392.05	382.66	380.93
45000	619.88	564.10	511.47	464.49	441.06	430.49	428.55
50000	688.76	626.78	568.30	516.10	490.06	478.32	476.17
55000	757.36	689.46	625.13	567.10	539.07	526.16	523.78
60000	826.51	752.14	681.96	619.32	588.07	573.98	571.40
65000	895.38	814.82	738.79	670.93	637.08	621.81	619.02
70000	964.28	877.46	795.62	722.54	686.08	669.65	666.63
75000	1033.13	940.17	852.45	774.15	735.09	717.48	714.25
80000	1102.01	1002.85	909.28	825.76	784.10	765.31	761.86
85000	1170.88	1065.53	966.11	877.37	833.10	813.14	809.48
90000	1239.76	1128.20	1022.94	928.97	882.11	860.97	857.10
95000	1308.63	1190.88	1079.77	980.58	931.11	908.80	904.71
100000	1377.51	1253.56	1136.60	1032.19	980.12	956.63	952.33

14%   MONTHLY PAYMENT
necessary to amortize a loan

Term Amt.	10 Years	12 Years	15 Years	20 Years	25 Years	29 Years	30 Years
25	.39	.36	.34	.32	.31	.30	.30
50	.78	.72	.67	.63	.61	.60	.60
75	1.17	1.08	1.00	.94	.91	.90	.90
100	1.56	1.44	1.34	1.25	1.21	1.19	1.19
200	3.11	2.88	2.67	2.49	2.41	2.38	2.37
300	4.66	4.32	4.00	3.74	3.62	3.57	3.56
400	6.22	5.75	5.33	4.98	4.82	4.76	4.74
500	7.77	7.19	6.66	6.22	6.02	5.94	5.93
600	9.32	8.63	8.00	7.47	7.23	7.13	7.11
700	10.87	10.06	9.33	8.71	8.43	8.32	8.30
800	12.43	11.50	10.66	9.95	9.64	9.51	9.48
900	13.98	12.94	11.99	11.20	10.84	10.69	10.67
1000	15.53	14.38	13.32	12.44	12.04	11.88	11.85
2000	31.06	28.75	26.64	24.88	24.08	23.76	23.70
3000	46.58	43.12	39.96	37.31	36.12	35.63	35.55
4000	62.11	57.49	53.27	49.75	48.16	47.51	47.40
5000	77.64	71.86	66.59	62.18	60.19	59.39	59.25
6000	93.16	86.23	79.91	74.62	72.23	71.26	71.10
7000	108.69	100.60	93.23	87.05	84.27	83.14	82.95
8000	124.22	114.98	106.54	99.49	96.31	95.02	94.79
9000	139.74	129.35	119.86	111.92	108.34	106.89	106.64
10000	155.27	143.72	133.18	124.36	120.38	118.77	118.49
11000	170.80	158.09	146.50	136.79	132.42	130.65	130.34
12000	186.32	172.46	159.81	149.23	144.46	142.52	142.19
13000	201.85	186.83	173.13	161.66	156.49	154.40	154.04
14000	217.38	201.20	186.45	174.10	168.53	166.27	165.89
15000	232.90	215.57	199.77	186.53	180.57	178.15	177.74
16000	248.43	229.95	213.08	198.97	192.61	190.03	189.58
17000	263.96	244.32	226.40	211.40	204.64	201.90	201.43
18000	279.48	258.69	239.72	223.84	216.68	213.78	213.28
19000	295.01	273.06	253.04	236.27	228.72	225.66	225.13
20000	310.54	287.43	266.35	248.71	240.76	237.53	236.98
21000	326.06	301.80	279.67	261.14	252.79	249.41	248.83
22000	341.59	316.17	292.99	273.58	264.83	261.29	260.68
23000	357.12	330.54	306.31	286.01	276.87	273.16	272.53
24000	372.64	344.92	319.62	298.45	288.91	285.04	284.37
25000	388.17	359.29	332.94	310.89	300.95	296.91	296.22
26000	403.70	373.66	346.26	323.32	312.98	308.79	308.07
27000	419.22	388.03	359.58	335.76	325.02	320.67	319.92
28000	434.75	402.40	372.89	348.19	337.06	332.54	331.77
29000	450.28	416.77	386.21	360.63	349.10	344.42	343.62
30000	465.80	431.14	399.53	373.06	361.13	356.30	355.47
31000	481.33	445.51	412.84	385.50	373.17	368.17	367.32
32000	496.86	459.89	426.16	397.93	385.21	380.05	379.16
33000	512.38	474.26	439.48	410.37	397.25	391.93	391.01
34000	527.91	488.63	452.80	422.80	409.28	403.80	402.86
35000	543.44	503.00	466.11	435.24	421.32	415.68	414.71
40000	621.07	574.86	532.70	497.41	481.51	475.06	473.95
45000	698.70	646.71	599.29	559.59	541.70	534.44	533.20
50000	776.34	718.57	665.88	621.77	601.89	593.82	592.44
55000	853.97	790.42	732.46	683.94	662.07	653.21	651.68
60000	931.60	862.28	799.05	746.12	722.26	712.59	710.93
65000	1009.24	934.14	865.64	808.29	782.45	771.97	770.17
70000	1086.87	1005.99	932.22	870.47	842.64	831.35	829.42
75000	1164.50	1077.85	998.81	932.65	902.83	890.73	888.66
80000	1242.14	1149.71	1065.40	994.82	963.01	950.12	947.90
85000	1319.77	1221.56	1131.99	1057.00	1023.20	1009.50	1007.15
90000	1397.40	1293.42	1198.57	1119.17	1083.39	1068.88	1066.39
95000	1475.04	1365.28	1265.16	1181.35	1143.58	1128.26	1125.63
100000	1552.67	1437.13	1331.75	1243.53	1203.77	1187.64	1184.88

12%   MONTHLY PAYMENT
necessary to amortize a loan

Term Amt.	10 Years	12 Years	15 Years	20 Years	25 Years	29 Years	30 Years
25	.36	.33	.31	.28	.27	.26	.26
50	.72	.66	.61	.56	.53	.52	.52
75	1.08	.99	.91	.83	.79	.78	.78
100	1.44	1.32	1.21	1.11	1.06	1.04	1.03
200	2.87	2.63	2.41	2.21	2.11	2.07	2.06
300	4.31	3.95	3.61	3.31	3.16	3.10	3.09
400	5.74	5.26	4.81	4.41	4.22	4.13	4.12
500	7.18	6.57	6.01	5.51	5.27	5.17	5.15
600	8.61	7.89	7.21	6.61	6.32	6.20	6.18
700	10.05	9.20	8.41	7.71	7.38	7.23	7.21
800	11.48	10.51	9.61	8.81	8.43	8.26	8.23
900	12.92	11.83	10.81	9.91	9.48	9.30	9.26
1000	14.35	13.14	12.01	11.02	10.54	10.33	10.29
2000	28.70	26.27	24.01	22.03	21.07	20.65	20.58
3000	43.05	39.41	36.01	33.04	31.60	30.98	30.86
4000	57.39	52.54	48.01	44.05	42.13	41.30	41.15
5000	71.74	65.68	60.01	55.06	52.67	51.62	51.44
6000	86.09	78.81	72.02	66.07	63.20	61.95	61.72
7000	100.43	91.94	84.02	77.08	73.73	72.27	72.01
8000	114.78	105.08	96.02	88.09	84.26	82.59	82.29
9000	129.13	118.21	108.02	99.10	94.80	92.92	92.58
10000	143.48	131.35	120.02	110.11	105.33	103.24	102.87
11000	157.82	144.48	132.02	121.12	115.86	113.56	113.15
12000	172.17	157.62	144.03	132.14	126.39	123.89	123.44
13000	186.52	170.75	156.03	143.15	136.92	134.21	133.72
14000	200.86	183.88	168.03	154.16	147.46	144.54	144.01
15000	215.21	197.02	180.03	165.17	157.99	154.86	154.30
16000	229.56	210.15	192.03	176.18	168.52	165.18	164.58
17000	243.91	223.29	204.04	187.19	179.05	175.51	174.87
18000	258.25	236.42	216.04	198.20	189.59	185.83	185.16
19000	272.60	249.55	228.04	209.21	200.12	196.15	195.44
20000	286.95	262.69	240.04	220.22	210.65	206.48	205.73
21000	301.29	275.82	252.04	231.23	221.18	216.80	216.01
22000	315.64	288.96	264.04	242.24	231.71	227.12	226.30
23000	329.99	302.09	276.04	253.25	242.25	237.45	236.59
24000	344.34	315.23	288.05	264.27	252.78	247.77	246.87
25000	358.68	328.36	300.05	275.28	263.31	258.09	257.16
26000	373.03	341.49	312.05	286.29	273.84	268.42	267.44
27000	387.38	354.63	324.05	297.30	284.38	278.74	277.73
28000	401.72	367.76	336.05	308.31	294.91	289.07	288.02
29000	416.07	380.90	348.05	319.32	305.44	299.39	298.30
30000	430.42	394.03	360.06	330.33	315.97	309.71	308.59
31000	444.76	407.16	372.06	341.34	326.50	320.04	318.87
32000	459.11	420.30	384.06	352.35	337.04	330.36	329.16
33000	473.46	433.43	396.06	363.36	347.57	340.68	339.45
34000	487.81	446.57	408.06	374.37	358.10	351.01	349.73
35000	502.15	459.70	420.06	385.39	368.63	361.33	360.02
40000	573.89	525.37	480.07	440.44	421.29	412.95	411.45
45000	645.62	591.04	540.08	495.49	473.96	464.57	462.88
50000	717.36	656.71	600.09	550.55	526.62	516.18	514.31
55000	789.10	722.39	660.10	605.60	579.28	567.80	565.74
60000	860.83	788.06	720.11	660.66	631.94	619.42	617.17
65000	932.57	853.73	780.11	715.71	684.60	671.04	668.60
70000	1004.30	919.40	840.12	770.77	737.26	722.66	720.03
75000	1076.04	985.07	900.13	825.82	789.92	774.27	771.46
80000	1147.77	1050.74	960.14	880.87	842.58	825.89	822.90
85000	1219.51	1116.41	1020.15	935.93	895.25	877.51	874.33
90000	1291.24	1182.08	1080.16	990.98	947.91	929.13	925.76
95000	1362.98	1247.75	1140.16	1046.04	1000.57	980.75	977.19
100000	1434.71	1313.42	1200.17	1101.09	1053.23	1032.36	1028.62

3.   Prepare a loan repayment schedule for the first three payments on a loan of $100,000 at 10% for 30 years.

4.   Prepare a loan repayment schedule for the first three payments on a loan of $100,000 at 12% for 30 years.

5.   Prepare a loan repayment schedule for the first three payments on a loan of $100,000 at 14% for 30 years.

Real Estate Taxes

Real estate taxes are the most common type of taxes imposed by cities, towns, counties, and school districts. They are levied against land and buildings on an annual basis. Five terms are constantly found in problems concerning real estate taxes:

Definitions:

1. *Market value.*   The actual worth of a property on the market. Market value is usually determined by a government tax appraiser and is often called *appraisal value.*

2. *Assessment rate.*   An arbitrary rate set by the taxing authority. Since a property appraisal is always an estimate, there is a risk that property might be appraised at a value greater than its true market value. To avoid over-taxing property because of human error, the market value is multiplied by an assessment rate which is less than 100%.

3. *Assessed valuation.*   A percentage of the true market value. Assessed valuation is determined by multiplying the market value by the assessment rate. It is the base upon which real estate taxes are calculated.

4. *Tax rate.*   The ratio that exists between the amount of tax and the assessed valuation. Normally, the tax rate is not stated as a percent. It is stated in dollar-and-cents terms—for example, $2.15 per $100 of assessed valuation or $21.50 per $1000 of assessed valuation.

5. *Tax.* The amount paid by the real estate owner. Tax is calculated by multiplying the assessed valuation by the tax rate.

Note: In some areas, the tax rate is applied directly to the market value (appraised value) of real estate. While this appears to be the trend, most localities still use assessed valuations.

Calculating the Unknowns for Real Estate Taxes

Any of the five terms defined above could be unknown. Thus, it is desirable to consider the terms in the following manner:

Market Value	MV	B
× Assessment Rate	×AR	×R
= Assessed Valuation	=AV OR	=P(B)
× Tax Rate	×TR	×R
= Tax	= T	=P

Example   Sam owns a house that has been appraised at $62,000. The county assessment rate is 60%. The tax rate is $2.12 per $100 of valuation. How much county tax will Sam have to pay?

Solution   Set up the format as shown below and substitute the numbers given in the example:

MV	$62,000
×AR	.60
=AV	$37,200
×TR	.0212 → ($\frac{\$2.12}{\$100}$ = .0212)
= T	$788.64

Example   A town collects $970,000 from property taxes. The assessed valuation of the town's property is $86,000,000. How much is the tax rate per $100?

Solution   Set up the format as shown below and substitute the numbers given in the example:

MV
×AR   **Note:** Solving this problem does not require this information

=AV $86,000,000
×TR $\frac{TR}{\$100}$

= T $ 970,000

Using the information above, notice that the rate has been written as stated in the example (that is, the rate per $100). Rewriting the information to solve for the rate, we have:

$$AV \quad \times \quad TR = \quad T$$
$$\$86,000,00\cancel{0} \times \frac{TR}{\$10\cancel{0}} = \$970,000$$
$$\text{cancel}$$

$$TR = \frac{\$970000}{\$860000} = \$1.13 \quad \text{Tax Rate per \$100 of assessed valuation}$$

Example   A county in Georgia has collected $2 billion in taxes. The county tax rate is $20 per $1000 of assessed valuation. The assessment rate is 80%. Calculate the market value of the property.

Solution   Set up the format as shown below and substitute the numbers given in the example:

MV	
×AR	80%
=AV	
×TR	$\frac{\$20}{\$1000}$
= T	$2,000,000,000

Before any calculations, the problem should be set up as above. Thus, the assessed valuation has to be calculated before we can calculate the market value. The correct procedure follows:

$$AV \times TR = T$$

$$AV \times \frac{\$20}{\$1000} = \$2,000,000,000$$

$$AV = \frac{\$2,000,000,000}{\frac{\$20}{\$1000}} \quad \text{or} \quad \frac{\$2,000,000,000}{.02}$$

$$AV = \$2,000,000,000 \times \frac{\$1000}{\$20}$$

$$AV = \$100,000,000,000$$

The format now looks this way:

MV	
×AR	80%
=AV	$100,000,000,000
×TR	
	$\frac{\$20}{\$1000}$ or .02
= T	$ 2,000,000,000

We can now solve for the MV as follows:

$$MV \times AR = AV$$

$$MV \times 80\% = \$100,000,000,000$$

$$MV = \frac{\$100,000,000,000}{80\%}$$

$$MV = \frac{\$100,000,000,000}{.8}$$

$$MV = \$125,000,000,000 \text{ or } \$125 \text{ billion}$$

Assignment 8-3

1. Cornelius owns a house with an assessed valuation of $84,000. If the tax rate is $3.80 per $100, how much tax will Cornelius pay?

2. Mazie owns an old house with a market value of $20,000. The city assessed such property at 65% of market value. If the tax rate is $2.80 per $100, how much tax will she pay?

3. Bruce pays $.27 per $100 county tax and $21.40 per $1000 school tax. His mansion is assessed at $2,160,000. How much are his combined county and school taxes?

4.   Gotham City needs $8.6 million. The assessed value of property is $360 million. What is the tax rate per $100?

.5.   The market value of property in Atlantis is $24 billion. For tax purposes, property is assessed at 60% of its market value. If the tax to be raised is $52 million, what will the tax rate per $100 need to be?

6.   The city of Mudville raised $14 million with a tax rate of $.47 per $100 valuation. The assessment rate is 60%. What is the market value of the property in Mudville? (Round off to the nearest $100,000.)

7.   Hazard County collected $2 million with a tax rate of $1.25 per $100 valuation. The assessment rate is 70%. What is the market value of the property in Hazard County? (Round off to the nearest $100,000.)

8.   Bob's house has a market value of $96,000. The county tax rate is $2.40 per $100 assessed valuation. The assessment rate is 65%. How much tax will Bob pay?

9.   The tax officials of Megopolis are told they will need to raise $120 million. The property to be taxed has a market value of $72 billion, and the assessment rate is 60%. What will the tax rate per $1000 be?

Insurance

Several types of insurance exist. When a business decides that the risk of loss is too great for it to assume, yet not so great that the risk should be avoided entirely, insurance companies are often sought as a means of shifting the risk. Insurance companies accept risks for others because they can spread the risk. It is unlikely, for example, that all of the thousands of homes an insurance company protects against the risk of fire will burn at one time.

The two types of insurance covered in this section are life insurance and fire insurance.

	Age	10-Year Term	Straight Life	20-Payment Life	Endowment
Table 8-2	20	$ 8.44	$16.06	$26.30	$47.08
Annual	21	8.66	16.44	26.78	47.15
Premium	22	8.87	16.83	27.28	47.28
Rates	23	9.09	17.23	27.78	47.31
per $1000	24	9.31	17.66	28.31	47.40
	25	9.53	18.10	28.85	47.49
	26	9.75	18.57	29.40	47.60
	27	9.97	19.06	29.98	47.71
	28	10.18	19.57	30.57	47.84
	29	10.51	20.10	31.18	47.98
	30	10.73	20.67	31.82	48.14
	31	11.08	21.33	32.52	48.35
	32	11.43	21.98	33.23	48.56
	33	11.78	22.64	33.93	48.78
	34	12.12	23.29	34.64	48.99
	35	12.47	23.95	35.34	49.20
	36	12.95	24.80	36.19	49.54
	37	13.43	25.65	37.04	49.89
	38	13.91	26.49	37.90	50.23
	39	14.39	27.34	38.75	50.58
	40	14.87	28.19	39.60	50.92
	41	15.48	29.29	40.63	51.44
	42	16.09	30.39	41.66	51.97
	43	16.71	31.48	42.69	42.49
	44	17.32	32.58	43.72	53.02
	45	17.93	33.68	44.75	53.54
	46		35.11	46.04	54.35
	47		36.55	47.32	55.16
	48		37.98	48.61	55.96
	49		39.42	49.89	56.77
	50		40.85	51.18	57.58

Semiannual rate = .51 times annual
Quarterly rate = .26 times annual
Monthly rate = .0875 times annual

These are rates for males. To find rates for females, use 3 years younger than actual age.

Life Insurance

Types of Policies

Straight life insurance requires the payment of a premium each year until the insured person dies, at which time the beneficiary collects the stated value of the policy. This type of policy has a cash surrender value, which can be collected if the insured person decides to stop paying premiums.

Term insurance protects the purchaser for a specified period of time. At the end of that time, the policy expires and can be converted to another type of policy, but at a higher rate.

Limited-payment life insurance requires the insured person to make payments for a limited number of years, after which the policy is paid up and no further premiums are required. The policy has a cash surrender value.

Endowment insurance policies accumulate money, and the face value of such a policy will be paid to the insured person at the end of a specified amount of time. If the insured person dies before the policy matures, a beneficiary collects the face value of the policy.

Calculating the Premium

Tables 8-2 and 8-3 are to be used for solving problems in this unit. Table 8-2 shows partial premium rates per $1000 of insurance for some types of life insurance policies.

Example   John is 25 years old. Determine the premium he would have to pay for a $12,000 straight life policy.

Solution   From Table 8-2, for a man age 25, straight life insurance costs $18.10 per $1000. There are 12 thousands in $12,000:

$$\begin{array}{r} \$18.10 \\ \times \quad 12 \\ \hline \$217.20 \end{array}$$

Assignment 8-4

1.   John Scarborough, who is 22 years old, wishes to buy $100,000 of life insurance. How much more per year will it cost him to buy 20-payment life instead of straight life?

2.   Mary Small, who is 30 years old, is going to buy $25,000 of 20-payment life insurance. How much will it cost her per year? How much more will it cost her per year to pay quarterly?

3.   Joseph Mannix is 40 years old. He wishes to purchase an $80,000 20-payment life policy. What is the annual premium? What is the quarterly premium?

4.   Lulu Miller is 29 years old. She is going to buy $40,000 worth of straight life insurance. How much will each payment be if she pays monthly?

Cash Surrender Value or Cash Value for Borrowing
The cash surrender value is what the insured receives upon cashing in the policy. At other times a person might need to know the cash value to use an insurance policy for borrowing purposes.

Example   Pete wishes to surrender his $16,000 straight life policy which he purchased when he was 20 years old and has held for 10 years. How much will be he receive?

Solution   Using Table 8-3, it is determined that the cash surrender value per $1000 for straight life is $87. Pete's policy is for $16,000. There are 16 thousands in $16,000.

$$\begin{array}{r} \$87 \\ \times \quad 16 \\ \hline \$1392 \end{array}$$

Table 8-3
Cash Values
for Selected
Types of Life
Insurance

Cash Values per $1,000—Male and Female
Straight Life
End of Year

Age	1	2	3	5	10	15	20
20			3	27	87	158	230
25			8	34	106	187	277
30			15	45	127	218	318
35		5	22	57	151	253	361
40		11	30	70	176	289	406
45		17	39	85	204	376	451
50		23	49	101	233	365	494
55	1	31	60	118	263	401	533
60	5	38	71	136	291	433	570

Cash Values per $1,000—Male and Female
20 Payment Life
End of Year

Age	1	2	3	5	10	15	20
20		10	29	70	183	315	468
25		14	35	81	206	351	518
30		18	42	93	231	390	571
35		24	50	106	257	429	625
40		29	58	118	282	467	679
45	3	34	66	131	307	503	731
50	5	39	73	143	329	534	779
55	8	44	80	154	347	559	822
60	10	49	87	164	360	573	860

Cash Values per $1,000—Male and Female
Endowment at 65
End of Year

Age	1	2	3	5	10	15	20
20			14	44	127	223	333
25		5	22	58	157	270	399
30		12	33	76	195	329	481
35		21	47	99	243	405	590
40	2	33	65	130	308	510	746
45	11	51	91	175	405	672	1000
50	25	81	138	257	591	1000	
55	53	143	235	430	1000		

Assignment 8-5

1. What is the cash surrender value on a 20-payment life policy which was purchased at age 25 and is surrendered for cash in 10 years? Face value of the policy is $14,000.

2. Jerry bought an $18,000 endowment at 65 policy when he was 20 years old. He is now 35 years old. What is the cash surrender value of the policy?

3. Freddie owns two life insurance policies. He purchased a $100,000 straight life policy when he was 20 years old and an endowment at 65 policy for $100,000 when he was 30. He is now 35 years old. How much total cash can he receive if he surrenders both policies now?

4. Donna bought two $10,000 policies 20 years ago when she was 20 years old. One is a straight life policy and the other is a 20-payment life policy. How much more is the 20-payment life policy now worth than the straight life policy?

Fire Insurance

Insurance is an agreement, made legal by the signing of a contract, in which a company guarantees to pay for losses incurred by the insured. In return for this guarantee, the insured pays premiums to the insurance company. The type of insurance under consideration here is payment for loss incurred as a result of fire.

Premiums

The insurance rates are usually stated in terms of a dollar value per $100 of insurance. These rates are multiplied by the amount to be insured to find the premium.

Example   The rate for insuring a brick building is $.345 per $100. Determine the annual premium for $25,000 of insurance.

Solution   Determine how many hundreds are in $25,000:

$25,000 ÷ 100 = 250$

Multiply by the rate per $100:

$250 × \$.345 = \$86.25$ annual premium

Assignment 8-6

1. What is the annual premium for a $48,000 fire insurance policy if the rate is $.562 per $100?

2. The rate of fire insurance on a frame building is $.784 per $100. How much will the annual premium be if the building is insured for $120,000?

3. The rate for fire insurance on a new building is $.465 per $100. The new building is worth $1,000,000. How much will the annual premium be?

4. The rate of fire insurance on an old building is $1.72 per $100. How much will the annual premium be to insure it for $200,000?

Fire Insurance Premiums for More Than 1 Year

It is less expensive to insure a building if the insured will pay premiums in advance for a period longer than 1 year. The rates for longer terms are

1 year	100% of yearly premiums
2 years	185% of yearly premiums
3 years	270% of yearly premiums
4 years	355% of yearly premiums
5 years	440% of yearly premiums

Example   The rate of fire insurance for a brick building is $.47 per $100. Calculate the premium to insure the building for $20,000 for 1, 2, 3, 4 and 5 years.

Solution $\dfrac{\$20,000}{100} = 200$ hundreds

$200 \times \$.47 = \$94$	annual premium
$\$94 \times 185\% = \$94 \times 1.85 = \$173.90$	premium for 2 years
$\$94 \times 270\% = \$94 \times 2.7 = \$253.80$	premium for 3 years
$\$94 \times 355\% = \$94 \times 3.55 = \$333.70$	premium for 4 years
$\$94 \times 440\% = \$94 \times 4.4 = \$413.60$	premium for 5 years

Assignment 8-7

1. The fire insurance rate for a run-down building on the old side of a city is $.96 per $100. How much will the premiums be to insure the building for $125,000 for

    a. 1 year   **b.** 2 years

    c. 3 years   **d.** 4 years

    e. 5 years

2. The fire insurance rate for a new building built of brick and steel and having an automatic sprinkler system is $.27 per $100. How much will the premium be to insure the building for $125,000 for

    a. 1 year   **b.** 2 years

    c. 3 years   **d.** 4 years

    e. 5 years

3. The fire insurance for a building in a part of town known for arson is $1.82 per $100. How much will an owner have to pay to insure a dilipidated building for $1,000,000 for 4 years?

4. The fire insurance rate in the expensive Ridgelea area across the street from a fire station is $.18 per $100. How much will it cost Mr. Schnob to insure his house for $300,000 if he pays his premium every 5 years?

Fire Insurance Premiums in Cases of Cancellation by the Insured Party

Short-term rate tables are provided by insurance companies for calculating rates for fire insurance covering less than 1 year. The same tables cover the amount of premiums the insurance company has earned in case the policy is canceled by the insured party. Table 8-4 is for this purpose. Refunds can be determined by using the table as follows:

1. Calculate the exact number of days the policy has been in effect.
2. Find the number of days in the first column on the left of the table.
3. Move across the table to the correct amount of time indicated on the policy—that is, 1 year, 2 years, 3 years, 4 years, 5 years.
4. At the junction of the number of days and the term of the policy is a number which indicates the percent of the premium the insurance company has earned.
5. Multiply the percent of the premium the insurance company has earned by the amount of premium paid to find the amount of the premium the insurance company has earned.
6. Subtract the amount of the premium earned by the insurance company from the total premium paid to determine the amount of the refund.

Example The Remington Company insured its office building for 2 years for a premium of $1725. The term of the policy was from June 8, 1987, (inception) to June 8, 1989, (expiration). On September 20, 1987, the Remington Company canceled the policy. Determine the amount of refund due.

Solution 1. Calculate the exact number of days the policy has been in effect:

$$
\begin{array}{ll}
\text{June} & 30 \text{ days} \\
& \underline{-8} \\
& 22 \text{ days in June} \\
& 31 \text{ days in July} \\
& 31 \text{ days in August} \\
& \underline{20} \text{ days in September} \\
& 104 \text{ days the policy was in effect}
\end{array}
$$

2. Find the number of days in the first column on the left of Table 8-4 (103-105 days).
3. Move across the table to the correct amount of time indicated on the policy (2 years).
4. At the junction of 103-105 days and 2 years is the number 21.1 which is the percent of premium the insurance company has earned.
5. Multiply the percent of the premium the insurance company has earned by the amount of the premium:

$21.1\% \times \$1725 = .211 \times \$1725 = \$363.98$ amount of the premium the insurance company has earned

6. Subtract the amount of the premium the insurance company has earned from the total premium:

$\$1725 - \$363.98 = \$1361.02$ amount of the refund

Table 8-4
Fire
Insurance

Cancellation or Short Rate Table Showing Percent of Premium Earned

Policy in Force	1 Yr.	2 Yrs.	3 Yrs.	Policy in Force	1 Yr.	2 Yrs.	3 Yrs.
Days	Percent of Premium Earned			Days	Percent of Premium Earned		
1	5	2.7	1.9	161-164	55	29.7	20.4
2	6	3.2	2.2	165-167	56	30.3	20.7
3-4	7	3.8	2.6	168-171	57	30.8	21.1
5-6	8	4.3	3.	172-175	58	31.4	21.5
7-8	9	4.9	3.3	176-178	59	31.9	21.9
9-10	10	5.4	3.7	179-182	60	32.4	22.2
11-12	11	5.9	4.1	183-187	61	33.	22.6
13-14	12	6.5	4.4	188-191	62	33.5	23.
15-16	13	7.0	4.8	192-196	63	34.1	23.3
17-18	14	7.6	5.2	197-200	64	34.6	23.7
19-20	15	8.1	5.6	201-205	65	35.1	24.1
21-22	16	8.6	5.9	206-209	66	35.7	24.4
23-25	17	9.2	6.3	210-214	67	36.2	24.8
26-29	18	9.7	6.7	215-218	68	36.8	25.2
30-32	19	10.3	7.	219-223	69	37.3	25.6
33-36	20	10.8	7.4	224-228	70	37.8	25.9
37-40	21	11.4	7.8	229-232	71	38.4	26.3
41-43	22	11.9	8.1	233-237	72	38.9	26.7
44-47	23	12.4	8.5	238-241	73	39.5	27.
48-51	24	13.	8.9	242-246	74	40.	27.4
52-54	25	13.5	9.3	247-250	75	40.5	27.8
55-58	26	14.1	9.6	251-255	76	41.1	28.1
59-62	27	14.6	10.	256-260	77	41.6	28.5
63-65	28	15.1	10.4	261-264	78	42.2	28.9
66-69	29	15.7	10.7	265-269	79	42.7	29.3
70-73	30	16.2	11.1	270-273	80	43.2	29.6
74-76	31	16.8	11.5	274-278	81	43.8	30.
77-80	32	17.3	11.9	279-282	82	44.3	30.4
81-83	33	17.8	12.2	283-287	83	44.9	30.7
84-87	34	18.4	12.6	288-291	84	45.4	31.1
88-91	35	18.9	13.	292-296	85	45.9	31.5
92-94	36	19.5	13.3	297-301	86	46.5	31.9
95-98	37	20.	13.7	302-305	87	47.	32.2
99-102	38	20.5	14.1	306-310	88	47.6	32.6
103-105	39	21.1	14.4	311-314	89	48.1	33.
106-109	40	21.6	14.8	315-319	90	48.6	33.3
110-113	41	22.2	15.2	320-323	91	49.2	33.7
114-116	42	22.7	15.6	324-328	92	49.7	34.1
117-120	43	23.2	15.9	329-332	93	50.3	34.4
121-124	44	23.8	16.3	333-337	94	50.8	34.8
125-127	45	24.3	16.7	338-342	95	51.4	35.2
128-131	46	24.9	17.	343-346	96	51.9	35.6
132-135	47	25.4	17.4	347-351	97	52.4	35.9
136-138	48	25.9	17.8	352-355	98	53.	36.3
139-142	49	26.5	18.1	356-360	99	53.5	36.7
143-146	50	27.	18.5	361-365	100	54.1	37.
147-149	51	27.6	18.9				
150-153	52	28.1	19.3				
154-156	53	28.6	19.6				
157-160	54	29.2	20.				

Assignment 8-8

1. A building was insured for a premium of $150 for 3 years. The policy was purchased on January 9, 1987. The policy was canceled on May 18, 1987. Determine the amount of refund due.

2. A building insured at the rate of $.48 per $100 is insured for $280,000. The owner bought a 3-year policy on May 2, 1986. On March 10, 1987, the owner canceled the policy. Determine the amount of refund due.

3. A building is insured for $240,000 at the rate of $.76 per $100. The policy is for 2 years. If the owner bought the policy on January 6, 1986, and cancelled it on January 4, 1987, how much refund is due?

4. A building is insured at the rate of $1.52 per $100 for 2 years. The policy is for $48,000. The policy was bought February 4, 1986 and cancelled February 2, 1987. How much is the refund?

Co-insurance

Most fire insurance policies for businesses contain a *co-insurance clause*. A *co-insurance* clause is a statement that requires the insured party to carry coverage of up to a specified percentage of the total value of property, but not more. Insurance companies rarely will insure buildings for 100% of their total worth because to do so would encourage arson by owners of unwanted real estate. By limiting an insurance company's liability, the owners are encouraged to take better care of their property.

The specified percentage is usually 80%. For example, a fire insurance policy containing an 80% co-insurance clause on a building worth $10,000 would require that the building be insured for $8000 ($10,000 × 80% = $8000). If the property was insured for less than $8000 (for example, $7000) and a loss was incurred, the insurance company would not pay the full amount of the loss. The insurance company, would prorate the loss on the basis of $\frac{7000}{8000} = \frac{7}{8}$ of the amount of the actual loss. Therefore, if a fire caused $5000 damage, the insurance company would pay $4375 ($\frac{7}{8}$ × $5000). The insurance company will not, of course, pay more than the face value of the insurance policy.

Example   A building worth $40,000 was insured for $24,000 under a policy containing an 80% co-insurance clause. A fire caused damages of $20,000. How much will the insurance company pay?

Solution   insurance company liability = loss $\times \dfrac{\text{amount of policy}}{80\% \text{ of value}}$

liability = $20,000 $\times \dfrac{\$24,000}{80\% \times \$40,000}$

liability = $20,000 $\times \dfrac{\$24,000}{\$32,000}$

liability = $20,000 $\times \dfrac{3}{4}$

liability = $15,000

Assignment 8-9

1. A building worth $54,000 is insured under a policy containing an 80% co-insurance clause for $37,800. A fire caused damages of $21,600. How much will the insurance company pay?

2. A building worth $240,000 is insured for $150,000. The policy contains an 80% co-insurance clause. If the building has a $100,000 fire loss, how much will the insurance company's liability be?

3. An office building worth $60,000 has been insured for $50,000 under a policy containing an 80% co-insurance clause. The building was completely destroyed by fire. How much will the insurance company pay?

4. An apartment house valued at $56,000 was insured for $44,800 under a policy containing an 80% co-insurance clause. What is the insurance company's share in the event a fire causes $17,500 damage?

Chapter 8   Self-Testing Exercises

1. Prepare a loan repayment schedule for the first three payments for a mortgage of $85,000 at 11% for 30 years.

2.   Jeannie's house has a market value of $70,000. The city-county tax authorities levy a tax of $.80 per $100 assessed valuation. The assessment rate is 75%. How much tax will Jeannie have to pay?

3.   Beeville needs $14 million to operate the city next year. Market value of all taxable property is $1.2 billion. The assessment rate is 75%. How much will the tax rate need to be per $100?

4.   The tax rate in Cleeborne is $.75 per $100 and returns the city $3 million each year. If the assessment rate is 60%, how much is the market value of the property in Cleeborne?

5.   The fire insurance rate for a building is $.48 per $100. How much will the premium be to insure the building for $62,500 for 1 year, 2 years, and 3 years?

6.   A building is insured for $120,000 at the rate of $.38 per $100. The policy is for 2 years. If the owner bought the policy on March 10, 1987 and canceled it on July 28, 1987, how much refund was due?

7.   A building worth $80,000 was insured for $48,000 under a policy containing an 80% co-insurance clause. A fire caused damages of $40,000. How much will the insurance company pay?

8.   Herman is 30 years old. He is going to buy $25,000 of 20-payment life insurance. How much will it cost him per year? How much more will it cost per year to pay quarterly?

9.   Sarah is interested in purchasing a $10,000 straight life insurance policy. If she is 23 years old, what will her premiums be if paid quarterly?

10. Sam wished to cash in a $15,000 endowment-at-65 insurance policy he purchased when he was 35. If he is presently 50 years old, what is the cash surrender value?

11. John is deciding between two different insurance policies: straight life and 20-payment life. If he purchases a $10,500 policy and pays monthly, what is the premium difference at age 26?

12. Tony wants to buy $50,000 of life insurance. He is 25 years old. How much will an endowment policy cost him monthly?

13. Rebecca is trying to decide between types of insurance policies. She is 28 years old and wants to purchase a $60,000 policy. What would be the difference in the cost of a monthly payment for an endowment policy and a 10-year term policy?

14. If Bill, who is 43 years old, buys a straight life policy instead of a 10-year term $100,000 policy, how much more will his quarterly payments be?

15. The tax on a building is $4987.50. The tax rate is $5.25 per $100 of assessed valuation. What is the assessed valued of the building?

16. The total market value of property in Bexar County is $20 billion. If property is assessed at 60% of its market value and the county needs $650,400,000 to carry out its programs, what is the tax rate per $1000?

17. Ms. Garcia owns a house that has an assessed value of $12,826. If the property tax rate is $7.24 per $100 valuation, how much tax will Ms. Garcia have to pay?

18. Mr. Maltese owns property accessed at $28,000. If he pays taxes of $1540, what is the tax rate per $1000?

19. The city of Lynchburg's proposed budget shows a deficit for the next fiscal year of $250,000. If the necessary increase in the tax rate is $.025 per $1000, what is the town's assessed valuation?

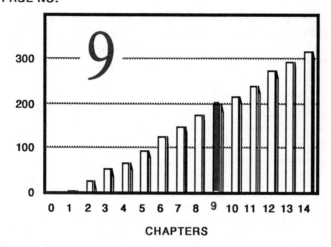

CHAPTERS

Payroll Applications

Student Objectives

Upon completion of this chapter the student should be able to

1. **Calculate** *an employee's gross earnings.*
2. **Calculate** *an employee's net earnings.*
3. **Define, illustrate,** *or* **use**

social security	*federal income tax*
FICA	*overtime*
hourly wage	*commission*
piecework	

Remuneration

For reasons of employee morale and for legal reasons, it is essential that a business keep accurate and complete payroll records. Most businesses keep records that show amounts and dates of earnings subject to payroll taxes; names, addresses, and jobs of employees; periods of employment; social security numbers; amounts of income; and payroll taxes withheld. Today, many large firms keep employee records with computers which can process data faster and usually more accurately than people can. It is still important, however, for people who expect to work in personnel to understand how remuneration is calculated.

Gross earnings is the term used to refer to earnings before any deductions are made. *Net earnings* refers to the amount left after all deductions (for example, withholding taxes, FICA, state payroll taxes, group insurance, payments to company retirement programs, union dues) are paid. Net earnings are commonly called *take-home pay.* Gross earnings must be calculated before net earnings can be calculated.

Gross Earnings

Gross earnings are usually stated in terms of *salary* and *wages.* Traditionally, the term *salary* has been applied to earnings paid on a monthly or annual basis, and *wages* has been applied to remuneration for workers who are paid for numbers of hours worked, weekly pay, or piecework. Today, the terms are often used interchangeably. Among economists, for example, the term *salary* seldom is used to refer to remuneration. Economists call all remuneration *wages*, regardless of how it is calculated.

Regardless of the name used, an employee's gross earnings are calculated on the basis of one of the following:

1. Amount of time on the job
2. Number of units produced (piecework)
3. Money value of goods and services sold (commission)
4. A combination of two or more of the above
5. The type or status of the position held by the employee in the organization

Amount of Time on the Job

The most common method of calculating earnings is on the basis of the amount of time on the job, usually called an *hourly wage.* Most workers who are paid on an hourly basis are covered by the Federal Fair Labor Standards Act (commonly called the Wage and Hour Law). According to the Wage and Hour Law, wages must be paid at a minimum rate of $1\frac{1}{2}$ times the regular hourly rate for all hours worked in excess of 40 hours per week. The formula for calculating gross earnings is

$$\text{gross earnings} = [\text{regular hours} + (1\tfrac{1}{2} \times \text{overtime hours})] \times \text{hourly rate}$$

Example

Mr. Schwartz worked 46 hours last week. His regular rate of pay is $8.40 per hour. How much were his gross earnings for the week?

Solution

$$\text{gross earnings} = [\text{regular hours} + (1\tfrac{1}{2} \times \text{overtime hours})] \times \text{hourly rate}$$

$$\text{gross earnings} = [40 + (1\tfrac{1}{2} \times 6)] \times \$8.40$$

$$\text{gross earnings} = (40 + 9) \times \$8.40$$

$$\text{gross earnings} = 49 \times \$8.40$$

$$\text{gross earnings} = \$411.60$$

Assignment 9-1

1. Mr. Stacey worked 52 hours last week. His regular wage is $9.36 per hour. What were his gross earnings for the week?

2. Miss Zapata is paid $7.74 per hour. Last week she worked 43 hours. What were her gross earnings for the week?

3. Complete the gross pay for the following employees:

	Hours worked						Total hours	Regular rate	Gross pay
	M	T	W	T	F	S			
a. Allen, Z	9	6	9	8	7	4	_____	$4.38	_____
b. Barskie, Y.	8	8	8	8	8	4	_____	5.08	_____
c. Cleveland, X.	6	8	5	4	3	2	_____	6.94	_____
d. Douglas, W.	9	10	8	10	9	0	_____	4.68	_____

Other Methods of Computing Overtime

In many cases today, overtime is calculated on a basis more favorable to the employee than the Wage and Hour Law prescribes. For example, it is not unusual for overtime to be defined as all time in excess of 8 hours per day or all time worked after 5, or for overtime to be paid at the rate of double or even triple time for holidays.

Example   Arthur's union contract calls for double time for all time worked in excess of 8 hours per day. Last week, Arthur worked the following hours: Monday 8, Tuesday 10, Wednesday 7, Thursday 9, Friday 4. His regular rate of pay is $9.36 per hour. How much are his gross earnings for the week?

Solution   overtime hours $10 - 8 = 2$ (Tuesday)
                              $9 - 8 = 1$ (Thursday)

hours at overtime rate $2 + 1 = 3$

hours at regular rate $8 + 8 + 7 + 8 + 4 = 35$

gross earnings = [regular hours + (2 × overtime hours)] × hourly rate

gross earnings = $[35 + (2 \times 3)] \times \$9.36$

gross earnings = $(35 + 6) \times \$9.36$

gross earnings = $41 \times \$9.36$

gross earnings = $383.76

Assignment 9-2

1. Herman's regular rate of pay is $8.38 per hour. Last week, he worked the following hours: Monday 9, Tuesday 7, Wednesday 10, Thursday 9, Friday 8. His union contract requires that he be paid at the rate of double time for overtime which is defined as all hours in excess of 8 hours per day. Compute his gross pay.

2. Matilda is paid $4.78 per hour. Last week, she worked 2 hours on Monday, 6 hours on Tuesday, 12 hours on Wednesday, 9 hours on Thursday, and took Friday off. Her employer pays her time and a half for overtime, and overtime is defined as all time in excess of 8 hours per day. Compute her gross pay.

3. Last week, Lawrence worked the following schedule: Monday 8 to 4, Tuesday 7 to 5, Wednesday 9 to 6, Thursday 8 to 5, Friday 7 to 12. His union contract defines overtime as all time before 8 in the morning and all time after 5 in the evening. He takes off 1 hour each day from 12 to 1 for which he is not paid. He is paid double time for all overtime, and his regular rate of pay is $9.54 per hour. Compute his gross earnings for the week

4. Al is a pipe fitter who is often called to work at irregular hours of the day. His union contract defines overtime as all time before 8 in the morning and all time after 5 in the afternoon. He is paid double time for overtime and triple time for weekends and holidays. According to his contract, if he is called out on a job, he cannot be paid for less than one half (4 hours) of a day of work. His regular rate of pay is $14.50 per hour. Last year, he worked the following schedule in one week during December.

Monday, Dec. 23	9 a.m. to 7 p.m.
Tuesday, Dec. 24	9 a.m. to 11 a.m.
Wednesday, Dec. 25	8 a.m. to 5 p.m.
Thursday, Dec. 26	8 a.m. to 5 p.m.
Friday, Dec. 27	8 a.m. to 6 p.m.
Saturday, Dec. 28	8 a.m. to 12 noon

    (**Note:** Dec. 25 is a holiday.)

    Al takes off 1 hour each day from 12 to 1 for lunch. He is not paid for that hour. Compute his gross pay for the week

5. Joan works on an assembly line in the Ford factory. Her regular rate of pay is $12 per hour. Her union contract defines all time in excess of 8 hours per day as overtime. She is paid double time for overtime and holidays, and time and a half when she works the graveyard shift. The graveyard shift begins at 11 p.m. and ends at 9 in the morning. She takes a 1-hour break at the middle of each shift. She is not paid for the break time. Last summer, she worked the following hours one week:

Monday, July 1	9 a.m. to 5 p.m.
Tuesday, July 2	8 p.m. to 5 a.m.
Wednesday, July 3	9 a.m. to 8 p.m.
Thursday, July 4	12 noon to 9 p.m.
Friday, July 5	9 a.m. to 5 p.m.

How much was her gross pay for the week?
(Note: July 4 is a holiday.)

6. Jacques is a lumberjack. He is paid $11.50 per hour for regular time and double time for weekends and holidays. For overtime, he is paid time and a half. He is not paid for the 1-hour break he takes halfway through the workday, and overtime is defined as all time in excess of 8 hours per day. His hours for one week last year were as follows:

Monday, Dec. 30	9 a.m. to 8 p.m.
Tuesday, Dec. 31	9 a.m. to 7 p.m.
Wednesday, Jan. 1	9 a.m. to 6 p.m.
Thursday, Jan. 2	8 a.m. to 8 p.m.
Friday, Jan. 3	10 a.m. to 7 p.m.
Saturday, Jan. 4	9 a.m. to 6 p.m.

How much was his gross pay for the week?
(Note: Jan. 1 is a holiday.)

Piecework

In a piecework system of remuneration, a worker is paid according to the number of units produced. The objective is to increase worker productivity, and it is commonly used in such industries as textiles and other shops that fabricate products.

Straight Piecework
One of the more desirable characteristics of straight piecework is the simplicity of calculating gross earnings. This is done by adding together the units produced in the pay period and multiplying the resulting sum by the piece rate.

Example Kate sews pockets on blue jeans at the rate of $.05 per pocket. One week she produced the following in 8 hours of work each day: Monday 485, Tuesday 643, Wednesday 521, Thursday 610, Friday 432. Compute Kate's gross earnings for the week.

The following formula is used to calculate gross earnings for piecework.

gross earnings = total number of units produced × rate per unit

gross earnings = (485 + 643 + 521 + 610 + 432) × $.05

gross earnings = 2691 × $.05

gross earnings = $134.55

Complete the gross earnings for the following employees:

		Production				Total units	Piece rate	Gross earnings
	M	T	W	T	F			
a. Adams	85	76	47	23	99	_____	$ .76	_____
b. Boskey	11	9	20	18	14	_____	2.14	_____
c. Carson	47	52	41	47	50	_____	.92	_____
d. Davida	1012	1121	969	898	1200	_____	.04	_____
e. Eyoto	146	235	117	198	201	_____	.32	_____
f. Franklin	40	35	65	23	40	_____	1.00	_____
g. Grekas	70	60	53	87	65	_____	.75	_____
h. Hortoni	12	9	10	8	7	_____	1.96	_____
i. Ingram	985	423	1125	462	1500	_____	.09	_____
j. Jackson	94	104	82	94	100	_____	.46	_____
k. Kimball	506	560	484	449	600	_____	.09	_____
l. Ling	438	705	351	598	603	_____	.11	_____

Differential Piecework
The intent of a differential piecework system is to encourage employees to produce more units during the pay period. In a differential piecework system, the rate per piece produced increases on a fixed scale as the number of pieces increases.

Example The differential piecework rates at the Alonzo sewing factory are

1-50 pieces @ $.25
51-100 pieces @ $.30
101 and over pieces @ $.35

Minnie produced 147 units of work last week. How much were her gross earnings?

Solution Determine how many units were produced at each of the different rates by subtracting from the total number of units produced:

Total pieces	147				
1-50 pieces	50	@ $.25	=	$12.50	
remaining pieces	97				
50-100 pieces	50	@ $.30	=	$15.00	
101 and over pieces	47	@ $.35	=	$16.45	
Total earnings				$43.95	

Assignment 9-4

1. Calculate gross earnings for the people listed below using the differential piecework rate at Lord and Bowden's factory:

    1-50 pieces @ $. 80
    51-100 pieces @ $1.00
    101 and over pieces @ $1.20

Worker	Units produced	Gross earnings
a. Anthony	180	_____
b. Bill	96	_____
c. Carla	48	_____
d. Doris	240	_____
e. Elmer	25	_____

2. The people listed below work in a gun factory. Use the following piecework rate schedule to calculate their gross earnings:

    1-20 pieces @ $1.50
    21-40 pieces @ $1.70
    41-60 pieces @ $1.90
    61 and over pieces @ $2.10

Worker	Pieces produced	Gross earnings
a. Adam	75	_____
b. Barbara	120	_____
c. Charley	36	_____
d. Dana	12	_____
e. Ernie	47	_____

3. The differential piecework rate at Arkansas Instrument Inc. is:

    1-500 pieces @ $ .10
    501-1000 pieces @ $ .15
    1001-1500 pieces @ $ .20
    1501 and over pieces @ $ .25

Worker	Pieces produced	Gross earnings
a. Alice	951	_____
b. Bob	1000	_____

c. Christy	1001	_____
d. Dick	1628	_____
e. Emma	2000	_____

Commissions

Remuneration on a commission basis is a method of determining gross earnings for people involved in sales. Two variations are discussed below.

Straight Commission

Straight commissions (P) are determined by multiplying the amount sold (B) by the commission rate (R). **Note:** If there is a salary plus commission, add the salary after calculating the commission to determine gross earnings.

Example   Don receives a straight commission of 6% on sales. During March, he sold $18,000 worth of goods. What were his gross earnings for the month?

Solution   gross earnings = amount sold × commission rate

$P = B \times R$

$P = \$18,000 \times 6\%$

$P = \$18,000 \times .06$

$P = \$1080$

Assignment 9-5

1. A salesman is paid a 7% commission on sales. Last month, he sold $25,000 worth of merchandise. How much were his gross earnings?

2. A sales clerk at Montgomery Ward is paid 9% commission on sales of appliances. Last week, he sold eight washing machines at $398 each. What were his gross earnings for the week?

3. Mildred is paid on a salary-plus-commission basis. She sold $8400 worth of tractor equipment last week, on which she is paid a commission of 2%. Her salary is $185 per week. Calculate her gross earnings for the week.

4. Clarence is paid $40 per week and 6% commission on sales. How much are his gross earnings if he sells $4200 of merchandise in 1 week?

5. Murray is paid 8% commission on sales and a salary of $120 per week. Last week, he sold $1600 worth of automobile parts. How much were his gross earnings?

6. Deborah is paid 6% commission on book sales. Last month, she sold 846 economics workbooks for $18.68 each. She is paid a salary of $600. What were her gross earnings last month?

Graduated Commissions

In a system of graduated commissions, a salesperson is paid at a higher commission rate as the amount of sales increases.

Example   Victor is a salesperson paid on the following system of graduated commissions over a week:

first $6000	@ 3%
$6001 to $16,000	@ 5%
$16,001 and over	@ 7%

What were his gross earnings in a week in which he sold $18,000 worth of merchandise?

Solution   first $6000 @ 3%
$6000 \times .03 = $180

next $10,000 @ 5%
$16,000 - $6,000 = $10,000
$10,000 \times .05 = $500

over $16,000 @ 7%
$18,000 - $16,000 = $2,000
$2000 \times .07 = $140

gross earnings = $180 + $500 + $140
gross earnings = $820

Assignment 9-6

1. Using the following graduated commission system, calculate the following gross earnings:

first $5000	@ 2%
$5001 to $11,000	@ 6%
$11,001 and over	@ 8%

	Salesperson	Amount sold	Gross earnings
a.	Arnold	$12,000	_____
b.	Ben	4,000	_____

    c. Clyde   8,000   _____

    d. Dan   11,000   _____

2. How much did each person earn using the following graduated commission system:

     first $3000   @ 4%
     $3001 to $6000   @ 6%
     $6001 to $11,000   @ 8%
     $11,001 and over   @10%

Salesperson	Amount sold	Gross earnings
a. Anne	$14,500	_____
b. Beth	2000	_____
c. Carole	7400	_____
d. Dora	4600	_____

3. The Wilson Company pays its salespeople by the following graduated commission system:

     first $5000   @ 3%
     $5001 to $13,000   @ 5%
     $13,001 to $22,000   @ 7%
     $22,001 and over   @ 8%

Calculate the earnings for Adolf who had sales of $4500, and Chris who had sales of $15,600.

Net Earnings

Very few workers receive the full amount of their gross pay at the end of a pay period. Employers are required by law to withhold a specified amount for Social Security and income taxes from a worker's gross pay. In addition to Social Security and income taxes, employers often make other deductions, such as for company retirement programs, union dues, medical insurance, or life insurance. The amount of money left after all deductions are made is *net earnings* or *take-home pay*.

Social Security (Employee Contribution)

Congress passed the Social Security Act in 1935. The original purpose of the act was to provide minimum benefits for people who are past their productive employment age and have no means of support. Since its modest beginnings, Social Security has grown into a federally supported retirement system with many other benefits for the support of Americans who are not in a position to support themselves effectively. The major benefits received from Social Security are

1. *Retirement benefits.* Monthly payments made to workers upon retirement.
2. *Disability benefits.* Monthly payments made to workers who are unable to work because of physical or mental disability.
3. *Survivor benefits.* Burial payments and monthly benefits made to the family of the deceased worker.
4. *Medical care for older citizens.*

The Social Security law provides for additional increases in the tax rate and the wage base in future years in order to keep the Social Security system on a sound financial footing.

The Social Security contribution is usually called *FICA* (meaning Federal Insurance Contributions Act) on payroll forms. The FICA tax is calculated differently from all other taxes that Americans pay. There is a standard rate, which applies to all incomes subject to the tax, and a maximum amount of income on which the tax is levied. The rate and base are subject to change by act of Congress, so that the rate 7.15%, and the base $42,000, the figures used to work the problems in this book, may not be the current rate and maximum income on which the tax is levied. However, the principle is always the same, regardless of the figures applied.

The employer is legally required to withhold a specified amount from an employee's gross earnings for FICA. The employer is also required to pay an amount equal to the tax on the employee.

Example

Dave's gross earnings for last week were $350. His earnings from January 1 to the beginning of last week were $12,500. Compute his FICA tax.

Solution

$12,500
+   350
=$12,850   (less than $42,000)

The entire income is therefore subject to the tax:

$350.00   earnings subject to FICA last week
×   .0715   rate of FICA tax
$25.03   FICA tax for the week

Example

Edward's gross pay for last week was $900. His earnings from January 1 to the beginning of last week were $41,800. Compute his FICA tax.

Solution

Since last week's earnings added to the previous earnings for the year are more than $42,000 (the maximum taxable income), only part of that income is subject to the tax. The amount subject to the tax can be calculated as follows:

$42,000   maximum earnings subject to FICA in 1 year
−41,800   earnings from January 1 to beginning of last week
$200   earnings subject to FICA last week
× .0715   rate of FICA tax
$14.30   FICA tax for last week

Assignment 9-7

1. Last week, Mr. Bimble earned $820. His gross earnings from January 1 to the beginning of the week were $41,900. Compute his FICA tax for the week.

2. Compute the amount of FICA tax due on the monthly earnings of $1200 if the employee earned $41,300 in the period from January 1 to the beginning of the month.

3. Fred earned $20,000 from January 1 to the beginning of last week. Last week he earned $435. How much was Fred's FICA tax for the week?

4. Mary earned $12,027.48 from January 1 to the beginning of last week. Last week, she earned $327.84. How much FICA tax did she pay last week?

Federal Income Tax Withholding

For most workers, the largest deduction made from their gross earnings is the federal income tax. Employers are required by law to withhold the tax from earnings of employees and forward it to the Internal Revenue Service. The amount of tax withheld is based on the amount of earnings and the number of allowances claimed by the employee.

Generally, the employee is allowed to claim one allowance for each person who depends on the income. However, the number of allowances claimed may be adjusted by: nonwage income on which tax has not been withheld, large amounts of itemized deductions, and more than one wage earned in the family. Taxpayers determine the number of allowances by following the instructions for the W-4 form.

After the taxpayer has determined the number of allowances to be claimed, the information is made available to the employer on a W-4 form. The employer determines the amount to subtract from the employee's gross earnings before calculating the tax by using the *Allowance Table* (Table 9-1). After the allowances have been made, the withholding tax is determined by using the Percentage Withholding Table (Table 9-2). Final answers are rounded to the nearest whole dollar as is allowed by the Internal Revenue Service.

All figures in these tables were correct at the time of publication of this book, but are subject to change by an act of Congress.

Example Bob's gross pay for the week was $350. He is single and claimed one personal allowance on his W-4 form. How much should be withheld?

Solution

Gross weekly wage	$350.00
Less allowances (weekly payroll period—one allowance)	36.54
Amount subject to withholding	$313.46

Withholding tax on $313.46 from Table 9-2 for a single person on weekly payroll falls between $47-$335, thus:

Tax on first $47.00	$ 3.85
Tax on remaining $266.46 ($313.46 − $47 = $266.46) @ 15%	39.97
	$43.82
Weekly withholding tax (rounded)	$44.00

Table 9-1 Allowance Table

Number of Withholding Allowances	Weekly	Biweekly	Semi-monthly	Monthly	Quarterly	Semi-annual	Annual	Daily or Misc.
0	$ 0	$ 0	$ 0	$ 0	$ 0	$ 0	$ 0	$ 0
1	36.54	73.08	79.17	158.33	475.00	950.00	1,900.00	7.31
2	73.08	146.16	158.34	316.66	950.00	1,900.00	3,800.00	14.62
3	109.62	219.24	237.51	474.99	1,425.00	2,850.00	5,700.00	21.93
4	146.16	292.32	316.68	633.32	1,900.00	3,800.00	7,600.00	29.24
5	182.70	365.40	395.85	791.65	2,375.00	4,750.00	9,500.00	36.55
6	219.24	438.48	475.02	949.98	2,850.00	5,700.00	11,400.00	43.86
7	255.78	511.56	554.19	1,108.31	3,325.00	6,650.00	13,300.00	51.17
8	292.32	584.64	633.36	1,266.64	3,800.00	7,600.00	15,200.00	58.48
9	328.86	657.72	712.53	1,424.97	4,275.00	8,550.00	17,100.00	65.79
10	365.40	730.80	791.70	1,583.30	4,750.00	9,500.00	19,000.00	73.10

Table 9-2
Percentage
Withholding
Table

Table 1—If the Payroll Period With Respect to an Employee is Weekly

(a) SINGLE person—including head of household:

If the amount of wages is:		The amount of income tax to be withheld shall be:	
Not over $12 0			
Over—	*But not over—*		*of excess over—*
$12	—$47	11%	—$12
$47	—$335	$3.85 plus 15%	—$47
$335	—$532	$47.05 plus 28%	—$335
$532	—$1,051	$102.21 plus 35%	—$532
$1,051	....	$283.86 plus 38.5%	—$1,051

(b) MARRIED person—:

If the amount of wages is:		The amount of income tax to be withheld shall be:	
Not over $36 0			
Over—	*But not over—*		*of excess over—*
$36	—$93	11%	—$36
$93	—$574	$6.27 plus 15%	—$93
$574	—$901	$78.42 plus 28%	—$574
$901	—$1,767	$169.98 plus 35%	—$901
$1,767	....	$473.08 plus 38.5%	—$1,767

Table 2—If the Payroll Period With Respect to an Employee is Biweekly

(a) SINGLE person—including head of household:

If the amount of wages is:		The amount of income tax to be withheld shall be:	
Not over $25 0			
Over—	*But not over—*		*of excess over—*
$25	—$94	11%	—$25
$94	—$671	$7.59 plus 15%	—$94
$671	—$1,063	$94.14 plus 28%	—$671
$1,063	—$2,102	$203.90 plus 35%	—$1,063
$2,102	....	$567.55 plus 38.5%	—$2,102

(b) MARRIED person:

If the amount of wages is:		The amount of income tax to be withheld shall be:	
Not over $72 0			
Over—	*But not over—*		*of excess over—*
$72	—$187	11%	—$72
$187	—$1,148	$12.65 plus 15%	—$187
$1,148	—$1,802	$156.80 plus 28%	—$1,148
$1,802	—$3,533	$339.92 plus 35%	—$1,802
$3,533	....	$945.77 plus 38.5%	—$3,533

Table 3—If the Payroll Period With Respect to an Employee is Semimonthly

(a) SINGLE person—including head of household:

If the amount of wages is:		The amount of income tax to be withheld shall be:	
Not over $27 0			
Over—	*But not over—*		*of excess over—*
$27	—$102	11%	—$27
$102	—$727	$8.25 plus 15%	—$102
$727	—$1,152	$102.00 plus 28%	—$727
$1,152	—$2,277	$221.00 plus 35%	—$1,152
$2,277	....	$614.75 plus 38.5%	—$2,277

(b) MARRIED person—:

If the amount of wages is:		The amount of income tax to be withheld shall be:	
Not over $78 0			
Over—	*But not over—*		*of excess over—*
$78	—$203	11%	—$78
$203	—$1,244	$13.75 plus 15%	—$203
$1,244	—$1,953	$169.90 plus 28%	—$1,244
$1,953	—$3,828	$368.42 plus 35%	—$1,953
$3,828	....	$1,024.67 plus 38.5%	—$3,828

Table 4—If the Payroll Period With Respect to an Employee is Monthly

(a) SINGLE person—including head of household:

If the amount of wages is:		The amount of income tax to be withheld shall be:	
Not over $53 0			
Over—	*But not over—*		*of excess over—*
$53	—$203	11%	—$53
$203	—$1,453	$16.50 plus 15%	—$203
$1,453	—$2,303	$204.00 plus 28%	—$1,453
$2,303	—$4,553	$442.00 plus 35%	—$2,303
$4,553	....	$1,229.50 plus 38.5%	—$4,553

(b) MARRIED person:

If the amount of wages is:		The amount of income tax to be withheld shall be:	
Not over $155 0			
Over—	*But not over—*		*of excess over—*
$155	—$405	11%	—$155
$405	—$2,488	$27.50 plus 15%	—$405
$2,488	—$3,905	$339.95 plus 28%	—$2,488
$3,905	—$7,655	$736.71 plus 35%	—$3,905
$7,655	....	$2,049.21 plus 38.5%	—$7,655

Assignment 9-8

1. George earned $472 last week. He claims his wife, their two children, and himself as allowances. His wife does not work outside the home. How much was withheld from his wages last week for taxes?

2. Gail's income was $8500 last month. She is divorced and she supports her four children. She claims four allowances. How much should be withheld from her salary each month for taxes?

3. Carol is single and lives alone. Her gross income for the biweekly pay period was $460. She claims one allowance. How much is withheld each pay period for taxes?

4. Robert is married and has three children. He claims five allowances. His income for the month was $3163. How much tax should be withheld from his paycheck?

5. Jerry and Kit are married. He earned $325 last week and she earned $478. How much income tax was withheld if they claim two allowances?

Miscellaneous Deductions

State Payroll Taxes

Most of the states impose some kind of payroll tax. Every state that does impose a payroll tax uses a system of its own. In some states, it is a straight payroll tax of a certain percent of gross earnings less standard deductions for the number of exemptions claimed by that employee. In some states, the payroll tax is based entirely on the federal income tax. In states that use a formula of this type, the state payroll tax is calculated after the person's federal income tax is calculated. It is typically a percent of the federal income tax.

Because of the differences in methods of calculation, it is not practical to show all the methods used in various states in this book. Consequently, any problems requiring a deduction to be made for state payroll tax will include the amount of the tax so that no calculation by the student will be necessary.

Group Insurance

Many employees today buy life and medical insurance as a group rather than as individuals. The advantages of group insurance over individual insurance are lower rates and greater benefits. For purposes of showing such deductions, the amounts of insurance premiums will be given in problems in this book.

Payment to Company Retirement Programs
Many business firms organize their own retirement programs. Typically, taking part in a company retirement program is voluntary on the part of the employee. Such retirement programs are usually good investments for the employee since the company is likely to match all contributions made by employees. There are many variations of company retirement programs, but most of them deduct a flat percent of an employee's gross earnings.

Example   Howard's gross earnings for last month were $800. His company deducts 3% of gross earnings for the company retirement program. How much was deducted from Howard's gross earnings last month for the company retirement program?

Solution   retirement deduction = rate × gross earnings

retirement deduction = .03 × $800

retirement deduction = $24

Union Dues
In vocations where workers are represented by labor unions, the companies often withhold an amount from the worker's gross earnings to pay the worker's dues to the union. Union dues are usually a percent of the gross earnings of the worker.

Example   Jake works in a factory and is a member of the labor union. The union contract contains an agency shop clause. Jake's union dues are 2% of his gross earnings. How much were his union dues last week when he earned $260?

Solution   dues = rate × gross earnings

dues = .02 × $260

dues = $5.20

Assignment 9-9

1. Last month, Sam's gross earnings were $2276. His withholding tax was $388.80, and FICA was $162.73. The group medical insurance program costs $79.66 per month. The state payroll tax is $38.88. His union dues were 2% of gross earnings. Calculate Sam's net earnings.

2. Jane earns a gross weekly wage of $196 as a clerk in a department store. Of this amount, $29.40 is withheld for income tax, 7.15% for FICA, and $18 for group medical insurance. The state payroll tax is $12, and 3% of gross earnings is deducted for a company-sponsored retirement program. Calculate Jane's net earnings.

3. Frank's take-home pay for one month last year was $1792. He paid $408 in income taxes, $141.60 FICA taxes, $72 to the company retirement program, $74 for medical insurance, and a state payroll tax of $24. What were Frank's gross earnings?

4. Matilda is a worker in a sewing factory. Her take-home pay one week was $220. From this had been deducted $59 for income tax, $17.70 for FICA, $16 for medical insurance, and $6 union dues. Calculate Matilda's gross earnings.

Chapter 9   Self-Testing Exercises

1. Sally works in a pajama factory. She is paid for completed pajama tops according to the following differential piecework schedule:

1-100 pieces	@ $.45
101-150 pieces	@ $.50
151 and over pieces	@ $.55

   If Sally sewed 200 tops, how much was she paid?

2. Jan has earned $16,300 so far this year. If she earns $685 gross in the coming month, how much FICA tax will she owe?

3. Larry is a construction worker who is called to work at irregular hours. His union contract defines overtime as all time before 7 in the morning and all time after 6 in the evening. He is paid double time for all overtime and all weekends. He is paid triple time for all holidays. Larry takes off 30 minutes for lunch every day in which he works more than 4 hours, and he is not paid for the lunch break. Larry's regular hourly wage is $6.42 per hour. If Larry is called out on a job, he cannot be paid for less than a half day (4 hours). One week in July, he worked the following schedule:

Sunday, July 1	7:00 a.m. to 3:30 p.m.
Monday, July 2	6:30 a.m. to 3:30 p.m.
Tuesday, July 3	9:30 a.m. to 7:00 p.m.
Wednesday, July 4	8:00 a.m. to 11:30 a.m.
Thursday, July 5	7:30 a.m. to 4:00 p.m.
Friday, July 6	7:30 a.m. to 6:00 p.m.
Saturday, July 7	8:00 a.m. to 4:30 p.m.

   Calculate Larry's gross earnings.

   (Note: July 4 is a holiday.)

4. Joe worked 49 hours last week. His regular wage is $3.52 per hour. How much were his gross earnings?

5. Bill's gross earnings for one month were $1100. His earnings up to the beginning of the month were $12,800. His withholding tax was $192.20. The group medical insurance program costs $34.65 per month. The state payroll tax was $16.50. His union dues were 2% of his gross earnings. Calculate Bill's net earnings (**Note:** Remember to deduct FICA.)

6. Mervin's regular rate of pay is $4.25 per hour. Last week, he worked the following hours: Monday 7, Tuesday 9, Wednesday 10, Thursday 11, Friday 8. His company defines overtime as all time worked in excess of 8 hours per day, and it is calculated at the rate of 1½ times regular pay. How much were Mervin's gross earnings for the week?

7. Melinda works in a factory using the following differential piecework system of rates:

1-100 pieces	@ $.12
101-200 pieces	@ $.20
201-300 pieces	@ $.30
301 and over pieces	@ $.35

   One week she produced 428 pieces. How much were Melinda's gross earnings?

8. Calculate commissions for the sales representatives listed using this commission schedule:

0-$1000	2%
$1001-$2000	2.5%
$2001-$3000	3%
all over $3000	4%

Salesperson	Total sales	Commission
DeWitt	$3250	_____
Avilla	2700	_____
Samuel	4050	_____
Wicker	3000	_____

9. Becky is paid $450 per week as a pianist with a rock group. From this, $106 is deducted for withholding tax, 7.15% for FICA, $18 for group medical insurance, $8 for union dues, and $30 for state income tax. Calculate Becky's net pay.

10. Tony is a professional football player who is paid $9615.38 per week. The income tax on this amount would be $2692.31. FICA is 7.15%, medical insurance is $25, and union dues are $100. Since this is the first week of the year, Tony's earnings to date have been zero. Calculate Tony's net pay.

11. Todd earned $423 last week. He is single, lives alone, and claims two allowances. How much should be withheld each week for taxes?

12. Joe and Myrtle are married and have two dependent children. Joe earned $1300 last month. Myrtle does not work. How much will be withheld for taxes if they claims four alowances?

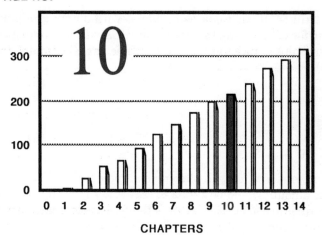

CHAPTERS

Accounting Applications

Student Objectives

Upon completion of this chapter, the student should be able to

1. Calculate yearly depreciation using the straight-line method.
2. Calculate yearly depreciation using the sum-of-the-years-digits method.
3. Calculate yearly depreciation using the units-of-production method.
4. Calculate yearly depreciation using the declining-balance method.
5. Calculate the value of inventory by the LIFO, FIFO, and weighted-average methods.
6. Reconcile a bank statement.
7. Define, illustrate, or *use*

expected life of an asset	depreciation
resale value	bank reconciliation
merchandise inventory	draft

Of all the functions of business, none could be of greater importance than accounting. Managers always need to know how well they are performing in the marketplace. Accounting provides the measurement and the communication of an organization's economic position according to standard accounting principles. A company's financial position is important to outsiders as well as to company officials and employees. The government, primarily the Internal Revenue Service and the Securities and Exchange Commission, and present or potential stockholders are also interested.

All employees of any business organization will be affected by, if not directly employed in, accounting. It is essential that any worker who wants to progress beyond the lowest level of an organization, or any present or potential investor in corporate stocks and/or bonds, understand some basic accounting principles.

This chapter deals with some of the important mathematical calculations and concepts in accounting.

Depreciation

Most business assets do not retain their original worth. Just as a car or clothing wears out or becomes less desirable because of style or technological changes, so, too, does some machinery, equipment, buildings, transportation facilities, furniture, fixtures, etc., of a business. Some assets may, however, increase or retain their value. They are, nevertheless, depreciated. Depreciation is, therefore, a process of allocating costs to periods of use. These assets are called *plant assets*. They are expenses to a business firm and reduce the amount of taxable income, but they do not reduce cash.

Current expenses, those that are expected to be incurred in 1 year or less, are claimed (written off) by the business. However, fixed assets are expected to last for more than 1 year. Therefore, the amount that can be written off in any year depends upon the *expected life* of the asset. The amount of expense write-off on fixed assets is called *depreciation*. Since no one really knows for sure how long an asset will be productive or how much money can be realized by selling or trading in the asset when it is no longer useful, the amount of depreciation taken is an estimate.

Depreciation is often accounted for differently for financial accounting and tax accounting purposes. Until recent tax law changes, financial accounting reflected accounting for tax purposes.

Depreciating for Financial Accounting
Several methods of calculating depreciation for financial accounting are used. Four of these will be discussed.

Straight-Line Method
The straight-line method of calculating depreciation is the easiest and the most commonly used. Three factors are used:

1. *Original cost* is the original amount paid for the asset plus the freight and installation costs if any were incurred.
2. *Resale value* (sometimes referred to as *salvage value, trade-in value, residual value,* or *scrap value*) is the estimated amount for which the asset can be sold at the end of its usable life.
3. *Usable life* is the estimated number of years the asset will remain in service.

The formula for determining the amount of yearly depreciation using the straight-line method is

$$\text{yearly depreciation} = \frac{\text{cost} - \text{resale value}}{\text{usable life}}$$

Example	What is the yearly depreciation expense for a $3500 planer that is expected to be in service for 5 years and have a resale value $500, using the straight-line method?

Solution

$$\text{yearly depreciation} = \frac{\text{cost} - \text{resale value}}{\text{usable life}}$$

$$\text{yearly depreciation} = \frac{\$3500 - \$500}{5}$$

$$\text{yearly depreciation} = \frac{\$3000}{5} = \$600$$

Assignment 10-1

1. Use the straight-line method to calculate the amount of yearly depreciation for the following:

	Original cost	Resale value	Usable life	Depreciation
a.	$ 1,500	$ 300	3 years	_____
b.	12,000	1,500	5 years	_____
c.	1,400	400	2 years	_____
d.	6,750	250	10 years	_____
e.	60,000	10,000	20 years	_____

2. A truck was purchased by Idlefast, Inc., at $14,800 plus $284 freight. Company records indicate that trucks of this type normally last for 3 years and can be traded in for $600. Determine the yearly amount of depreciation using the straight-line method.

3. A stamping machine was purchased by Wilson Plate Glass, Inc., for $8595. When the machine arrived, Wilson had to pay freight of $215. Installation and preparation costs for the machine were $75. If the machine is expected to be in service for 12 years and to possess an estimated residual value of $1250, what is the amount of yearly depreciation using the straight-line method?

4. Southwest Bank bought a new addressograph machine for $7000. Delivery cost was $40, and installation was $260. Experience has shown that such equipment usually lasts 12 years and that the old machine can be sold for junk for $250. What is the amount of yearly depreciation using the straight-line method?

5. The Goodwrench Garage purchased a hydraulic lift for $6500. Installation cost was $2500. The lift is expected to last 8 years and have a junk value of $200. What is the yearly depreciation using the straight-line method?

Sum-of-the-Years-Digits Method

One of the main reasons the straight-line method of estimating depreciation is the most often used is that the depreciable amount is the same for each year of its estimated usable life. However, as anyone who has ever bought a new car knows, most assets lose more of their value in the first year of life and less in each succeeding year. Since money today is more valuable than it will be in the future, if for no other reason than because it can earn interest, it is usually advantageous to use a method of depreciation that reflects this depreciation pattern. Such a method is the sum-of-the-years-digits method of calculating depreciation. The steps required for this method are:

1. List the digits in the asset's usable life in reverse order. For example, if a machine has an estimated usable life of 5 years, the digits would be listed 5, 4, 3, 2, 1.
2. Add the digits. The sum of the digits will be the denominator for all calculations. $(5 + 4 + 3 + 2 + 1 = 15)$
3. Place each year's digit over the denominator found in Step 2, that is, $\frac{5}{15}$, $\frac{4}{15}, \frac{3}{15}, \frac{2}{15}, \frac{1}{15}$. Each fraction then becomes the rate for the year to which it corresponds, that is, the first-year rate is $\frac{5}{15}$, the second $\frac{4}{15}$, and so on.
4. Subtract the resale value from the original cost of the asset.
5. Multiply the result of the subtraction in Step 4 by the rate for each successive year obtained in Step 3.

Note: If the asset's life is long, the sum-of-the-digits formula can be used to simplify the calculation of the denominator. The formula is

$$\frac{n\,(n + 1)}{2}$$

where n is the estimated usable life. For example, the denominator for 30 years would be

$$\frac{\overset{15}{\cancel{30}}\,(30 + 1)}{2} = 15 \times 31 = 465$$

Example What is the yearly depreciation expense for $3500 planer that is expected to be in service for 5 years and have a resale value of $500, using the sum-of-the-years-digits method?

Solution $3500 − $500 = $3000 total depreciation

Year	Digits	Rate ×	Total depreciation =	Yearly depreciation
1	5	$\frac{5}{15}$	$3000	$1000
2	4	$\frac{4}{15}$	3000	800
3	3	$\frac{3}{15}$	3000	600
4	2	$\frac{2}{15}$	3000	400
5	1	$\frac{1}{15}$	3000	200
total	15	$\frac{15}{15}$	$3000	$3000

Assignment 10-2

1. Martha's Machine Shop bought a new lathe for $4000. The shop replaces such machines every 4 years and sells the old ones for $400. What is the yearly depreciation using the sum-of-the-years-digits method?

2. Joe's Bar and Grill purchased a new beer dispenser for $22,225. The manufacturer charged $275 to install the machine. Joe estimates it will last 6 years and can then be sold to a local junkyard for $1500. What will be the yearly depreciation using the sum-of-the-year-digits method?

3. Every 5 years, Bruce's Beauty Salon buys all new hair dryers. The new dryers cost $9500, and the old ones can be sold for $500. What is the yearly depreciation using the sum-of-the-years-digits method?

4. Using the sum-of-the-years-digits method, determine the estimated depreciation for the sixth year of a building with a usable life of 15 years. The building cost $200,000 and has a residual value of $80,000.

5. An asset costing $23,000 with a $500 freight charge was installed at a cost of $300. It is estimated that the asset will last for 10 years and will have a salvage value of $3000. Calculate the depreciation for the fifth year, using the straight-line method and the sum-of-the-years-digits method.

Units-of-Production Method

When depreciating machinery and equipment, an attempt is sometimes made to actually match the expense and revenues for the period in which they are incurred. To do this, an estimate of the actual number of units the machinery or equipment will produce is made upon purchase. (Units can be in any reasonable measurement applicable to the asset under consideration, such as hours, miles, or product output.) This estimate is made on a yearly or some other periodic basis for the entire expected life of the asset. Depreciation is then calculated on the basis of the estimate of units produced during the expected life of the asset. The following steps are required:

1. Calculate the cost of the equipment per unit of production

$$\text{cost per unit of production} = \frac{\text{equipment cost} - \text{resale value}}{\text{total units of production}}$$

2. Multiply each year's actual production during the usable life of the asset by the answer obtained in step 1.

Example   A planer costing $3500 is expected to produce the following number of units during its life: first year 2500, second year 2350, third year 2000, fourth year 1500, and fifth year 650. Calculate the amount of yearly depreciation using the units-of-production method if the planer is expected to have a resale value of $500.

Solution   Find the total expected number of units that will be produced over the planer's expected life:

First year	2500
Second year	2350
Third year	2000
Fourth year	1500
Fifth year	650
Total	9000

Calculate the cost of the planer per unit of production:

$$\text{cost per unit of production} = \frac{\text{cost of planer} - \text{resale value}}{\text{total units of production}}$$

$$\text{cost per unit of production} = \frac{\$3500 - \$500}{9000}$$

$$\text{cost per unit of production} = \frac{\overset{1}{\cancel{3,000}}}{\underset{3}{\cancel{9,000}}}$$

$$\text{cost per unit of production} = \$.33\tfrac{1}{3}$$

Multiply each year's production, assuming actual production followed the expected production patterns, by the cost per unit of production

Year	Yearly production	×	Cost per unit of production	=	Depreciation
First	2500		33\tfrac{1}{3}$		$ 833.33
Second	2350		33\tfrac{1}{3}$		$ 783.33
Third	2000		33\tfrac{1}{3}$		$ 666.67
Fourth	1500		33\tfrac{1}{3}$		$ 500.00
Fifth	650		33\tfrac{1}{3}$		$ 216.67
Total	9000		33\tfrac{1}{3}$		$3000.00

Assignment 10-3

1. Jones Electronics purchased a delivery truck for $16,000. The truck is expected to be worn out when it has been driven 100,000 miles. Experience has shown that such trucks can be sold to a salvage yard for $200. Using the units-of-production method, determine the depreciation for a year when the truck was expected to be driven 12,000 miles.

2. A new electric generator cost the city the Muleshoe $204,000. Such generators last for 60,000 hours. The last generator of the same type was sold as junk by the city for $4000. What would the depreciation be in a year when the generator is expected to operate 4000 hours, using the units-of-production method?

3. Marvin's Plastic Products acquired a new stamping machine for $20,000. The machine is expected to be worn out and in need of replacement after it has stamped 500,000 plastic parts. It can then be sold as scrap for $2000. Using the units-of-production method, how much can the machine be depreciated in a year in which it has been estimated that 18,000 plastic parts will be produced?

4. Margaret's Waffle Shop depreciates cooking equipment using the units-of-production method. The average productive use of a waffle iron is 435,000 waffles. New waffle irons cost $2200 and can be sold as junk for $25. How much can a waffle iron be depreciated in a year when it is expected to produce 48,500 waffles?

5. Total production during the life of an asset is estimated to be 250,000 units. The fifth year's production is estimated to 20,000 units. If the asset cost $58,000 and is expected to have a trade-in value of $8000, what is the fifth year's depreciation?

Declining-Balance Method

The declining-balance method of calculating depreciation is another accelerated method—that is, the depreciation is higher the first year and less in each succeeding year. As in all the other methods of determining depreciation, the maximum an asset can be depreciated is the total cost less the resale value. However, unlike the other depreciation methods, the base upon which the rate is taken in the declining-balance method begins with cost, not the cost less the resale value. The rate is taken on the *book value** of the asset in each period, and the book value declines by the amount of previous period's depreciation. Thus, the method is called the declining-balance method.

The rate of depreciation generally used for illustrative purposes for the declining-balance method is twice the straight-line rate. On most assets, however, the rate used in practice is less than twice the straight-line rate, usually $1\frac{1}{2}$ times.

> **Note:** The straight-line rate can always be determined by placing 1 in the numerator position and the years of usable life in the denominator position of a common fraction. Thus, an asset having a usable life of 5 years has a straight-line rate of $\frac{1}{5}$, one having a usable life of 12 years has a straight-line rate of $\frac{1}{12}$, and so on.

To compute the depreciation using the declining-balance method, the following steps are required:

1. Calculate the rate by multiplying the straight-line rate by the amount allowed; that is, if an asset's expected life is 5 years and it is to be depreciated using the declining-balance method at twice the straight-line rate, the calculation is

    $$\text{straight-line rate} \times 2 = \frac{1}{5} \times 2 = \frac{2}{5} = 40\%$$

2. Multiply the original cost by the rate found in step 1. The answer will be the amount of depreciation allowable for the first year of the asset's life.

3. Deduct the first year's depreciation (found in step 2) from the original cost of the asset; that is, find the book value for the second period.

4. Continue alternating steps 2 and 3 until all allowable depreciation (original cost less resale value) has been taken or until the last year's depreciation is to be calculated. The last year's depreciation is the difference between the allowable depreciation and the amount of depreciation taken in the previous years.

Example   Using the declining-balance method at twice the straight-line rate, calculate the annual depreciation for a planer costing $3500 with a resale value of $500 if its expected life is 5 years.

Solution   Find the rate (straight-line rate = $\frac{1}{5}$):

$$\frac{1}{5} \times 2 = \frac{2}{5} = 40\%$$

*Book value is the amount at which an asset is valued in the accounting records. It is the total cost of the asset less the total of the accumulated depreciation expense in past accounting periods.

Calculate the yearly depreciation:

Year	Balance (book value)	×	Rate	=	Yearly depreciation	Total depreciation	Allowable depreciation ($3500 - $500)
1	$3500		40%		$1400	$1400	$3000
2	2100		40%		840	2240	3000
3	1260		40%		504	2744	3000
4	756		40%		256	3000	3000
5*					0	3000	3000

Assignment 10-4

1. The Goop Oil Corporation purchased a new computer for $210,000. The firm wishes to use the computer for 3 years and expects it to have a residual value of $10,000. Find the depreciation for each year using the declining-balance method at twice the straight-line rate.

2. Bimble's grocery chain depreciates cash registers using the declining-balance method at twice the straight-line rate. Calculate the yearly depreciation for $120,000 worth of cash registers which have a resale value of $5000 and a useful life expectancy of 5 years.

3. A peanut mill bought a new drying machine for $60,000. The machine is expected to last 8 years and have a junk value of $5000. Calculate the depreciation for the first 3 years using the declining-balance method at twice the straight-line rate.

*756 × 40% would be $302.40, but at the end of the third year $2744 of the allowable $3000 had been taken. Therefore, the maximum depreciation in the fourth year is $3000 less $2744, or $256. No depreciation can be taken in the fifth year.

4. Calculate the annual depreciation for a machine that cost $30,320 and has a scrap value of $820 if its expected life is 4 years. Use the declining-balance method at $1\frac{1}{2}$ times the straight-line rate.

5. The Burnit Corporation owns a building that it wants to write off as rapidly as possible. The building cost $8250, has a resale value of $1250, and is expected to last 5 years. If the declining-balance method must be at $1\frac{1}{2}$ times the straight-line rate, calculate the depreciation for the first year using the straight-line method, the sum-of-the-years-digit method, and the declining-balance method. Which method has the fastest write-off and by how much?

Merchandise Inventory Valuation

Inventories are the merchandise on hand at a specific time in a business. The amount of inventory carried by a business is very important. If too much is on hand, the firm has "tied up" money that it could be using for some other purpose, and it might have to pay higher taxes because the inventory is an asset. If the inventory is too low, the company may have to backorder customer orders—that is, the order is accepted but the merchandise cannot be shipped until a later date. Not having sufficient inventory on hand could also result in lost sales. The method of valuing an inventory can reflect directly on the profits of a company, since the value of the inventory is one of the amounts used to determine net income.

During any period, a business may purchase merchandise several times. At the end of the period, the ending inventory must be determined. The question is, at what cost should the inventory be valued? While there are other methods of calculating the value of an inventory, the three most common will be discussed in this chapter. They are first in, first out (FIFO); last in, first out (LIFO); and weighted average.

FIFO

The FIFO method of inventory valuation assumes that the merchandise was sold in the order it was received, that is, the merchandise received first is sold first. The FIFO method of inventory valuation should be used when a product is expected to decline in price. For tax purposes, the least possible inventory value is desirable and, if a product is decreasing in price, the lowest value will be on the purchases made last.

Example   Use the FIFO inventory valuation method to find the value of the following inventory:

Date of purchase	Units purchased	Unit cost
2/1	30	$5
5/15	25	6
9/1	40	5
12/6	50	7

On 12/31, a merchandise inventory count shows that there are 55 units on hand.

Solution   Since 50 of the 55 units of inventory using the FIFO method of valuation are from the order received on 12/6, multiply the number of units (50) by the cost per unit ($7). Multiply the number of remaining units (5) by the cost per unit of the order received on 9/1 ($5), and add the products:

from 12/6 order   50 × $7 = $350
from 9/1 order   5 × 5 =   25
FIFO inventory   = $375

Assignment 10-5

1. Quality Seal, Inc., imported the following merchandise for resale: on 6/1, six seals @ $125 each; on 9/3, ten seals @ $110 each; and on 11/31, eight seals @ $115 each. Use the FIFO method to determine the value of the inventory if there are ten seals still in the inventory.

2. During a 1-month period, Fast Shop Specialty Grocery Store purchased canned green beans as follows:

    first order   5 cases @ $6.00 per case
    second order 7 cases @ 6.25 per case
    third order   7 cases @ 6.40 per case
    fourth order 8 cases @ 6.50 per case

    The month-end inventory showed 11 cases in inventory. Fast Shop uses the FIFO method to calculate its inventories. Calculate the value of the green bean inventory.

3. A retail tire center specializes in selling steel-belted radials. Purchases are made in rather large quantities to take advantage of quantity discounts. Purchase records for last year showed the following for the highest-quality model:

    2/18   200 tires @ $90 each
    5/7   150 tires @ 94 each
    8/21   220 tires @ 85 each
    11/30 180 tires @ 95 each

    The year-end inventory count showed that 190 tires were in stock. Use the FIFO method to calculate the inventory value.

4. P.S.W., a large chain department store, purchases specialty fad items, especially for the Christmas season, if trial sales prove successful. Purchases of the Bhambo Whoopsie Hoop are as follows:

3/6	20 cases @ $40 per case
4/1	50 cases @ 38 per case
4/26	50 cases @ 38 per case
5/5	70 cases @ 36 per case
6/1	100 cases @ 35 per case
6/20	100 cases @ 35 per case
7/20	200 cases @ 33 per case
8/4	100 cases @ 37 per case
9/20	4000 cases @ 30 per case

Unfortunately for P.S.W., the fad ended in September. The year-end inventory showed 4450 cases in stock. Value the inventory using the FIFO method.

5. Use the FIFO method to value the 20-unit inventory remaining at the end of the month if purchases were as follows:

4/9	17 units @ $6.85 each
4/18	21 units @ 6.92 each
4/24	42 units @ 6.20 each
4/27	10 units @ 7.00 each
4/29	5 units @ 7.20 each

LIFO

The last-in, first-out inventory valuation method assumes that the last merchandise received is the first to be sold. Some students usually question the reality of such a system. While it is not likely that the last merchandise received would be the first sold, the point to remember is that inventory is a cost flow assumption and not necessarily related to actual physical flow. LIFO is an acceptable accounting procedure for assigning costs to inventories.

Example Use the LIFO method to find the value of an inventory of 55 units when purchases have been

2/1	30 units @ $5 per unit
5/15	25 units @ 6 per unit
9/1	40 units @ 5 per unit
12/6	50 units @ 7 per unit

Solution LIFO assumes that the last merchandise purchased is sold first. Therefore, the last 50 units, purchased on 12/6, have been sold and so have the 40 units purchased on 9/1. The 55 units on hand include the 30 units purchased on 2/1 and the 25 units purchased on 5/15. The value of the inventory is

from order on 2/1   30 × $5 = $150
from order on 5/15   25 × 6 =   150
LIFO inventory   = $300

Assignment 10-6

1. Use the LIFO method to determine the value of 48 units left in inventory when purchases are as follows:

2/19	25 cases @	$10 per case
3/12	15 cases @	11 per case
4/14	50 cases @	10 per case
5/6	30 cases @	12 per case

2. Determine the value of an inventory using both the FIFO and the LIFO method if purchases have been

first purchase	10 units @	$100 each
second purchase	12 units @	105 each
third purchase	10 units @	110 each

   An inventory count shows 15 units in stock.

3. Calculate the inventory for the Moonbeam Corporation using both LIFO and FIFO, and tell which method you would suggest Moonbeam use and why. Purchases for the period are

3/4	150 packages @	$30 per package
6/8	200 packages @	31 per package
9/12	175 packages @	32 per package
12/5	180 packages @	33 per package

   There are 215 packages left in inventory on 12/31.

4. Ambassador's Reducing Salon stocks rubbing alcohol to treat tired, aching muscles. The purchases for January and February follow:

1/1	4 cases @	$35 per case
1/5	5 cases @	34 per case
1/12	9 cases @	33.50 per case
2/4	1 case @	37 per case
2/12	2 cases @	36.50 per case
2/25	1 case @	38 per case

   There are ten cases left in inventory. Value the inventory using both LIFO and FIFO.

5. Use the LIFO method to calculate the value of 200 pounds of round steak in inventory at the end of July. The purchase record for the month is

7/3	120 pounds @	$2.00 per pound
7/7	70 pounds @	2.10 per pound
7/19	100 pounds @	2.02 per pound
7/24	100 pounds @	2.02 per pound
7/29	180 pounds @	1.91 per pound

Weighted-Average

The weighted-average method of inventory valuation is probably the most accurate method for most businesses. Unless strict controls are enforced on stock rotation, it is quite likely that some of the inventory on hand at any given time will include some stock from each purchase made.

The weighted-average method comes by its name because the cost of each unit purchased is "weighted" by the number of units purchased at that time. Thus, the steps to be followed to determine the value of an inventory using the weighted-average method are as follows:

1. Multiply the number of units purchased by the price of each unit to determine the total cost of each purchase.
2. Add the total costs of each purchase to arrive at the total cost of goods purchased during the valuation period.
3. Find the sum of total units purchased during the period.
4. Divide the total cost of the units purchased during the period (Step 2) by the total number of units purchased during the period (Step 3).
5. Multiply the quotient obtained in Step 4 (the weighted-average cost) by the number of units in the inventory at the end of the period.

Example Determine the value of an inventory of 55 units, using the weighted-average method, if purchases for the period have been

2/1	30 units @	$5 per unit
5/15	25 units @	6 per unit
9/1	40 units @	5 per unit
12/6	50 units @	7 per unit

Solution

2/1	30 units @	$5 per unit =	$150
5/15	25 units @	6 per unit =	150
9/1	40 units @	5 per unit =	200
12/1	50 units @	7 per unit =	350
total	145 units		$850

Divide the total cost of merchandise, $850, by the total number of units purchased, 145 units:

$850 ÷ 145 = $5.862   carried to the third place

Multiply $5.862, the weighted-average unit cost, by the number of units left in inventory (55):

$5.862 \times 55 = 322.41 weighted-average inventory

Note: If a simple average of the prices had been taken ($5 + $6 + $5 + $7 = $23; $23 \div 4 = $5.75), the unit cost of the inventory would have been understated and, therefore, the inventory valuation would be understated.

Assignment 10-7

1. Value the inventory, using the weighted-average method, if purchases are as follows:

    1/1   10 units @ $15 per unit
    1/8   10 units @ 16 per unit
    1/15   15 units @ 15 per unit
    1/22   8 units @ 14 per unit
    1/29   10 units @ 16 per unit

    There are 22 units left in inventory.

2. Use the weighted-average method to value an inventory of 280 units if purchases have been as follows:

    first purchase   200 units @ $4.10 per unit
    second purchase   175 units @ 4.00 per unit
    third purchase   215 units @ 4.25 per unit

3. Calculate the weighted average value of Cheese House's monthly Edam cheese inventory of 250 pounds if purchases for December were as follows:

    12/1   185 pounds @ $.75 per pound
    12/15   300 pounds @ .70 per pound
    12/23   75 pounds @ .78 per pound

4. Calculate the value of an ending inventory of 20 units, using the FIFO, LIFO, and weighted-average methods, when purchases for the period have been as follows:

    1/26   10 units @ $13.85 per unit
    4/5   8 units @ 14.00 per unit
    8/29   12 units @ 13.75 per unit
    12/15 15 units @ 13.50 per unit

5. Determine the inventory value by the FIFO, LIFO, and weighted-average methods, using these period purchases:

1/4   100 cartons @ $1.00 per carton
1/29   110 cartons @ 1.05 per carton
2/16   150 cartons @ 1.07 per carton
3/1   115 cartons @ 1.09 per carton
3/29   140 cartons @ 1.10 per carton
4/10   160 cartons @ 1.30 per carton

The ending inventory was 300 cartons.

Retail Method of Estimating Inventory

Businesses often have to prepare interim reports. The Internal Revenue Service, for example, requires businesses to file quarterly tax statements. To do so, they must estimate their income. Accurate records are kept on many revenue (sales) and expense items. Inventory, however, is usually estimated.

Retail firms often use the retail method to estimate the value of inventory. The retailer knows the *cost* and the *retail price of merchandise available for sale* during the period. The retailer also knows the *amount of sales* during the inventory period. With this information, an estimate of the value of inventory can be made without laboriously counting the merchandise on the shelves. Using the following steps, the retailer can estimate the cost value of the merchandise in inventory:

1. Divide the cost of the merchandise available for sale during the inventory period by the retail price of the merchandise.
2. Subtract the amount sold from the amount available for sale at retail to find the retail value of unsold inventory.
3. Multiply the value obtained in Step 1 by the value obtained in Step 2.

Example   During an inventory period, a hardware store had available for sale merchandise that cost $24,000 and was marked to sell for $40,000. Total sales at retail for the period were $14,000. What was the estimated cost value of the inventory at the end of the period?

Solution
1. Divide the cost of the merchandise available for sale during the inventory period by the retail price of the merchandise:

$$\frac{\text{cost of merchandise available for sale}}{\text{retail value of merchandise}} = \frac{\$24,000}{\$40,000} = .6$$

2. Subtract the amount sold from the amount available for sale at retail:

amount available for sale	$40,000
− amount sold	14,000
= retail value of unsold inventory	$26,000

3. Multiply Step 1 by Step 2:

retail value of unsold inventory	$26,000
× ratio of merchandise available at cost to retail value of merchandise	.6
= estimated cost value of inventory	$15,600

Assignment 10-8

1. During an inventory period, a retail department store had available for sale merchandise that cost $390,000 and was marked to sell for $520,000. Total sales for the period were $240,000. What was the approximate cost of inventory at the end of the period?

2. Total merchandise available for sale at Quatro Rosas package store cost $80,000 and was marked to sell for $120,000. Sales were $45,000. What is the estimated cost of the inventory for the period?

3. A sporting goods store had equipment costing $160,000 available for sale. Its retail price was $320,000. If sales were $120,000, what is the estimated cost of the inventory?

4. Find the estimated cost of the inventory in the following:

	Cost of merchandise	Retail price of merchandise	Sales	Estimated cost of inventory
a.	$ 25,000	$ 40,000	$ 30,000	_____
b.	65,000	75,000	38,000	_____
c.	2,591	7,849	1,500	_____
d.	189,000	378,000	100,000	_____
e.	1,000	4,000	100	_____
f.	25,000	50,000	15,000	_____
g.	100,000	160,000	100,000	_____
h.	12,000	20,000	10,000	_____
i.	350,000	500,000	300,000	_____

Bank Reconciliation

Bank Statement

Each month, individuals and businesses with checking accounts receive a statement from the bank. This statement lists all amounts added to the account (deposits) and all amounts subtracted from the account (checks, drafts, and bank charges). It also includes a monthly opening and closing statement balance. An example of a bank statement is shown in Figure 10-1.

Check Register

Though banks record all transactions and send a statement to each depositor, good business practice requires that, in addition, each depositor keep accurate records also. Banks can and do make errors. More important, however, is the fact that there is a lapse between the time the statement is prepared and the time it is received by the depositor. In the meantime, many transactions may have taken place, resulting in either a higher or a lower balance than the one shown on the bank statement. Obviously, it is also important that the depositor know the amount on deposit at any given time between bank statements. Thus, a check register, such as the one illustrated in Figure 10-2, should be kept by all depositors.

Bank Reconciliation Statement

For most bank customers, it would be unusual if the bank statement showed an amount in its closing balance that equaled the balance in the depositor's check register. The most common reasons for any discrepancy are the following:

1. Most banks charge a fee (called a *service charge*) for handling the depositor's transactions during the month. Generally, the depositor does not know the amount of the service charge until the bank statement is received.
2. Checks written by the depositor were not received by the bank in time to be included on the bank statement. These checks are called *checks outstanding*.
3. A deposit may have been made too late to appear on the bank statement. Deposits of this type are referred to as *deposits in transit*.
4. Loans from the bank, insurance premiums, and, at some banks, utility bills may be automatically deducted from the depositor's checking account balance. These deductions are like checks and are treated in the same way, but the depositor may not know the exact amount or may as a matter of policy record them when they are received in the bank statement. These deductions are called *drafts*.
5. Checks received from third parties in payment for merchandise or other debts are often deposited. Unfortunately, one or more of these checks may not be good. When it was deposited, it was added to the depositor's account. When it failed to be negotiable, it was deducted from the depositor's account by the bank and returned to the depositor. Such a check is called an *uncollectible check*.
6. Recording or arithmetic errors are frequently made.

Since neither the bank statement nor the check register is likely to accurately reflect the exact checking account balance at any one time, it is desirable to determine that balance. Though neither alone contains all the information necessary to calculate the correct current balance, together they do. Hence, when the bank statement is received, it and the check register should be adjusted to properly reflect the correct balance. This process, usually done on the form called a *bank reconciliation statement*, entails the following steps:

1. Locate all items recorded in the bank statement but not in the check register. If the item reduced the bank statement balance, it will be deducted from the check register balance. If the item increased the bank statement balance, it will be added to the check register balance.
2. Locate all items recorded in the check register but not in the bank statement. An item that increased the check register balance will be added to the bank statement balance. If the item reduced the check register balance, it will be deducted from the bank statement balance.

An example of a bank reconciliation statement is presented in Figure 10-3.

NATIONAL BANK OF ANY CITY

— ооо —

1234 LIME ST. • PHONE 800 555 – 3456 • ANY CITY, OHIO 87654

Charles D. Jones
or Mary E. Jones
2603 Oak Street
Millville, Ohio 87655

Account No. 222 – 318 – 8

Statement Rendered 12/13/87

Number of Transactions   19

BALANCE LAST STATEMENT	DEPOSITS		CHECKS AND CHARGES		SERVICE CHARGE	BLANCE THIS STATEMENT
	NO.	AMOUNT	NO.	AMOUNT		
2388.69	3	2711.07	16	854.59	0.00	4245.17

CHECKS AND OTHER DEBITS			DEPOSITS AND OTHER CREDITS	DATE	BALANCE
21.00 ✓	19.61 ✓	22.00 ✓	191.37 ✓	03117	2388.69
100.00 ✓				03147	2559.06
2.81 ✓	64.23 ✓	74.99 ✓		03157	2459.06
60.00 ✓				03177	2414.64
38.37 ✓	25.14 ✓			03287	2078.04
100.00 ✓				03317	2923.70
	378.77 ✓		845.66 ✓	04047	4556.94
15.66 ✓				04067	4406.94
150.00 ✓			1674.04 ✓	04087	4345.17
24.00 ✓				04117	4245.17
100.00 ✓					

PLEASE EXAMINE AT ONCE AND REPORT ANY ERROR IMMEDIATELY.

LAST AMOUNT IN
THIS COLUMN IS YOUR
BALANCE

PLEASE NOTIFY US OF ANY CHANGE IN ADDRESS ٭ USE REVERSE SIDE FOR RECONCILING YOUR ACCOUNT

Figure 10-1 Bank statement.

PLEASE BE SURE TO <u>DEDUCT</u> ANY PER CHECK CHARGES OR SERVICE CHARGES THAT MAY APPLY TO YOUR ACCOUNT

CHECK NO.	DATE	CHECKS ISSUED TO OR DESCRIPTION OF DEPOSIT	(−) AMOUNT OF CHECK		✓ T	(−) CHECK FEE (IF ANY)	(+) AMOUNT OF DEPOSIT	BALANCE	
								583	80
262	11/15	Valley Realty RENT	300	00				−300	00
								283	80
263	11/15	Scotts Service "925"	7	40				− 7	40
								276	40
264	11/21	Deposit					39	20	+39	20
								315	60

Figure 10-2 Check register.

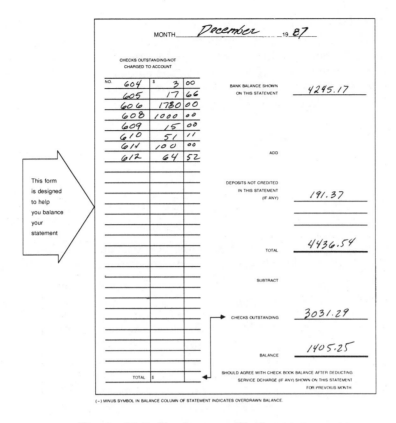

Figure 10-3 Bank reconciliation statement.

Example   Statement balance   •$193.50
Checkbook balance   144.05
Outstanding checks   26.75, 31.20
Service charge   8.50

Using the above information, prepare a bank reconciliation statement.

Solution
Bank balance per statement		$193.50
Less outstanding checks	$26.75	
	31.20	57.95
Adjusted bank balance		$135.55
Bank balance per checkbook		$144.05
Less service charge		8.50
Adjusted checkbook balance		$135.55

Assignment 10-9

1. Using the following information, reconcile the bank statement with the checkbook:

Statement balance	$671.80
Outstanding checks	10.85
	16.41
	57.75
Service charge	1.40
Checkbook balance	588.19

2. Jack received his bank statement on May 18. The statement balance was $1371.37. A deposit on May 17 for $123.86 was not recorded on the bank statement. The outstanding checks were for $15.82, $27.83, $33.50, and $137.50. A service charge of $4.70 appeared on the bank statement. The bank returned an uncollectible check in the amount of $66.05. The checkbook balance was $1351.33. Reconcile the balance.

3. Charles Dickens, Inc., received its bank statement today. Before reconciling the statement, the bookkeeper found the following differences between the bank statement and the check register:

In register but not in statement		*In statement, but not in register*	
a. four checks:	#1828 for $25	**a.** service charge	$ 3
	#1831 for $82.50	**b.** drafts from	
	#1832 for $56.65	life insurance co.	$295
	#1834 for $23.85	bank loan	$190
b. two deposits:	on 2/15 for $365	**c.** a charge for extra	$ 10
	on 2/17 for $510	check blanks	

In addition to the above, the bookkeeper found that check #1820 had been written for $12.95 but incorrectly recorded in the register as $12.59. The bank statement was $2015.00. The check register balance was $3200.36. Reconcile the balances.

4. Sandman Bros. received a bank statement for the month of August. The statement balance was $293.00 The check register balance was also $293.00. The bookkeeper decided that a bank reconciliation statement was unnecessary since the balances agreed. Was this right? Why or why not?

5. The accounting supervisor at Sandman Bros. insisted that a bank reconciliation statement be prepared. The bank statement and check register are as follows Reconcile them.

Bank Statement for August 1986

Your beginning balance of [$385.22] was increased by [2] deposits totaling [$250] and decreased by [11] checks totaling [$338.52] and a service charge of [$4.00], resulting in an ending balance of [$293.00].

Checks		Deposits	Balance
			$385.52
$19.00	$25.00		341.52
$32.00	$10.50	$185.00	484.02
$ 3.15	$ 6.45		474.42
$13.90			460.52
$44.50	$ 6.02	$ 65.00	475.00
$90.00	$88.00		297.00
$ 4.00 sc			$293.00

Check Register for August 1986

Check Number	Date	Description	Amount of Check	Amount of Deposit	Balance
					$385.52
25	8/1	Charley O.	$36.00		349.52
26	8/2	Henry A.	19.00		330.52
27	8/5	Reggie J.	25.00		305.52
28	8/7	Louis A.	32.00		273.52
29	8/8	Sal B.	10.50	$185.00	448.02
30	8/9	Johnny B.	3.15		444.87
31	8/12	Brooks R.	6.45		438.42
32	8/16	Jeff B.	13.90		424.52
33	8/18	Catfish H.	44.50		380.02
34	8/19	The Bird F.	6.02	65.00	439.00
35	8/23	Toby H.	88.00		351.00
36	8/24	Billy M.	90.00		261.00
37	8/25	Murry W.	70.02	200.00	390.98
38	8/30	Sam G.	97.98		293.00

Chapter 10   Self-Testing Exercises

1. At the end of a 3-month period, Exelsor Company had 30 cases of gloves in its inventory. During the period, its glove orders were as follows:

   20 cases @ $15 per case
   28 cases @   14 per case
   25 cases @   16 per case
   20 cases @   17 per case

   Figure the value of the inventory using the FIFO method, the LIFO method, and the weighted-average method.

238   *Accounting Applications*

2.   A machine cost $32,000. It is expected to have a usable life of 5 years with a scrap value of $2000. During its 5-year life, the output, in units, is expected to be as follows: first year 75,000, second year 72,000, third year 67,000, fourth year 61,000, and fifth year 45,000. What is the second year's depreciation using the straight-line method, the sum-of-the-years-digits method, the declining-balance method at twice the straight-line rate, and the units-of-production method?

3.   A used delivery truck costing $6300 was purchased on April 1. The truck's life expectancy is 3 years, at which time its resale value will be $300. Calculate the depreciation for each year using the straight-line method, the sum-of-the-years-digits method, and the declining-balance method at twice the straight-line rate.

4.   Using the FIFO method of inventory valuation, determine the value of an inventory of 120 units, given the following information.

Purchase date	Amount	Unit price
4/6	150	$.75
5/5	125	.80
6/14	160	.78

5.   In Problem 4, what is the value of the inventory using the weighted-average method?

6.   Using the sum-of-the-years-digits method of calculating depreciation, determine the depreciation for the third year of a $200,000 building with a $50,000 salvage value being depreciated over 10 years.

7.   A salesperson paid $12,750 for his car. He plans to keep it for 3 years, and experience has shown that he will receive $3750 on a trade-in at the end of 3 years. Figure the annual depreciation using the straight-line method, the sum-of-the-years-digits method, the declining balance method at $1\frac{1}{4}$ the straight-line rate, and the units-of-production method (first year 50,000 miles, second year 52,000 miles, third year 48,000 miles.)

8. The following is a partial purchase record for Adams Electronics:

   50 transformers @ $25 each
   35 transformers @ 28 each
   60 transformers @ 23 each

   If there are 65 transformers in the year-end inventory, what is the value of the inventory using FIFO, LIFO, and weighted average?

9. Prepare a bank reconciliation using the following information:

Statement balance	$154.80
Checkbook balance	115.24
Outstanding checks	24.96
	21.40
Service charge	6.80

10. Purchases of $40,000 were marked to sell for $60,000. If the first week's sales were $15,000, what was the inventory at cost?

11. What is the inventory cost when sales for the period were $40,000 and the total merchandise available for sale cost $50,000 and is marked to sell for $80,000?

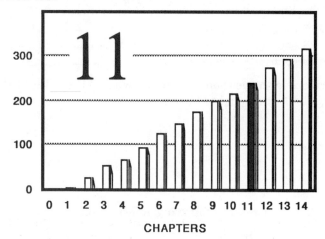

PAGE NO.

CHAPTERS

Management Applications

Student Objectives

Upon completion of this chapter, the student should be able to

1. **Use** *the basic accounting formula to calculate*
   a. *assets when liabilities and capital are known.*
   b. *liabilities when assets and capital are known.*
   c. *owner's equity when assets and liabilities are known.*
2. **Conduct** *a horizontal analysis of a comparative balance sheet.*
3. **Perform** *a vertical analysis of a balance sheet.*
4. **Construct** *an income statement when given sufficient revenue and expense data.*
5. **Perform** *a horizontal analysis of an income statement.*
6. **Conduct** *a vertical analysis of an income statement.*
7. **Calculate** *the following:*
   a. *current ratio*
   b. *acid-test ratio*
   c. *inventory turnover ratio*
   d. *rate of return on ownership capital ratio*
   e. *accounts receivable to net sales ratio*
8. **Define, illustrate, or use**

balance sheet
assets
current assets
long-term assets
liabilities
current liabilities
long-term liabilities
owner's equity
comparative balance sheet
income statement

revenues
sales allowances
cost of goods sold
net income
comparative income statement
expenses
sales returns
current ratio
acid-test ratio

inventory turnover ratio.
rate of return on owner-ship capital ratio
accounts receivable to net sales ratio
debt
ownership
quick assets

240

Accounting Equation

The *accounting equation* is a simple mathematical formula that can be presented in a number of ways. The most common way is as follows:

assets = liabilities + owner's equity

From the most common equation, two other formulas can be derived:

liabilities = assets − owner's equity

owner's equity = assets − liabilities

Assets

Assets are things of value owned by the business. Complete legal ownership is not necessary for an item to be considered an asset. Thus, goods purchased on the installment plan are reported as assets of the business firm from the moment of purchase. Examples of typical business assets include cash, buildings, land, fixtures, and office supplies.

Liabilities

Liabilities are debts owed to creditors. Liabilities represent the claims of the creditors against a business for cash or goods. Normally, liabilities must be paid at some definite time in the future according to the agreement made with the creditors. Most liability obligations result from legally enforceable contracts. Examples of common liabilities are accounts payable, notes payable, interest payable, rent payable, taxes payable, bonds, and mortgages.

Owner's Equity

Owner's Equity is the interest or ownership in the assets by the owner or owners of the business firm. Other frequently used terms for owner's equity are *capital, ownership capital, proprietorship,* and *stockholders' equity.* Owner's equity includes items such as common stock, preferred stock, owner's investment and retained earnings.

Example A business has the following account balances: cash, $3000; accounts receivable, $2000; machinery and equipment, $10,000; accounts payable, $1000; notes payable, $1500; salaries payable, $3500. What is the amount of owner's equity that would be shown on a balance sheet?

Solution Organize the assets and add them together:

Cash	$ 3,000
Accounts receivable	2,000
Machinery and equipment	10,000
Total assets	$15,000

Organize the liabilities and add them together:

Accounts payable	$1000
Notes payable	1500
Salaries payable	3500
Total liabilities	$6000

Subtract the total liabilities from the total assets:

$15,000 − $6000 = $9000   owner's equity

Assignment 11-1

1. Determine owner's equity from the following:

Cash	$8000	Accounts receivable	$2000
Accounts payable	3000	Notes receivable	1000
Merchandise inventory	4000	Notes payable	7000
Interest payable	500		

2. Find total liabilities from the following:

Cash	$22,000	Owner's equity	$75,000
Accounts receivable	64,000	Notes receivable	18,000
Merchandise inventory	38,000	Equipment	30,000
Plant	95,000	Land	60,000

3. Calculate total assets from the following:

Salaries payable	$315,000	Notes payable	$29,000
Insurance payable	21,000	Interest payable	7,500
Taxes payable	57,500	Accounts payable	17,000
Owner's equity	138,000		

4. Compute owner's equity from the following:

Cash	$12,000	Merchandise inventory	$162,000
Accounts payable	24,000	Land	40,000
Interest payable	2,000	Insurance payable	20,000
Equipment	38,000	Accounts receivable	50,000
Notes payable	115,000	Plant	300,000
Notes receivable	65,000	Interest receivable	5,000

Financial Statements

Accounting data must be summarized and presented in the form of *financial statements* so decision makers can truly utilize information provided by the accounting system. Two financial statements are of extreme importance. They are the balance sheet and the income statement. These statements are used by investors, creditors, governmental agencies, and other interested parties to determine and analyze the financial condition of a business.

Balance Sheet

The *balance sheet* is a formal presentation of the basic accounting equation. A balance sheet will normally be prepared more frequently, but it must be prepared at least once a year to meet various governmental reporting requirements. A balance sheet for Bixby Tooling, Inc., is presented in Table 11-1.

A balance sheet is only a representation or image of a business *at a particular point in time.* In other words, many items shown for Bixby Tooling on December 31 were different on December 30, and those figures will change again on January 1.

Below is a brief descussion of each of the major items found in the Bixby Tooling, Inc., balance sheet, Table 11-1.

1. **Current Assets** *Current assets* are cash and other goods expected to be converted into cash, sold, or consumed within a period of one year.
2. **Fixed Assets** *Fixed assets* are assets which were acquired to use in the business rather than for resale. Examples are land, buildings, and machinery. The life expectancy of the assets, when acquired, must exceed one year to be classified as a fixed asset. Land is relatively permanent and does not ordinarily lose value over time. However, some other kinds of assets, such as buildings and machinery, decrease in value over time. The decrease in value may be the result of physical wear and tear or technical obsolescence. The decrease in value is called *depreciation.* Depreciation is accumulated over the years and is deducted as a separate amount from the assets subject to depreciation.
3. **Intangible Assets** *Intangible assets* are assets lacking physical substance, which have value as a result of the rights and benefits that the owner derives from them. Examples of intangible assets are goodwill, patents, copyrights, and trademarks. Intangible assets are carried on the balance sheet at cost. Cost is their purchase price or the cost incurred to develop them.
4. **Other Assets** The *other asset* category includes all assets which will not fit into any of the three prior classifications. Examples of other assets are long-term investments in stocks and bonds of other corporations, land held for plant expansion, and an abandoned plant held for disposal.
5. **Current Liabilities** *Current liabilities* are debts or obligations due within one year. Current liabilities are normally paid from existing current assets or by creating other current liabilities. The amount shown on the balance sheet for each current liability is the amount owed on the balance sheet date. Amounts owed to banks, suppliers of goods, and taxes are examples of current liabilities.
6. **Long-Term Liabilities** *Long-term liabilities* are debts or obligations not due for a relatively long period of time, usually more than one year. Cash borrowed by issuing bonds or signing a note or mortgage are illustrations of long-term liabilities. Long-term liabilities are shown as the amount owed as of the balance sheet date.
7. **Owner's Equity** *Owner's equity* is the owner's interest in the assets of the business. In Table 11-1, common stock represents ownership in a corporation. Common stock is divided into shares. Investors purchasing shares of stock are called stockholders or shareholders. A corporation may issue more than one class of stock to attract a broader group of investors. One class of stock will have preferential rights over the other class. The stock having preferential rights is called *preferred stock. Additional paid-in capital* represents the amounts received by selling stock at more than par value. That is, Bixby has sold stock for an additional $51,600 above its par value of $25 per share. *Retained earnings* is the amount of earnings of prior years which have been kept or retained in the business and not returned to the stockholders.

Table 11-1

Bixby Tooling, Incorporated
Balance Sheet as of 31 December 1987

Assets

1. Current Assets:

Cash		$ 48,000	
Marketable securities		187,500	
Accounts receivable	$255,400		
Less estimated uncollectibles	6,300	249,100	
Merchandise inventory		403,700	
Prepaid expenses		29,300	
Total current assets			$917,600

2. Fixed assets:

Land		$416,000	
Buildings	$432,000		
Less accumulated depreciation	57,500	374,500	
Machinery and equipment	$612,200		
Less accumulated depreciation	97,400	514,800	
Total fixed assets			$1,305,300

3. Intangible assets:

Goodwill	$86,000	
Patent	29,400	
Total intangible assets:		115,400

4. Other assets:

Investment in Longjohn Corporation	68,500
Total assets:	$2,406,800

Liabilities

5. Current liabilities:

Notes payable to banks	$198,300	
Accounts payable	47,300	
Taxes payable	108,200	
Current portion of mortgage on equipment and buildings	32,600	
Total current liabilities:		$386,400

6. Long-term liabilities:

Mortgage on buildings and equipment	463,900
Total liabilities:	$850,300

Owner's Equity

7. Common stock, par value $25.00/share,

20,000 shares issued and outstanding	$ 500,000	
Additional paid-in capital	51,600	
Retained earnings	1,004,900	
Total owner's equity		1,556,500
Total liabilities and owner's equity		$2,406,800

Horizontal Analysis of a Balance Sheet
Accounting data are usually more meaningful when they are compared with data from other accounting periods. An abnormally large percent increase or decrease should alert a manager to perform a more detailed analysis. Any problems can then be corrected before they become serious.

The horizontal analysis of comparative balance sheet figures is accomplished by first finding the difference between last year's business and this year's business. The *percent* increase or decrease is then found by dividing the difference by last year's business.

Example Prepare a horizontal analysis of the data in the comparative balance sheet shown below. (**Note:** A *decrease* is indicated by placing an * after the amount and the percent.)

Basic Rock Company
Comparative Balance Sheet — December 31, 1987

	1986	1987	Increase or Decrease* Amount	Percent
Assets				
Current assets				
Cash	$ 31,000	$ 27,000	$ 4,000*	12.9%*
Accounts receivable	99,000	80,000	19,000*	19.2%*
Notes receivable	5,000	3,000	2,000*	40.0%*
Total current assets	$135,000	$110,000	$25,000*	18.5%*
Plant assets				
Land	$ 35,000	$ 40,000	$ 5,000	14.3%
Building	100,000	90,000	10,000*	10.0%*
Equipment	25,000	30,000	5,000	20.0%
Total plant assets	$160,000	$160,000	—0—	—0—
Total assets	$295,000	$270,000	$25,000*	8.5%*
Liabilities and Owner's equity				
Current liabilities				
Accounts payable	$ 18,000	$ 13,000	$ 5,000*	27.8%*
Notes payable	40,000	25,000	15,000*	37.5%*
Insurance payable	8,000	7,000	1,000*	12.5%*
Total current liabilities	$ 66,000	$ 45,000	$21,000*	31.8%*
Long-term liabilities				
Mortgage payable	$ 90,000	$ 80,000	$10,000*	11.1%*
Bonds payable	30,000	20,000	10,000*	33.3%*
Total long-term liabilities	$120,000	$100,000	$20,000*	16.7%*
Total liabilities	$186,000	$145,000	$41,000*	22.0%*
Owner's equity				
7% preferred stock	$ 30,000	$ 50,000	$20,000	66.7%
Common stock	75,000	75,000	—0—	—0—
Retained earnings	4,000	—0—	4,000*	100%*
Total Owner's equity	$109,000	$125,000	$16,000	14.7%
Total liabilities and Owner's equity	$295,000	$270,000	$25,000*	8.5%*

Solution The amount of increase or decrease is the difference between the 1986 figure and the 1987 figure. The difference is then divided by the earlier figure—in this case, the 1986 figure. For example, cash in the balance sheet is $31,000 in 1986 and $27,000 in 1987. The difference is a decrease of $4000:

(1986) $31,000 − (1987) $27,000 = $4000 decrease

The decrease, $4000, is then divided by $31,000, the 1986 cash balance, to obtain the percent decrease of 12.9%:

$$\frac{\$4000}{\$31,000} = .129 = 12.9\% \text{ decrease}$$

All the remaining balance sheet figures are handled in the same manner until every category has been calculated.

The company's management is very concerned about any figure showing a significant percent change. The reason or reasons for these variations would be analyzed very carefully to find a solution to problems that first become apparent in a horizontal balance sheet analysis.

Assignment 11-2

1.   Perform a horizontal analysis on the following comparative balance sheet:

Sam's Appliance
Comparative Balance Sheet

	1986	1987	Increase or Decrease* Amount	Percent
		Assets		
Current assets				
Cash	$ 5,000	$ 6,000	$_____	_____
Accounts receivable	10,000	11,000	$_____	_____
Total current assets	$15,000	$17,000	$_____	_____
Plant assets				
Building and equipment	$55,000	$48,000	$_____	_____
Land	18,000	20,000	$_____	_____
Total plant assets	$73,000	$68,000	$_____	_____
Total assets	$88,000	$85,000	$_____	_____
		Liabilities and Owner's equity		
Current liabilities				
Accounts payable	$ 7,000	$ 10,000	$_____	_____
Notes payable	6,000	4,000	$_____	_____
Total current liabilities	$13,000	$14,000	$_____	_____
Long-term liabilities				
Long-term debt	$40,000	$35,000	$_____	_____
Total long-term liabilities	$40,000	$35,000	$_____	_____
Total liabilities	$53,000	$49,000	$_____	_____
Owner's equity				
Capital stock	$20,000	$25,000	$_____	_____
Retained earnings	15,000	11,000	$_____	_____
Total Owner's equity	$35,000	$36,000	$_____	_____
Total liabilities and Owner's equity	$88,000	$85,000	$_____	_____

2.   Two account balances from the Harcourt Bit Company's balance sheets of 1986 and 1987 are (1) cash: 1986, $4650; 1987, $5895; (2) accounts payable: 1986, $24,000; 1987, $18,000. Perform a horizontal analysis of these two account balances.

3. From the following data, construct the appropriate portion of a balance sheet and perform a horizontal analysis:

Cash, 1986	$ 25,000
Accounts payable, 1987	17,000
Accounts receivable, 1987	38,000
Buildings and equipment, 1986	135,000
Accounts payable, 1986	19,000
Buildings and equipment, 1987	130,000
Cash, 1987	27,000
Accounts receivable, 1986	40,000

Steeles' Market
Comparative Balance Sheet

	1986	1987	Increase Amount	Decrease* Percent

Vertical Analysis of a Balance Sheet

A vertical analysis of a balance sheet is a *comparison of each component* in the balance sheet with the total assets or the total liabilities plus owner's equity in one accounting period. Remember, total assets equal total liabilities plus owner's equity. The analysis is more meaningful when the percent relationships can be compared with percent relationships in another accounting period. It is then possible to see any significant changes.

Perform a vertical analysis of the comparative balance sheet below.

The Steep Slope Ski Shop
Comparative Balance Sheet — December 31, 1986 and 1987

	1986 Amount	Percent	1987 Amount	Percent
	Assets			
Current assets				
Cash	$ 9,200	8.6%	$ 11,800	10.9%
Accounts receivable	21,200	19.9%	22,400	20.7%
Merchandise inventory	26,000	24.4%	26,400	24.4%
Total current assets	$ 56,400	52.9%	$ 60,600	56.0%
Plant assets				
Land	$ 4,000	3.8%	$ 4,000	3.7%
Building	28,600	26.8%	28,000	25.9%
Equipment	17,600	16.5%	15,600	14.4%
Total plant assets	$ 50,200	47.1%	$ 47,600	44.0%
Total assets	$106,600	100%	$108,200	100%
	Liabilities and Owner's equity			
Current liabilities				
Accounts payable	$ 27,900	26.2%	$ 17,000	15.7%
Notes payable	11,000	10.3%	$ 10,000	9.2%
Taxes payable	3,500	3.3%	4,000	3.7%
Total current liabilities	$ 42,400	39.8%	$ 31,000	28.7%
Long-term liabilities				
Bonds payable	$ 20,000	18.8%	$ 20,000	18.5%
Total liabilities	$ 62,400	58.5%	$ 51,000	47.1%
Owner's equity				
Preferred stock	$ 15,000	14.1%	$ 25,000	23.1%
Common stock	30,000	28.1%	30,000	27.7%
Retained earnings	(800)	(.8%)	2,200	2.0%
Total Owner's equity	$ 44,200	41.5%	$ 57,200	52.9%
Total liabilities and Owner's equity	$106,600	100%	$108,200	100%

Note: Numbers within parentheses are negative.

Solution   Using the information above, the vertical analysis is performed by dividing each component of the balance sheet by either the total assets or the total liabilities plus stockholders' equity. For example, merchandise inventory in 1986 was $26,000. Total assets in 1986 were $106,000. Therefore,

$$\frac{\text{merchandise inventory (1986)}}{\text{total assets (1986)}} = \frac{\$26,000}{\$106,600} = .2439 = 24.4\%$$

Likewise, notes payable in 1987 were $10,000, and total liabilities and stockholders' equity in 1987 were $108,200. Therefore,

$$\frac{\text{notes payable (1987)}}{\text{total liabilities and stockholders' equity (1987)}} = \frac{\$10,000}{\$108,200} = .0924 = 9.2\%$$

All other calculations are done in the same manner.

Assignment 11-3

1. Perform a vertical analysis on the following:

Time Lauris
Comparative Balance Sheet

	1986		1987	
	Amount	*Percent*	*Amount*	*Percent*
	Assets			
Current assets				
Cash	$ 38,000	_____	$ 50,000	16.1%
Accounts receivable	100,000	_____	90,000	29.0%
Other current assets	20,000	_____	30,000	9.7%
Total current assets	$158,000	_____	$170,000	54.8%
Plant assets	$150,000	_____	$140,000	45.2%
Total assets	$308,000	_____	$310,000	100%
	Liabilities and Owner's equity			
Current liabilities				
Accounts payable	$ 17,000	_____	$ 20,000	6.5%
Notes payable	20,000	_____	14,000	4.5%
Total current liabilities	$ 37,000	_____	$ 34,000	11.0%
Long-term liabilities	$ 50,000	_____	$ 45,000	14.5%
Total liabilities	$ 87,000	_____	$ 79,000	25.5%
Owner's equity				
Capital stock	$200,000	_____	$190,000	61.3%
Retained earnings	21,000	_____	41,000	13.2%
Total Owner's equity	$221,000	_____	$231,000	74.5%
Total liabilities and Owner's equity	$308,000	_____	$310,000	100%

2.   Perform a vertical analysis on the following comparative balance sheet:

Botanical Exposition, Inc.
Comparative Balance Sheet

| | 1986 | | 1987 | |
	Amount	Percent	Amount	Percent
		Assets		
Current assets				
Cash	$ 44,000	_____	$ 50,000	_____
Accounts receivable	75,000	_____	88,000	_____
Notes receivable	20,000	_____	18,000	_____
Merchandise inventory	44,000	_____	53,000	_____
Prepaid expenses	3,000	_____	5,000	_____
Total current assets	$186,000	_____	$214,000	_____
Plant assets				
Land	$ 60,000	_____	$ 60,000	_____
Buildings	185,000	_____	195,000	_____
Equipment	47,000	_____	50,000	_____
Fixtures	17,000	_____	15,000	_____
Total plant assets	$309,000	_____	$320,000	_____
Total assets	$495,000	_____	$534,000	_____
		Liabilities and Owner's equity		
Current liabilities				
Accounts payable	$ 25,000	_____	$ 28,000	_____
Notes payable	10,000	_____	8,000	_____
Insurance payable	4,000	_____	6,000	_____
Taxes payable	15,000	_____	18,000	_____
Payroll payable	30,000	_____	45,000	_____
Total current liabilities	$ 84,000	_____	$105,000	_____
Long-term liabilities				
Bonds payable	$ 40,000	_____	$ 35,000	_____
Total liabilities	$124,000	_____	$140,000	_____
Owner's equity				
Preferred stock	$ 50,000	_____	$ 70,000	_____
Common stock	100,000	_____	150,000	_____
Retained earnings	221,000	_____	174,000	_____
Total Owner's equity	$371,000	_____	$394,000	_____
Total liabilities and Owner's equity	$495,000	_____	$534,000	_____

3. From the following information, construct a comparative balance sheet for the Kem Card Company and perform a horizontal and a vertical analysis of it. (Retained earnings must be calculated in both years.)

1986		1987	
Cash	$ 1,000	Accounts receivable	$12,000
Accounts payable	7,500	Prepaid expenses	100
Bonds	7,000	Notes receivable	5,000
Preferred stock	8,000	Accounts payable	7,800
Accounts receivable	7,900	Buildings	14,000
Machinery and equipment	14,000	Payroll payable	1,500
Notes receivable	2,000	Bonds	6,000
Insurance payable	80	Land	6,000
Notes payable	4,000	Cash	3,000
Prepaid expenses	60	Insurance payable	100
Payroll payable	1,000	Machinery and equipment	15,000
Land	4,000	Preferred stock	8,000
Common stock	25,000	Notes payable	3,500
Buildings	16,000	Common stock	30,000
Merchandise inventory	11,000	Merchandise inventory	14,000

Kem Card Company
Comparative Balance Sheet

	Vertical Analysis				Horizontal Analysis	
	1986		1987		*Increase or Decrease**	
	Amount	Percent	Amount	Percent	Amount	Percent

Income Statement

The balance sheet records the position of a company at any given time. The *income statement* is a summary of all business transactions affecting operations that have taken place during an accounting period. If the revenues, the resources coming in from providing the product or service, are greater than the expenses, the money going out, the result is a *profit*. A firm that has expenses greater than its revenues suffers a *loss* for the time period being measured. Since the purpose of the income statement is to record how a profit or loss came about, it is often called a *profit and loss statement*. The basic income statement formula is

net income (or net loss) = revenues − expenses

The basic income statement format is shown in Table 11-2 for Bixby Tooling.

Table 11-2	Bixby Tooling, Incorporated Income Statement for the Year Ending December 31, 1987		
1.	Sales		$2,880,500
2.	Sales Returns	$3000	
3.	Sales Allowances	1400	4,400
4.	Net Sales		$2,876,100
5.	Cost of Goods Sold		2,287,300
6.	Gross Margin		$ 588,800
7.	Operating Expenses		321,400
8.	Operating Income		$ 267,400
9.	Other Income and Expenses (net)		25,900
10.	Income Before Taxes		$ 241,500
11.	Federal Income Taxes		115,900
12.	Net Income		$ 125,600

Below is a brief discussion of each of the major items found in the Bixby Tooling, Incorporated income statement, Table 11-2.

1. **Sales**   *Sales* represent the total revenue received or to be received (sales made on credit) by Bixby Tooling, Inc.
2. **Sales Returns**   *Sales returns* are the amount of merchandise sold to, but returned by, customers.
3. **Sales Allowances**   *Sales allowances* are discounts granted to customers because of damage to merchandise, error in shipment, defective merchandise, and so forth.
4. **Net Sales**   *Net sales* is the value of sales revenue after the value of all returned goods and discounts have been deducted.
5. **Cost of Goods Sold**   *Cost of goods sold* is normally the largest expense for a business that sells a product. It is the cost of goods sold during the period covered by the income statement. A business engaged solely in providing services would not have a cost of goods sold.
6. **Gross Margin**   *Gross margin* is determined by subtracting the cost of goods sold from net sales. If the business had no extraordinary or unusual items and no operating expenses, the gross margin amount would also be the net income figure.
7. **Operating Expenses**   *Operating expenses* are the costs incurred in actually running the business. These would be, for example, advertising, selling, and administrative expenses.
8. **Operating Income**   *Operating income* is determined by deducting the operating expenses from gross margin. If operating expenses are larger than gross margin the result is an *operating loss*. Most business firms have several items of nonoperating income and expense. In the event they do not, the operating income would also be the net income.
9. **Other Income and Expenses**   *Other income and expenses* are revenues and expenses that are not a part of the main operating activities of the business. For most business firms, for example, interest income and interest expense would fall into this category.

10. **Income Before Taxes** *Income before taxes* results by finding the difference between operating income and other income and expense. If no tax is due or the company has an operating loss, this would be the net income or net loss.
11. **Federal Income Taxes** *Federal income taxes* are paid by corporations because they are "legal persons." Other forms of business organization, proprietorships, and partnerships must pay taxes as personal income tax.
12. **Net Income** *Net income* is the amount remaining after all expenses have been deducted from the total revenue. Of course, if the total expenses are more than the total revenue, a *net loss* will result.

Example Construct an income statement from the following information: sales, $146,000; sales returns and allowances, $3000; cost of goods sold, $65,000; operating expenses, $42,000.

Solution Determine the amount of net sales:

Jack's Tire Store
Income Statement for the Period January 1, 1986 to December 31, 1987

Sales	$146,000
Less sales returns and allowances	3,000
Net sales	$143,000

Calculate the gross margin:

Net sales	$143,000
Less cost of goods sold	65,000
Gross margin	$ 78,000

Find the net income:

Gross margin	$ 78,000
Less operating expenses	42,000
Net income	$ 36,000

In summary:

Sales	$146,000
Less sales returns and allowances	3,000
Net sales	$143,000
Less cost of goods sold	65,000
Gross margin	$ 78,000
Less operating expenses	42,000
Net income	$ 36,000

Assignment 11-4

1. Find the net income, given the following: net sales, $127,000; cost of goods sold, $32,000; operating expenses, $45,000.

2. Determine net sales from the following information: net income, $1,153,000; operating expenses, $538,000; cost of goods sold, $397,000.

3. Calculate the net income from the following: sales, $77,000; sales returns and allowances, $15,000; cost of goods sold, $42,000; operating expenses, $27,000.

4. Given the following, find the gross margin: cost of goods sold, $12,700; sales, $21,600; operating expenses, $6850.

5. Find the net income from the following: sales $9,430; sales returns and allowances, $50; cost of goods sold, $4290; operating expenses, $4000.

6. Calculate the net income from the following: sales, $32,000; sales returns and allowances, $4000; cost of goods sold, $20,000; operating expenses, $11,000.

Horizontal Analysis of an Income Statement

A horizontal analysis of the income statement is performed just as it is for the balance sheet. That is, the difference, the increase or decrease*, is found between the component parts in a base year and a comparison year. The base year is the earlier year in the comparison. The difference is then divided by the base year to determine the percent change.

When the amounts being compared are positive or when the base year is positive, there is no difficulty in calculating the percent change. However, if the base year is zero or negative, the percent change cannot be calculated. These problems are illustrated in the first three of the following four examples.

Example   Calculate the amount and percent change in the following portion of a comparative income statement:

	1986	1987	Increase or Decrease* Amount	Percent
Net income	$15,000	($10,000)	$25,000*	166.7% *

Solution   The difference between a $15,000 profit in 1986 and a $10,000 loss in 1987 is $25,000. Dividing the decrease by the base year's net income results in

$$\frac{\$25,000}{\$15,000} = 1.6666 = 166.7\% \text{ decrease}$$

Example Compute the amount and percent change in the following portion of a comparative income statement:

	1986	1987	Increase or Decrease* Amount	Percent
Net income	$—0—	$10,000	$10,000	—

Solution The difference between a $0 profit in 1986 and a $10,000 profit in 1987 is an increase of $10,000, but the percent increase cannot be calculated because anything divided by zero is infinite and therefore has no application in this type of problem.

Example Find the amount and percent change in the following portion of a comparative income statement:

	1986	1987	Increase or Decrease* Amount	Percent
Net income	($10,000)	$15,000	$25,000	—

Solution The difference between the net profit of $15,000 in 1987 and the net loss of $10,000 in 1986 is $25,000. The percent increase cannot be calculated because $\frac{\$25,000}{-\$10,000} = -2.5 = -250\%$, and an increase of -250% is impossible.

Example Perform a horizontal analysis on the following comparative income statement.

Motor City, Incorporated
Comparative Income Statement
for the Years Ending December 31, 1986 and 1987

	1986	1987	Increase or Decrease* Amount	Percent
Sales	$192,500	$208,250	$15,750	8.2%
Less sales returns and allowances	4,000	6,250	2,250	56.3%
Net sales	$188,500	$202,000	$13,500	7.2%
Cost of goods sold				
Inventory, January 1	$ 50,000	$ 60,000	$10,000	20.0%
Purchases	100,000	110,000	10,000	10.0%
Freight-in	5,000	7,000	2,000	40.0%
Goods available for sale	$155,000	$177,000	$22,000	14.2%
Inventory, December 31	60,000	65,500	5,500	9.2%
Cost of goods sold	$ 95,000	$111,500	$16,500	17.4%
Gross margin	$ 93,500	$ 90,500	$ 3,000*	3.2%*
Operating expenses				
Salaries expense	$ 30,000	$ 35,000	$ 5,000	16.7%
Advertising expense	8,500	10,000	1,500	17.6%
Depreciation expense	4,800	4,500	300*	6.3%*
Supplies expense	7,350	8,180	830	11.3%
Bad debt expense	1,925	2,080	155	8.1%
Taxes expense	12,200	4,150	8,050*	66.0%*
Total operating expenses	$ 64,775	$ 63,910	$ 865*	1.3%*
Net income	$ 28,725	$ 26,590	$ 2,135*	7.4%*

Solution Each component of the income statement is analyzed by first finding the difference between the component in the base year, 1986, and the comparison year, 1987. The second step is to divide the increase or decrease* by the component in the base year, 1986. For example, the net sales in the comparative income statement are analyzed as follows:

$$\frac{\text{net sales, 1987} - \text{net sales, 1986}}{\text{net sales, 1986}} = \frac{\$202,000 - \$188,500}{\$188,500} = \frac{\$13,500}{\$188,000} = .0716 = 7.2\%$$

All other components are analyzed in the same manner.

Assignment 11-5

1. Perform a horizontal analysis on the following comparative income statement:

Joe's Ice Cream Shop
Comparative Income Statement

	1986	1987	Increase or Decrease* Amount	Percent
Sales	$1,000,000	$1,260,000	$_____	_____
Less sales returns	5,000	4,960	$_____	_____
Net sales	$ 995,000	$1,255,040	$_____	_____
Less cost of goods sold	537,500	564,340	$_____	_____
Gross margin	$ 457,500	$ 690,700	$_____	_____
Less operating expenses	328,250	335,600	$_____	_____
Net income	$ 129,250	$ 355,100	$_____	_____

2. Conduct a horizontal analysis on the following comparative income statement:

Margot's Plumbing
Comparative Income Statement

	1986	1987	Increase or Decrease* Amount	Percent
Sales	$75,000	$82,000	$_____	_____
Less sales returns	$ 3,000	$ 3,250	$_____	_____
Less sales allowances	1,500	1,475	$_____	_____
Total	$ 4,500	$ 4,725	$_____	_____
Net sales	$70,500	$77,275	$_____	_____
Less operating expenses				
Salaries expense	$18,000	$18,260	$_____	_____
Advertising expense	20,000	17,500	$_____	_____
Depreciation expense	4,000	3,295	$_____	_____
Bad debt expense	750	820	$_____	_____
Office supplies expense	1,485	1,600	$_____	_____
Rent expense	6,000	6,000	$_____	_____
Utilities expense	1,215	1,200	$_____	_____
Miscellaneous expense	3,630	3,745	$_____	_____
Total operating expenses	$55,080	$52,420	$_____	_____
Net income	$15,420	$24,855	$_____	_____

3. From the following information, construct a comparative income statement and perform a horizontal analysis for Rollerland:

	1986	1987
Sales returns and allowances	$ 3,000	$ 3,500
Net sales	120,000	134,000
Rent expense	12,000	12,000
Salaries expense	40,000	41,000
Cost of goods sold	30,000	37,000
Advertising expense	10,000	12,000
Delivery expense	5,000	4,500

Rollerland
Comparative Income Statement

	1986	1987	Increase or Decrease* Amount	Percent

Vertical Analysis of an Income Statement

In addition to the horizontal analysis, which shows at a glance any significant variations that might require further managerial investigation, a vertical analysis of the income statement should be made. The base in a vertical analysis is always net sales. Businesses can compare various rates obtained in the vertical analysis with their own past performance, with the rates of similar companies within their geographic area, or with industry-wide rates to help determine their position and progress in relation to other organizations. Various sources are available to managers for these comparisons. Some of the sources are Dun and Bradstreet's, the Mail-Me-Monday Barometer (Accounting Corporation), and the National Retail Merchants Association.

The analysis is performed by dividing each item in the income statement by the net sales in the same year.

Example Conduct a vertical analysis on the following comparative income statement:

Burne's Bowling
Comparative Income Statement

	1986 Amount	Percent	1987 Amount	Percent
Sales	$123,000	_____	$137,500	_____
Less sales returns	3,000	_____	3,500	_____
Net sales	$120,000	_____	$134,000	_____
Less cost of goods sold	30,000	_____	37,000	_____
Gross margin	$ 90,000	_____	$ 97,000	_____
Less operating expenses	67,000	_____	69,500	_____
Net income	$ 23,000	_____	$ 27,500	_____

Solution   Each component in the vertical analysis is divided by the net sales in the same year. For example, cost of goods sold in 1986 as a percent of the net sales in 1986 is

$$\frac{\text{cost of goods sold}}{\text{net sales}} = \frac{\$30,000}{\$120,000} = .25 = 25\%$$

Net income in 1987 as a percent of the net sales in 1987 is

$$\frac{\text{net income}}{\text{net sales}} = \frac{\$27,500}{\$134,000} = .2052 = 20.5\%$$

The remaining calculations are performed in the same manner; the results are shown in the comparative income statement below.

Bruce's Men's Store
Comparative Income Statement

	1986 Amount	1986 Percent	1987 Amount	1987 Percent
Sales	$123,000	102.5%	$137,500	102.6%
Less sales returns	3,000	2.5%	3,500	2.6%
Net sales	$120,000	100.0%	$134,000	100.0%
Less cost of goods sold	30,000	25.0%	37,000	27.6%
Gross margin	$ 90,000	75.0%	$ 97,000	72.4%
Less operating expenses	67,000	55.8%	69,500	51.9%
Net income	$ 23,000	19.2%	$ 27,500	20.5%

Assignment 11-6

1. Perform a vertical analysis of the following comparative income statement:

Bill's Lawnmower Repair
Comparative Income Statement

	1986 Amount	1986 Percent	1987 Amount	1987 Percent
Sales	$1,497,000	_____	$1,250,300	_____
Less sales returns	7,000	_____	5,300	_____
Net sales	$1,490,000	_____	$1,245,000	_____
Less cost of goods sold	1,035,500	_____	836,600	_____
Gross margin	$ 454,500	_____	$ 408,400	_____
Less operating expenses				
Selling expense	$ 190,700	_____	$ 155,600	_____
Administrative expense	104,300	_____	99,800	_____
Total operating expenses	$ 295,000	_____	$ 255,400	_____
Net operating income	$ 159,500	_____	$ 153,000	_____

2. From the following, conduct a vertical analysis:

Sue's Dress Store
Comparative Income Statement

	1986		1987	
	Amount	Percent	Amount	Percent
Sales	$10,000	_____	$11,000	_____
Sales returns	90	_____	110	_____
Sales allowances	50	_____	50	_____
Net sales	$ 9,860	_____	$10,840	_____
Cost of sales				
Opening inventory	$ 5,860	_____	$ 6,520	_____
Net purchases	6,000	_____	5,000	_____
Total merchandise handled	$11,860	_____	$11,520	_____
Closing inventory	6,520	_____	5,520	_____
Cost of sales	$ 5,340	_____	$ 6,000	_____
Gross margin	$ 4,520	_____	$ 4,840	_____
Operating expenses				
Selling expenses				
Sales salaries	$ 500	_____	$ 560	_____
Advertising	240	_____	250	_____
Promotion	80	_____	100	_____
Entertaining	100	_____	90	_____
Automobile	70	_____	75	_____
Total selling expenses	$ 990	_____	$ 1,075	_____
Administrative expenses				
Administrative salaries	$ 450	_____	$ 475	_____
Office supplies	20	_____	25	_____
Utilities	80	_____	90	_____
Rent	120	_____	110	_____
Depreciation	160	_____	150	_____
Bad debt	200	_____	220	_____
Total administrative expenses	$ 1,030	_____	$ 1,070	_____
Total operating expenses	$ 2,020	_____	$ 2,145	_____
Operating profit	$ 2,500	_____	$ 2,695	_____
Extraordinary expenses	70	_____	—0—	_____
Net profit before taxes	$ 2,430	_____	$ 2,695	_____
Federal, state, and local taxes	1,380	_____	1,545	_____
Net profit after taxes	$ 1,050	_____	$ 1,150	_____

3. Construct a comparative income statement and perform a vertical analysis from the following data for the Bertrum Co.:

	1986	1987
Administrative expense	$ 700	$ 1,000
Sales returns and allowances	100	200
Total expenses	1,200	1,500
Sales	15,000	20,000
Cost of goods sold	8,000	10,000

Jones Drug Store
Comparative Income Statement

	1986		1987	
	Amount	*Percent*	*Amount*	*Percent*

4. From the following, prepare a comparative income statement for Smith Hardware and analyze it both vertically and horizontally:

	1986	*1987*
Net sales	$650,000	$600,000
Net profit	80,000	75,000
Gross margin	360,000	350,000
Sales returns and allowances	20,000	70,000

Smith Hardware
Comparative Income Statement

	Vertical Analysis				Horizontal Analysis Increase or Decrease*	
	1986		*1987*			
	Amount	Percent	Amount	Percent	*Amount*	*Percent*

Ratio Analysis

The horizontal and vertical analyses of the balance sheet and the income statement provide managers with valuable problem-solving tools. Other tools in the form of ratios (a ratio is the relationship of one number to another) are used by accountants and financial officers to analyze the financial condition of a business. These ratios are used by bankers in deciding on loans, by investors to help decide upon a reasonable purchase price, and, of course, by management to help identify a company's strengths and weaknesses.

Many ratios are used in decision-making. Five of the most important ratios are discussed in this section. The *current ratio* and the *acid-test ratio* are calculated by using balance sheet information. The *inventory turnover ratio* is figured using data from the income statement. Finally, the *rate of return on owner's equity ratio* and the *accounts receivable to net sales ratio* use information from both the balance sheet and the income statement.

Many of the examples in this section will be based on the following balance sheet and income statement for the Simpson Manufacturing Company.

Simpson Manufacturing Company
Balance Sheet, December 31, 1986

Assets		Liabilities and Owner's equity	
Current assets		Current liabilities	
Cash	$250,000	Accounts payable	$140,000
Accounts receivable	200,000	Notes payable	80,000
Inventory	100,000	Taxes payable	30,000
Prepaid expense	15,000	Total current liabilities	$250,000
Total current assets	$565,000	Long-term liabilities	
Plant assets		Bonds	150,000
Land	$ 30,000	Total liabilities	$400,000
Buildings	210,000		
Equipment	120,000		
Total plant assets	$360,000	Owner's equity	
		Preferred stock	$150,000
		Common stock	200,000
		Retained earnings	175,000
		Total Owner's equity	525,000
Total assets	$925,000	Total liabilities and Owner's equity	$925,000

Simpson Manufacturing Company
Income Statement for the Year Ending December 31, 1986

Net sales		$800,000
Cost of goods sold		
Beginning inventory	$ 50,000	
Purchases	550,000	
Available for sale	$600,000	
Ending inventory	100,000	
Cost of goods sold		500,000
Gross margin		$300,000
Operating expenses		200,000
Net income		$100,000

Current Ratio

The current ratio, sometimes referred to as the *working capital ratio*, is an indicator of a company's ability to meet its current expenses and is measured by comparing current assets to current liabilities. Generally speaking, a ratio of 2 to 1, that is, current assets of two times current liabilities, is considered adequate. However, the desired amount can be more or less than 2, depending on the type of business.

The current ratio for the Simpson Manufacturing Company is

$$\text{current ratio} = \frac{\text{current assets}}{\text{current liabilities}} = \frac{\$565,000}{\$250,000} = \frac{2.26}{1}$$

Note: Ratios are generally written, for example, 2.26:1. The colon (:) is the sign used to denote the word *to*. It is a division sign (÷) with the bar removed, but still indicates division. The ratio 2.26:1 would be read "two point two six to one."

Assignment 11-7

1. Calculate the current ratio in each of the problems below: (Round to the nearest hundredth)

	Current assets	Current liabilities	Current ratio
a.	$ 124.000	$ 62,000	_____
b.	58,000	26,500	_____
c.	1,450,000	563,000	_____
d.	165,858	93,000	_____
e.	28,500	7,460	_____

2. The XYZ Corporation, manufacturers of zippers and other tailoring accessories, has current liabilities of $62,500. Its current ratio is 2:1. What is the amount of the current assets?

3. From the following information, determine the current ratio: (Round to the nearest hundredth)

Sales	$1,300,000	Cash	$ 14,500
Furniture and equipment	152,000	Accounts payable	132,000
Accounts receivable	325,000	Bonds payable	50,000
Capital	600,000	Merchandise inventory	63,000
Notes payable	82,500	Taxes payable	32,000

4. Using the portion of the balance sheet shown below, calculate the current ratio:

Assets		Liabilities	
Cash	$ 33,000	Accounts payable	$25,000
Accounts receivable	42,000	Notes payable	23,000
Notes receivable	15,000	Insurance payable	12,000
Merchandise inventory	50,000	Total current liabilities	$60,000
Total current assets	$140,000		

5. Use Table 11-1, the balance sheet for Bixby Tooling, to calculate the current ratio (round to the nearest hundredth).

Acid-test Ratio

The acid-test ratio is similar to the current ratio but is a more severe test of a firm's ability to meet its obligations. To calculate the acid-test ratio, divide quick assets by current liabilities. Quick assets include only cash, readily marketable securities, and receivables. A ratio of 1:1 is generally acceptable, but comparisons to industry standards would be more meaningful.

The acid-test ratio for Simpson Manufacturing company is

$$\text{acid-test ratio} = \frac{\text{quick assets (cash and marketable securities + receivables)}}{\text{current liabilities}}$$

$$= \frac{\$250,000 + \$200,000}{\$250,000}$$

$$= \frac{\$450,000}{\$250,000} = 1.8:1$$

Assignment 11-8

1. Calculate the acid-test ratio in the following problems. Round your answers to the nearest hundredth):

	Current Liabilities	Cash	Accounts Receivable	Notes Receivable	Prepaid Expenses	Merchandise Inventory	Acid Test Ratio
a.	$200,000	$80,000	$300,000	$12,000	$4,000	$500,000	_____
b.	300,000	300,000	50,000		5,000	750,000	_____
c.	52,500	7,500	20,000	25,000		70,000	_____
d.	100,000	25,000	125,000	5,000	10,000	55,000	_____
e.	700,000	140,000	500,000	15,000	14,000	800,000	_____

2. Using the partial balance sheet given in problem 4, assignment 11-7, calculate the acid-test ratio.

3. Using the data given in problem 3, assignment 11-7, determine the acid-test ratio.

4. From the following information, determine the acid-test ratio:

Cash	$ 40,000
Accounts receivable	850,000
Accounts payable	750,000
Merchandise inventory	1,493,500
Sales	94,350,000
Owner's equity	20,000,000
Salaries payable	75,000
Notes receivable	100,000
Notes payable	50,000
Taxes payable	115,000

5.   Use Table 11-1, the balance sheet for Bixby Tooling, Inc., to calculate the acid-test ratio (round to the nearest hundredth).

Inventory Turnover Ratio

Companies usually have a large amount of money invested in inventory. In addition, there are expenses to maintaining inventory—the cost of insurance, warehouse space, etc. The amount of inventory on hand must be large enough, however, to effectively carry on daily business. By knowing the inventory turnover ratio, a business can know how efficiently its inventory is being handled.

The inventory turnover ratio is also a useful tool for estimating the markup percent on the merchandise the business sells. A business that has a high inventory turnover ratio is likely to have a lower markup percent than a business that has a low inventory turnover ratio. For example, a grocery store is likely to have a high inventory turnover ratio and a low markup percent, whereas a jewelry store is likely to have a low inventory turnover ratio and a high markup percent.

To determine the inventory turnover ratio, divide the cost of goods sold by the average cost of the inventory:

$$\text{inventory turnover ratio} = \frac{\text{cost of goods sold}}{\text{average cost of inventory}}$$

1. *Cost of goods sold* is the cost of all of the merchandise sold during the accounting period.
2. *Average inventory* is usually determined by adding the opening inventory to the closing inventory and dividing the sum by 2:

$$\text{average cost of inventory} = \frac{\text{opening cost of inventory} + \text{closing cost of inventory}}{2}$$

The inventory turnover ratio for the Simpson Manufacturing Company is calculated as follows:

1. Find the average cost of inventory:

$$\text{average cost of inventory} = \frac{\text{opening cost of inventory} + \text{closing cost of inventory}}{2}$$

$$= \frac{\$50,000 + \$100,000}{2}$$

$$= \frac{\$150,000}{2}$$

$$= \$75,000$$

2. Find the inventory turnover ratio:

$$\text{inventory turnover ratio} = \frac{\text{cost of goods sold}}{\text{average inventory}}$$

$$= \frac{\$500,000}{\$75,000}$$

$$= 6\frac{2}{3} : 1$$

Management is interested in knowing the *number of times* the firm sold the average inventory on hand during an accounting cycle. Hence, for convenience, the ratio would be written $6\frac{2}{3}$ times.

Assignment 11-9

Unless otherwise stated, round your answers to the nearest hundredth.

1. At the beginning of an accounting period, a retailer found that his inventory was worth $58,000. At the close of the period, the stock was worth $20,000. During the period, the retailer sold merchandise costing $156,000. What was the inventory turnover ratio?

2. Last year Kohoutek's Telescope shop had an opening inventory of $30,000 and a closing inventory of $50,000. During the year, Kohoutek sold telescopic equipment costing $150,000. What was the inventory turnover ratio?

3. The sales at Goldstein's jewelry store were $24,000 at cost during an accounting period. The opening inventory was $14,000 and the closing inventory was $22,000. What was the inventory turnover ratio?

4. Find the inventory turnover ratio for the following:

	Opening inventory	Closing inventory	Goods sold	Inventory turnover ratio
a.	$ 9,920	$ 6,080	$ 33,600	_____
b.	23,200	8,000	62,400	_____
c.	7,000	13,800	52,000	_____
d.	52,000	28,000	104,000	_____
e.	3,000	1,500	24,000	_____
f.	2,800	2,900	3,500	_____
g.	26,108	5,892	73,600	_____

5. Calculate the inventory turnover ratio for both 1986 and 1987 using the comparative income statement in problem 2, assignment 11-6.

6. Use Table 11-2, the income statement for Bixby Tooling, to calculate the inventory turnover ratio.

Inventory Turnover Ratio with More Than Two Inventory Periods
A more accurate average inventory can be found if a company counts its inventory more than once a year. It would add together all the beginning inventories in a series of inventory periods and the ending inventory for the last inventory period and divide by the number of inventories.

Example

Inventory at cost		Cost of goods sold	
March 1	$ 6,800	March	$ 6,400
April 1	12,800	April	7,200
May 1	16,000	May	9,200
May 31	3,700	Total merchandise sold	$22,800
Total inventory	$39,300		

Solution

$$\text{average cost of inventory} = \frac{\text{total inventory}}{\text{number of inventories}}$$

$$= \frac{\$39,300}{9} = \$9825$$

$$\text{inventory turnover ratio} = \frac{\text{cost of goods sold}}{\text{average cost of inventory}}$$

$$= \frac{\$22,800}{\$9825}$$

$$= 2.32 \text{ times}$$

Assignment 11-10

1. Determine the inventory turnover ratio for the following merchandise sold over a 5-month period:

Inventory at cost		Cost of goods sold	
May 1	$28,000	May	$15,000
June 1	30,000	June	29,000
July 1	41,000	July	32,000
August 1	18,000	August	16,000
Sept. 1	25,000	September	25,000
Sept. 30	38,000		

2. Determine the inventory turnover ratio for the following merchandise. (Round to the nearest hundredth.)

Inventory at cost		Cost of goods sold	
June 1	$568,947.18	June	$259,623.17
July 1	218,437.25	July	127,549.33
August 1	629,312.87	August	437,921.57
August 31	38,406.17		

Rate of Return on Owner's Equity Ratio

The rate of return on owner's equity is a major guide to investors. All investors have a large number of alternative investment possibilities: common stock, preferred stock, corporate bonds, governmental bonds (federal, state, and local), or bank savings accounts to name a few.

The *rate of return on owner's equity ratio* shows the profitability of the stockholders' investment. All other things remaining equal, the higher the rate of return on an investment, the greater the risk. Therefore an investor is not necessarily looking for the highest possible rate of return. For all but a few, called *speculators*, the highest possible rate of return would involve too much risk. However, the rate of return should be at least as high as the prevailing interest rate.

The rate of return on owner's equity ratio is determined by dividing the net income (from the income statement) by the owner's equity (from the balance sheet). For the Simpson Manufacturing Company, the ratio is

$$\text{rate of return on owner's equity ratio} = \frac{\text{net income}}{\text{owner's equity}}$$

$$\text{rate of return on owner's equity} = \frac{\$100,000}{\$525,000} = .1904{:}1$$

$$\text{rate of return on owner's equity} = 19.0\%$$

In the calculation of most ratios, if the ratio is less than 1, it is written as a percent.

Assignment 11-11

1. Calculate the rate of return on owner's equity in each of the following problems:

	Preferred stock	Common stock	Retained earnings	Net income	Rate of return on owner's equity
a.	$100,000	$540,000	$60,000	$ 20,000	_____
b.	60,000	100,000	40,000	15,000	_____
c.	200,000	800,000	75,000	38,000	_____
d.	50,000	950,000	20,000	75,000	_____
e.	130,000	300,000	29,500	38,750	_____
f.	75,000	200,000	74,300	80,000	_____
g.	80,000	238,430	67,980	48,000	_____
h.	400,000	562,750	38,450	12,560	_____
i.	70,000	388,540	98,765	24,700	_____
j.	90,000	756,990	44,797	114,700	_____

2. From the following information, determine the rate of return on owner's equity:

Bonds	$ 100,000
Preferred stock	150,000
Current liabilities	195,000
Net sales	1,000,000
Common stock	1,000,000
Gross margin	460,000
Operating expenses	330,000
Retained earnings	70,000

3. Use Table 11-1, the balance sheet of Bixby Tooling, and Table 11-2, the income statement for Bixby Tooling, to calculate the rate of return on owner's equity.

Accounts Receivable to Net Sales Ratio

The percent of net sales for an accounting period still tied up in accounts receivable is a valuable comparison. An investor wants to be certain that enough cash is being generated by sales to continue to meet future obligations. Also, management and interested outsiders can gain some insight into a company's credit policy. The more liberal the credit policy, the higher the potential loss in accounts receivable should economic conditions take a turn for the worse.

The *ratio of accounts receivable to net sales* is calculated by dividing the accounts receivable by the net sales. The Simpson Manufacturing Company's ratio is

$$\text{accounts receivable to net sales ratio} = \frac{\text{accounts receivable}}{\text{net sales}}$$

$$\text{accounts receivable to net sales ratio} = \frac{\$200,000}{\$800,000}$$

$$\text{accounts receivable to net sales ratio} = .25$$

$$= 25\%$$

The appropriateness of this ratio can be determined by comparison to industry standards.

Assignment 11-12

1. Calculate the accounts receivable to net sales ratio in the following:

	Accounts receivable	Net sales	Ratio of accounts receivable to net sales
a.	$330,000	$1,498,000	_____
b.	224,000	783,000	_____
c.	98,500	802,000	_____
d.	81,200	780,000	_____
e.	212,000	744,000	_____
f.	390,630	950,000	_____
g.	592,410	1,650,000	_____
h.	461,700	1,425,000	_____

2. Use Table 11-1 and 11-2 of Bixby Tooling to calculate the accounts receivable to net sales ratio.

Chapter 11 Self-Testing Exercises

1. Prepare both a vertical and a horizontal analysis of the following portion of a balance sheet:

Dennis Realty Company
Comparative Balance Sheet — December 31, 1986 and 1987

| | Vertical Analysis | | | | Horizontal Analysis | |
| | 1986 | | 1987 | | Increase or Decrease* | |
	Amount	Percent	Amount	Percent	Amount	Percent
Assets						
Current assets						
Cash	$ 3,000		$ 3,200			
Accounts receivable	2,000		4,000			
Notes receivable	15,000		10,000			
Inventory	5,000		8,000			
Total current assets	$ 25,000		$ 25,200			
Plant assets						
Land	$ 50,000		$ 75,000			
Building	20,000		25,000			
Furniture	10,000		12,000			
Equipment	5,000		7,500			
Total plant assets	$ 85,000		$119,500			
Total assets	$110,000		$144,700			

2. Using the following income statement, perform both a vertical and a horizontal analysis (round off to the nearest whole percent):

Acme Chemical
Comparative Income Statement
for the Years Ended June 30, 1986 and 1987

	1986	1987
Sales	$350,000	$400,000
Returns and allowances	25,000	10,000
Net sales	$325,000	$390,000
Cost of goods sold	105,000	136,500
Gross margin	$220,000	$253,500
Operating expenses		
Selling expense	$ 85,000	$101,200
Administrative expense	70,000	76,000
Total operating expenses	$155,000	$177,200
Net profit	$ 65,000	$ 76,300

3. From the following balance sheet and income statement, calculate
    a. the current ratio
    b. the acid-test ratio
    c. the rate of return on owner's equity
    d. the accounts receivable to net sales ratio

Balance Sheet

Assets		Liabilities and Owner's Equity	
Current assets		Current liabilities	
Cash	$ 50,000	Accounts payable	$ 20,000
Accounts receivable	80,000	Taxes payable	40,000
Merchandise inventory	40,000	Total current liabilities	$ 60,000
Total current assets	$170,000	Long term liabilities	
Plant assets		Bonds payable	$ 80,000
Furniture	$100,000	Total liabilities	$140,000
Equipment	50,000		
Total plant assets	$150,000	Owner's equity	
		Preferred stock	$ 70,000
		Common stock	90,000
		Retained earnings	20,000
		Total Owner's equity	$180,000
Total assets	$320,000	Total liabilities and Owner's equity	$320,000

Income Statement

Net sales	$180,000
Cost of goods sold	95,000
Gross margin	$ 85,000
Operating expenses	70,000
Net income	$ 15,000

4. From the following information, calculate the inventory turnover ratio:

	Inventory at cost	Cost of goods sold for the month
January 1	$23,000	$26,000
February 1	26,000	18,000
March 1	18,000	30,000
March 31	23,000	

5. Calculate owner's equity from the following:

Cash	$ 20,000	Accounts payable	$700,000
Accounts receivable	200,000	Notes payable	100,000
Merchandise inventory	300,000	Interest payable	50,000
Plant and equipment	500,000		

6. Determine net income from the following:

Sales	$1,000,000
Cost of goods sold	600,000
Operating expenses	100,000
Sales returns	20,000
Sales allowances	30,000

7. Accounts payable are $20,000 for 1986 and $24,000 for 1987; perform a horizontal analysis.

8. What is the current ratio given the following:

Sales	$80,000
Current assets	50,000
Net income	3,000
Current liabilities	30,000

9. From the following:

   a. prepare an income statement
   b. analyze the statement vertically
   c. calculate the inventory ratio

Sales	$100,000
Inventory, January 1, 1986	20,000
Purchases	70,000
Inventory, December 31, 1986	30,000
Sales returns and allowances	10,000
Operating expenses	12,000

10. Using the following comparative balance sheet and comparative income statement for Domestic Services, Inc:

a. Perform a horizontal analysis on the comparative balance sheet.
b. Conduct a vertical analysis on the comparative balance sheet.
c. Perform a horizontal analysis on the comparative income statement.
d. Conduct a vertical analysis on the comparative income statement.
e. Calculate the current ratio for 1986 and 1987.
f. Calculate the acid-test ratio for 1986 and 1987.
g. Determine the inventory turnover ratio for 1986 and 1987.
h. Figure the rate of return on owner's equity for 1986 and 1987.
i. Calculate the ratio of accounts receivable to net sales for 1986 and 1987.

Domestic Services, Inc.
Comparative Balance Sheet, December 31, 1986 and 1987

	1986	1987
Current assets		
Cash	$ 30,000	$ 25,000
Accounts receivable	50,000	60,000
Merchandise inventory	80,000	70,000
Total current assets	$160,000	$155,000
Plant assets		
Land	$ 60,000	$ 60,000
Building	200,000	250,000
Equipment	40,000	50,000
Total plant assets	$300,000	$360,000
Total assets	$460,000	$515,000
Current liabilities		
Accounts payable	$ 80,000	$ 70,000
Notes payable	40,000	30,000
Salaries payable	30,000	40,000
Taxes payable	10,000	20,000
Total current liabilities	$160,000	$160,000
Long-term liabilities		
Bonds	$ 50,000	$ 55,000
Total liabilities	$210,000	$215,000
Owner's equity		
Common stock	$140,000	$150,000
Preferred stock	50,000	55,000
Retained earnings	60,000	95,000
Total Owner's equity	$250,000	$300,000
Total liabilities and Owner's equity	$460,000	$515,000

Domestic Services, Inc.
Income Statement for the Years Ending December 31, 1986 and 1987

	1986	1987
Sales	$1,200,000	$1,300,000
Less sales returns and allowances	20,000	10,000
Net sales	$1,180,000	$1,290,000
Cost of goods sold		
Inventory, January 1	$ 90,000	$ 80,000
Purchases	500,000	570,000
Goods available for sales	$ 590,000	$ 650,000
Inventory, December 31	80,000	70,000
Cost of goods sold	$ 510,000	$ 580,000
Gross margin	$ 670,000	$ 710,000
Operating expenses		
Salaries expense	$ 280,000	$ 320,000
Advertising expense	150,000	200,000
Depreciation expense	100,000	120,000
Supplies expense	10,000	12,000
Bad debt expense	1,000	800
Taxes expense	19,000	22,200
Total operating expenses	$ 560,000	$ 675,000
Net income	$ 110,000	$ 35,000

PAGE NO.

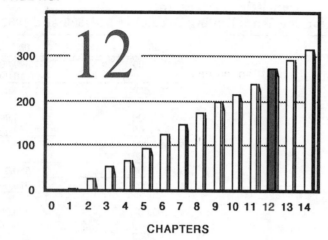

CHAPTERS

Statistical Applications and Metric Measurement

Student Objectives

Upon completion of this chapter, the student should be able to

1. **Arrange** *data in an array.*
2. **Perform** *a frequency distribution of data.*
3. **Find** *the range in data.*
4. **Calculate** *the mean, median, and mode.*
5. **Construct** *line graphs, bar graphs, and circle graphs.*
6. **Make** *everyday calculations using metric weights and measures.*
7. **Define, illustrate,** *or* **use**

graph	*frequency distribution*
line graph	*mean*
multiple-line graph	*median*
bar graph	*mode*
comparative bar graph	*central tendency*
circle graph	*gram*
array	*liter*
range	*meter*

Basic Business Statistics

In the modern business community, managers must know how to analyze statistical data accurately. Business decisions today depend on judgments based on definite, measurable facts rather than on intuition, as has often been the case in the past.

Statistics is that branch of mathematics that is concerned with collecting, classifying, analyzing, and interpreting data. The purpose of statistics is to order data, which makes them useful.

Terminology

To understand statistics, it is necessary to know the meaning of some basic terminology that appears frequently.

Definitions

1. *Data* Facts, information, or values derived by experiment.
2. *Array* An arrangement of data according to numerical size:

Example

```
    11
    11
     9
     8
     8
     7
     7
     7
     4
   ───
     9   number of values
```

---

3. *Frequency Distribution* An arrangement of data with the numerical values grouped to show the frequency with which each size of data occurs:

Example (using the same data as above)

value	frequency
11	2
9	1
8	2
7	3
4	1
	9 number of values

---

4. *Range* The difference between the smallest and the largest value in a set of data:

Example (using the same data as above)

```
   11   largest value
 −  4   smallest value
  ───
    7   range
```

Assignment 12-1

1. Given the following data, arrange them in an array, perform a frequency distribution, and find the range.

    a. 8, 12, 3, 8, 53, 12, 8, 3

    b. 87, 42, 112, 37, 42, 87

    c. 1, 7, 13, 5, 13, 1, 5

    d. 4768, 1123, 4768, 3523, 1123, 4768

Measures of Central Tendency

Central tendency is a value that is used to represent a group of values within a range. There are three commonly used measures of central tendency. These are the arithmetic mean, the median, and the mode. Each can be useful in certain instances, depending upon the data being analyzed and upon what is to be determined from the data.

Arithmetic Mean

The most commonly used measure of central tendency is the *arithmetic mean*. In most cases, an arithmetic mean is what people refer to as an *average*. The arithmetic mean is found by adding together all the values in a series of data and dividing by the number of values in the series. The formula for finding the arithmetic mean is

$$\text{arithmetic mean} = \frac{\text{sum of values}}{\text{number of values}}$$

Example Find the arithmetic mean of the following array: 11, 11, 9, 8, 8, 7, 7, 7, 4.

Solution

$$
\left.\begin{array}{r}
11 \\
11 \\
9 \\
8 \\
8 \\
7 \\
7 \\
7 \\
+\ 4 \\
\end{array}\right\} \text{number of values} = 9
$$

$$\overline{72} \quad \text{sum of values}$$

$$\text{arithmetic mean} = \frac{\text{sum of values}}{\text{number of values}}$$

$$= \frac{72}{9}$$

$$= 8$$

Assignment 12-2

1. Abdul's oil well produced the following number of barrels of oil in 1 week: Sunday, 640; Monday, 580; Tuesday, 745; Wednesday, 628; Thursday, 470; Friday, 929; and Saturday, 348. Find the arithmetic mean for daily production for the week.

2. Jerry had the following grades in business math: 86, 45, 97, 73, 86, 54. What is his average grade for the course?

3. Find the arithmetic mean for the following series of numbers:

		Arithmetic mean
a.	295, 497, 632, 101, 98	_____
b.	12, 16, 18, 42, 31, 18, 17	_____
c.	83.5, 65.2, 18.7, 9.98	_____
d.	$100,000, $2	_____
e.	196, 194, 197, 195, 52	_____
f.	2, 4, 6, 8, 10, 12, 14	_____

Median

The *median* is the value at the midpoint in an array. The median is found by counting the number of values in an array of data and applying the formula $\frac{n+1}{2}$, where n is the number of values, to find the position of the middle value. If there are an odd number of values, the median will be the middle value. If the array contains an even number of values, the median will be the halfway point between the two middle values.

Example Find the median for the following data: 11, 8, 12, 9, 12, 8, 7.

Solution

  1. Arrange the data in an array:

   7, 8, 8, 9, 11, 12, 12

  2. Count the number of values (there are seven).
  3. The middle value would be in the fourth position counting from either end:

   $\frac{7+1}{2} = 4$

  4. The median is 9 (the fourth value from either end of the array).

Example Find the median for the following data: 11, 7, 12, 10, 6, 4, 11, 5.

Solution

  1. Arrange the data in an array:

   4, 5, 6, 7, 10, 11, 11, 12

  2. Count the number of values (there are eight).
  3. The middle value would be halfway between the fourth value from each end:

   $\frac{8+1}{2} = 4.5$

4. Find the mean for the values 7 and 10:

$$\frac{7 + 10}{2} = 8.5$$

5. The median is 8.5.

Assignment 12-3

1. Find the median salary of the workers in Zeke's print shop. Their salaries are as follows:

Albert	$104
Bennie	$ 96
Clara	$110
Dora	$ 90
Emmet	$100

2. Find the median output for the workers at Zelda's custom sewing shop in a week in which they produced the following:

Anita	8 dresses
Bruce	10 dresses
Cora	6 dresses
Diane	4 dresses
Elane	12 dresses
Flora	9 dresses

3. Find the median in each of the following:

		Median
a.	6, 1, 7, 5, 4	_____
b.	66, 12, 42, 98, 3	_____
c.	31, 218, 4, 65	_____
d.	14, 9, 4, 8, 6, 12	_____
e.	8, 7, 12, 9, 16	_____
f.	11, 7, 14, 35, 19, 6	_____

Mode

The value that occurs the greatest number of times in a series is the *mode*.

Example   Find the mode for the following data: 12, 12, 10, 9, 9, 8, 8, 8, 5.

Solution   Arrange the data in a frequency distribution. The mode is the value occurring the greatest number of times:

Value	Frequency
12	2
10	1
9	2
8 = mode	3
5	1

In some cases, there may be no mode in a series of numbers and, in other cases, a series of numbers may contain two or more modes:

Example

	13	
12	12	mode
10	12	
9 no mode	8	
8	7	mode
7	7	
	6	

Assignment 12-4

1. The cashiers in a supermarket are paid the following hourly wages: $3.25, $3.25, $3.25, $4.50, $4.50, $4.50, $4.75, $4.75, $4.75, $4.75. What is the mode?

2. A toy shop sells several different styles of Barbie doll kits, depending on the number of accessories that go into a particular kit. This past Christmas, the store sold kits for the following prices: $3.98, $3.98, $3.98, $3.98, $3.98, $2.19, $2.19, $2.19, $2.99, $2.99, $2.99, $2.99, $6.99, $6.99. Find the modal price.

3. Find the mode in the following series of numbers:

		Mode
a.	6.25, 5, 3.86, 7, 3.37, 5	_____
b.	2.14, 2.14, 3.75, 3.75, 1.3	_____
c.	75, 81, 23, 75, 81, 75, 23	_____
d.	38, 41, 39, 42, 40, 43	_____
e.	4, 1, 3, 7, 6, 3, 4, 5, 4	_____
f.	225, 224, 225, 226, 225	_____

Graphs

The main purpose of a *graph* is to aid in the interpretation and comparison of data. A table that contains the same information as a graph is not likely to make as strong an impression as the graph. This is not meant to suggest that graphs should always replace tables. Graphs cannot usually be as accurate as tables and are usually used only as supplements to them.

Line Graphs

The most adaptable of the commonly used types of graphs is the *line graph*. Line graphs are useful in situations where time is one of the major elements in the table. This is especially true when an attempt is made to compare two or more kinds of data over the same time period.

A *multiple-line graph* is a line graph that contains more than one series of data. The data are easily compared in this type of graph, as shown in the following example.

Example   Prepare a multiple-line graph using the data in the following table:

Comparison of Total U.S. Investment and Residential Construction, 1977-1987 (in billions of dollars)

Year	Total U.S. Investment	Residential Construction
1977	$ 68	$20
1978	61	21
1979	75	26
1980	75	23
1981	72	23
1982	83	25
1983	87	27
1984	94	27
1985	107	27
1986	118	24
1987	112	25

Solution

1. Show the time element on the horizontal scale of the graph and the quantities or values on the vertical scale, beginning with zero at the bottom.
2. On the vertical scale, list the quantities or values in some convenient interval for plotting the data (2, 5, 10, and so on).
3. At each point where the time and quantity relationships intersect, place a dot.
4. Connect the dots with a straight edge.

The completed graph is shown at the top of the next page.

TOTAL U.S. INVESTMENT AND
RESIDENTIAL CONSTRUCTION, 1972-1982

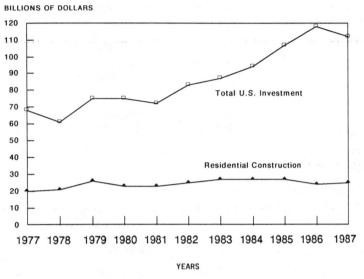

The graph exemplifies vividly what can be found only through close study of the table: over the 10-year period from 1977 to 1987, residential construction did not fluctuate as much as did total U.S. investment.

Assignment 12-5

1. Prepare a multiple-line graph for the net sales and net income of the Kennedy Alcoholic Beverage Corporation using the following data:

Year	Net sales	Net income
1981	$ 75,000	$ 6,000
1982	74,000	7,500
1983	71,000	7,300
1984	79,000	10,000
1985	95,000	11,250
1986	100,000	6,300
1987	119,000	7,000

2. Prepare a line graph showing the income from residential and commercial accounts for the Muleshoe, Texas, Telephone Company:

Month	Income from residential accounts	Income from commercial accounts
July	$156,000	$100,000
August	148,000	84,000
September	200,000	175,000
October	180,000	140,000
November	204,000	182,000
December	260,000	280,000

3. The Goldwater Department Store is attempting to compare gross sales for the first 6 months of 1986 and 1987. Sales for the two periods were as follows:

Month	1986 sales	1987 sales
January	$100,000	$110,000
February	90,000	70,000
March	130,000	135,000
April	145,000	150,000
May	160,000	170,000
June	200,000	190,000

Prepare a multiple-line graph to show the comparison.

Bar Graphs

Bar graphs are used for many of the same purposes as line graphs, to show simple comparisons of size and to make time comparisons. In a bar graph, the length of each bar corresponds to the size of the data it represents.

Example Using the following data, prepare a bar graph of total U.S. investment from 1977 to 1987:

Year	Total U.S. investment (in billions)
1977	$ 68
1978	61
1979	75
1980	75
1981	72
1982	83
1983	87
1984	94
1985	107
1986	118
1987	112

Solution
1. Divide a horizontal scale into 11 equal parts and label the parts for the years from 1977 to 1987.
2. Using a convenient interval (in this problem, 10), mark off intervals from 0 to 120 on the vertical scale (120 is the next 10 interval greater than the largest value in the series, which is 118).
3. Draw the equally spaced bars in proportion to the data being represented.

The completed graph is shown below.

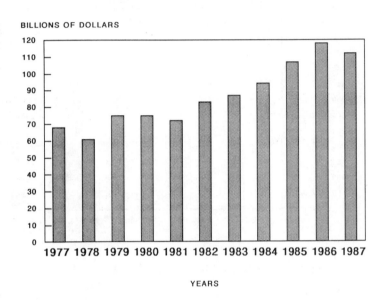

Total U.S. Investment and
Residential Construction, 1977-1987

Comparative Bar Graphs
Another type of bar graph is one that shows comparisons of data for more than one period.

Example   Using the data given below, prepare a bar graph of third-quarter profits for six competing companies for 1986 and 1987:

| Company | Third-quarter profits (in millions of dollars) | |
	1986	*1987*
Exxon	$353	$638
Gulf	110	210
Mobil	141	231
Phillips	37	53
Royal Dutch	110	413
Texaco	207	307

Solution
1. Divide a horizontal scale into six equal parts and label for each of the companies.
2. Using a convenient interval (in this case, 50), mark off intervals from 0 to 650 on the vertical scale.
3. Plot the appropriate amount of profits for each company for each year.

4. Select two different types of bars (in this case, one is shaded and the other is white).

The completed graph is shown below.

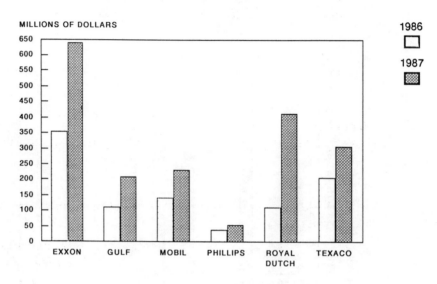

Assignment 12-6

1. Prepare a bar graph showing a comparison of sales for the month of January for the following salespeople.

Salesperson	Sales in January
Alphonzo	$36,400
Beatrice	30,800
Cranston	33,600
Delilah	29,400
Effrin	23,800
Grayson	26,600

2. Prepare a comparative bar graph for the Goldwater department store sales for the first 6 months of 1986 and 1987. Sales for the period were

Month	1986 sales	1987 sales
January	$100,000	$110,000
February	90,000	70,000
March	130,000	135,000
April	145,000	150,000
May	160,000	170,000
June	200,000	190,000

Circle Graphs

Circle graphs are most useful for showing a percentage distribution of the parts of a whole.

Example   Using the following data about U.S. federal tax receipts, construct a circle graph of federal revenue:

	U.S. federal revenue (billions of dollars)
Personal income taxes	$450
Corporation income taxes	150
Payroll taxes	300
Excise taxes	50
Other taxes	50
Total	$1000

Solution   1. Draw a circle
2. Convert each part of the data to percents of the total:

$$\text{Personal income taxes} \quad \frac{\$450}{\$1000} = 45\%$$

$$\text{Corporation income taxes} \quad \frac{\$150}{\$1000} = 15\%$$

$$\text{Payroll taxes} \quad \frac{\$300}{\$1000} = 30\%$$

$$\text{Excise taxes} \quad \frac{\$50}{\$1000} = 5\%$$

$$\text{Other taxes} \quad \frac{\$50}{\$1000} = 5\%$$

3. The whole circle contains $360°$. Multiply the percent of each part of the data by $360°$.

Personal income taxes	$45\% \times 360° = 162°$
Corporation income taxes	$15\% \times 360° = 54°$
Payroll taxes	$30\% \times 360° = 108°$
Excise taxes	$5\% \times 360° = 18°$
Other taxes	$5\% \times 360° = 18°$

4. Using a protractor, divide the circle into sections that correspond to the number of degrees needed to represent the proportional segment for each part of the data.
5. Label the graph.

The completed graph is shown below.

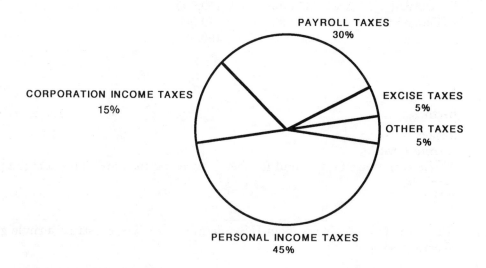

PAYROLL TAXES
30%

CORPORATION INCOME TAXES
15%

EXCISE TAXES
5%

OTHER TAXES
5%

PERSONAL INCOME TAXES
45%

Assignment 12-7

1.   Draw a circle graph showing the breakdown of shoe sales at Bimble's Department Store:

Women's shoes	50%
Men's shoes	25%
Children's shoes	25%

2.   Bilge Publishing Company has the following long-term debt and equity (in millions of dollars):

Long-term liabilities	$30
Preferred stock	15
Common stock	25
Retained earnings	20

Prepare a circle graph based on these data.

Metric Measurement

The metric system of weights and measures was developed by a commission of French scientists in the late 18th century following a period in which mathematicians had made some very important discoveries about the use of the base-10 numbering system. The main advantage of the metric system is that it is based upon algebraic thinking rather than geometric thinking.

Basic Units
In the metric system there are three basic units of measure:

meter for length or distance
gram for weight
liter for capacity or volume

The names of units larger and smaller than the basic units are formed by adding the Greek and Latin prefixes shown in Table 12-1. The measures themselves are shown in Table 12-2.

Table 12-1
Metric
System
Prefixes

Prefix	Abbreviation	Number $\times$ Basic Unit	
kilo-	k	(10^3)	$1000 \times$ basic unit
hecto-	h	(10^2)	$100 \times$ basic unit
deka-	dk	(10^1)	$10 \times$ basic unit
deci-	d	(10^{-1})	$\frac{1}{10} \times$ basic unit
centi-	c	(10^{-2})	$\frac{1}{100} \times$ basic unit
milli-	m	(10^{-3})	$\frac{1}{1000} \times$ basic unit

Table 12-2
Units of the
Metric
System

Length		Weight		Capacity	
Unit	*Abbreviation*	*Unit*	*Abbreviation*	*Unit*	*Abbreviation*
kilometer	km	kilogram	kg	kiloliter	kl
hectometer	hm	hectogram	hg	hectoliter	hl
dekameter	dkm	dekagram	dkg	dekaliter	dkl
meter	m	gram	g	liter	l
decimeter	dm	decigram	dg	deciliter	dl
centimeter	cm	centigram	cg	centiliter	cl
millimeter	mm	milligram	mg	milliliter	ml

The distinct advantage of the metric system should already be apparent. Each unit is ten times greater than the next smaller unit. This eliminates the need to make conversions from inches to feet, ounces to pounds, feet to miles, and so on. The name of each unit indicates exactly how many units as well as what kind of unit. To convert from one unit to another, move a decimal point one space for each level on the scale.

Example   How many grams are there in 3 kilograms?

Solution

kilogram	3 kilograms	(given)
hectotgram	= 30 hectograms	↓
dekagram	= 300 dekagrams	
gram	= 3000 grams	(answer)
decigram		
centigram		
milligram		

Example	How many meters are there in 2 centimeters?

Solution	kilometer
	hectometer
	dekameter
	meter = .02 meters (answer)
	decimeter = .2 decimeters ↑
	centimeter 2 centimeters (given)
	millimeter

Example	How many hectoliters are there in 700 deciliters?

Solution	kiloliter
	hectoliter = .7 hectoliter (answer)
	dekaliter = 7 dekaliters ↑
	liter = 70 liters	
	deciliter 700 deciliters (given)
	centiliter
	milliliter

Assignment 12-8

1.   Complete the following conversions:

   a. 1000 meters = _____ kilometers
   b. .2 gram = _____ decigrams
   c. 3 hectoliters = _____ liters
   d. .001 centigram = _____ milligrams
   e. 27 meters = _____ millimeters
   f. 463 liters = _____ kiloliters
   g. .72 dekameter = _____ centimeters
   h. 38.65 grams = _____ kilograms
   i. .001 milliliter = _____ kiloliters
   j. 5623 kilograms = _____ milligrams

Solving Problems Using Metric Measurement

Solving problems using metric measurement is no different from solving other problems with the base-10 numbering system. When the student has become thoroughly familiar with its use, metric measurement is much easier and quicker to use than the system Americans have been using.

To solve such problems, it is first necessary to convert all figures in the problem into the same units. Americans are tempted to do this by multiplication or division by powers of 10. It is much easier, and more in keeping with the way other people in the world work with measurements, to make the conversions by moving the decimal point up or down the scale of the metric prefixes.

Example	Schmaltz Inc. is selling a new formula of mouthwash. Each liter contains 25 milliliters of glycerin. How many deciliters of glycerin would be in 2 kiloliters of the mouthwash?

Solution
1. All figures must be converted into the same units. Since the final answer is going to be in deciliters, convert the 2 kiloliters and the 25 milliliters into deciliters:
   a. Move the 2 from the kiloliter position to the dekaliter position. At each step going down the scale, move the decimal point one place to the right.
   b. Move the 25 from the milliliter position to the dekaliter position. At each step going up the scale, move the decimal point one place to the left.

   kl ⌐   2
   hl │   20
   dkl │   200
   l ↓   2000
   dl ↓   20,000   ↑ .25
   cl   │ 2.5
   ml   ⌐┘ 25

2. Divide 20,000 by .25:

   $$\begin{array}{r} 80{,}000 \\ \overline{.25)20{,}000.00} \end{array}$$

3. The answer is 80,000 deciliters of glycerin.

Assignment 12-9

1. It is 56 kilometers from Fort Worth to Dallas, and Arlington is between the two cities. Arlington is 25 kilometers from Fort Worth. How far is Arlington from Dallas?

2. Pharmaceuticals International has developed a new drug. The drug will sell for $.20 per capsule, and each capsule contains 10 milligrams of the drug. How much will 15 grams sell for?

3. A car traveling at the rate of 86 kilometers per hour will go how far in 12 hours?

4. A board is 4 meters long. How many pieces 8 centimeters long can be cut from the board?

5. Gasoline costs $.36 per liter. How much does a kiloliter cost?

6. A tank holds 47 kiloliters of water. How many deciliters does it hold?

7. A book is 3 centimeters thick. How many books are there in a stack 6 meters tall?

8. A sprinter in a track meet goes 2 meters with each step. How many kilometers will she go in 2638 steps?

9. George's Inc. sells eggs that weigh .8 kilogram per average dozen. How many grams does one average egg weigh?

10. Matilda's bakery produces cakes that weigh 2 kilograms each. Joe bought one of the cakes for a party and cut it into 20 equal portions. How many grams did each piece of cake weigh?

11. Myrtle's Machine Shop makes pipe hangers from steel rods. A rod is 10 meters long. How many hangers can be produced from a rod if each hanger requires a piece 5 decimeters long?

12. Paul lives 12 kilometers from his job. Last year, he worked 215 days. How many kilometers did he drive going to and from work last year?

13. Deana's cow pasture measures 2 hectometers by 3 hectometers. She wants to put a four-strand barbed-wire fence around it. A roll of wire is 250 meters long. How many rolls will she have to buy?

14. Juanita bought 14 packages of hamburger meat. The average package weighed 420 grams. How many kilograms of hamburger did Juanita buy?

15. Mr. Benavides has a new Chevrolet which used 1.5 kiloliters of gasoline on his 12,000-kilometer vacation last year. What was the average gasoline consumption in kilometers per liter?

Conversion

Since in the not-too-distant future, metric measurement will become a common practice in the United States, it is *not* advantageous for Americans to make conversions. We should attempt to accustom ourselves to thinking in terms of meters, grams, and liters rather than in terms of feet, ounces, and gallons. However, to provide a reference point with which Americans are already familiar, a few conversions are useful.

The equivalents for commonly used metric measures are

meter = 39.37 inches
gram = .0353 ounce
liter = 1.057 quarts
kilogram (kilo) = 2.21 pounds
kilometer = .621 mile

Note: In countries that use the metric system, it is a common practice to refer to a kilogram as a *kilo* in everyday transactions.

Example   1 dekameter = _____ yards

Solution   1 meter = 39.37 inches
1 dekameter = 10 meters
10 × 39.37 = 393.7 inches
1 yard = 36 inches
$\frac{393.7}{36}$ = 10.94 yards

Assignment 12-10

1. Make the following conversions (carry out the answers to the nearest one hundredth):

   a. 240 kilometers = _____ miles
   b. 6 meters = _____ inches
   c. 72 ounces = _____ grams
   d. 25 yards = _____ meters
   e. 20 liters = _____ gallons
   f. 80 kiloliters = _____ gallons
   g. 18 quarts = _____ liters
   h. 16 liters = _____ pints
   i. 12 kilos = _____ pounds
   j. 47 grams = _____ ounces

2. An American tourist is buying sugar in a supermarket in Germany. If the sugar costs $.49 per kilo, how much does it cost per pound? (Round off to the nearest cent.)

3. Cans of beans sold by the Green Thumb Company are available internationally. If the beans are packed in 18-ounce cans, what metric weight must be shown on the label?

4. Vodka sells for $1.50 per liter in Mexico. How much does it cost per quart?

It should be obvious from the preceding assignment that converting from the metric system to the U.S. system is difficult and essentially inaccurate. Americans should be discouraged from attempting to convert when the nation does adopt the metric system of measurement. It is obvious, however, that some converting will inevitably be attempted. To facilitate converting when a calculator is not available, the following approximate equivalents can be used when accuracy is not important:

meter $\quad$ = approximately $1\frac{1}{10}$ yards

gram $\quad$ = approximately $\frac{1}{30}$ ounce

liter $\quad$ = approximately 1 liquid quart

kilogram = approximately 2 pounds

kilometer = approximately $\frac{3}{5}$ mile

Assignment 12-11

1. Approximately how many pounds are there in a bag of flour that weighs 4 kilos?

2. Approximately how many liters are there in $\frac{1}{2}$ gallon of milk?

3. Two cities are 15 kilometers apart. Approximately how many miles is this?

4. A can of soup weighs $10\frac{1}{2}$ ounces. Approximately how many grams does it weigh?

5. An athletic field is 90 meters long. Approximately how many yards long is it?

Chapter 12   Self-Testing Exercises

1. Find the mean:

    a. 25, 41, 18, 61, 32, 27   **b.** 24.649, 235.69, 2293.7, 2.5769

2. A lazy student had test scores of 67, 42, 70, and 59 on his first four tests. By
    final exam time, he decided he had better start studying if he expected to make
    a grade better than D. He made 96 on the exam. If the teacher counted all tests
    the same, what was his mean grade for the course?

3. Compute the mean, median, and mode for the following grade distribution: 85,
    48, 82, 74, 76, 93, 58, 76.

4. Calculate the mean, median, and mode of the following sales figures:

Dept. A	$4500	Dept. E	$3850
Dept. B	2350	Dept. F	1250
Dept. C	6000	Dept. G	5700
Dept. D.	2350	Dept. H	3000

5. Show the relationship between each salesman's sales volume on a bar graph:

John	$158,000	Sid	$146,000
Sam	210,000	Joe	150,000
Bill	167,000	Eric	200,000

6. Your tax dollar goes to provide many government services. Draw a circle graph
    showing the relationship of the following services, assuming they total 100%
    (figures in millions of dollars):

Roads	$55
Education	35
Police protection	25
Fire protection	10

7. Draw a line graph using the following sales comparisons for 1986 and 1987:

	1986	1987
January	$18,000	$20,000
February	15,000	19,000
March	20,000	20,000
April	22,000	24,000
May	25,000	29,000
June	30,000	35,000
July	24,000	30,000
August	25,000	28,000
September	26,000	25,000
October	20,000	18,000
November	27,000	25,000
December	35,000	38,000

8. A pipeline is 12 hectometers long. How many pieces of pipe, each 4 meters long, does the line contain?

9. The gasoline tank on Marvin's car holds 20 gallons. How many liters will the tank hold?

10. Minnie is concerned about her weight problem. Ten days ago, she weighed 900 hectograms. She has been losing 500 grams per day since then. How many kilograms does Minnie now weigh?

11. It is 300 kilometers from Little Rock to Memphis. Approximately how many miles is it?

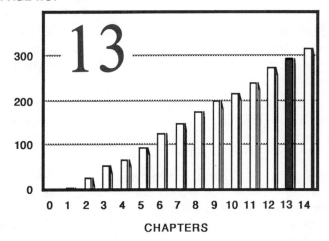

CHAPTERS

Securities Market Applications

Student Objectives

Upon completion of this chapter, the student should be able to

1. **Calculate** *common stock dividend payments in cash and in stock.*
2. **Determine** *the amount of stock and bond premiums and stock and bond discounts.*
3. **Compute** *preferred stock dividends if the stock is noncumulative, cumulative, or participating.*
4. **Determine** *all costs associated with stock purchases and sales and with bond purchases and sales.*
5. **Calculate** *the current yield of bonds.*
6. **Amortize** *bond premiums and discounts.*
7. **Define, illustrate,** *or* **use**

common stock	*premium*	*odd-lot differential*
preferred stock	*discount*	*current yield*
dividends	*noncumulative preferred*	*bond*
cash dividends	*cumulative preferred*	*amortization*
stock dividends	*participating preferred*	*bond-carrying value*
par value	*odd lot*	*premium amortization*
market value	*round lot*	*discount amortization*
no-par stock		

Stocks and Bonds

Corporations obtain needed funds to purchase long-term (fixed) assets from two main sources, stocks and bonds. While the sale of both stocks and bonds provides funds for long-term financing, there are many differences between these two types of securities. The main differences are presented in Table 13-1.

Decisions to purchase particular stocks or bonds are based on many different goals and objectives. These decisions are so important, however, that most large organizations have departments that specialize in stock and bond analysis. The chief financial officers within these departments are often corporate vice-presidents.

Whether you have ambitions to be a corporate vice-president, an individual stockholder sharing in American business, or simply an observer, it is almost impossible not to become involved in some way with stocks and bonds. Insurance companies, banks, trust companies, pension funds, etc., touch almost everyone in some way. Each is heavily involved with stock and bond investment decisions.

Stocks

For a business to become a corporation, it must be chartered by the state or states in which it does business. The corporate charter provides for the number of shares of stock that can be issued. However, not all stock that has been authorized for issue is always sold. The amount that is sold is called *outstanding*. There are two types of stock, *common* and *preferred*. All corporations have common stock outstanding, and some have preferred stock outstanding.

Stockholders are the owners of a corporation. When corporations earn a profit, they either *retain* the profits for future operations and/or expansion or *distribute* the profits to the stockholders in the form of *dividends*. As the name implies, preferred stock has preference over common stock when dividends are paid. That is, holders of preferred stock are paid the dividends due them before any dividends are paid to holders of common stock.

Common Stock Dividends

Payment in Cash

When management declares a cash dividend payment, the dividends are distributed proportionately among stockholders of record on the date of declaration. This means that when dividends are declared, the board of directors will select a specific date on which to determine the identity of all its stockholders. People owning stock on this date will receive a specific amount of money for each share of the corporation's stock they own. Dividends are normally paid quarterly.

	Stocks	Bonds
Table 13-1 Comparison Between Stocks and Bonds	1. Shares of stock represent ownership of the business. *Stockholders* are *owners* of the business.	1. Bonds represent debt of the business. Bondholders are *creditors* of the business.
	2. *Cash payments* are called *dividends*.	2. *Cash payments* are referred to as *interest*.
	3. Stockholders receive dividends if any are declared, but *no dividends need to be paid*.	3. A *fixed* amount of *interest must be paid* to bondholders *each* year, and it must be paid before any dividends can be declared.
	4. There is *no maturity* date on stocks	4. Bonds have a *specified maturity date*.
	5. There is *no promise to pay a certain amount in the future*	5. The *face value must be paid on the maturity date*.
	6. *Stockholders of common stock* are *entitled to vote* on corporate matters. *Stockholders of preferred stock* are usually *not entitled to vote.*	6. *Bondholders* are *not entitled to vote* on corporate matters unless the interest or the face value are not paid when due.
	7. If the business is liquidated, *stockholders are paid after bondholders.*	7. If the business is liquidated, *bondholders are paid before stockholders.*

Example	The Excelsor Corporation declared dividends of $100,000 on its common stock to be paid to shareholders of record on April 1. There were 50,000 shares of common stock outstanding. Sam Clemmet had 100 shares of Excelsor's stock. How much did Sam receive in dividends?
Solution	1. Divide the amount of the declared dividend payment by the number of shares outstanding:

$100,000 \div 50,000 = \$2$

2. Multiply the number of shares of Excelsor stock owned by Sam by the $2 per share dividend (the $2 is the amount of cash to be paid for each share held by stockholder):

$100 \times \$2 = \$200$

Assignment 13-1

1. Compute the amount of dividends to be paid in the following:

	Shares outstanding	*Dividend declared*	*Dividend per share*
a.	100,000	$ 50,000.00	_____
b.	1,000,000	100,000.00	_____
c.	3,295,415	3,789,727.20	_____
d.	15,314,798	12,251,838.00	_____
e.	143,622	611,829.72	_____

2. Sunrise Doughnuts declared dividends of $3,215,892 on 1 million shares of stock, authorized and issued. Determine the amount of dividends to be received by the following stockholders of record:

		Dividend
J. Standish	1000 shares	_____
P. Aldon	105 shares	_____
P. Hontis	8000 shares	_____
C. Leggs	3210 shares	_____

Payment in Stock

Sometimes a corporation that has stock authorized but not issued will declare a stock dividend. The dividend payment will then be made in additional shares of stock to each stockholder of record on the declaration date, in proporotion to the number of shares held. This declaration is made in accordance with a stated percent. For example, a corporation may declare a 5% stock dividend.

Example   A corporation declared a 5% common stock dividend. Calculate the amount of the dividend paid to a stockholder who owns 1000 shares of common stock.

Solution   Multiply the stock dividend rate by the number of shares owned:

5% × 1000 = .05 × 1000 = 50 shares

The stockholder now owns 1050 shares of the corporation's common stock.

Assignment 13-2

1. Stephens Consolidated declared a 3% common stock dividend. If the total common stock outstanding is 5,500,000 shares, what is the total number of common stock shares to be issued in the form of dividends?

2. Calculate the common stock dividend received by the following stockholders if a 2.5% stock dividend has been declared:

		Dividend
#146432	400 shares	_____
#186291	1,000 shares	_____
#141725	1,300,000 shares	_____
#362918	9,000 shares	_____
#143679	250,000 shares	_____

3. The Watsamata Corporation declared cash dividends of $350,000 on the 200,000 shares of outstanding stock and a 5% stock dividend to stockholders of record. Joe Amata owned 50,000 shares of common stock. What were his dividend payments?

Par Value

The par value of a stock is not an indication of its market value or selling price. The *par value* is a value arbitrarily assigned to stock upon its issue. This protects corporate creditors by preventing the distribution of dividends to a point where the stockholder's equity would be below the par value of the stock. Some corporations issue no-par stock. In some states, a no-par stock is given a stated value, usually $100, for tax and other liability purposes.

When a stock sells at a price *above* the stated par value, which is most often the case, the difference is called the *premium*. If a stock sells at a price *below* the par value, the difference is known as the *discount*. Commonly, the total difference is divided by the total number of shares outstanding to show the premium or discount per share.

Example   The par value of the common stock of Land Development Company is $10. There are 25,000 shares of stock outstanding, and the total receipts from sales of stock are $300,000. Calculate the premium or discount per share of outstanding stock.

Solution   Multiply the per-share par value by the total number of stocks outstanding:

$10 × 25,000 = $250,000 total par value

Find the difference between the total par value and the total receipts from stock sales:

$300,000 − $250,000 = $50,000   premium (total receipts are higher than par value)

Divide the total premium by the total number of outstanding shares:

$50,000 ÷ $25,000 = $2   premium per share

Assignment 13-3

1. Compute the total premium or discount and the premium or discount per share in the table below:

	Par value	Outstanding shares	Total receipts	Total premium or discount	Premium or discount per share
a.	$ 1	350,000	$ 550,000	_____	_____
b.	10	1,550,000	25,500,000	_____	_____
c.	10	38,000	370,000	_____	_____
d.	100	525,000	97,500,000	_____	_____
e.	1	3,650,500	42,398,000	_____	_____

2. William Slagg, Inc., has sold 2000 shares of $10 par value stock for $25 per share. Calculate the total and per-share premium or discount.

Preferred Stock Dividends

Noncumulative Dividends

Preferred stock dividends are usually a fixed percent of their par value. Therefore, unlike common stock, par value for preferred stock does have a meaning. This meaning, however, is not the selling price of the stock, except by chance.

Some preferred stock is *noncumulative*, which means that *if* dividends are not declared by the corporate board of directors, the dividends are lost forever to the stockholder.

Example   Bolen Sage, Inc., declared preferred stock dividends to be paid to stockholders of record on June 30. The preferred stock has a par value of $100, and dividends are 5% of par value. Calculate the amount of dividends to be paid if there are 20,000 shares of outstanding stock.

Solution   Dividends for each share of stock:

par value × dividend rate = $100 × 5% = $5   dividend per share

Total dividends to be paid:

outstanding stock × dividend per share = 20,000 × $5
= $100,000   total dividends

Assignment 13-4

1. An investor bought 100 shares of 5% noncumulative $100 par value preferred stock. When dividends are declared, what will be the amount received by this investor?

2. The Bronx Manufacturing Company issued 30,000 shares of 6% noncumulative $100 par value preferred stock. Five of the stockholders are

A Siegel	1,500 shares
P. White	1,000 shares
J. Sanchez	900 shares
S. O'Brien	500 shares
H. Shultz	200 shares

   At the end of the year, Bronx declared dividends on the issue. Calculate the total amount of dividends to be paid and how much each of the above stockholders would receive.

Cumulative Dividends

Most preferred stock is *cumulative*. If the issuing company declares dividends in a given year, this assures the holders of preferred stock that they will receive all dividends not declared in previous years plus the current year's dividends before the holders of common stock are paid any dividends.

Example   Stephens Electronics sold 7000 shares of 6% cumulative preferred stock having a $100 par value. No dividends were paid last year but, because of a very profitable current year, Stephens has declared dividends to bring the dividend payments on the preferred stock issue up to date. Compute the total amount of dividends declared.

Solution   Multiply 6% by the par value, $100:

$$.06 \times \$100 = \$6$$

Multiply the dividend per share by total shares:

$$\$6 \times 7000 = \$42,000$$

$42,000 is the total amount of dividends per year but, since the preferred stock is cumulative, to bring the dividend payments up to date they must be paid for last year as well as for the current year. Therefore, multiply the yearly dividend by 2:

$$\$42,000 \times 2 = \$84,000$$

Assignment 13-5

1. Alex Schroeder's four children each gave him 175 shares of cumulative $6\frac{1}{2}\%$ preferred stock with a par value of $100. He has not received dividends for the past 3 years. During the fourth year, the corporation that issued Mr. Schroeder's stock announced that it would pay dividends sufficient to bring them up to date at the end of the current year. How much will he receive?

2. Calculate the amount of dividends payable in the table below:

	Cumulative preferred stock outstanding	Par value	Dividend rate	Time since last payment	Total dividends due
a.	8,000	$100	5%	3 years	_____
b.	3,000	100	6%	1 year	_____
c.	17,000	100	$6\frac{1}{2}\%$	4 years	_____
d.	63,000	100	7%	2 years	_____
e.	19,000	100	$5\frac{3}{4}\%$	3 years	_____

Participating Dividends

Participating preferred stock allows the stockholder to receive more than the stipulated percent of par value if sufficient dividends are declared. Usually, the extra dividend is on an equal-share basis with common stock. Therefore, after holders of preferred stock have received the stated percent share of par value and holders of common stock have received the same dollar amount per share, any dividends remaining to be distributed will be distributed on a proportionate basis to all stockholders. These are the steps to be followed:

1. Calculate the dividend due to the holders of the preferred stock based on the stipulated percent of par value.
2. Multiply the per-share dividend amount found in Step 1 by the total of the outstanding preferred stock.
3. Multiply the total shares of outstanding common stock by the dollar amount per share found in Step 1. (**Note:** If there have not been sufficient total dividends declared so that the result of this step is greater than or equal to the dividends remaining after the holders of the preferred stock have been paid, then the holders of the common stock share the remaining amount proportionately on a per-share basis).
4. Subtract the sum of Steps 2 and 3 from the total dividends declared.
5. Add the number of holders of preferred stock to the number of holders of common stock.
6. Divide the answer found in Step 4 by the result of Step 5. (Dividends remaining to be distributed divided by the total number of shares of stock.)
7. Add the result of Step 6 to the result of Step 1. This is the amount of dividends to be paid to each stockholder, both of common and of preferred stock.

Example   Dividends of $625,000 are to be distributed by Zipp, Inc. The corporation has 12,500 shares of 4% participating $100 par value preferred stock and 50,000 shares of $10 par value common stock outstanding. Calculate the dividend per share of preferred stock and the dividend per share of common stock.

Solution
1. Dividend per share of preferred stock at 4% with a $100 par value:

    $100 \times 4\% = \$4$

2. Preferred stock distribution:

    $\$4 \times 12,500 = \$50,000$

3. Common stock distribution:

    $\$4 \times 50,000 = \$200,000$

4. Add preferred stock and common stock distribution:

$50,000 + $200,000 = $250,000

5. Subtract total dividends thus distributed from total dividends declared:

$625,000 − $250,000 = $375,000

6. Calculate total number of shares of stock:

12,500 + 50,000 = 62,500

7. Divide dividends remaining to be distributed by total number of stock-holders:

$375,000 ÷ 62,500 = $6

8. Add per-share distribution found in Step 1 to per-share distribution found in Step 7 to find the total per-share dividend to be distributed to holders of both types of stock:

$4 + $6 = $10

Note: A short-cut method is to first divide the dividends to be distributed by the total of all shares of stock outstanding. If the quotient is larger than the dividend per share for the preferred stock before participation, the quotient is the amount of the dividend per share for both the common and the preferred stock.

Assignment 13-6

Calculate the dividend for each share of common stock and preferred stock in the following table:

	Common stock shares	Participating preferred stock Shares	Par value	Dividend rate	Dividends to be distributed	Dividend per share Common	Preferred
a.	100,000	10,000	$100	6%	$2,000,000	_____	_____
b.	50,000	6,000	100	7%	400,000	_____	_____
c.	150,000	20,000	100	5%	800,000	_____	_____
d.	60,000	2,000	100	4%	248,000	_____	_____
e.	315,000	1,500	100	$5\frac{1}{2}$%	1,900,000	_____	_____
f.	80,000	10,000	100	6%	500,000	_____	_____
g.	110,050	17,500	100	5%	750,000	_____	_____
h.	145,000	7,500	100	7%	2,250,000	_____	_____
i.	1,250,000	28,000	100	$4\frac{1}{2}$%	5,751,000	_____	_____
j.	24,000	3,250	100	$6\frac{3}{4}$%	183,937.50	_____	_____

Buying and Selling Stock

Stock quotations can be found in many sources. The best-known source is the *Wall Street Journal*. However, all major newspapers publish stock price quotations daily. An example of stock quotations is shown in Table 13-2. Beginning at the left and proceeding to the right, stock quotations can be read as follows.

*Table 13-2
Sample Stock
Quotations*

Stocks	Div	P-E Ratio	Sales 100s	High	Low	Close	Net Chg
AbtLb	.84	19	6612	44	43	43⅜	+½
Disney	.32	27	4129	44¼	43⅞	44	+½
Exxon	3.60	9	11934	68	66⅛	67⅝	+1⅞
IBM	4.40	12	17018	123	121⅜	122	−1⅛
Occi Ppf	6.25		122	57⅞	57	57⅞	+½

1. *Stocks* The companies for which the quotes are given are listed in this column. The first stock listed in Table 13-2 is Abbott Laboratories (AbtLb). It is a common stock issue. A preferred stock issue is followed by a *pf*, as is the last stock listed, Occi P (Occidental Petroleum).
2. *Div* The figure .84 for AbtLb is the annual dividend. In this instance, $.84 is the current dividend.
3. *P-E Ratio* The price-to-earnings ratio is calculated by dividing the closing price of the stock by the earnings per share. The P-E ratio is often used by investors to judge whether the stock is selling at a bargain price or if it is particularly vulnerable to changing economic conditions. Since the ratio is given (19 for AbtLb), it is possible to calculate the current earnings per share as follows:

$$\frac{\text{price}}{\text{earnings}} = \text{ratio}$$

Therefore:

$$\frac{\text{price}}{\text{ratio}} = \text{earnings}$$

The price is the day's closing price. Hence, the earnings per share for Abt Lb is

$$\$43.375 \div 19 = \$2.28$$

4. *Sales 100s* The 6612 means that, on this particular day, 661,200 shares of AbtLb stock changed hands.
5. *High* The highest price AbtLb sold for during the day was $44.00.
6. *Low* The lowest price AbtLb sold for during the day was $43.00.
7. *Close* The closing price (the day's last transaction) was $43.375.
8. *Net Chg* Net change is the amount of change between one day's closing price and the closing price from the previous workday. AbtLb increased $\frac{1}{2}$, or $.50.

The four major stock exchanges in the United States are the New York Stock Exchange, the American Stock Exchange, the Pacific Stock Exchange, and the Midwest Stock Exchange. Most stockbrokers trade on all of these exchanges. A broker acts as an agent, performing various transactions between buyer and seller. For these services, the broker receives a commission based on the dollar value of the stocks bought or sold.

Stocks may be purchased in *odd lots* or *round lots*. An odd lot is usually a transaction of fewer than 100 shares. A round lot is usually a transaction of exactly 100 shares. For some stock that is traded infrequently, a round lot is considered to be ten shares. However, for purposes of this book, a round lot will be 100 shares. Of course, it is possible for an investor to purchase a combination of a round lot and an odd lot of stock.

Calculating Commission
Round-Lot Sales
The commission on a stock transaction is computed as follows. First, the per-share price of the stock is multiplied by the number of shares to be bought or sold. Then the total stock price is multiplied by the commission rate, which can be negotiated with the broker.

Example   Calculate the broker's commission for 100 shares of common stock if the price per share is $56 and the commission rate is 1.5%.

Solution   Multiply the price per share by the number of shares:

$56 × 100 shares = $5600

Multiply this amount by the commission rate:

$5600 × 1.5% = $84 broker's fee

Asignment 13-7

1.   Calculate the broker's commission in the following:

	Shares sold	Price	Commission rate	Money involved	Broker's commission
a.	100	5	1.5%	$_____	$_____
b.	100	$14\frac{5}{8}$	1.5%	_____	_____
c.	200	$24\frac{7}{8}$	1.3%	_____	_____
d.	100	115	1.0%	_____	_____
e.	300	$18\frac{7}{8}$	1.1%	_____	_____
f.	100	59	1.2%	_____	_____
g.	500	$21\frac{1}{4}$	1.0%	_____	_____
h.	100	$15\frac{1}{2}$	1.4%	_____	_____
i.	200	$8\frac{1}{2}$	1.6%	_____	_____
j.	300	$31\frac{3}{4}$	1.2%	_____	_____

2.   Assume a commission rate of 2.0% and calculate the total purchase price for 100 shares of each of the stocks in Table 13-2. Use the closing price for your calculations.

Odd-Lot and Combination Sales

An odd-lot differential fee is added to the price of stock being purchased. The differential is subtracted from the price of a stock being sold. The odd-lot differential is $\frac{1}{8}$ ($.125) for each share traded under $55. For each share of stock traded at or above $55, the differential is $\frac{1}{4}$ ($.25).

If a combination of a round lot and an odd lot is sold, say 150 shares, the commission fee is the sum of the fee for the round lot and the fee for the odd lot.

Example   An investor bought 50 shares of stock selling at $30\frac{1}{8}$. What was the commission on the transaction if the commission rate was 1.6%?

Solution

$30.125   selling price
+   .125   differential fee ($30.125 is under $55 — fee is $\frac{1}{8}$)
$30.25   price per share

Multiply the price per share by the number of shares purchased:

$30.25 × 50 = $1512.50   cost of stock

Determine the commission:

commission = commission rate × cost of stock
= $1512.50 × 1.6%
= $24.20

Example   An investor sold 30 shares of stock at 78. Calculate the broker's commission if the commission rate was 1.7%.

Solution

$78.00   selling price
−   .25   differential fee ($78 is over $55 — fee is $\frac{1}{4}$)
$77.75   price per share

receipts from stock = price per share × shares sold
= $77.75 × 30 = $2332.50

commission = commission rate × receipts from stock
= $2332.50 × 1.7%
= $39.65

Example   Steve sold 120 shares of stock selling at $23\frac{1}{2}$. Find the broker's commission if the commission rate was 1.5%.

Solution

1. Round lot:

$23.50   selling price
×   100   shares sold
$2350.00   receipts from round lot

2. Odd lot:

$ 23.50   selling price
−   .125   differential fee ($23.50 is under $55)
$23.375   price per share

receipts from stock = price per share × shares sold
= $23.375 × 20
= $467.50

3. Total sales receipts:

$2350.00   from round lot
+ 467.50   from odd lot
$2817.50

4. Total commission:

commission = commission rate × receipts from stock
= 1.5% × $2817.50
= $42.26

Assignment 13-8

1. Find the broker's commission in each of the following:

	Transaction	Number of shares	Price	Commission rate	Commission
a.	purchased	150	$14\frac{1}{8}$	2.0%	_____
b.	sold	30	$29\frac{1}{2}$	1.9%	_____
c.	sold	120	$104\frac{1}{4}$	1.6%	_____
d.	purchased	60	65	1.8%	_____
e.	sold	140	$65\frac{5}{8}$	1.5%	_____
f.	sold	180	$17\frac{1}{2}$	1.6%	_____
g.	purchased	275	$57\frac{5}{8}$	1.4%	_____
h.	sold	320	$8\frac{1}{4}$	2.0%	_____
i.	sold	250	$54\frac{1}{2}$	1.4%	_____
j.	purchased	425	$28\frac{3}{8}$	1.6%	_____

Bonds

Bonds are a major source of corporate and government financing. A bond issued by public or private institutions is bought and sold through security brokers, much like corporate stocks. Bonds generally are issued in $1000 denominations, although the denomination, which is called the *face value*, can be more or less than $1000.

Even though the redemption value of the bond, the amount received by the investor on the maturity date, is always the face value, the bond's value commonly fluctuates on the market. This fluctuation may be caused by the issuing agency's financial condition or by changes in the current interest rate.

A bond selling at below its face value is selling at a discount, and one selling at above its face value is selling at a premium. Bonds are quoted as a percent of their face value instead of in a dollar amount. Therefore, a bond quoted at 102 and having a face value of $1000 would be selling at 102% of $1000, or $1020. If the bond was quoted at 98, it would be selling at 98% of its face value, or $980. The premium or discount is the difference between the face value of the bond and the market value.

Example   A $1000 bond is selling at 103. Calculate the premium

Solution   Multiply the face value by the quoted percent:

$1000 × 103% = 1000 × 1.03 = $1030

Subtract the face value from the market value:

$1030 − $1000 = $30 premium

Example   A $1000 bond is quoted at $93\frac{5}{8}$. Calculate the amount of the discount.

Solution   Multiply the face value by the quoted percent:

$1000 \times 93\frac{5}{8}\% = 1000 \times .93625 = \$936.25$

Subtract the market value from the face value:

$1000 - \$936.25 = \$63.75$ discount

Assignment 13-9

1.   Calculate the premium or discount for the following:

		Face value	Market quote	Market value	Premium	Discount
a.		$1000	97	$_____	$_____	$_____
b.		1000	106	_____	_____	_____
c.		1000	$102\frac{5}{8}$	_____	_____	_____
d.		1000	$76\frac{3}{4}$	_____	_____	_____
e.		500	$101\frac{1}{8}$	_____	_____	_____
f.		500	$94\frac{1}{2}$	_____	_____	_____
g.		100	104	_____	_____	_____
h.		1000	$111\frac{7}{8}$	_____	_____	_____
i.		5000	$88\frac{1}{4}$	_____	_____	_____
j.		1000	$93\frac{3}{8}$	_____	_____	_____

Bond Transactions

As with stocks, the buyer or seller of bonds must pay a commission to the broker handling the transactions. The commission fee for bonds is as follows:

1-49	$1000 bonds	$5 each
50 and over	$1000 bonds	2.50 each

In addition, since bonds pay interest at specified periods, the amount of accumulated unpaid interest at the date of transaction completion must be added to the market price of the bonds. Bond interest for this purpose is always calculated using ordinary time, 30-day months, and ordinary interest, 360-day years. The principal is always the face value of the bond.

Example   Calculate the total transaction cost of purchasing ten $1000 bonds selling at $104\frac{3}{8}$.

The last interest payment was on January 1, and the transaction settlement date is April 1. The interest rate on the bonds is 12%.

Solution   1. Determine the market price:

$$\text{market price of bonds} = \text{number of bonds} \times \text{face value} \times \text{quoted percent}$$
$$= 10 \times \$1000 \times 104\tfrac{3}{8}\%$$
$$= 10 \times \$1000 \times 1.04375$$
$$= \$10,437.50$$

2. Calculate the accumulated unpaid interest:

Time from January 1 to April 1:

January 1 to February 1	30 days
February 1 to March 1	30 days
March 1 to April 1	30 days
Total	90 days

$$I = P \times R \times T$$

$$I = \$1000 \times 12\% \times 90 \text{ days}$$

$$I = \$1000 \times .12 \times \frac{90}{360}$$

$$I = \$30 \text{ per bond, or } \$300 \text{ for ten bonds}$$

3. Add market price and accumulated interest:

$$\$10,437.50 + \$300 = \$10,737.50 \quad \text{purchase price}$$

4. Find the commission:

$$10 \times \$5 = \$50$$

5. Add the commission and the answer arrived at in Step 3:

$$\$10,587.50 + \$50 = \$10,637.50 \quad \text{total purchase price}$$

Example   Determine the total receipts to an investor selling twenty $1000 $4\tfrac{1}{2}\%$ bonds quoted at 70 on September 12 if the last interest payment was on July 1.

Solution   1. Find the market price of the bonds:

$$20 \times \$1000 \times 70\% = 20 \times \$1000 \times .70 = \$14,000$$

2. Calculate the accumulated unpaid interest:

Time from July 1 to September 12:

July 1 to August 1	30 days
August 1 to September 1	30 days
September 1 to September 12	12 days
Total	72 days

$$I = P \times R \times T$$

$$I = \$1000 \times 4\tfrac{1}{2}\% \times 72 \text{ days}$$

$$I = \$1000 \times \frac{45}{1000} \times \frac{72}{360}$$

$$I = \$9 \text{ per bond, or } \$180 \text{ for 20 bonds}$$

3. Add the market price and the accumulated interest:

$$\$14,000 + \$180 = \$14,180$$

4. Find the commission:

$20 \times \$5 = \$100$

5. Subtract the commission from the answer arrived at in Step 3:

$\$14,180 - \$100 = \$14,080$ total receipts

Assignment 13-10

1. Use the following information to complete the table shown below:

	Number of bonds	Face value	Interest rate	Market quote	Last interest payment	Transaction date	Transaction
a.	2	$1000	10%	98	1/1	3/1	purchase
b.	10	1000	7%	76	1/1	3/12	sale
c.	5	1000	12%	101	1/1	4/1	sale
d.	40	1000	8%	$87\frac{1}{2}$	7/1	11/1	purchase
e.	25	1000	$11\frac{1}{2}\%$	$92\frac{3}{8}$	7/1	8/15	sale
f.	100	1000	14%	$103\frac{1}{8}$	7/1	9/1	sale
g.	50	1000	$12\frac{1}{2}\%$	$102\frac{5}{8}$	3/1	4/10	sale
h.	5	1000	16%	$105\frac{1}{4}$	3/1	4/6	purchase
i.	20	1000	9%	$85\frac{3}{4}$	9/1	11/1	purchase
j.	100	1000	$11\frac{1}{4}\%$	$60\frac{7}{8}$	9/1	10/15	sale

	Market price	Accumulated interest	Commission	Total cost or receipts
a.	$_____	$_____	$_____	$_____
b.	_____	_____	_____	_____
c.	_____	_____	_____	_____
d.	_____	_____	_____	_____
e.	_____	_____	_____	_____
f.	_____	_____	_____	_____
g.	_____	_____	_____	_____
h.	_____	_____	_____	_____
i.	_____	_____	_____	_____
j.	_____	_____	_____	_____

2. Sheila O'Connell sold twenty $1000 18% bonds at $105\frac{3}{8}$ on May 1. She received her last interest payment on January 1. Calculate her net receipts.

3. An investor purchased 1000 bonds having a face value of $1000 and an interest rate of 9% at $83\frac{1}{2}$ on July 7. The last interest payment was on July 1. What was the total cost?

Current Yield

An investor certainly cares about a bond's interest rate, but it should be obvious that a bond selling at a price above (for a premium) or below (at a discount) its face value changes the amount of actual effective interest, which for a bond is called its *yield*. That is, a 6% bond is truly a 6% bond only if it is selling at face value. On a 6% $1000 bond, the bond owner will receive interest payments totaling $60 every year until the bond matures, regardless of the market value of the bond.

Therefore, an investor is more concerned about the rate of return, or the yield, of a bond. The current yield can be determined by dividing the annual interest by the market price of the bond (the face value times the quoted percent).

Example   Find the current yield of a $1000 6% bond quoted at 105.

Solution   Find the market value of the bond:

$1000 × 105% = $1000 × 1.05 = $1050

Determine the annual interest:

$1000 × 6% = $1000 × .06 = $60

Divide the annual interest by the market value:

$\frac{\$60}{\$1050}$ = .057 = 5.7% current yield

Example   Find the current yield of the above bond if it was quoted at 95.

Solution   Find the market value of the bond:

$1000 × 95% = $1000 × .95 = $950

Determine the annual interest:

$1000 × 6% = $1000 × .06 = $60

Divide the annual interest by the market value:

$\frac{\$60}{\$950}$ = .063 = 6.3% current yield

Assignment 13-11

Calculate the market value and the current yield in each of the following:

	Face value	Market quote	Annual interest rate	Market value	Current yield
a.	$1000	90	$9\frac{1}{2}\%$	$_____	_____%
b.	1000	110	16%	_____	_____
c.	1000	85	10%	_____	_____
d.	1000	$94\frac{3}{8}$	11%	_____	_____
e.	100	$106\frac{1}{2}$	14%	_____	_____
f.	1000	100	13%	_____	_____
g.	1000	$55\frac{1}{4}$	$11\frac{1}{4}\%$	_____	_____
h.	5000	114	20%	_____	_____
i.	1000	$105\frac{5}{8}$	13%	_____	_____
j.	500	$74\frac{3}{4}$	$16\frac{1}{4}\%$	_____	_____

Amortization of Bond Premium

Amortization is the process of spreading a bond premium over the life of the bond. It is the same as depreciating a fixed asset using the straight-line method. Therefore, the yearly amortization is calculated by dividing the total premium by the number of years or months from the date of purchase to the date of bond maturity. The *book value*, or *bond carrying value*, in the accounting records at any given time is the market price of the bond less the accumulated amortization from previous periods. At the bond's maturity date, then, the carrying value will equal the face value of the bond.*

Example   A 10-year 12% $1000 bond was purchased at 110 on the date of issue, January 1. Calculate the amount of annual amortization and the carrying value at the end of the first 2 years.

Solution   Calculate the market value of the bond:

$1000 × 110% = 1000 × 1.10 = $1100

Calculate the amount of the premium:

$1100   market value
− 1000   face value
$ 100   premium

Annual amortization equals total premium divided by number of years from date of purchase to date of bond maturity:

$$\text{annual amortization} = \frac{\$100 \text{ premium}}{10 \text{ years}} = \$10$$

*In current practice, many bond costs are calculated using present-value techniques, and the bond amortization of the premium/discount is calculated using an effective interest method. Similar concepts were demonstrated in Chapter 7 and will not be discussed here. Both methods result in the same total amount of interest expense over the term of the bonds, and the annual amounts of interest expenses are generally quite similar. However, when the annual amounts are materially different, the effective interest method is required under generally accepted accounting principles.

Carrying value equals market value less accumulated depreciation:

end of first year:

$1100 − $10 = $1090

end of second year:

$1100 − $20 = $1080

or

$1090 book value (carrying value) at end of first year
−   10 annual amortization
$1080

Assignment 13-12

1. Use the following information to complete the table shown below:

		Face value	Market quote	Date of purchase	Date of maturity
a.		$1000	110	1/1/85	1/1/95
b.		1000	114	1/1/86	1/1/97
c.		1000	120	1/1/84	1/1/94
d.		1000	105	1/1/86	1/1/06
e.		500	112	1/1/85	1/1/00
f.		1000	115	1/1/86	1/1/93
g.		1000	106	1/1/85	1/1/04
h.		1000	108	1/1/86	1/1/96
i.		1000	130	1/1/85	1/1/13
j.		1000	$109\frac{3}{4}$	1/1/87	1/1/92

	Market value	Premium	Annual amortization	Carrying value End of 1st year	End of 2nd year
a.	$_____	$_____	$_____	$_____	$_____
b.	_____	_____	_____	_____	_____
c.	_____	_____	_____	_____	_____
d.	_____	_____	_____	_____	_____
e.	_____	_____	_____	_____	_____
f.	_____	_____	_____	_____	_____
g.	_____	_____	_____	_____	_____
h.	_____	_____	_____	_____	_____
i.	_____	_____	_____	_____	_____
j.	_____	_____	_____	_____	_____

Amortization of Bond Discounts

The mathematics involved in computing the amortization of bond discounts is the same as that for calculating the amortization of bond premiums, except that the annual or monthly amortization is added to the market value instead of being subtracted from it. Since a bond selling at a discount will have a market value lower than the face value, the total amortization when added to the market value will equal the bond's face value at maturity.

Example   A discount of $50 is to be amortized for 10 years. If the face value of the bond is $1000, what is the annual amortization and the carrying value at the end of the first year if the bond was issued and bought on January 1, 1986?

Solution   The annual amortization is

$$\frac{\$50}{10} \quad \frac{\text{discount}}{\text{years}}$$

$$= \$5$$

The carrying value at the end of the first year is

market value = face value − discount
$$= \$1000 - \$50$$
$$= \$950$$

carrying value = market value + accumulated discounts
$$= \$950 + \$5$$
$$= \$955$$

Assignment 13-13

Use the following information to complete the table shown below:

	Face value	Market quote	Date of purchase	Date of maturity
a.	$1000	94	1/1/86	1/1/96
b.	1000	90	1/1/87	1/1/97
c.	1000	85	1/1/85	1/1/95
d.	1000	96	1/1/87	1/1/07
e.	500	75	1/1/86	1/1/01
f.	1000	57	1/1/87	1/1/04
g.	1000	88	1/1/86	1/1/05
h.	100	66	1/1/87	1/1/97
i.	1000	92	1/1/86	1/1/14
j.	1000	72	1/1/87	1/1/92

	Market value	Discount	Annual amortization	Carrying value End of 1st year	Carrying value End of 2nd year
a.	$_____	$_____	$_____	$_____	$_____
b.	_____	_____	_____	_____	_____
c.	_____	_____	_____	_____	_____
d.	_____	_____	_____	_____	_____
e.	_____	_____	_____	_____	_____
f.	_____	_____	_____	_____	_____
g.	_____	_____	_____	_____	_____
h.	_____	_____	_____	_____	_____
i.	_____	_____	_____	_____	_____
j.	_____	_____	_____	_____	_____

Chapter 13   Self-Testing Exercises

1.   A cautious investor was considering the purchase of 20 Lotsaluck Inc. bonds on January 1, 1987. The bonds are $1000 10% 20-year bonds issued January 1, 1978. Interest on the bonds is paid every 6 months, and the last payment was made on June 30, 1986. The bonds were quoted at 90. Determine the following:

   a. total market value

   b. total discount

   c. total annual amortization

   d. total annual interest

   e. total carrying value on December 31, 1986

   f. total carrying value on December 31, 1987

   g. current yield

   h. broker's commission

   i. investor's total cost

2.   The Rainy Day mutual Fund made the following stock and bond purchases on April 4, 1987.

   a. 1000 shares of common stock at $24\frac{1}{4}$

b. 250 shares of common stock at $38\frac{7}{8}$

c. 150 shares of preferred stock at 61

d. 100 $1000 12% bonds at 94, issued January 1, 1974, with interest paid semiannually on January 1 and July 1

Determine the total purchase costs for each issue and the total purchase cost for all issues. Assume the broker's commission for stock purchases is 2.0%.

3. The Axelrod Corporation has the following stock outstanding:

a. 50,000 shares of 6% cumulative $100 par value preferred stock

b. 20,000 shares of 8% noncumulative $100 par value preferred stock

c. 15,000 shares of 5% participating $100 par value preferred stock

d. 1 million shares of common stock

No dividends have been paid since January 1, 1984, but on January 1, 1987, dividends of $10 million were declared. Calculate the total and per-share dividends of each stock issue.

4. An investor sold 130 shares of stock at $28\frac{3}{8}$. What were her total receipts?

5. Wilma Hager Clothes Corporation sold 20,000 shares of $5 par value stock for $15.50 per share. Calculate the total premium.

6. Standly Bros. Inc. declared a total dividend of $3 million. A total of 500,000 shares of common stock and 200,000 shares of 8% $100 par value participating preferred stock was outstanding. Calculate the dividend for each share of common stock and preferred stock.

7. Sara Browder bought 450 shares of Saxon, Inc., at $4 per share. Calculate the total cost, including odd-lot differential and broker's commission at 1.8%.

8. Determine the market value and the current yield of a $1000 18% bond selling at 110.

9. Zorok Corporation declared cash dividends of $400,000 and stock dividends of 5% to stockholders of record. Zorok had a total of 200,000 shares outstanding. Calculate both the cash and stock dividend payments for an investor owning 800 shares.

10. Athen's Mutual Fund sold 5000 bonds ($1000, 14%) at 95 on May 1. Interest was last paid on January 1. What are the net receipts?

11. Sam Bolten owns 1000 shares of 14% noncumulative $100 par value preferred stock. Dividends have recently been declared. How much will Sam receive?

12. Circus Entertainers Company declared dividends of $800,000 on its common stock to be paid to stockholders of record on June 1. One million shares of stock were outstanding. The Edison Company held 15,000 shares. How much will Edison receive?

13. A $1000 bond is selling at 104. Calculate the premium.

14. Calculate the broker's commission on an order to buy 350 shares of stock at $32\frac{3}{8}$ if the commission rate is 1.7%.

15. Elmer's Auto Repair owns 6000 shares of cumulative preferred stock. It has been 4 years since the last dividend payment. The stock is $100 par value and the dividend rate is 13%. What is the total amount of dividends due?

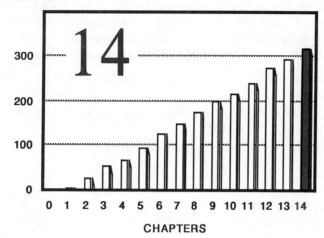

PAGE NO.

CHAPTERS

Computer Science Applications

Student Objectives

Upon completion of this chapter, the student should be able to

1. **Convert** *binary numbers to decimal numbers and decimal numbers to binary numbers.*
2. **Add, subtract, multiply,** *and* **divide** *with binary numbers.*
3. **Define** *or* **illustrate**

binary	*powers of 10*
base 2	*powers of 2*
base 10	

Binary Digits and the Computer

Computer science is a continually expanding field. Virtually no person is immune to its applications. No business mathematics textbook can be complete without an introduction to the binary system, the second most important place-value system of numeration.

Symbols are used in written communications. We generally use alphabetic characters (A, B, C ... Z), the decimal numbering system (0, 1, 2, 3, 4, 5, 6, 7, 8, and 9), and several special characters (#, ?, ;, :, $, @, etc.).

Input in and output out of a computer also use these alphanumeric characters. Internally, however, the computer uses a special numeric computer notation. All other symbols (alphabetic characters, decimal numbers, and special characters) are converted to a binary representation for each symbol. Table 14-1 illustrates this process.

The computer has only two symbols for representing data, 0 and 1. Because there are two digits in computer notation, computer language is referred to as the *binary system* (the prefix *bi* means "two"). Different configurations, or codes, are used to represent each alphanumeric character. For example, the configuration 11000001 might represent an A, the configuration 11000010 might represent a B, the configuration 01011011 might represent a $, and so forth. The word *might* is used because there are different codes depending on the type of computer system and the type of equipment.

Computers use binary digits (0 and 1) because these can most easily be used by the two electronic or magnetic states used in computer circuits and storage. In a punched card, for example, a binary digit is represented by the presence of a hole (1) or by the absence of a hole (0). Basically, a hole (1) allows electronic contact that turns a switch *on* and the absence of a hole (0) prohibits electronic contact and keeps a switch *off*.

While virtually any code can be used to represent alphabetic characters and special characters, numeric data is different. Numeric data must be used in computations. Thus, the coded representations must also be suited to arithmetic. The remainder of this chapter explains the concept of the binary number system and binary arithmetic.

The Binary System

The binary system is a positional system of numeration. That is, the numbers (0 and 1) take on different values when moved from one position to another. The same is true, of course, for the decimal system. For example, the number 5 in the decimal system has a different value when its position is changed. The value is *fifty* when the five is moved one place to the left and written 50. When moved one more position to the left, the 5 takes on the value *five hundred*, 500.

Table 14-1

INPUT DEVICE (punched card, tape, disk, etc.)	INTERNAL PROCESSING			OUTPUT DEVICE (visual display, documents, typewriter, etc.)
INPUT read in alphanumeric characters (A, B, C, 1, 2, 3, #, $, @, etc.)	CONVERT to a binary representation for each alphanumeric character (Special numeric computer notation)	PERFORM computation and manipulation	CONVERT to alphanumeric characters	OUTPUT printed or displayed in alphanumeric characters (A, B, C, 1, 2, 3, #, $, @, etc.)

Table 14-2
Place Values
in the Base-10
System

AND SO ON	10^6	10^5	10^4	10^3	10^2	10^1	10^0	Powers of 10
	1,000,000	100,000	10,000	1,000	100	10	1	Decimal System

Base 10

The decimal system is a base-10 system. Therefore, the first position, the units position, is 10^0. Other positions have successively higher powers of 10 (10^1, 10^2, 10^3, etc.). Positions in the base-10 system have the values given in Table 14-2.

Note: Any number to the zero power is 1 ($10^0 = 1$, $2^0 = 1$, etc.).

Base 2

Binary numbers are constructed the same way as decimal numbers but, instead of using powers of 10 in the position, powers of 2 are used. Thus, there is the units position (2^0), the twos position (2^1), the fours position (2^2), the eights position (2^3), and so forth. Positions in the base-2 system have the values given in Table 14-3.

Note: $2^0 = 1$ just as $10^0 = 1$.

Converting from Binary to Decimal

Tables 14-2 and 14-3 illustrate a comparison between the positions of the numbers in the decimal and binary systems. For example, the number 5092 in the decimal system can be shown to take its value from the positions occupied by the numbers 5, 0, 9, and 2, as demonstrated below:

$$
\begin{array}{ccccc}
10^3 & 10^2 & 10^1 & 10^0 & \text{positional value} \\
\times\ 5 & \times\ 0 & \times\ 9 & \times\ 2 & \text{number} \\
\hline
5000 & +\quad 0 & +\ 90 & +\quad 2 & = 5092
\end{array}
$$

That is:

$$
\begin{array}{lll}
2 \times 10^0 = 2 \times 1 & = & 2 \\
9 \times 10^1 = 9 \times 10 & = & 90 \\
0 \times 10^2 = 0 \times 100 & = & 0 \\
5 \times 10^3 = 5 \times 1000 & = & \underline{5000} \\
& & 5092
\end{array}
$$

If you understand the above explanation, the method of conversion from binary to decimal will follow logically.

Table 14-3
Place Values
in the Base-2
System

AND SO ON	2^5	2^4	2^3	2^2	2^1	2^0	Powers of 2
	32	16	8	4	2	1	Binary System

Example Convert the binary number 1101101_2 to a decimal number.

Solution

(2^6)	(2^5)	(2^4)	(2^3)	(2^2)	(2^1)	(2^0)	positional value in the base-2 (binary) system
64	32	16	8	4	2	1	
$\times 1$	$\times 1$	$\times 0$	$\times 1$	$\times 1$	$\times 0$	$\times 1$	number to be converted

$$64 + 32 + 0 + 8 + 4 + 0 + 1 = 109_{10}$$

That is:

$$1 \times 2^0 = 1 \times 1 = 1$$
$$0 \times 2^1 = 0 \times 2 = 0$$
$$1 \times 2^2 = 1 \times 4 = 4$$
$$1 \times 2^3 = 1 \times 8 = 8$$
$$0 \times 2^4 = 0 \times 16 = 0$$
$$1 \times 2^5 = 1 \times 32 = 32$$
$$1 \times 2^6 = 1 \times 64 = \underline{64}$$
$$109_{10}$$

Note: The subscripts (1101101_2 and 109_{10}) indicate the numbering system's base. That is, the subscript 2 represents the base-2 system (binary) and the subscript 10 represents the base-10 system (decimal).

Assignment 14-1

1. Convert the following binary numbers to their decimal equivalents:

   a. 111_2 **b.** 1010_2 **c.** 11_2

   d. 11100_2 **e.** 11011_2 **f.** 10111001_2

   g. 110110_2 **h.** 10101_2 **i.** 1_2

Converting from Decimal to Binary

The simplest method for converting decimal numbers to binary numbers is the remainder method. The remainder method entails dividing the decimal numeral by 2 (the binary system base). The quotient and all succeeding quotients are also divided by 2 until a quotient of zero is obtained. The remainder will always be either 1 or 0, which are the digits of the binary system. The remainders are recorded in the reverse order from which they are derived, resulting in the binary equivalent.

Example   Find the binary equivalent of 19_{10}.

Solution

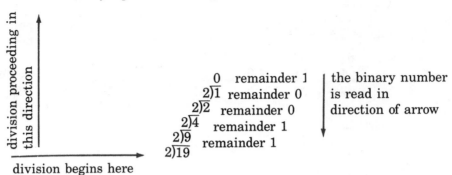

division begins here

Therefore $19_{10} = 10011_2$.

Alternative Method of Conversion from Decimal to Binary   The fastest method of converting decimal numbers to binary numbers consists of the steps listed below.

1.   Write the positional values of the binary system, beginning from the lowest, $2^0 = 1$, on the right side of the page and continuing with higher values to the left until the value of the decimal number to be converted would be exceeded by the next positional value. For example, if the decimal number to be converted is 25, the binary positional values would be

2^4 2^3 2^2 2^1 2^0 (these powers of 2 need not be written)
16   8   4   2   1

Since $2^5 = 32$ is higher than the decimal number to be converted, 25, it is not used.

2.   Place a 1 under the highest value written. The example in Step 1 would now look like this:

2^4 2^3 2^2 2^1 2^0
16   8   4   2   1
 1

3.   Subtract the highest positional value from the decimal number to be converted. In our example, that would be

$25 - 16 = 9$

4.   Place a 1 under the highest positional value that does not exceed the value obtained in Step 3. Our example now looks like this:

2^4 2^3 2^2 2^1 2^0
16   8   4   2   1
 1   1

5.   Subtract the positional value from the number obtained in Step 3. In our example, that would be

$9 - 8 = 1$

6.   Continue repeating Steps 4 and 5 until the subtraction results in a difference of zero (0). Our example is now

2^4 2^3 2^2 2^1 2^0
16   8   4   2   1
 1   1   1

7. Place zeros in all positions not used in the previous steps. The final answer for our example is

2^4 2^3 2^2 2^1 2^0
16 8 4 2 1
1 1 0 0 1   answer

This method may appear complicated, but the most complicated thing about it is attempting to explain it. With a little practice, it is fast and simple to use.

Example Find the binary equivalent of 19_{10}.

Solution

1. Write the positional values that do not exceed 19_{10}.

16 8 4 2 1

2. Put a 1 under 16:

16 8 4 2 1
1

3. Subtract 16 from the decimal number being converted, 19:

$19 - 16 = 3$

4. Place a 1 under the positional value that does not exceed 3:

16 8 4 2 1
1   1

5. Subtract 2 from 3:

$3 - 2 = 1$

6. Place a 1 under the positional value that does not exceed 1:

16 8 4 2 1
1   1 1

7. Subtract 1 from 1:

$1 - 1 = 0$

8. Since the difference in step 7 is zero, place zeros under all other positional values:

16 8 4 2 1
1 0 0 1 1

9. Thus, $19_{10} = 10011_2$.

Assignment 14-2

1. Find the binary equivalents of the following decimal numbers:

a. 27_{10} b. 41_{10}

c. 126_{10} d. 147_{10}

e. 7_{10} **f.** 308_{10}

g. 11_{10} **h.** 875_{10}

i. 2_{10} **j.** 1_{10}

Adding Binary Numbers

Adding binary numbers is not essentially different from adding decimal numbers except that, in principle, it is simpler. Four combinations are possible rather than the 100 possible combinations in the decimal system. The four combinations in the binary system are

$$0 + 0 = 0$$
$$0 + 1 = 1$$
$$1 + 0 = 1$$
$$1 + 1 = 0 \text{ carry } 1$$

or

$$
\begin{array}{cccc}
 & & & c \\
0 & 0 & 1 & 1 \\
+0 & +1 & +0 & +1 \\
\hline
0 & 1 & 1 & 10
\end{array}
$$

Explanation

The c is the "carry 1" resulting from the addition of $1 + 1$. Its value is 1, and it is used mainly for clarification purposes.

Example   Add 1010 and 1011.

Solution
$$
\begin{array}{r}
c\ c \\
1010 \\
+\ 1011 \\
\hline
10101_2
\end{array}
$$

Example   Add the following binary numbers:

$$
\begin{array}{r}
1111 \\
1000 \\
1110 \\
+1011
\end{array}
$$

Solution   Addition always involves several values, as shown here. The same rules of binary addition apply. Remember, however, that the only numbers in the binary system are 0 and 1. That requires a slightly different method of carrying than in the decimal system.

It is often difficult to keep in mind the proper number of c's (one's) to carry from the right column into the column immediately to its left. It sometimes helps to place brackets around each combination of two one's in the same column. Next, count the number of brackets in a column and carry that number of *c*'s into the column immediately to its left. This process is shown below.

```
      c                           c
    c c c                       c )c  c
  c c c c c                   c c c )c )c
    1 1 1 1                     1 1 1 )1
    1 0 0 0                     1 0 )0 0
    1 1 1 0                     1 1 1 0
    1 0 1 1                     1 0 1 )1
  _____                 _____
  1 1 0 0 0 0                 1 1 0 0 0 0
```

Add anything not bracketed and place that sum in the proper column.

Assignment 14-3

1. Add the following binary numbers.

    a.   1101
           +1001

    b.   10010
           +11011

    c.   1110
          10110
             11
        + 1011

    d.   1
           111
           101
        +1111

    e.   101
        11011
        10011
       + 1111

    f.   11101
        1010
         111
      + 111

    g.   1101
         101
      10101
      + 11

    h.   101
         11
         11
      +1011

    i.   1000
        1000
        1000
        1000
      +1000

    j.   1111
        1111
        1111
        1111
      +1111

Subtracting Binary Numbers

Subtracting binary numbers is the same as subtracting decimal numbers, if no borrowing is necessary. That is,

$$
\begin{array}{ccc}
0 & 1 & 1 \\
\underline{-0} & \underline{-0} & \underline{-1} \\
0 & 1 & 0
\end{array}
$$

Example   Subtract

$$
\begin{array}{r}
111001 \\
-\ 10001 \\
\end{array}
$$

Solution
$$
\begin{array}{r}
111001 \\
-\ 10001 \\
\hline
101000 \\
\end{array}
$$

Assignment 14-4

1. Subtract the following binary numbers:

   a. 1010
       <u>1000</u>

   b. 1110
       <u>100</u>

   c. 101101
       <u>1001</u>

   d. 11110
       <u>10100</u>

   e. 111001
       <u>10001</u>

Borrowing

The rule when borrowing is necessary is

$$
\begin{array}{r}
10 \\
-\ 1 \\
\hline
1 \\
\end{array}
$$

The other rules remain the same, that is,

$$
\begin{array}{ccc}
0 & 1 & 1 \\
\underline{-0} & \underline{-0} & \underline{-1} \\
0 & 1 & 0
\end{array}
$$

Example   Subtract

$$
\begin{array}{r}
1001000 \\
-\ 10101 \\
\end{array}
$$

Solution First, since the 1 in the extreme right column cannot be subtracted from 0, borrow the first 1 found to the left of that 0. Write 0 in the place of the borrowed 1. Change any 0 in between to a 1. Change the 0 at the point of subtraction to a 10:

$$
\begin{array}{r}
011 \\
100100^{1}0 \\
- \quad 1010\ 1 \\
\hline
\end{array}
$$

Next, moving from right to left and borrowing when necessary, as described above, subtract each column until the problem is solved. (Remember the subtraction rules.)

$$
\begin{array}{r}
01\ \ 011 \\
10^{1}0100^{1}0 \\
- \quad 1010\ 1 \\
\hline
1\ 1001\ 1
\end{array}
$$

Assignment 14-5

1. Subtract the following binary numbers:

a.
$$
\begin{array}{r}
11000 \\
-10010 \\
\hline
\end{array}
$$

b.
$$
\begin{array}{r}
11001 \\
-\ 1110 \\
\hline
\end{array}
$$

c.
$$
\begin{array}{r}
110111 \\
-\ 1011 \\
\hline
\end{array}
$$

d.
$$
\begin{array}{r}
11100 \\
-\ 101 \\
\hline
\end{array}
$$

e.
$$
\begin{array}{r}
11011 \\
-\ 100 \\
\hline
\end{array}
$$

f.
$$
\begin{array}{r}
11001 \\
-10110 \\
\hline
\end{array}
$$

g.
$$
\begin{array}{r}
1011 \\
-\ 111 \\
\hline
\end{array}
$$

h.
$$
\begin{array}{r}
10001 \\
-1101 \\
\hline
\end{array}
$$

i.
$$
\begin{array}{r}
11001 \\
-10111 \\
\hline
\end{array}
$$

j.
$$
\begin{array}{r}
111011 \\
-1111 \\
\hline
\end{array}
$$

k.
$$
\begin{array}{r}
100010 \\
-\ 1001 \\
\hline
\end{array}
$$

l.
$$
\begin{array}{r}
100000101 \\
\end{array}
$$

328   *Computer Science Applications*

Multiplying Binary Numbers
Multiplying binary numbers is the same as multiplying decimal numbers. However, far fewer combinations exist in the binary multiplication table. The complete binary multiplication table is as follows:

$0 \times 0 = 0$
$0 \times 1 = 0$
$1 \times 0 = 0$
$1 \times 1 = 1$

Example   Multiply 1011_2 and 110_2.

Solution
```
     1011
×    110
 cccc
    0000
   1011
  1011
 1000010
```

The addition of the partial products follows binary addition rules.

Assignment 14-6

1. Multiply the following binary numbers:

    a.   11
        ×10

    b.   101
        × 11

    c.   1010
        × 110

    d.   1111
        × 111

    e.   1001
        × 101

    f.   1011
        ×1101

    g.   1011
        ×1111

    h.   1101
        × 111

    i.   101
        ×111

    j.   1000
        × 111

Dividing Binary Numbers
Division of binary numbers is done in essentially the same way as is division with decimal numbers. The greatest difference is that in the binary system a number will divide into another number either one time (1) or not at all (0), since 1 and 0 are the only numbers in the binary system. Also, remember the method of subtracting binary numbers.

Example   Solve 10011 ÷ 110.

Solution

```
              11   remainder 1
           ┌────
           │01
      110│10¹011
           1 10
           ─────
            111
            110
           ─────
             1   remainder
```

Assignment 14-7

1. Divide the following binary numbers:

   a. 1010 ÷ 101   b. 1100 ÷ 11

   c. 1101 ÷ 11   d. 11011 ÷ 110

   e. 1101110 ÷ 1011   f. 11101001 ÷ 11011

   g. 10110 ÷ 1011   h. 110110 ÷ 1001

   i. 10011 ÷ 1100   j. 11001 ÷ 101

   k. 101010110 ÷ 100101

Chapter 14   Self-Testing Exercises

1.   Convert the following binary numbers to decimal numbers:

   a. 110101_2 b. 101111_2

   c. 110000_2 d. 101010_2

2.   Convert the following decimal numbers to binary numbers:

   a.   76   b.   31

   c.   12   d.   15

3.   Add the following binary numbers

   a.   110   b.   11010
        101   10111
        111   11111
       $\underline{\quad 1}$ $\underline{11110}$

   c.   110111   d.   1000001
        101010   100001
        110110   10001
         10000   1001
        $\underline{\quad 1010}$ 101
                                                            10
                                                       $\underline{\qquad 1}$

4.   Subtract the following binary numbers:

   a.   11101   b.   10010
        $\underline{-\ 1011}$ $\underline{-\ 1011}$

c.   110
    −101

d.   1001101
    − 110110

e.   11000100110
    −110101101

5. Multiply the following binary numbers:

a.   1011
   × 110

b.   10101
   × 1001

c.   1101
   × 101

d.   101101
   × 10110

6. Divide the following binary numbers:

a. 101)‾1010‾

b. 1110)‾110100‾

c. 1010)‾111010‾

d. 1101)‾11011101‾

e. 1001)‾1000110‾

f. 1110)‾100011001‾

7.   Perform the indicated operations:

a.   10101
      − 1010

b.   1110
      × 101

c.   110001 ÷ 111

d.   101
        110
      +111

e.   1001101 ÷ 1011

f.   10111
      ×11001

g.   101101
      − 1011

h.   1111
         101
        1010
      +1001

i.   100010
        10100
         1011
      +101010

j.   10101010 ÷ 111

k.   100111
      ×   1011

l.   1000000101
      −   1101010

m. 101001
      $\times$ 1001

n. 1010010
       -101001

o. 11101 ÷ 1011

p. 1000
       1001
      $+1110$

8. Convert the following as indicated:

   a. $10110_2 = \underline{\hspace{1cm}}_{10}$ **b.** $87_{10} = \underline{\hspace{1cm}}_2$ **c.** $41_{10} = \underline{\hspace{1cm}}_2$

   d. $100100_2 = \underline{\hspace{1cm}}_{10}$ **e.** $11101_2 = \underline{\hspace{1cm}}_{10}$ **f.** $30_{10} = \underline{\hspace{1cm}}_2$

   g. $1001_{10} = \underline{\hspace{1cm}}_2$ **h.** $22_{10} = \underline{\hspace{1cm}}_2$ **i.** $10101_2 = \underline{\hspace{1cm}}_{10}$

   j. $1001_2 = \underline{\hspace{1cm}}_{10}$ **k.** $256_{10} = \underline{\hspace{1cm}}_2$ **l.** $11111_2 = \underline{\hspace{1cm}}_{10}$

   m. $146_{10} = \underline{\hspace{1cm}}_2$ **n.** $1000001_2 = \underline{\hspace{1cm}}_{10}$ **o.** $58_{10} = \underline{\hspace{1cm}}_2$

Answers

Chapter 1

Answers to Odd-Numbered Questions

Assignment 1-1

1. 8763
3. 49,000,412,000,027
5. 1,000,215

Assignment 1-2

1. .2
3. .0005
5. .102
7. fifteen hundredths
9. one hundred twenty millionths

Assignment 1-3

1. 1.06
3. 3,000,025.0201
5. 79.1002
7. one thousand two hundred fifteen and three thousandths
9. one hundred sixty-seven and nine tenths

Assignment 1-4

1. 5000
3. 577 trillion
5. 60
7. 572,000
9. 1270

Asignment 1-5

1. 201.2537
3. 3765.3858
5. 1054.297
7. 218.5052
9. $123,045.84

Assignment 1-6

1. Actual — 843 Estimated — 810
3. Actual — $8146.21 Estimated — $8360
5. Actual — 177.25 Estimated — 160

Assignment 1-7

1. 29,172
3. 3297
5. 12.1
7. .0001
9. 612

Assignment 1-8

1. Actual — 9425.675 Estimated — 5000
3. Actual — 5454.1344 Estimated — 6000
5. Actual — $1595 Estimated — $2000

Assignment 1-9

1. $491.26
3. 12,062
5. 73,947,048
7. 3006.852
9. 1778.4468

Assignment 1-10

1. 295,000
3. 2,895,060
5. 870,900
7. 46,527,900
9. 60,600

Assignment 1-11

1. Actual — 2892 Estimated — 2800
3. Actual — 2562 Estimated — 3000
5. Actual — 2592 Estimated — 5000

Assignment 1-12

1. 248   3. .03782
5. .0003   7. 37
9. 253

Assignment 1-13

1. 84.643   3. .137
5. 1112.412   7. 160 minutes

Assignment 1-14

1. Actual — 123   Estimated — 100
3. Actual — 1012 Estimated — 1000
5. Actual — 2.25 Estimated — 1

Chapter 2

Answers to Odd-Numbered Problems

Assignment 2-1

1. I   3. I   5. I
7. I   9. M

Assignment 2-2

1. $\frac{17}{6}$ 3. $\frac{13}{3}$ 5. $\frac{767}{5}$

Assignment 2-3

1. $3\frac{1}{5}$ 3. $19\frac{1}{3}$ 5. $2\frac{127}{519}$

Assignment 2-4

1. $\frac{1}{2}$ 3. $\frac{2}{7}$ 5. $\frac{3}{7}$
7. $\frac{13}{40}$ 9. $\frac{8}{9}$

Assignment 2-5

1. $\frac{2}{7}$ 3. $\frac{1}{4}$ 5. $\frac{5}{11}$
7. $\frac{9}{10}$ 9. $\frac{7}{11}$

Assignment 2-6

1. $\frac{12}{20}$ 3. $\frac{39}{66}$ 5. $\frac{595}{1037}$

Assignment 2-7

1. 120   3. 90   5. 112

Assignment 2-8

1. $\frac{7}{8}$ 3. $2\frac{19}{20}$ 5. $\frac{39}{64}$

Assignment 2-9

1. $9\frac{3}{4}$ 3. $18\frac{13}{56}$ 5. $63\frac{61}{80}$
7. $570\frac{2}{5}$ 9. $14\frac{25}{432}$ 11. $56\frac{3}{8}$ pounds
13. $93\frac{41}{120}$ miles

Assignment 2-10

1. $\frac{5}{7}$ 3. $\frac{8}{63}$ 5. $\frac{1}{12}$
7. $\frac{5}{12}$ 9. $\frac{1}{6}$ 11. $\frac{5}{12}$

Assignment 2-11

1. $4\frac{2}{5}$ 3. $10\frac{29}{45}$ 5. $2\frac{19}{20}$
7. $99\frac{3}{16}$ 9. $36\frac{1}{3}$ 11. $9\frac{15}{16}$ inches
13. $16\frac{3}{10}$ miles

Assignment 2-12

1. $\frac{1}{2}$ 3. $\frac{7}{50}$ 5. $\frac{1}{1728}$
7. $\frac{1}{24}$ 9. $\frac{1}{30}$ 11. $\frac{1}{12}$

Assignment 2-13

1. 32   3. 4   5. 15
7. $\frac{5}{6}$ 9. $900   11. $180\frac{5}{6}$ yards

Assignment 2-14

1. $2\frac{13}{25}$ 3. $4\frac{23}{31}$ 5. $3\frac{73}{189}$
7. 3

Assignment 2-15

1. $4\frac{1}{5}$ 3. $\frac{117}{224}$ 5. $\frac{1}{114}$
7. $\frac{1}{2}$ 9. $1\frac{5}{184}$ 11. 32 lengths
13. 400 copies   15. $990

Assignment 2-16

1. $\frac{13}{50}$ 3. $\frac{3}{8}$ 5. $\frac{1}{8}$
7. $\frac{749}{1000}$ 9. $\frac{213}{500}$

Assignment 2-17

1. .4   3. .545   5. 3.889
7. 15.625   9. 388.833

Chapter 3

Answers to Odd-Numbered Problems

Assignment 3-1

1. -6 3. -26 5. 8457

Assignment 3-2

1. 42   3. -42 5. -96
7. -147 9. 63

Assignment 3-3

1. -6 3. 6   5. -134
7. -5 9. 8

Assignment 3-4

1. $A = 9$ 3. $N = 27$ 5. $L = \frac{3}{8}$
7. 41   9. $12.50

Assignment 3-5

1. $N = 12$ 3. $Y = 6336$ 5. $M = \frac{G}{N}$
7. $S = \frac{R}{T}$ 9. 3600   11. $R = \frac{3}{100}$

Assignment 3-6

1. 19   3. 10
5. $\frac{(L + S)(C - Z)}{B}$ 7. 10
9. $B[(D + S) - (Z \cdot Y)]$ 11. 108

Assignment 3-7

1. Stan 11   3. gas $305
   Carla 33   elect. $762.50
                  tele. $796.50
5. 600 shift 2
   300 shift 1
   553 shift 3

Chapter 4

Answers to Odd-Numbered Problems

Assignment 4-1

1. .08   3. .005   5. .1225
7. 24.2975

Assignment 4-2

1. 1%   3. .2%   5. 4212%
7. 34%

Assignment 4-3

1. $\frac{1}{4}$ 3. $\frac{1}{20}$ 5. $\frac{3}{1000}$
7. $\frac{1}{40}$

Assignment 4-4

1. 40%   3. 12%   5. 150%
7. 25%

Assignment 4-5

1. a. $22.50   c. $25.20   e. $.21
   g. $446.25   i. $25
3. $524.80   5. $936   7. .3 gallon
9. $405,000   11. $1085   13. $228
15. 8

Assignment 4-6

1. a. 25%   c. 80%   e. 5%
   g. .8%   i. $66\frac{2}{3}$%
3. 6%   5. 80%   7. 75%
9. 50%   11. 40%   13. 3.3%
15. 254.5%

Assignment 4-7

1. a. $420   c. $20   e. $26.80
   g. $800   i. $3071
3. $86   5. $10,750   7. 25,000
9. 120,000,000   11. $2000   13. 400,000
15. $60,000

Assignment 4-8

1. a. $336   c. $.91   e. $1513.75
   g. $4905.44   i. $378
3. $47,300   5. $1.25   7. $8680
9. $264,000   11. $705,250   13. 117 months
15. $60,000

Assignment 4-9

1. a. $177.60   c. $.16   e. $1752.60
   g. $1248.45   i. $1620.50
3. $1720   5. $16,800   7. 18 miles
9. 2773   11. $756,500   13. 7.2 hours
15. $31.96

Assignment 4-10

1. a. 12.5%   c. 28%   e. 100%
   g. 25%   i. 50%
3. 25%   5. $33\frac{1}{3}$%
7. 50%   9. 2%

Chapter 5

Answers to Odd-Numbered Problems

Assignment 5-1

1. $34   3. $184

Assignment 5-2

1. a. $33\frac{1}{3}\%$ 3. a. 40%
5. a. 17.6%

Assignment 5-3

1.
Retail	Markup	Cost %
a. $60	$15	75%
c. $400	$120	70%
e. $60	$30	50%
g. $500	$175	65%
i. $35	$8.75	75%

3. $50   5. $8

Assignment 5-4

1.
Retail	Markup	Cost %
a. $15	$10	60%
c. $35	$35	50%
e. $10.40	$5.60	65%
g. $38.50	$16.50	70%
i. $4.34	$2.66	62%

3. $192   5. $1725

Assignment 5-5

1.
Cost	Markup	Retail %
a. $40	$20	150%
c. $10	$2.50	125%
e. $2	$1	150%
g. $21	$7	$133\frac{1}{3}\%$
i. $.40	$.10	125%

3. $11.25   5. $100

Assignment 5-6

1.
Retail	Markup	Retail %
a. $10	$5	200%
c. $24	$9	160%
e. $9.80	$2.80	140%
g. $507.50	$157.50	145%
i. $332.50	$157.50	190%

3. $136   5. $19.95

Assignment 5-7

1. $90   3. $108.75   5. $133.33
7. 44.4%   9. $400   11. $528.08

Assignment 5-8

1. $66\frac{2}{3}\%$ 3. 40.8%   5. 60%
7. a. 10%   b. 61%   c. 21%   d. 93%

Assignment 5-9

1. $33\frac{1}{3}\%$ 3. 42.9%   5. 50%

Assignment 5-10

1. $339.50   3. $509.70
5. EOM 10/10, ROG 9/25, payment $980

Assignment 5-11

1. $4300.80
3. Wholesaler — $12,600   Retailer — $15,140.63
5. a. $530.78   c. $547.20

Chapter 6

Answers to Odd-Numbered Problems

Assignment 6-1

1. a. $90   c. $50   e. $14
3. $6

Assignment 6-2

1. a. $20   c. $13   e. $43.13
3. $43.13

Assignment 6-3

1. a. $30   c. $12   e. $37.33
3. $30.66 (E.O.) $30.25 (E.E.)

Assignment 6-4

1. a. $640   c. $1875   e. $300
    g. $4100   i. $2400
3. $234,800   5. $8525.00

Assignment 6-5

1. a. 10%   c. 8%   e. 12%
    g. 18%   i. 6%
3. 18.5%

Assignment 6-6

1. a. 20 days   c. 44 days   e. 45 days
    g. 60 days   i. 30 days
3. 66 days   5. 30 days

Assignment 6-7

1. *Discount   Net proceeds*
    a. $40 $960
    c. $400 $19,600
    e. $30 $1470
3. $D = \$52.50$
     $NP = \$2947.50$
      $R = 14.25\%$

Assignment 6-8

1.

	Total amount to be paid	*Total interest*	*Effective interest rate*
a.	$416	$41	29%
c.	$800	$50	41%
e.	$1,800	$300	13%
g.	$12,000	$2800	24%
i.	$720	$22	2%

3. 6.4%   5. 13%

Assignment 6-9

1. between 14.25% and 14.50%
3. between 18.75% and 19.00%
5. between 28.75% and 29.00%

Assignment 6-10

1. a. $530 $30   12.9%
    c. 414   64   22.0%
    e. 120,000   35,000   18.1%

Chapter 7

Answers to Odd-Numbered Problems

Assignment 7-1

1. a. 8%   c. 10%   e. 1%

Assignment 7-2

1. a. 60   c. 12   e. 12

Assignment 7-3

1.

	Number of periods	*Period interest rate*
a.	16	3%
c.	24	$.33\frac{1}{3}\%$
e.	60	3%
g.	40	1%
i.	36	1.5%

Assignment 7-4

1.

	Maturity value	*Compound interest*
a.	$883.05	$83.05
c.	$3230.67	$230.67
e.	$1458.61	$258.61
g.	$330.75	$30.75
i.	$432.97	$32.97

Assignment 7-5

1.

	Maturity value	*Compound interest*
a.	$1757.49	$257.49
	$10,158.50	$4558.50
	$8663.35	$1563.35
	$49,071.15	$46,571.15
	$19,161.81	$17,961.81

3. $MV = \$161,222.61$
    $I = \$61,222.61$

Assignment 7-6

1. a. $822.70   c. $2355.40   e. $839.57
   g. $918.16   i. $446.13
3. $36,198.91   **5.** 22 periods or $5\frac{1}{2}$ years

Assignment 7-7

1. a. $23,275.97 c. $2715.38 e. $74,445.20
   g. $889.23   i. $2128.80
3. $671.69

Assignment 7-8

1. a. $1846.27   c. $3721.57   e. $2749.20
   g. $4742.16   i. $3627.60
3. $2963.85

Assignment 7-9

1. a. $24,672.50 c. $2851.13 e. $77,423.00
   g. $875.46   i. $2192.67
3. $1368.03

Assignment 7-10

1. a. $7823.71   c. $9969.78   e. $920.01
3. $15,990.22

Chapter 8

Answers to Odd-Numbered Problems

Assignment 8-1

1. $65.65 $23,634
3. $123 $36,900
5. $201.59 $72,572.40

Assignment 8-2

1.

Size of Payment	Interest Portion	Principal Portion	Balance of Principal
$702.06	$666.67	$35.39	$79,964.61
702.06	666.37	35.69	79,929.92
702.06	666.07	35.99	79,892.93

3.

Size of Payment	Interest Portion	Principal Portion	Balance of Principal
$877.58	833.33	$44.25	$99,955.76
877.58	832.96	44.62	99,911.15
877.58	832.59	44.99	99,866.16

5.

Size of Payment	Interest Portion	Principal Portion	Balance of Principal
$1184.88	$1166.67	$18.21	$99,981.79
1184.88	1166.45	18.43	99,963.37
1184.88	1166.24	18.64	99,944.73

Assignment 8-3

1. $3192   **3.** $52,056   **5.** $.36
7. $228,600,000   **9.** $2.78

Assignment 8-4

1. $1045   **3.** $3,168.00, $823.68

Assignment 8-5

1. $2884   **3.** $23,400

Assignment 8-6

1. $269.76   **3.** $4650

Assignment 8-7

1. a. $1200   c. $3240   e. $5280
3. $64,610

Assignment 8-8

1. $124.50   **3.** $154.85

Assignment 8-9

1. $18,900   **3.** $50,000

Chapter 9

Answers to Odd-Numbered Problems

Assignment 9-1

1. $542.88
3.

Total hours	Gross pay
a. 43	$194.91
b. 28	$194.32

Assignment 9-2

1. $393.86   **3.** $381.60   **5.** $630

Assignment 9-3

	Total units	Gross earnings
a.	330	$250.80
b.	237	$218.04
c.	897	$287.04
d.	335	$251.25
e.	4495	$404.55
f.	2599	$233.91

Assignment 9-4

1. a. $186.00   c. $38.40   e. $20.00
3. a. $117.65   c. $125.20   e. $350.00

Assignment 9-5

1. $1750   **3.** $353   **5.** $248

Assignment 9-6

1. a. $540   c. $280
3. Adolf $135, Chris $732

Assignment 9-7

1. $7.15   **3.** $31.10

Assignment 9-8

1. $4664.66   **3.** $7048.30   **5.** $16,096.50

Assignment 9-9

1. $1560.41   **3.** $2511.60

Chapter 10

Answers to Odd-Numbered Problems

Assignment 10-1

1. a. $400   c. $500   e. $2500
3. $636.25   **5.** $1100

Assignment 10-2

1. $1440   **3.** $3000
$1080 $2400
$720 $1800
$360 $1200
$600
5. SL = $2080
SOTYD = $2269.09

Assignment 10-3

1. $1896   **3.** $648   **5.** $4000

Assignment 10-4

1. $140,000   **3.** $15,000
$46,666.67 $11,250
$13,333.33 $8437.50
5. SL = $1400
SOTYD = $2333.33
DB = $2475
DB by $141.67 over SOTYD
and by $1075 over SL

Assignment 10-5

1. $1140   **3.** $17,950   **5.** $137

Assignment 10-6

1. $495   **3.** LIFO = $6515
FIFO = $7060
LIFO for a lower inventory
valuation for income tax
5. $407.20

Assignment 10-7

1. $334.97   **3.** **$181.81**
5. FIFO = $362
LIFO = $311.80
WA = $334.20

Assignment 10-8

1. $210,000   **3.** $100,000

Assignment 10-9

1. Bank balance per statement $671.80

   Less outstanding checks $10.85

                                     16.41

                                     57.75   85.05

   Adjusted bank balance $586.79

   Bank balance per checkbook $588.19

   Less service charge   1.40

   Adjusted checkbook balance $586.79

3. Bank balance per statement $2015.00

   Less outatanding checks   #1828 $ 25.00

                           #1831   82.50

                           #1832   56.65

                           #1834   23.85   188.00

                                              $1827.00

   Add deposits in transit   2/15 $365.00

                             2/17   510.00   875.00

   Adjusted bank statement balance $2702.00

   Bank balance per check register $3200.36

   Less service charge $ 3.00

   Less drafts: life insurance co.   295.00

                      bank loan   190.00

   Less charge for extra checks   10.00

   Less check #1820 written for $12.95

                    recorded at 12.59   .36   498.36

   Adjusted check register balance $2702.00

5. Bank balance per statement $293.00

   Less outstanding checks   #25 $36.00

                            #37   70.02

                            #38   97.98   204.00

                                              $ 89.00

   Add deposit in transit 8/25   200.00

   Adjusted bank statement balance $289.00

   Bank balance per check register $293.00

   Less service charge   4.00

   Adjusted check register balance $289.00

Chapter 11

Answers to Odd-Numbered Problems

Assignment 11-1

1. $4500   **3.** $585,000

Assignment 11-2

1.

	Increase or Decrease*	
	Amount	*Percent*
Assets		
Current assets		
Cash	$1000	20.0%
Accounts receivable	1000	10.0%
Total current assets	$2000	13.3%
Fixed assets		
Building and equipment	$7000*	12.7%*
Land	2000	11.1%
Total fixed assets	$5000*	6.8%*
Total assets	$3000*	3.4%*
Liabilities and owner's equity		
Current liabilities		
Accounts payable	$3000	42.9%
Notes payable	2000*	33.3%*
Total current liabilities	$1000	7.7%
Fixed liabilities		
Long-term debt	$5000*	12.5%*
Total fixed liabilities	$5000*	12.5%*
Total liabilities	$4000*	7.5%*
Owner's equity		
Capital stock	$5000	25.0%
Retained earnings	4000*	7.5%*
Total owner's equity	$1000	2.9%
Total liabilities and owner's equity	$3000*	3.4%*

3.

	1986	1987	Increase or Decrease* Amount	Percent
Assets				
Current assets				
Cash	$ 25,000	$ 27,000	$2000	8.0%
Accounts receivable	40,000	38,000	2000*	5.0%*
Total current assets	$ 65,000	$ 65,000	—0—	—0—
Fixed assets				
Buildings and equipment	$135,000	$130,000	$5000*	3.7%*
Total assets	$200,000	$195,000	$5000*	3.7%*
Total assets	$200,000	$195,000	$5000*	2.5%*
Liabilities				
Current liabilities				
Accounts payable	$ 19,000	$ 17,000	$2000*	10.5%*
Total current liabilities	$ 19,000	$ 17,000	$2000*	10.5%*
Fixed liabilities	—0—	—0—	—0—	—0—
Total liabilities	$19,000	$ 17,000	$2000*	10.5%*

Assignment 11-3

1.

	1986 Amount	Percent	1987 Amount	Percent
Assets				
Current assets				
Cash	$ 38,000	12.3%	$ 50,000	16.1%
Accounts receivable	100,000	32.5%	90,000	29.0%
Other current assets	20,000	6.5%	30,000	9.7%
Total current assets	$158,000	51.3%	$170,000	54.8%
Fixed assets	$150,000	48.7%	$140,000	45.2%
Total assets	$308,000	100%	$310,000	100%
Liabilities and owner's equity				
Current liabilities				
Accounts payable	$ 17,000	5.5%	$ 20,000	6.5%
Notes payable	20,000	6.5%	14,000	4.5%
Total current liabilities	$ 37,000	12.0%	$ 34,000	11.0%
Long-term liabilities	$ 50,000	16.2%	$ 45,000	14.5%
Total liabilities	$ 87,000	28.2%	$ 79,000	25.5%
Owner's equity				
Stock	$200,000	64.9%	$190,000	61.3%
Retained earnings	21,000	6.8%	41,000	13.2%
Total owner's equity	$221,000	71.8%	$231,000	74.5%
Total liabilities and owner's equity	$308,000	100%	$310,000	100%

Kem Card Company
Comparative Balance Sheet
December 31, 1986 and 1987

| | Vertical Analysis | | | | Horizontal Analysis | |
| | 1986 | | 1987 | | Increase or Decrease* | |
	Amount	Percent	Amount	Percent	Amount	Percent
		Assets				
Current assets						
Cash	$ 1,000	1.8%	$ 3,000	4.3%	$ 2,000	200%
Accounts receivable	7,900	14.1%	12,000	17.4%	4,100	51.9%
Notes receivable	2,000	3.6%	5,000	7.2%	3,000	150%
Prepaid expenses	60	.1%	100	.1%	40	66.7%
Merchandise inventory	11,000	19.7%	14,000	20.3%	3,000	27.3%
Total current assets	$21,960	39.2%	$34,100	49.3%	$12,140	55.3%
Fixed assets						
Machinery and equipment	$14,000	25.0%	$15,000	21.7%	$ 1,000	7.1%
Land	4,000	7.1%	6,000	8.7%	2,000	50.0%
Buildings	16,000	28.6%	14,000	20.3%	2,000*	12.5%*
Total fixed assets	$34,000	60.8%	$35,000	50.7%	$ 1,000	2.9%
Total assets	$55,960	100%	$69,100	100%	$13,140	23.5%
		Liabilities and owner's equity				
Current liabilities						
Accounts payable	$ 7,500	13.4%	$ 7,800	11.3%	$ 300	4.0%
Notes payable	4,000	7.1%	3,500	5.1%	500*	12.5%*
Insurance payable	80	.1%	100	.1%	20	25.0%
Payroll payable	1,000	1.8%	1,500	2.2%	500	50.0%
Total current liabilities	$12,580	22.5%	$12,900	18.7%	$ 320	2.5%
Long-term liabilities						
Bonds	$ 7,000	12.5%	$ 6,000	8.7%	$ 1,000*	14.3%*
Total liabilities	$19,580	35.0%	$18,900	27.4%	$ 680*	3.5%*
Owner's equity						
Preferred stock	$ 8,000	14.3%	$ 8,000	11.6%	$ —0—	—0—
Common stock	25,000	44.7%	30,000	43.4%	5,000	20.0%
Retained earnings	3,380	6.0%	12,200	17.7%	8,820	260.9%
Total owner's equity	$36,380	65.0%	$50,200	72.6%	$13,820	38.0%
Total liabilities and owner's equity	$55,960	100%	$69,100	100%	$13,140	23.5%

Assignment 11-4

1. $50,000   **3.** ($7000)   **5.** $1090

Assignment 11-5

1.

| | Increase or Decrease* | |
	Amount	Percent
Sales	$260,000	26.0%
Less sales returns	40*	.8%*
Net sales	$260,040	26.1%
Less cost of goods sold	26,840	5.0%
Gross profit	$233,200	51.0%
Less operating expenses	7,350	2.2%
Net income	$225,850	174.7%

3.

	1986	1987	Increase or Decrease* Amount	Increase or Decrease* Percent
Sales	$123,000	$137,500	$14,500	11.8%
Sales returns and allowances	3,000	3,500	500	16.7%
Net sales	$120,000	$134,000	$14,000	11.7%
Cost of goods sold	30,000	37,000	7,000	23.3%
Gross profit	$ 90,000	$ 97,000	$ 7,000	7.8%
Operating expenses				
Rent expense	$ 12,000	$ 12,000	$ —	—
Salaries expense	40,000	41,000	1,000	2.5%
Advertising expense	10,000	12,000	2,000	20.0%
Delivery expense	5,000	4,500	500*	10.0%*
Total operating expenses	$ 67,000	$ 69,500	$ 2,500	3.7%
Net income	$ 23,000	$ 27,500	$ 4,500	19.6%

Assignment 11-6

1.

	1986 Percent	1987 Percent
Sales	100.5%	100.4%
Less sales returns	.5%	.4%
Net sales	100.0%	100.0%
Less cost of goods sold	69.5%	67.2%
Gross profit	30.5%	32.8%
Less operating expenses		
Selling expense	12.8%	12.5%
Administrative expense	7.0%	8.0%
Total operating expenses	19.8%	20.5%
Net operating income	10.7%	12.3%

3.

	1986 Amount	1986 Percent	1987 Amount	1987 Percent
Sales	$15,000	100.7%	$20,000	101.0%
Sales returns and allowances	100	.7%	200	1.0%
Net sales	$14,900	100.0%	$19,800	100.0%
Cost of goods sold	8,000	53.7%	10,000	50.5%
Gross profit	$ 6,900	46.3%	$ 9,800	49.5%
Operating expenses				
Selling expense	$ 500	3.4%	$ 500	2.5%
Administrative expense	700	4.7%	1,000	5.1%
Total operating expenses	$ 1,200	8.1%	$ 1,500	7.6%
Net profit	$ 5,700	38.3%	$ 8,300	41.9%

Assignment 11-7

1. a. 2:1   **3.** 1.63:1
    c. 2.58:1
    e. 3.82:1   **5.** 2.37:1

Assignment 11-8

1. a. 1.96:1   **3.** 1.38:1
    c. 1:1
    e. .94:1   **5.** 1.25:1

Assignment 11-9

1. 4 times   3. 1.33 times
5. 1986, .863 time
   1987, 1.0 time

Assignment 11-10

1. 3.9 times

Assignment 11-11

1. a. 2.9%   c. 3.5%   3. 8.1%
   e. 8.4%   g. 12.4%
   i. 4.4%

Assignment 11-12

1. a. 22.0%   c. 12.3%
   e. 28.5%   g. 35.9%

Chapter 12

Answers to Odd-Numbered Problems

Assignment 12-1

1. a.

Array	Frequency distribution		Range
	value	frequency	
3	3	2	50
3	8	3	
8	12	2	
8	53	1	
8			
12			
12			
53			

c.

Array	Frequency distribution		Range
	value	frequency	
1	1	2	12
1	5	2	
5	7	1	
5	13	2	
7			
13			
13			

Assignment 12-2

1. 620
3. a. 324.6
   c. 44.345
   3. 166.8

Assignment 12-3

1. $100
3. a. 5   c. 48
   e. 9

Assignment 12-4

1. $4.75
3. a. 5   c. 75
   e. 4

Assignment 12-5

1.

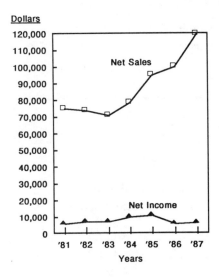

3.

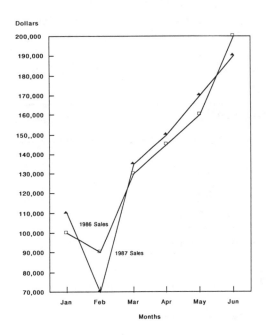

Assignment 12-6

1.

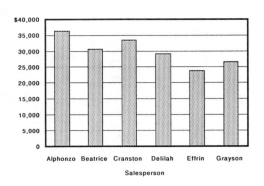

Assignment 12-7

1.

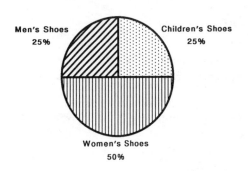

Assignment 12-8

1. a. 1   c. 300
   e. 27,000   g. 720
   i. .000000001

Assignment 12-9

1. 31 kilometers
3. 1032 kilometers
5. $360
7. 200 books
9. 66⅔ grams
11. 20 hangers
13. 8 rolls
15. 8 kilometers per liter

Assignment 12-10

1. a. 149.04   c. 2,039.66
   e. 5.29   g. 17.03
   i. 26.52
3. 509.92 grams

Assignment 12-11

1. 8 pounds   3. 9 miles
5. 99 yards

Chapter 13

Answers to Odd-Numbered Problems

Assignment 13-1

1. a. $.50   c. $1.15
   e. $4.26

Assignment 13-2

1. 165,000
3. $87,500 and 2500 shares

Assignment 13-3

1.

	Total premium or discount	Premium or discount per share
a.	$200,000 P	$.57 P
c.	$10,000 D	$.26 D
e.	$38,747,500 P	$10.61 P

Assignment 13-4

1. $500

Assignment 13-5

1. $18,200

Assignment 13-6

1.

	Dividend per share	
	Common	Preferred
a.	$18.18	$18.18
c.	$ 4.67	$5
e.	$ 6	$6
g.	$ 5.88	$5.88
i.	$ 4.50	$4.50

Assignment 13-7

1.

	Money involved	Broker's commission
a.	$500	$7.50
c.	$4975	$64.68
e.	$5662.50	$62.29
g.	$10,625	$106.25
i.	$1700	$27.20

Assignment 13-8

1. a. $42.50   c. $200.08
   e. $137.66   g. $222.12
   i. $190.66

Assignment 13-9

1.

	Market value	Premium	Discount
a.	$970		$30
c.	$1026.25	$26.25	
e.	$505.63	$5.63	
g.	$104	$4	
i.	$4412.50		$587.50

Assignment 13-10

1.

	Market price	Accumulated interest	Commission	Total cost or receipts
a.	$1960	$33.33	$10	$2003.33 C
c.	$5050	$150	$25	$5157 R
e.	$23,093.75	$359.38	$125	$23,328.13 R
g.	$51,312.50	$694.44	$125	$51,881.94 R
i.	$17,150	$300	$100	$17,550 C

3. $839,000

Assignment 13-11

1.

	Market value	Current yield
a.	$900	10.6%
c.	$850	11.8%
e.	$106.50	13.1%
g.	$552.50	20.4%
i.	$1056.25	12.3%

Assignment 13-12

1.

	Market value	Premium	Annual amortization	Carrying value End of 1st yr	End of 2nd yr
a.	$1100	$100	$10	$1090	$1080
c.	$1200	$200	$20	$1180	$1160
e.	$560	$60	$4	$556	$552
g.	$1060	$60	$3.16	$1056.84	$1053.68
i.	$1300	$300	$10.71	$1289.29	$1278.58

Assignment 13-13

1.

	Market value	Discount	Annual amortization	Carrying value End of 1st yr	End of 2nd yr
a.	$940	$60	$6	$946	$952
c.	$850	$150	$15	$865	$880
e.	$375	$125	$8.33	$383.33	$391.67
g.	$880	$120	$6.32	$886.32	$892.64
i.	$920	$80	$2.86	$922.86	$925.72

Chapter 14

Answers to Odd-Numbered Questions

Assignment 14-1

1. a. 7   c. 3
   e. 27   g. 54
   i. 1   k. 33

Assignment 14-2

1. a. 11011_2 c. 1111110_2
   e. 111_2 g. 1011_2
   i. 10_2

Assignment 14-3

1. a. 10110_2 c. 110010_2
   e. 1000010_2 g. 101010_2
   i. 101000_2

Assignment 14-4

1. a. 10_2 c. 100100_2
   e. 101000_2

Assignment 14-5

1. a. 110_2 c. 101100_2
   e. 10111_2 g. 100_2
   i. 10_2 k. 11001_2

Assignment 14-6

1. a. 110_2 c. 111100_2
   e. 101101_2 g. 10100101_2
   i. 100011_2

Assignment 14-7

1. a. 10_2 c. $100_2 R\ 1_2$
   e. 1010_2 g. 10_2
   i. $1_2 R\ 111_2$ k. $1001_2 R\ 1001$

Index

352

1 – 1 –96

NORMANDALE
COMMUNITY COLLEGE
9700 France Avenue South
Bloomington, Minnesota 55431

DEMCO